SHARING OUR STORIES
OF SURVIVAL

TRIBAL LEGAL STUDIES SERIES

SERIES EDITOR: Jerry Gardner (Cherokee), Tribal Law & Policy Institute

This series began as a collaborative initiative with the UCLA Native Nations Law and Policy Center and four tribal colleges. It is designed to promote education and community empowerment through the development of resources for and about tribal justice systems. This project was supported by Grant No. 2003-WT-BX-K001, Grant No. 2004-WT-AX-K045, and Grant No. 2006-MU-AX-K028, awarded by the Office on Violence Against Women, U.S. Department of Justice. The opinions, findings, conclusions and recommendations expressed in this publication are those of the authors and do not necessarily reflect the views of the Department of Justice, Office on Violence Against Women.

American Indian tribal court systems deal with a wide range of difficult criminal and civil justice problems on a daily basis. Culturally-based legal training is one of Indian country's most pressing needs, as tribes assume responsibility for a growing number of government functions, such as child welfare and environmental control, and tribal courts continue to expand as the primary sources of law enforcement and dispute resolution for tribal communities. This book series is designed to develop legal and technical resources for tribal justice course offerings and materials so that they reflect community thought, philosophy, traditions, and norms, and serve to strengthen tribal government and leadership.

BOOKS IN THE SERIES
1. *Introduction to Tribal Legal Studies* (2004), by Justin B. Richland and Sarah Deer
2. *Tribal Criminal Law and Procedure* (2004), by Carrie E. Garrow and Sarah Deer
3. *Sharing Our Stories of Survival: Native Women Surviving Violence* (2007), edited by Sarah Deer, Bonnie Clairmont, Carrie A. Martell, and Maureen L. White Eagle

ADVISORY BOARD – VOLUME III
Eileen Hudon (Anishinabe), Advocate
Genne James (Navajo), Advocate
Tina Olson (Yaqui), Mending the Sacred Hoop TA Project
Mary Pearson (Musckogee Creek), Tribal Court Judge
Beryl Rock (Chippewa), Tribal Law and Policy Institute
Rose Mary Shaw (Osage), Osage Nation Counseling Center
Rebecca St. George (Anishinabe), Mending the Sacred Hoop/Advocate
Tammy M. Young (Tlingit), Alaska Native Women's Coalition

SHARING OUR STORIES OF SURVIVAL

Native Women Surviving Violence

EDITED BY
SARAH DEER, BONNIE CLAIRMONT
CARRIE A. MARTELL, AND
MAUREEN L. WHITE EAGLE

ALTAMIRA PRESS
A Division of Rowman & Littlefield Publishers, Inc.
Lanham • New York • Toronto • Plymouth, UK

ALTAMIRA PRESS
A division of Rowman & Littlefield Publishers, Inc.
A wholly owned subsidiary of The Rowman & Littlefield Publishing Group, Inc.
4501 Forbes Boulevard, Suite 200, Lanham, MD 20706
www.altamirapress.com

Estover Road, Plymouth PL6 7PY, United Kingdom

Copyright © 2008 by Tribal Law and Policy Institute

All rights reserved. No part of this publication may be reproduced, stored in a retrieval system, or transmitted in any form or by any means, electronic, mechanical, photocopying, recording, or otherwise, without the prior permission of the publisher.

British Library Cataloguing in Publication Information Available

Library of Congress Cataloging-in-Publication Data
Sharing our stories of survival : native women surviving violence / edited by Sarah Deer, Bonnie Clairmont, and Carrie A. Martell. . . . (et al.)
   p. cm. — (Tribal legal studies series)
   Includes bibliographical references and index.
   ISBN-13: 978-0-7591-1124-0 (cloth : alk. paper)
   ISBN-10: 0-7591-1124-3 (cloth : alk. paper)
   ISBN-13: 978-0-7591-1125-7 (pbk. : alk. paper)
   ISBN-10: 0-7591-1125-1 (pbk. : alk. paper)
 1. Indian women—North America—Social conditions. 2. Indian women—Violence against—North America. 3. Indians, Treatment of—North America. I. Deer, Sarah, 1972- II. Clairmont, Bonnie, 1950- III. Martell, Carrie A., 1978-

E99.W8S43 2008
305.48'969208997073—dc22
                                        2007018798

Printed in the United States of America

∞™ The paper used in this publication meets the minimum requirements of American National Standard for Information Sciences—Permanence of Paper for Printed Library Materials, ANSI/NISO Z39.48-1992.

This book is dedicated to the millions of Native women who've been harmed by violence, including those who have passed to the spirit world along with their stories.

CONTENTS

Foreword   xi

Preface   xv

Eagle's Wings by Petra L. Solimon (Laguna/Zuni)

Part I: Introduction to Violence Against Native Women

Native Women by Jayci Malone (Stockbridge-Munsee Mohican)

CHAPTER 1

Beloved Women: Life Givers, Caretakers, Teachers of Future Generations   3
Jacqueline Agtuca

Skin on Skin by Sally Brunk (Lac du Flambeau Ojibwa)

CHAPTER 2

Sexual Violence: An Introduction to the Social and Legal Issues for Native Women   31
Charlene Ann LaPointe

Rape by Eileen Hudon (White Earth Ojibwe)

CHAPTER 3

Domestic Violence: An Introduction to the Social and Legal Issues for Native Women   49
Victoria Ybanez

Run by Lea Krmpotich Carr (White Earth Ojibwe)

CHAPTER 4

Special Issues Facing Alaska Native Women Survivors of Violence   71
Eleanor Ned-Sunnyboy

Kitchen Table Wisdom by Margaret "Augie" Kochuten (Quinault)

CHAPTER 5

Overview of Issues Facing Native Women Who Are Survivors of Violence in Urban Communities   87
Rose L. Clark and Carrie L. Johnson

Part II: Stories of Survival

The Dance of Violence by Tracie Jones Myrick Meyer (Kalapuya)

CHAPTER 6

From a Woman Who Experienced Violence   105
Anonymous

Bouncy, Lively by Juanita Pahdopony (Comanche)

CHAPTER 7

Walking in the Darkness, Then Finding the Light   115
Lisa Frank

Intimate Disfigurement by Amanda D. Faircloth (Lumbee)

CHAPTER 8

Violence across the Lifecycle   131
Diane E. Benson

WRONG!!! by Frances M. Blackburn (Northern Arapahoe)

CHAPTER 9

Prisoner W-20170/Other   149
Stormy Ogden

Lecturing in Indian Studies on the Eve of the Millennium by Kim Shuck (Tsalagi, Sauk/Fox)

CHAPTER 10

Living in Fear   167
Karlene

Wolf by Coya Hope White Hat-Artichoker (Lakota)

Part III: Advocacy

How Madwomen Survive by MariJo Moore (Cherokee)

CHAPTER 11

Introduction to Advocacy for Native Women Who Have Been Raped   181
Bonnie Clairmont and Sarah Deer

Conversations Between Here and Home by Joy Harjo (Mvskoke)

CHAPTER 12

The Role of Advocates in the Tribal Legal System: Context Is Everything   193
Brenda Hill

the house of comfort by Nila NorthSun (Shoshone/Chippewa)

CHAPTER 13

Overview of Sexual Violence Perpetrated by Purported Indian Medicine Men   215
Bonnie Clairmont

Did I Know Your Dad? by Diane E. Benson (Tlingit)

Part IV: Tribal Legal Systems

Survival by Venus St. Martin (Colville/Nez Perce)

CHAPTER 14

Jurisdiction and Violence Against Native Women   233
B. J. Jones

Free Man Walking by Mary BlackBonnet (Sicangu Lakota)

CHAPTER 15

Representing Native American Victims in Protection Order Hearings   249
Kelly Gaines Stoner

Untitled by Sharon Lynn Reyna (Stockbridge-Munsee/Mohican)

CHAPTER 16

Using Full Faith and Credit to Protect Native American Survivors of Domestic Violence, Stalking, and Sexual Assault   267
Danielle G. Van Ess and Sarah Deer

CHAPTER 17

Divorce, Child Custody, and Support Issues in Tribal Courts 281
Hallie Bongar White

The Deafness of Domestic Violence by Kimberly Mullican Querdibitty

CHAPTER 18

The Indian Child Welfare Act and Violence Against Women 297
James G. White and Sarah Michèle Martin

NO ESCAPE by Anonymous

CHAPTER 19

The Role of Probation in Providing Safety for Native Women 311
George Twiss

Testament by Judi Brannan Armbruster (Karuk)

Glossary 337

Index 343

About the Advisory Board 347

About the Contributors 351

About the Editors 361

Foreword

Violence against tribal women has developed as a result of several factors, including colonization and Christianization, which are poignantly addressed in the chapters of this book. Tribal women have traveled a hard road toward rescuing their sacredness and sovereignty, which were usurped by the influence of European contact. For many years, our communities internalized the dominant culture's belief that women are subordinate to men. Ultimately, however, tribal women have never lost their sacredness or sovereignty. This text reflects tribal women's belief that we are sacred and sovereign, which includes our right to our property and personhood.

Restoring tribal women to our rightful place as safe and sovereign beings requires efforts at the tribal, state, and federal levels. Education and consciousness-raising is the critical link between survivors' voices and social change movements. This textbook is an important addition to materials and curricula developed by organizations such as Sacred Circle, Mending the Sacred Hoop, and Clan Star. By providing an academic context, this book can serve to bring new voices into the fold.

In Part I, "Introduction to Violence Against Native Women," authors Jacqueline R. Agtuca, Charlene A. LaPointe, Victoria Ybanez, Eleanor Ned-Sunnyboy, Rose L. Clark, and Carrie Johnson share the herstorical analysis that violence against tribal women is now widespread throughout all tribes of Turtle Island. The poetry of pain and feelings interspersed within these teachings reflect the awakening of tribal women to proclaim their sacredness and sovereignty.

Part II, "Stories of Survival," provides models of hope for victims/survivors of violence. These stories illustrate how violence has escalated in family systems, communities, and society, and how it erodes the sovereignty and sacredness of tribal women. This section confirms how violence is learned and how society has long supported the belief that violence against women is a "family" matter and not a crime. In traditional tribal societies, the woman holds a place of authority in her home and only has to place her husband's personal belongings outside her dwelling, and he quickly learns that he no longer has a place in her home. Storytellers like Lisa Frank, Diane E. Benson, Stormy Ogden, Karlene, and the anonymous writer depict how violence against tribal women often plays itself out today with no support for the victim/survivor except sometimes from friends and families. Karlene and Coya White Hat-Artichoker share stories that are often only told to intimate trusted friends. In traditional tribal societies two-spirited sisters/brothers were not an anomaly. Their stories need to be told and heard by everyone.

Part III is titled "Advocacy," and advocacy is the key to addressing the obstacles faced by tribal women who are dealing with the pain of the violence against them and its effects on their personal well-being. Advocates who have experienced the ramifications of domestic and/or sexual violence in their own lives have a special passion for assisting others in their healing. It has been through the creation of such organizations as the White Buffalo Calf Woman Society, Inc. (1977), the National Coalition Against Domestic Violence (1978), and the South Dakota Coalition Against Domestic Violence (1978) that advocacy has developed a voice in tribal communities and in Indian Country. Leaders such as Karen Artichoker had the tenacity to help with the first passage of the Violence Against Women Act in 1995. Advocates continued to take on leadership roles and have been joined by tribal women working in the legal system to alert the tribes to the call of women whose stories of survival permeate this text. These tribal women from the legal system, in collaboration with tribal women working in the trenches and behind shelter doors, have brought to the forefront the information that violence against tribal women is a crime in Indian Country. The movement to end domestic violence in Indian Country has only recently been expanded to include sexual violence. We must ensure that our efforts encompass both forms of violence. Tribal advocates throughout Turtle Island brought these plights to tribal leadership and have worked with our male counterparts in the reauthorization of the Violence Against Women Act of 2005, in particular to advocate for an increase in resources for tribal governments.

In Part IV, "Tribal Legal Systems," the writers show how advocacy for tribal women experiencing violence must continue in restoring tribal women to their rightful place in tribal societies, by retaining all their rights to sovereignty and their sacredness as women. Domestic and sexual violence is more than a physical assault but fits within a larger pattern of dominance, power, and control. Federal, state, and tribal laws should be crafted very carefully so that they do not undermine our sacredness and sovereignty as women. B. J. Jones, Kelly Gaines Stoner, Danielle G. Van Ess, Sarah Deer, Hallie Bongar White, James G. White, Sarah Michèle Martin, and George Twiss provide readers with a comprehensive insight into the impact that legal systems have made in addressing violence faced by tribal women.

Throughout this text, special reminders are shared by the sisters who are eloquent in their sharing of survival through their poetry: Petra L. Solimon-Yeager, Jayci Malone, Sally Brunk, Eileen Hudon, Lea Carr, Kochuten (Quinault) writer, Tracie Meyer, Juanita Pahdopony, Amanda D. Faircloth, Frances Monroe, Kim Shuck, Coya Hope White Hat-Artichoker, MariJo Moore, Joy Harjo, Nila NorthSun, Diane E. Benson, Venus St. Martin, Mary Black Bonnet, Sharon Lynn Reyna, Kim Querdibitty, and Judi Armbruster. These poems cover the whole spectrum of issues affecting tribal women in our communities.

Our struggle continues beyond this text, to protect our rights as tribal women to our sacredness and our sovereignty. It is my hope that this textbook will be read and taught in the spirit that it was written—with survivors at the center of the analysis. The effort to end violence against tribal women is a rich, multifaceted social change movement. The authors and poets highlighted in this text have provided a moving and profound foundation for discussion, academic inquiry, and activism. Tribal women need and deserve this book. It is long overdue.

Tillie Black Bear, Sicangu Lakota
Founder and Director, White Buffalo Calf Woman Society, Inc.

Preface

The nature of violent crime against women is a well-established discipline in many respects. There are several hundred books and at least five scholarly journals dedicated to the topic. However, the nature of violence against particular groups of women is still an emerging field. Recently, several books have been published that analyze issues of violence within the context of a particular race and/or geographic origin. For example, Margaret Abraham published *Speaking the Unspeakable: Marital Violence among South Asian Immigrants in the United States* in 2000. In 1998, Charlotte Pierce-Baker published *Surviving the Silence: Black Women's Stories of Rape*. These and other books have made a significant contribution to the field of antiviolence literature by giving voice to marginalized women in American society. In 2005, Andrea Smith (Cherokee) published *Conquest: Sexual Violence and American Indian Genocide*—a groundbreaking book focusing on the historical and contemporary issues surrounding the rape of Native women. It is our hope that this textbook will build upon and continue the scholarship established by this seminal work.

Sharing Our Stories of Survival: Native Women Surviving Violence is the result of a unique opportunity that arose from federal funding under the Violence Against Women Act of 1994. In 2002, the Tribal Law and Policy Institute (see www.tlpi.org), a Native-owned-and-operated nonprofit organization, entered into the first of a series of cooperative agreements with the U.S. Department of Justice, Office on Violence Against Women to develop a college curriculum on violence against Native women. This grant was part of a larger effort by the Justice Department to enhance training and technical assistance for tribal grantees. The textbook grew out of an online class first taught by Sarah Deer in fall 2003 through UCLA Extension.

Sharing Our Stories of Survival: Native Women Surviving Violence is the third book in the Tribal Legal Studies Series. The first two books—*Introduction to Tribal Legal Studies* and *Tribal Criminal Law and Procedure*—were published in 2004. Additional books in the Tribal Legal Studies Series are being developed.

This book is designed as an introductory textbook to the sociolegal issues that arise in the context of violence against Native women. A course on this topic might be taught in any number of disciplines: for example, social work, psychology, history, legal studies, nursing, or medicine. While there is a focus on legal issues in some of the text, we've tried to provide discussion of a wide variety of issues and topics that touch many disciplines. The reader may encounter any number of new concepts or vocabulary words; wherever possible, we have attempted to provide glossary definitions for these words.

Writing about violence and victims is never easy, but we have been fortunate to work with a series of writers and poets who are both knowledgeable about and sensitive to this topic. Many of the authors are survivors of violence, have worked directly with victimized women, or have close friends or family members who have experienced violence.

Much of the material in this book is very raw and exposed. We intentionally have not edited out any material that may be provocative and/or upsetting. Part of the reason we have chosen to reveal this sometimes dark material is to highlight the emergency level of the problem facing Native women in the United States. Statistics indicate that Native women are more likely than any other racial or gender group to be the victims of violent attacks. Some studies indicate that at least one in three women will be raped during their lifetimes.

Another reason for retaining the original tone and tenor of the writings is to allow each voice and each author to speak truth. The nature of the truth is sometimes unappealing or unattractive, but the telling of truth is a beautiful act of self-love. We choose to acknowledge and honor the authors for surviving the acts of violence. Native women too often suffer in silence. This silence resonates throughout Indian Country, from the lack of appropriate responses from law enforcement and judicial systems to the deafening silence faced by some women—even from their own families.

Tribal justice systems play a central role in responding to and intervening in criminal acts against women. This book, in addition to giving voice to those who have experienced violence, also provides information on tribal justice systems and their responses. Chapters on tribal jurisdiction, practicing in tribal courts, and the role of tribal probation and parole are included because the issues provide a critical link to safety. No book can cover every aspect of this complex topic. There are undoubtedly some areas that we were unable to include. We hope that this volume will be the inspiration for others, and that the areas we missed will be included in one of these future volumes.

Karren Baird-Olson and Carol Ward define "survival" as "the process of handling life with various degrees of constructive adaptation; to live with some dignity, to do more than just exist, to attempt to live a balanced life."[1] More than anything, we hope this book will serve as a testament to survival. Each story and poem included within this anthology represents hundreds and thousands of women who may never have had a chance to have their stories told.

Jerry Gardner, Cherokee, Series Editor
December 2006

Acknowledgments

Many Tribal Law and Policy Institute staff members and consultants assisted with the development of this book, including Arlene Downwind-White (Red Lake Band of Chippewa), April Clairmont (Lakota/HoChunk), Heather Valdez Singleton, Lou Sgroi, Diane Payne, Mona Evan (Tlingit/Haida/Yupik/Inupiat), Lavern Yanito Dennison (Navajo), and Terrilena Dodson (Navajo). We also wish to thank Erik Stegman (Nakota), who has been an intern in our office for the past two years, and Patricia Sekaquaptewa (Hopi) for her ongoing support of our work.

This book would not have been possible without the many contributing writers and poets—especially the survivors of violence—who have generously told their stories. We would also like to acknowledge the Advisory Board. Poet and actor Diane E. Benson (Tlingit) provided invaluable advice in soliciting and selecting poetry for this book. We are grateful for her artistic and cultural insight in the preparation of the final manuscript. Thanks also to George Boeck for his copyediting skills and David Sekaquaptewa (Hopi) for his graphic skills.

Sarah Deer thanks her parents, Jan and Montie Deer; her grandparents, Isaac "Kelso" and Wanda Lee Deer; her husband, Neal Axton; and her Indian law mentor, Robert Odawi Porter. Also a special thank you to Jerry Gardner for his vision of Tribal Legal Studies textbooks.

Bonnie Clairmont thanks her friend and colleague, Sarah Deer, for giving her the opportunity to contribute to this book. Bonnie thanks her partner of thirty-five years, Jim Clairmont, for his steadfast support and for representing the true hallmark of a Lakota man. She thanks her mother, Elizabeth Deere, for teaching her the value of standing up for what you believe in and speaking your truth at all costs. She thanks her son, Lakota, for growing up to be the fine young family man that he is, respected by Indian people, young and old; and her daughter, April Rainbow, for growing up to be the principled, activist-minded young woman that she has become. She thanks the many women and advocates who have chosen to tell their truths in this book and in their communities on behalf of murdered, missing women and women who cannot speak out due to the fear of further violence.

Carrie Martell thanks Sarah Deer for giving her the opportunity to work together on issues of violence against Native women. Carrie also thanks the writers for sharing their stories, which help the rest of us to survive and serve to educate society about the violence Native women face. She would also like to acknowledge DeAnna Rivera and the Tribal Learning Community and Educational Exchange (TLCEE) program at UCLA for supporting the Violence Against Native Women online course, and her family for their love.

There are many people who have aided in the production and completion of this work. Of special note is the contribution of the Tribal Unit at the Office on Violence Against Women (OVW, U.S. Department of Justice), including Lorraine Edmo, Kimberly Woodard, Kathy Howkumi, and Lauren Nassikas. The leadership of the former director of OVW, Diane M. Stuart, and the current acting director of OVW, Mary Beth Buchanan, have been instrumental in the development and publication of this book.

Further information and resources concerning this textbook and the Tribal Legal Studies Series are available on the Tribal Court Clearinghouse website (www.tlpi.org) and on the Tribal Legal Studies website (www.triballegalstudies.org).

Notes

1. Karren Baird-Olson and Carol Ward, "Recovery and Resistance: The Renewal of Traditional Spirituality among American Indian Women," *American Indian Culture & Research Journal* 24, no. 4 (2000): 7.

Eagle's Wings

Give me eagle wings
Great Spirit
Take me away from this hurt
Take me away from pain

Pray for me
That I will survive another day
That my child will not see
That the bruises will heal
That no one will ask questions
That no one will hear
Pray for me

Give me eagle wings

To soar above and beyond
My situation
Give me strength
Give me power
Give me courage
Help me heal

Give me eagle wings

                Petra L. Solimon (Laguna/Zuni)

INTRODUCTION TO VIOLENCE AGAINST NATIVE WOMEN

I

Native Women

Is it the hardships we face, or the hardships we survive?
Is it the bruises we don't allow or the bruises we sometimes hide?
Is it the men we put up with, or the red road most choose to ignore?
Is it the reservations we're confined to, or the fear of what is behind the other door?

It has to be something in our blood
Or something in our song
It has to be something in our soul
That makes Native Women strong

Is it the sound of the drum, or the grace of our step?
Is it the wisdom of our elders or the traditions we have kept?
Is it the closeness of our families knowing we will never be turned away?
Is it the excitement of pulling into a pow-wow on a hot summers day?

It has to be something in our blood
Or something in our song
It has to be something in our soul
That makes Native Women strong

I'll tell you what it is and I hope you will all agree.
It's the sound I hear at pow-wow's and the beauty
I see at grand entry
It's the feel of leather when I wear moccasins on my feet
It's the jokes that I tell and the highness of my cheeks
It's the taste of hull corn soup, wild rice and fry bread
It's knowing on the "rez" I'll never go unfed

It is something in our blood
It is something in our song
It is something in our soul
that makes Native Women strong.

       Jayci Malone (Stockbridge-Munsee Mohican)

Chapter 1

Beloved Women: Life Givers, Caretakers, Teachers of Future Generations

JACQUELINE AGTUCA

> *The unique legal relationship of the United States to Indian tribes creates a Federal trust responsibility to assist tribal governments in safeguarding the lives of Indian women.*[1]

In 1994, the U.S. Congress passed the Violence Against Women Act (VAWA),[2] marking the federal government's recognition of the extent and seriousness of violence against women. In 2005, Congress reauthorized VAWA, with the inclusion of a Safety for Indian Women Title[3] recognizing the unique legal relationship of the United States to Indian tribes and women. One purpose set forth by Congress for the creation of the title is "to strengthen the capacity of Indian tribes to exercise their sovereign authority to respond to violent crimes committed against women."[4] In this light, the VAWA of 2005 marks a shift in recognition by Congress of the seriousness of violence committed against Native[5] women and an attempt to fulfill the federal responsibility for their safety. The act, like other federal legislation, is an extension of a historical relationship between Indian nations and the United States as governments. It is this legal relationship that altered over time the existence of Native women and continues to affect their safety as a population.[6]

It is the history of this legal relationship that constitutes the social fabric of the current violence perpetrated against Native women as a population. The findings contained in the Safety for Indian Women Title refer to research by governmental agencies that unveils the level of danger confronting Native women as a population.[7] The U.S. Department of Justice (USDOJ) reports that the rate of violent crime victimization of Native women is higher than for all other populations in the United States.[8] These statistics estimate that the rate of violent crime perpetrated against American Indian females is 2½ times the rate for all females.[9]

More specifically, research by the Department estimates that one of three Native women will be raped,[10] that three of four will be physically assaulted,[11] and that Native women are stalked at a rate more than double that of any other population.[12] These estimates reflect a constant danger in the lives of Native woman and a threat to the stability of Indian nations. The reports also reflect a high number of interracial crimes, with white or black offenders committing 88 percent of all violent victimizations from 1992 to 2001.[13] Nearly four in five American Indian victims of sexual assault described the offender as white.[14] Although these statistics establish that violence against Native women is dramatically higher than for any other population in the United States, most advocates believe that crimes against Native women are actually underreported and underestimated.[15]

Within the United States three sovereigns exist: the federal government, tribal governments, and state governments.[16] Governmental responses available to assist Native women seeking safety from violence are defined not by a single body of law, but frequently by a combination of tribal, federal, and state laws. This combination of jurisdictional authority is the direct result of the legal relationship between Indian nations and the United States as governments. The jurisdictional gaps and inconsistent handling of violent crimes against Native women reach far beyond the failure of individuals to respond appropriately. It is the historical relationship between governments that shapes current legal authority over such crimes. This same historical legal relationship serves as the foundation for American cultural tolerance of violence against Native women.

Such violence is the contemporary mirror of the violence adopted by European nations[17] to achieve domination of Indian nations of North America.[18] Deer writes, "[W]hen speaking with Native American women who have survived rape, it is often difficult for them to separate the more immediate experience of their assault from the larger experience that their people have experienced through forced removal, displacement, and destruction."[19] While legal reform is essential to enhancing the responses of government agencies and services available to Native women, such reform must be combined with cultural change that increases respect for Native women and intolerance of violence against them. An ending point cannot exist without a beginning point, and ending violence against Native women requires an understanding of its historical beginning. The root of violence against Native women is not found in any single code, act, or policy but is revealed in the layers of governmental laws and policies known as Federal Indian Law.[20]

Safety and justice in the lives of Native women, while related, exist as separate realities. Safety, or the prevention of immediate violence against a Native woman, is within our reach. It is the goal driving advocates, justice personnel, and tribal leaders to work endless hours with scarce resources. Brutal beatings, rapes, and murders have been prevented because of the efforts of these dedicated women and men. Justice, on the other hand, is more complicated. In the words of Moana Jackson, a Maori leader in Aotearoa,[21] "colonization is only over when the colonized persons say it is over."[22] Reaching physical safety is but one part of the path to justice in the lives of Native women.

Following the legal, cultural, and spiritual journeys Native women have taken is a revealing story of strength, courage, and wisdom. Understanding the journeys of the grandmothers and Indian nations to defend and protect women is a challenge to the living. The first journey in this chapter is one to understand the concept of safety for Native women in a time prior to foreign domination by Europe or the United States. It was a time during which Native women experienced safety within their nations as **covenants** of their respective peoples. The second journey is one to understand the cultural changes that socially normalized violence against Native women.

Tillie Black Bear, founding member of the White Buffalo Calf Women Society, links her day-to-day work to enhance the safety of Native women to traditional teachings of White Buffalo Calf Woman.[23] "It is our belief that we are spirits on a human journey. In that way every step we take in our human life is a spiritual act. Every word we speak is a conversation with the creator." In this context, this chapter attempts to share the impact of the laws and policies of governments upon the lives of American Indian and Alaska Native women.

The Time before Colonization: Understanding That Violence Against Women Is Not Traditional

Two types of important resources are available to help explain the original status of Native women prior to contact with Europeans. While they represent divergent worldviews, both the foreign and indigenous sources agree that Native women have always performed essential, multifaceted roles within their nations.

Written historical documents of early contact between Indian nations and explorers chronicle Europeans' first impressions of the relations between Native men and women; specifically the authority women held within their nations. These observations, although sometimes skewed by Eurocentrism and racism, serve as documentation of the original status of Native women of North America.

In 1724, a Jesuit missionary named Lafitau wrote a detailed account of the customs of the Iroquois and other northern Indian nations. In his writing, Lafitau made specific reference to the status of Native women within Iroquois society. Lafitau's record demonstrates the importance and corresponding social status of Iroquois women.

> [T]here is nothing more real than this superiority of the women. It is they who constitute the tribe, transmit the nobility of blood, keep up the genealogical tree

and the order of inheritance, and perpetuate the family. They possess all actual authority; own the land, and the fields and their harvests; they are the soul of all councils, the arbiters of peace and war; they have the care of the public treasury. . . .[24]

The original status of Native women is also preserved in the teachings handed down over generations by the oral historians of Indian nations. These teachings from the cultural life bearers convey beliefs that define the lives and roles of women and their nations. These beliefs did not isolate women from their societies, but instead reflected the reality that Native women were essential to the existence of their nations. In many ways these beliefs are still operational in what is known today as **customary law**. This body of law is based upon the beliefs and practices developed within the respective Indian nations in many instances over thousands of years. Today, customary law continues to operate effectively as tribal **common law** within many Indian nations. Unlike the written reports of foreign explorers and missionaries, oral teachings are the living memories indigenous to each Indian nation. The conceptual foundations of these teachings are helpful in understanding the safety Native women experienced prior to European contact.

In general, Native women experienced the concept defined by the English word "safety." This was not due to individual actions but to cultural beliefs and practices that defined societies. This relationship is described in the words of Christine Zuni: "The word that comes closest to 'law' in Tiwa is the word for tradition—*keynaithue-wa-ee*, which translates 'this is our way of living'. That way of life is elaborated upon in prayer."[25] The way of living was not defined by a single individual's life but was reflective of the relationships between all members and things. Therefore, the concept of safety as a "way of living" was present in a Native woman's life as part of her existence within her tribal society.

The concept defined by the English word "respect" has been a foundational belief that prevented the abuse of and assured the safety of Native women. Marlin Mousseau,[26] quoting elder Jessie Johnnie,[27] describes the relationship of respect to safety as "whatever you respect, you don't mistreat" and "if we lived by our value of respect we wouldn't mistreat our partners by abusive behaviors."[28] Although the concept of respect is universal, the roles and responsibilities of women were defined by each individual nation. Karen Artichoker explains, "In the circle, everyone and thing had a role and function. None was above or below. The gifts that anyone or thing had to offer were valued and validated."[29] Within these worldviews, Native women had a place that was respected. Behavior that did not support their status was considered socially unacceptable and responded to accordingly.

A fuller understanding of the original social position of Native women can be understood by exploring the concept of the English word "spirituality." Pauma

Yuima leader Juana Majel-Dixon explains, "Indian nations after all the things we have experienced ... after all our differences ... languages ... religions ... it seems spirituality is our universal bond."[30] From their unique historical experiences, Indian nations developed specific spiritual beliefs and lifeways that came to define social norms and roles within their societies, such as the identities of women and men; the proper relationship between women and men, boys and girls; and relations within immediate and extended families. These relationships were critical to the stability of the entire community and therefore to each Indian nation in its entirety. The story of White Buffalo Calf Woman is one example of the relationship of the spiritual beliefs of the Lakota people to the safety of Lakota women. Tillie Black Bear,[31] speaking of the work of the White Buffalo Calf Woman's Society shares:

> They tell us in this camp the people were running out of food. And they decided that they would send two men out to hunt for food. And they went all over the canyon and up and down hills, looking for game. And they came upon this high hill and when they got on top of the hill they saw from the west this cloud was coming. And as the cloud got closer to them, in this cloud was a woman. And as the cloud got closer, one of the young scouts had unhealthy thoughts about her. And they tell us that she didn't speak our language. And so she signed to the man in the universal language and challenged the young man to come forward. The young scout being foolish went towards her. And the elements came together and protected this woman. When they all quieted down all that was left of this man was his bones and maggots. So one of the first teachings she brought to us as a people was that even in thought women are to be respected ... Probably, the biggest teaching of all she brought to us, that is still with us today, was as a nation we pray because if we are spiritual beings on a human journey, everything we do on this journey is a prayer. We teach this to our children, we teach this to our grandchildren, so that those generations to come will know what is expected of them and will know how to treat each other as relatives.[32]

European government officials and settlers did not understand these spiritual beliefs and lifeways as the operational basis of Indian nations. Deloria and Lytle note:

> Given the absence of formally structured institutions within the Indian tribes they encountered, it appeared to the earliest settlers that the tribes existed without any forms of government. The Indians were generally viewed as living almost in a state of anarchy and some early political writers, seeking to conceive a "state of nature" upon which they could build the philosophical framework for their natural law—social contract theories of government, frequently referred to Indians as "children of nature" and applauded their apparent ability to live without the confining and complex rules that had been devised within the European system of government.

Tribal governments of enormous complexity did exist but they differed so radically from the forms used by the Europeans that few non-Indian observers could understand them.[33]

The complexity of tribal governance was misunderstood in part due to the essential multifaceted roles of Native women within their respective nations. The social organization of many Indian nations dramatically differed from European societies. Many Indian nations held the mother's role as culturally and structurally central to their societies. In addition, many Indian nations had woman-centered economic systems. Women had authority over the home, production of foods, and oftentimes activities associated with trade. Although women headed many European monarchies, colonial governments could not conceive of a nation following descent through one's mother. The reality that many Indian nations were organized as matrilineal[34] societies seemed incomprehensible to the foreign observer. The Native customary practice of daughters taking their husbands or men to live at their mothers' homes was also viewed as unacceptable. In addition, women in many Indian nations retained the right to separate from an unwanted husband and retain her property.[35]

Europeans found the role of Native women perplexing, often describing it as uncivilized. Many rights of Native women within their nations were not recognized, and in some cases were declared illegal in European and American law. Native women were socially measured according to European standards of how women should behave. The differences that existed between women of Indian nations and European women were not only misunderstood as uncivilized, but also perceived to be unchristian.

In particular, the use of violence to control the behavior of a woman was not a belief or practice common to Indian nations. While British common law and early United States cases permitted abuse and violence against a wife by a husband,[36] such behavior was unacceptable within Indian nations. When individual incidents of violence against Native women occurred in precolonial times, they were addressed in the context of the worldview and spiritual beliefs of the tribe.[37] Unlike non-Indian jurisdictions, the commission of an act of violence held harsh consequences for the abuser, and the right of a husband to beat his wife was not legally sanctioned.

Prior to contact, such spiritual beliefs and cultural practices formed the basis of the customary law of Indian nations that created safety and respect for Native women within their homes and nations. European and later American governments misunderstood this combination of concepts that were reflected in the social structure of Indian nations. Native women, because of their strong identities and important roles, were perceived to be uncivilized and subsequently became targets of the federal efforts to civilize the Indian populations. The following petition for citizenship by the Alaska Natives of the Village of Hydaburg is but one of many examples of the erosion of the rights of Native women as terms of conquest.

> We the undersigned, Alaskan Natives of Hydaburg, Alaska, hereby declare that we have given up our old tribal relationships; that we recognize no chief of clan or tribal family; that we have given up all claim to or interest in tribal and communal houses; that we live in one family house in accordance with the customs of civilization; that we observe the marriage laws of the United States; that our children take the name of the father and belong equally to the father and mother, and that the rights of the maternal uncle to direct the children are no longer recognized and that in the case of death of either parent we recognize the laws of the United States relative to inheritance of property; that we have discarded the totem and recognize the Stars and Stripes as our only emblem; and that we are a law abiding and self-supporting people. We therefore believe that we have fulfilled all requirements necessary to citizenship in the United Sates, and we respectfully request that the Congress of the United States to pass a law granting to us the full rights of citizenship.[38]

Colonization and the Erosion of Safety for Native Women

Let your women's sons be ours; our sons be yours. Let your women hear our words.[39]

In 1781, a Cherokee woman named Nancy Ward spoke these good words in addressing the United States Treaty Commission at Holston. She believed that peace could only be sustained if the Cherokees and their enemies became one people bound by the ties of kinship. As a leader of the Cherokee nation she called upon the women of the United States because, in her worldview, only the women could accomplish this goal. At a subsequent meeting in 1785 at Hopewell, South Carolina, Nancy Ward was again introduced by the Cherokee Chiefs to speak to U.S. treaty commissioners as a "beloved woman who has borne and raised up warriors."[40] Perdue writes, "The political power of Ward and other Cherokee women rested on their position as mothers in a matrilineal society that equated kinship and citizenship. In such a society, mothers—and by extension, women—enjoyed a great deal of honor and prestige, and references to motherhood evoked power rather than sentimentality."[41] She did not know that the women of the United States did not possess the authority to respond to her call for peace.

In 2005, 224 years after Nancy Ward's appeal to the women of the United States, Tex Hall, former president of the National Congress of American Indians (NCAI) stated: "Our women are abused at far greater rates than any other group of women in the United States. The rate of violent assault is so high because (the) lack of authority given to tribal police has created a system destined to fail our people and our women."[42]

The journey from 1781 to 2005 is one of the physical, cultural, and spiritual survival of Native women. It is markedly similar to the process that occurred around the world, as indigenous nations became colonies of Europe. In response to the imposition of foreign governments, Indian nations were forced to dismantle or modify their systems of governance. This disruption included a breaking down of customary law and tribal lifeways that safeguarded Native women from crimes of physical and sexual abuse. The legalization and cultural acceptance of violence perpetrated against Native women as populations began with the conquest of Indian nations by colonial governments such as Spain, France, Russia, and England.[43] An outstanding characteristic of conquest was the physical and cultural genocide of indigenous women of the Americas. Historian Bouvier writes:

> Spain's conquest of California, like that of its other American colonies, occurred in three phases: exploration (often referred to as "discovery"), colonization, and evangelization, the last two overlapping considerably.... During the late fifteenth and early sixteenth centuries, Spain's golden age of exploration, rumors spread that lands inhabited by women lay undiscovered just beyond the reaches of the charted territory. On his first trip across the Atlantic Ocean, Christopher Columbus wrote of the existence of such an island.[44]

Such rumors piqued the curiosity of Spanish monarchs, who began to request that explorers search specifically for these mythic women, whom they called Amazons.[45] The purpose of their conquest was to claim the vast riches of a new land and its strong women.

Under the dominion of each conquering nation, Native women became targets of the colonizer in the quest to conquer and assimilate Indian nations. Within the United States, the body of law and policy that governs the legal relationship between Indian nations and the United States is known as Federal Indian Law. It is within this legal context that Native women have witnessed a dramatic shift in their quality of life as a population. This legal relationship, established over hundreds of years, separates Native women from any other population of women, as illustrated in the following historical episodes.

Erosion of the Authority of Indian Nations to Protect Women

As the aboriginal[46] people, Indian nations have always exercised the right of self-government, including authority over all persons committing acts of violence against women within their territorial lands. This authority of Indian nations over their members and land is known as **inherent authority**.[47] It is the natural and permanent authority that Indian nations have held over their members as governments for thousands of years. In 1831, in a case arising between the Cherokee Indian Nation and the State of Georgia, Chief Justice Marshall acknowledged, "The Cherokee Nation, then, is a distinct community, occupying its own territory, with boundaries accurately described, in which the laws of Georgia can have no force, and which the citizens of Georgia have no right to enter but with the assent of the Cherokees themselves or in conformity with the treaties and the acts of Congress."[48]

Independent of European nations, Indian nations make specific reference to the fact that they retain power to govern their land and the people who come within it. For example, among the Iroquois Confederacy, the Great Law addressed the Confederacy's jurisdiction:

> Roots have spread out from the Tree of the Great Peace, one to the north, one to the east, one to the south, one to the west. The name of these roots is The Great White Roots and their nature is Peace and Strength. If any man or any nation outside the Five Nations shall obey the laws of the Great Peace and make known their disposition to the Lords of the Confederacy, they may trace the Roots to the Tree and if their minds are clean and they are obedient and promise to obey the wishes of the Confederate Council they shall be welcome to take shelter beneath the Tree of the Long Leaves.[49]

Women under the Great Law were granted rights and privileges that outlawed violent and abusive behavior, thereby creating a culture within the Five Nations that afforded fundamental safety to women.

Historical accounts of nations punishing offenders for abusing women exist on the opposite side of the continent as well. In the land now known as Alaska, Russian sailors were held accountable for abuse of Native women, as told in the story "Taa'ii' Ti'":

> When the Russians landed they fooled around with the Indian women during the night. There were lots of men in the big ship. The Chief named Taa'ii'Ti' told them not to bother the women, but they still did it, so he told them, "Don't ever do that again." He spoke very loudly. The Russian men he was talking to at that time were feeling his body muscles like this (gesturing) and said to him: "You have a weak body, why are you talking?" He was like a President himself so he was really mad when they told him that. He didn't say another word until everyone went to bed. The next morning, he reminded them not to do it again, but they still fooled around with the women, even the married women. The people in the village told him about it. The Russian men were sleeping at that time. They were

sleeping in tents, and Taa'ii'Ti' got his cane and hit all of them. They all cried out in pain. While doing that he reminded them that they underestimated him and that his body was not weak. He only spared four men. They didn't like it, but what could they do about it. He ordered the rest of the men away to continue what they were being punished for. So the four men invited him to return with them since they knew he knew their own leader too. "Okay, yes," he said. So he went over with them (laughs). When they arrived (in Russia) they took him to the President there. Taa'ii'Ti' told him about the shipload of men that went over to Alaska and how he killed them all that one morning.[50]

Violence against Native women was rare because such behavior was inconsistent with the role of women within the worldview of Indian nations. When such behavior occurred, the nation addressed the offender's action appropriately. For example, among the Tlingit people, perpetrators of domestic violence crimes were tied to stakes during low tide and justice was left to greater powers. If the perpetrator survived, then he survived. If not, then he did not. The punishment was well known for such crimes.[51] The wishes and roles of the aggrieved woman were central to the response from the community. Violence was considered inappropriate behavior and the well-being of the woman was central to restoring the balance of the community. Thus, the family, the clan, as well as spiritual and tribal leaders held essential roles in the process of holding offenders accountable for their actions.

Offenders were often removed from the tribe through banishment or execution, whipped, or publicly humiliated, within the specific practice of the tribe. The Payne Papers contain the following report of the death of a Cherokee chief:

> Doublehead had beaten his wife cruelly when she was with child, and the poor woman died in consequence. The revenge against the murder now became, in the Indian's conscience, imperative. The wife of Doublehead was the sister of the wife of (James) Vann. Vann's wife desired with her own hand to obtain atonement for her sister's death. Vann acquiesced; and he and a large party of friends set away with his wife upon the mission of blood.[52]

The safety of women was and continues to be directly linked to the inherent authority of Indian nations to use the power of government to protect their wellbeing. The erosion of rights after the arrival of Europeans made it more difficult for nations to protect their women.

In exchange for lands and resources, the United States guaranteed to protect the sovereignty of Indian nations. The language of treaties signed by the United States and Indian nations indicates that lands were set aside for the exclusive use of Indian nations.[53] The U.S. Supreme Court has also affirmed that tribes retain the inherent right of self-government unless explicitly removed by Congress.[54] Specifically, the Court has stated that tribal government authority includes "the power to punish tribal offenders . . . to regulate domestic relations among members."[55] In addition, the Court added that tribes retained inherent sovereign power, even on **fee lands**, to regulate conduct of non-Indians that threatens or directly affects "the health or welfare of the tribe."[56] All of this envelops the federal trust responsibility of the United States, which Congress has defined to include "the protection of the sovereignty of each tribal government."[57] The federal trust responsibility assures tribes that the United States will defend the right of Indian nations to self-government. The United States has a trust responsibility to promote the welfare of Indian tribes, which includes a duty to assist tribes in making their reservations livable homes.[58] Within this large context lies the responsibility of the United States to assist Indian nations in safeguarding the physical safety and well-being of Native women from violence.

Regardless of the trust responsibility, both Congress and the Supreme Court have gradually restricted the jurisdictional authority of Indian nations, resulting in the erosion of the legal ability of tribal governments to protect women citizens. This pattern is highlighted by a review of the impact on Native women by the following federal actions.

The first is the Major Crimes Act, passed in 1885, wherein the U.S. government assumed jurisdiction over serious crimes[59] committed by an Indian in Indian Country (specifically in relation to acts of violence commonly committed against women: the crimes of murder, kidnapping, maiming, assault with intent to commit murder, assault with a dangerous weapon, assault resulting in serious bodily injury, and, later, sexual abuse).[60] This was devastating, because these are crimes that relate to acts of violence commonly committed against women. Although Indian tribes retain **concurrent** authority over such crimes, the act severely undermined tribal authority.[61] The Major Crimes Act thus **eroded** the traditional response of tribal governments to such crimes by sending a clear (but incorrect) message to Indian nations that they could not properly handle such cases.

The second act of erosion is contained in sections of the Indian Civil Rights Act, passed in 1968, which limits the sentencing authority of tribal courts to "in no event impose for conviction of any one offense any penalty or punishment greater than imprisonment for a term of one year and a fine of $5,000, or both." This limitation severely restricts the ability of tribal governments to appropriately respond to crimes of violence against Native women such as sexual assault and domestic abuse.[62] The limitations also reinforce the myth that offenders of such crimes will not incur any significant consequence.

The third act of erosion occurred in 1978, when the Supreme Court ruled in *Oliphant v. Suquamish Indian Tribe* that Indian nations did not have authority to prosecute crimes committed by non-Indians.[63] This landmark shift in criminal jurisdiction by the Court altered the ability of Indian nations to hold non-Indian offenders committing violent acts accountable. Indian tribes, while continuing to exercise civil jurisdiction over these offenders, also encounter the public perception that non-Indians can commit such crimes without significant consequences.

In 1953, Congress increased the jurisdictional complexity confronting Indian nations by enacting Public Law 83-280 (PL 280).[64] As an extension of the federal policy to "terminate" Indian tribes, Congress withdrew federal criminal jurisdiction on reservations in six states[65] and authorized those states to assume criminal jurisdiction over Indian nations[66] and permitted all other states to acquire it at their option. Under PL 280 federal responsibility for the prosecution of serious crimes under the Major Crimes Act,[67] such as sexual assault, was transferred to state law enforcement agencies. While PL 280 did not alter the civil or criminal jurisdictional authority of tribal governments, tribes located in PL 280 jurisdictions were denied federal funds to support the development of tribal justice systems.[68] In addition, the transfer of federal responsibility to the state governments to provide law enforcement services to Indian nations was not accompanied by the allocation of any funds to support such services. Today, many tribes located in PL 280 states have no emergency or other law enforcement services that should be provided by states and do not receive funding from the federal government to develop such services. Native women living within PL 280 states frequently report that crimes of physical or sexual assault are not addressed. The consequences of PL 280 are far-reaching and tragic.[69]

In addition to these congressional and Supreme Court actions, the ability of Indian nations to protect women citizens was also eroded through misinterpretation of treaties. Indian nations that entered into treaties with the United States did so on a nation-to-nation basis.[70] This **government-to-government** relationship recognized the inherent sovereign authority of Indian nations over their lands and peoples. In this context, Indian nations held full authority to protect women citizenry from foreign individuals choosing to enter their lands and commit acts of violence against women. The Choctaw and Chickasaw nations, for example, safeguarded authority to protect women citizens by including language providing for jurisdiction over non-Indian persons choosing to reside within the boundaries of the nation.

> Every white person who, having married a Choctaw or Chickasaw, resides in the said Choctaw or Chickasaw Nation, or who has been adopted by the legislative authorities, is to be deemed a member of said nation, and shall be subject to the laws of the Choctaw and Chickasaw Nations according to his domicile, and to prosecution and trial before their tribunals, and to punishment according to their laws in all respects as though he was a native Choctaw or Chickasaw.[71]

According to these agreements, Native women could rely upon their governments for protections from individual acts of abuse from their husbands. In earlier treaties Indian nations also provided for protections for women citizenry by including clauses specific to women.[72]

The Relationship to the Land and the Status of Native Women

Attacks on Native culture began with land acquisition. The legal fiction for creating a basis for land title in North America was the "doctrine of discovery." Under this doctrine, the sovereign discoverer could occupy land already occupied by infidels to extend their Christian sovereignty over the land and the indigenous people who resided there.[73]

The initial dispute between foreign conquerors and Indian nations over land has continued over time. In 1823, the Supreme Court adopted into U.S. law the "doctrine of discovery." Chief Justice John Marshall wrote in *Johnson v. McIntosh*, "As the United States marched across the continent, it was creating an empire by wars of foreign conquest just as England and France were doing in India and Africa. In every case the goal was identical: land."[74] The taking of tribal lands through these wars altered the relationship of Indian nations and specifically Native women to their homelands.

Originally, in the Eastern region of the North American continent, many Indian nations viewed cultivation of the soil as the responsibility of women.[75] In this region:

> [They] developed two forms of land tenure, one communal and the other individual. The village or cultural group claimed sovereignty over a particular area, and individual women controlled the use of specific fields. As long as a woman used a portion of land for agriculture, she had the continuing right of usage. If she stopped cultivating that land, however, either someone else would take the plot or it would revert to communal or village control.[76]

European and later American governments, on the other hand, considered farming the domain of a man and land the private property of individuals. Altering the identity of Native women as caretakers and cultivators of the land and instituting individual ownership was a vehicle for "civilizing" and assimilating the Indians. Because the worldview of many Indian nations held the earth as feminine, the spiritual mother, private ownership of land was culturally destructive to Indian nations and Native women.

Through treaties, Indian nations exchanged lands and resources for peace and recognition of their sovereignty. The language contained in such treaties frequently was not interpreted according to the lifeways of the Indian nation but that of the United States. One example of this is the claim of Sally Ladiga and her heirs to land under the Treaty of New Echota enacted in 1832.

> Under the treaty, Indian heads of families were to be allotted 320 acres of land to live on and cultivate. Local federally appointed "locating agents" decided who was an Indian and who was the head of a family and allotted heads of families the land on which they resided and had made improvements. When Ladiga was enrolled, she had a cabin and a cultivated field on her land, had raised a family of several children, but had no husband of record. The only people recorded living with her were another woman, Sarah Letter, and a boy named Ar-chee-chee. In spite of evidence that Ladiga bought clothes for Ar-chee-chee, as well as conflicting evidence that he was Ladiga's orphaned grandson, the locating agent found that Ladiga was not the head of a family and was not entitled to a half section of the land. . . . Despite all Sally Ladiga's efforts to continue living upon her land a soldier forcibly removed her from it. A white man named Smith entered her land and took over her cabin and field. Armed troops forced Ladiga to immigrate to Indian Territory in Arkansas.[77]

In 1844 the U.S. Supreme Court held that Sally Ladiga was indeed the head of a family. "We cannot seriously discuss the question, whether a grandmother and her grandchildren compose a family, in the meaning of that word in the treaty, it must shock the common sense of all mankind to even doubt it."[78] Although years later the Supreme Court recognized Sally Ladiga as "a head of family," it did not benefit her or her heirs. Sally Ladiga apparently died on the Trail of Tears and her grandchildren could not legally prove that she was their ancestor.

Native women also suffered the loss of their communally held tribal homelands through the General Allotment Act (passed by Congress), which conveyed personal ownership of land to individual Indians.[79] Prior to the Allotment Act, most Indian nations held land collectively. It is estimated that Indian nations lost 90 million acres of land due to the act, displacing hundreds of Native women and families. The act was inconsistently interpreted in different regions of the United States. In some regions, women could not receive allotments as head of household. As a result of the act many tribal women became landless. Additionally, Native women who did receive individual allotments frequently lost land to non-Indian men. In many cases non-Indian men married Native women to gain access to land and resources.[80] The large number of murdered women of the Osage Nation of Oklahoma finally sparked a federal investigation.[81] While the Allotment Act was later abolished, it had a devastating impact upon Indian nations, especially upon the lives of Native women. Many Native women went from holding a strong role in a communal land to being landless.

The alteration of the legal relationship of Native women to the land was another dimension in the erosion of the status and identity of Native women. In many instances it eliminated self-sufficiency, created economic and legal dependency upon a male head-of-household, and, in the case of Sally Ladiga, imposed the status of "homeless."

Impact of Federal Indian Policy on the Safety of Native Women

Historically, federal policy toward Indian nations has eroded the protections and status of Native women within their respective nations and within the United States. Federal policy served as an additional legal dimension that supported the normalization and cultural acceptance of violence committed against Native women. The policies during the Indian Wars, the Boarding School Era, the Adoption Era, and the Forced Sterilization Era highlight the impact of some federal policies upon the lives of Native women.

During the Indian Wars, Native women and their children were targeted. Phrases such as "kill and scalp all, big and little" and "nits make lice" became a rallying cry for the troops. "Since Indians were lice, their children were nits—the only way to get rid of lice was to kill the nits as well."[82] This policy of extermination legalized the killing of Native women. To avoid being killed or having their children murdered, Indian women were forced to assimilate. Assimilation for Native women meant relinquishing honored multifaceted roles within their nations for the role of non-Indian women within the United States. As a result Native women were instructed in the domestic tasks of servants.

The Boarding School Era, from the 1880s to the 1950s, followed by the Adoption Era from the 1950s to the 1970s, removed the children of Native women in order to further the federal policy of assimilation. This policy was clearly a violation of the concept of **mother's right**. Further, the cultural responsibility for raising children, according to customs and traditions of many Indian nations, is that of the mother and the maternal relatives. Therefore, these policies took from women the privilege of raising and passing on cultural traditions to their children. The intent of these two eras is captured in the following statement of the 1886 Commissioner of Indian Affairs:

> It is admitted by most people that the adult savage is not susceptible to the influence of civilization, and we must therefore turn to his children, that they might be taught to abandon the pathway of barbarism and walk with a sure step along the pleasant highway of Christian civilization. . . . They must be withdrawn, in tender years, entirely from the camp and taught to eat, to sleep, to dress, to play, to work, to think after the manner of the white man.[83]

There was a specific intent to disrupt the bond in order to assimilate Indian children. The cultural genocide committed through the forced removal of Native children is well documented as having lifelong detrimental effects on Indian families. One girl later wrote, "I cried aloud, shaking my head all the while until I felt the cold blades of the scissors against my neck, and heard them gnaw off one of my thick braids. Then I lost my spirit."[84] The consequences for resisting the removal of their children to government boarding schools were severe for parents.[85] Further, the physical and sexual violence committed against girls within the government schools by employees further normalized violence committed against Native women.[86]

More recently, Native women were the subjects of a policy described as "forced sterilization"[87] by the Department of Health and Human Services, Indian Health Services, and other health care facilities. Congress investigated the permanent sterilization of Native women at Indian Health Service facilities and contract facilities. In 1976, the comptroller general released a summary report.[88] The investigation, while limited to four areas of the United States for a period of three years, revealed that Native women, without their informed consent, were being permanently sterilized. The report states:

> Indian Health Service records show that 3,406 sterilization procedures were performed on female Indians in the Aberdeen, Albuquerque, Oklahoma City, and Phoenix areas during fiscal years 1973-76. Data for fiscal year 1976 is for a 120 month period ending June 30, 1976. Of the 3,406 procedures performed, 3,001 involved women of child-bearing age (ages 15-44) and 1,024 were performed at Indian Health Service contract facilities. On April 18, 1974, the U.S. District Court for the District of Columbia issued regulations to address the sterilization of persons by the Indian Health Service.

The policy of "sterilization" was operational beyond Indian Health Service facilities as recounted by a victim of the policy:

> I was badly beaten by my husband and left on the street outside our apartment building. An ambulance took me to the hospital. When I woke up I felt my stomach and there were stitches. I asked the nurse, "Did my husband do this?" She said, "No, the doctor did that." I asked why. The nurse said, "The doctor gave you a hysterectomy." I didn't know the meaning of the word. No one in my family knew the meaning of the word.[89]

The depth of the erosion of the physical safety and respect for Native women caused by this genocidal practice is societal and intergenerational.

These legislative acts of Congress, Supreme Court cases, and policies implemented by the executive branches of the U.S. government are not directly responsible for current statistics showing that Native women are the most victimized population in the United States.[90] The social extension of the federal laws and policies discussed above is, however, culturally significant to the acceptance of violence committed against Native women. The fact that Native women are victimized at a rate more than double that of any other population must be understood in this historical context.

The Journey Home

The Violence Against Women Act of 2005 provides Indian nations unprecedented access to resources to improve the governmental response to violence against Native women.[91] The accomplishments of this decade, 1995–2005, provide life-saving services to Native women seeking safety. The shift in federal law and policy over the last ten years is a beginning. Indian nations not only receive unprecedented resources under the act, but an affirmation of their inherent sovereign authority to respond to crimes of violence against women such as domestic violence, dating violence, sexual assault, and stalking.[92]

Indian nations and advocates for the safety of Native women are pursuing a strategy reflective of this reality. Similar to slaying a mythical two-headed monster, Indian nations and advocates must hold accountable both the individual perpetrator and also the justice systems charged with the responsibility of protecting Native women. While individual perpetrators are held accountable for specific acts of violence, legal reforms must be implemented to address gaps in tribal, federal, and state justice systems that increase the vulnerability of Native women to violent victimization as a population. As women's advocate Karen Artichoker remarks:

> We are working to re-shape a western, imposed, punitive criminal justice system into a system that utilizes consequences for bad behavior in combination with the tribal concept of relatives. A system based on this concept allows us to show compassion for offending relatives and will offer the opportunity for offenders to look at themselves and the impact of their behavior on themselves, others, the community, nation, and cosmos.[93]

The prevalence and severity of such crimes committed against Native women today cannot be disconnected from the process of colonization that has occurred since contact with European countries. It is not merely a distant historical period, but a continuing process lived and remembered by Native people on a daily basis. This living memory is evident in the stories and experiences of the survivors. Effie Williams, an Athabascan elder of the Native Village of Allakaket, recounts her first encounter with non-Natives and watching as children were forcibly removed to boarding schools. Marlin Mousseau, an Oglala Sioux traditional pipe bearer, remembers his great-great grandmother, who survived the mass graves of the Wounded Knee massacre at Pine Ridge, South Dakota. Juana Majel-Dixon, of the Pauma-Yuima Band Luiseño Indians, speaks of her forced sterilization in 1967 at an Indian Health Service contract care facility in Escondido, California.

Through education and increased awareness of the origins of violence against Native women, tribal nations can create a path toward its elimination. Understanding the connection of contemporary violence to policies of colonization is a social process important to reforming justice systems and unraveling myths that support cultural acceptance of violence against Native women. The Violence Against Women Acts of 1994, 2000, and 2005 are important historic points to begin the legal process of restoring social protectors of safety for Native women. The act can go further by continuing to support essential services that assist Native women in danger, strengthening the authority of tribal governments to address the safety of women, and establishing a policy that develops services to assist Native women directed by the customs, practices, and beliefs of that community.

The election of advocates for the safety of Native women to positions of tribal leadership is perhaps the clearest political statement by Indian nations of the commitment to eliminating violence against Native women.[94] Federal Indian Law is often analogized to the swinging of the pendulum. The last ten years is clearly one reflection of that swing in federal policy. For all that understand this reality the successes of the last ten years represent a challenge to continue to move forward until Native women and all women can live free of violence. In the words of Tillie Black Bear:

> As Indian women we have survived, as Indian nations we have survived. We have survived because of our beliefs, teachings and traditions. One of our strongest beliefs is in the teachings of White Buffalo Calf Woman. One of the first teachings brought to the Lakota people is that, even in thought, women are to be respected.[95]

Notes

1. *Violence Against Women and Department of Justice Reauthorization Act of 2005* (H.R. 3402).

2. *Violence Against Women Act*, Title IV of the *Violent Crime Control and Law Enforcement Act of 1994* (Pub. L. 103–322), as amended by the *Victims of Trafficking Protection Act of 2000* (Pub. L. 106–386), as amended by the *Violence Against Women and Department of Justice Reauthorization Act of 2005* (H.R. 3402).

3. H.R. 3402, Title IX, Safety for Indian Women.

4. H.R. 3402, Sec. 902 (2). See also inherent right of self-government codified in the *Indian Reorganization Act of 1934*, ch. 576, 48 Stat. 984 (codified as amended at 25 U.S.C. §§ 461-479 (1994 & Supp. IV 1998)); *Indian Civil Rights Act of 1968*, Pub. L. No. 90-284, 82 Stat. 77 (codified as amended at 25 U.S.C. §§ 1301-1341 (1994 & Supp. IV 1998)); *Indian Education Act of 1972*, Pub. L. No. 992-318, 86 Stat. 873 (codified as amended in scattered sections of 7,12,16, and 20

U.S.C.); *Indian Self-Determination and Education Assistance Act of 1975*, Pub. L. No. 93-638, 88 Stat. 2206 (codified as amended in scattered sections of 5 U.S.C. and 25 U.S.C.); and *American Indian Religious Freedom Act of 1978*, Pub. L. No. 95-341, 92 Stat. 469 (codified as amended at 42 U.S.C. § 1996 (Supp. IV 1998)).

5. Throughout this chapter, the term "Native" is used in lieu of "American Indian" or "Alaska Native" when not specifically citing or paraphrasing other work. Native Hawaiians are not included in this reference because they have a distinct historical and contemporary legal relationship to the United States. See *Liliuokalani, Hawaii's Story by Hawaii's Queen* (Honolulu: Mutual Publishing, 1990[1898]) (International plea for justice by Queen Liluokalani for restoration of the Hawaiian throne and her nation to determine its own destiny); *Apology Resolution of 1993*, Pub. L. 103-150 (S.J. Res. 19) (Apology to Native Hawaiians on behalf of the United States for the overthrow of the Kingdom of Hawaii); *Policy of the United States Regarding Its Relationship with Native Hawaiians*, Hearing on S. 2899 Before the Subcommittee on Indian Affairs (2000) (statement of Jacqueline Agtuca, Acting Director of Office of Tribal Justice, USDOJ).

6. See U.S. Commission on Civil Rights, *A Quiet Crisis: Federal Funding and Unmet Needs in Indian Country* (2003), available at http://www.usccr.gov/pubs/na0703/na0204.pdf.

7. H.R. 3402, Title IX, Safety for Indian Women, Sec. 901, Findings.

8. See Lawrence A. Greenfeld and Steven K. Smith, *American Indians and Crime* (Washington, DC: Bureau of Justice Statistics, USDOJ, February 1999, NCJ 173386); Steven W. Perry, *American Indians and Crime* (Washington, DC: Bureau of Justice Statistics, USDOJ, December 2004); Calli Rennison, *Violent Victimization and Race, 1993–1998* (Washington, DC: Bureau of Justice Statistics, USDOJ, 2001); Ronet Bachman, *National Crime Victimization Survey Compilation* (Washington, DC: Bureau of Justice Statistics, USDOJ, 2004).

9. See Patricia Tjaden and Nancy Thoennes, *Full Report of the Prevalence, Incidence, and Consequences of Violence Against Women: Findings from the National Violence Against Women Survey* (National Institute of Justice and Centers for Disease Control and Prevention, NCJ 183781, November 2000), p. 22.

10. See Greenfeld and Smith, p. 4.

11. See Tjaden and Thoennes, p. 22.

12. See USDOJ, *Domestic Violence and Stalking, Second Annual Report to Congress Under the Violence Against Women Act* (1997); USDOJ, *Stalking and Domestic Violence, Third Annual Report to Congress Under the Violence Against Women Act* (1998).

13. Supra note 8.

14. Tjaden and Thoennes, p. 22.

15. One example is that "There were 9,520 incidents of domestic violence reported to Navajo Nation Department of Law Enforcement in 2003. The good news is that number declined from the 11,086 incidents reported in 2002. These figures by no means represent the total number of cases on the reservation, because many incidents go unreported." Kathy Helms, "Tribe Battles High Domestic Violence Rate," *Gallup Independent*, March 18, 2005, available at: www.gallupindependent.com/2005/mar/031805dviolence.html.

16. Hon. Sandra Day O'Connor, "Lessons from the Third Sovereign: Indian Tribal Courts," *Tribal Court Record* 9, no.1 (National Indian Justice Center, 1996).

17. Russia, France, England, and Spain negotiated with and followed similar patterns of violence through warfare against Indian nations and Native women. See Herman J. Viola, *Diplomats in Buckskins: History of Indian Delegations in Washington City* (Bluffton, SC: Rivilo Books, 1995, originally published by the Smithsonian Institution Press, 1981).

18. David E. Stannard, *American Holocaust: The Conquest of the New World* (New York: Oxford University Press, 1992).

19. Sarah Deer, "Sovereignty of the Soul: Exploring the Intersection of Rape Law Reform and Federal Indian Law," *Suffolk University Law Review* vol. 38 (2005): 455.

20. Federal Indian Law refers to codes, cases, and executive orders of the United States and not the tribal law of specific Indian nations.

21. *Aotearoa* is the aboriginal name for New Zealand.

22. Moana Jackson, *Address at the National Collective of Independent Women's Refuges Conference and Annual General Meeting*, Rotorua, Aotearoa (October 15, 2003).

23. Tillie Black Bear is a founding member of the White Buffalo Calf Woman Society of the Rosebud Sioux Tribe (1978) and a founding member of the National Coalition Against Domestic Violence (1978). She is considered one of the grandmothers of the Battered Women's Movement in the United States.

24. Lafitau, *Moeurs des Sauvages*, vol. I (Paris, 1724), pp. 71 and 72, as cited in *Iroquois Women, An Anthology; On the Social and Political Position of Women Among the Huron-Iroquois Tribes* (Iroqrafts, Traditional & Ceremonial Iroquois Crafts & Arts from the Six Nations Reserve Reprint, 1990), p 36.

25. Christine Zuni Cruz, "Tribal Law as Indigenous Social Reality and Separate Consciousness[Re]Incorporating Customs and Traditions into Tribal Law," *UNM Tribal Law Journal* 1 (2000/2001), available at http://tlj.unm.edu/articles/volume_1/zuni_cruz/index.php. (The Tiwa words and translations used here are from a discussion and interview between Isleta Pueblo member and Tiwa instructor Doris Lucero with Christine Zuni, October 14–15, 2000.)

26. Marlin Mousseau is a traditional pipe bearer of the Oglala Sioux Tribe of the Pine Ridge Reservation, South Dakota. Mousseau developed the Medicine Wheel Approach to working with domestic violence, which incorporates traditional Lakota beliefs, philosophies, and ceremonies. He has worked in the field of domestic violence for over twenty years.

27. Jessie Johnnie, Chookaneidee Elder, Sitka Tribe of Alaska; Kayaani Commissioner; Rural Human Services Program Council Member.

28. "Alaska Native Women's Coalition Against Domestic Violence & Sexual Assault" (Statewide Conference Documentary Video, September 2003).

29. Karen Artichoker, *The Criminal Justice System: Indian Country and Domestic Violence Response* (unpublished 1991).

30. Interview with Juana Majel-Dixon, Tribal Council Member, Pauma Yuima Indian Nation (November 2004).

31. Tillie Black Bear, Interview, August 2004.

32. "Beyond the Shelter Doors," Office on Violence Against Women, USDOJ, documentary video in celebration of the ten-year anniversary of the passage of the Violence Against Women Act (Produced by Clan Star, Inc., September 2004).

33. Vine Deloria Jr. and C. Lytle, *American Indian, American Justice* (Austin: University of Texas Press, 1983), pp. 80–109.

34. "The Cherokees traced kinship solely through women. This circumstance gave women considerable prestige, and the all-encompassing nature of the kinship system secured for them a position of power" (Perdue, 1998; see note 41). "In the matrilineal societies of the Hopi in the Southwest, where the status of women was high, a woman wished to give birth to many girl babies, for it was through her daughters that a Hopi woman's home and clan were perpetuated" (Niethammer, 1977).

35. "Divorce was common and easy for most Native American women. If a woman was living with her husband's family, she simply took her belongings and perhaps the children and went to her parents' home. If a couple was living with the wife's parents or if the dwelling was considered hers,

she told the man to leave . . ." Carolyn Niethammer, *Daughters of the Earth: The Lives and Legends of American Indian Women* (New York: Collier Books, 1977) p. 3.

36. Beirne Stedman, "Right of Husband to Chastise Wife," *Virginia Law Register* 3 (1917): 241; *State v. Oliver* (1874) 70 N.C. 44; *State v. Rhodes* (1868) 61 N.C. 445.

37. Killing of a woman's sister under Cherokee law allowed the sister to take blood revenge herself.

38. Marian L. Swain, *Gilbert Said* (Walnut Creek, CA: Hardscratch Press Book, 1992).

39. Nathaniel Green Papers (Library of Congress), quoted in Samuel Cole Williams, *Tennessee during the Revolutionary War* (Knoxville: University of Tennessee Press, 1974), p. 201.

40. Ibid.

41. Theda Perdue, *Cherokee Women: Gender and Cultural Change 1700–1835*, (Lincoln: University of Nebraska Press, 1998), p. 101.

42. Tex "Red Tipped Arrow" Hall, *President's Report*, 2005 Executive Council Winter Session (February 28, 2005).

43. See Virginia M. Bouvier, *Women and Conquest of California, 1542–1840: Codes of Silence* (Tucson: University of Arizona Press, 2001); Karen Anderson, *Chain Her By One Foot, The Subjugation of Native Women in Seventeenth-Century New France* (New York: Routledge, 1991); Ann Fienup-Riordan, *Boundaries and Passages: Rule and Ritual in Yup'ik Eskimo Oral Tradition* (Norman: University of Oklahoma Press, 1994).

44. Bouvier, *Women and Conquest of California*, p. 3.

45. Bouvier, *Women and Conquest of California*, p. 5.

46. *Ab origine*, meaning "from the beginning."

47. *United States v. Wheeler*, 435 U.S. 313 (1978). Here, it is evident from the treaties between the Navajo Tribe and the United States and from the various statutes establishing federal criminal jurisdiction over crimes involving Indians, that the Navajo Tribe has never given up its sovereign power to punish tribal offenders, nor has that power implicitly been lost by virtue of the Indian's dependent status; thus, tribal exercise of that power is presently the continued exercise of retained tribal sovereignty. Pp. 323-326. Respondent, a member of the Navajo Tribe, pleaded guilty in Tribal Court to a charge of contributing to the delinquency of a minor and was sentenced. Subsequently, he was indicted by a federal grand jury for statutory rape of a fifteen-year-old girl arising out of the same incident.

48. *Cherokee Nation v. Georgia*, 30 U.S. (5 Pet.) 1 (1831).

49. The Iroquois Constitution, The Great Binding Law, Gayanashagowa, Number 2, University of Oklahoma Law Center, available at www.law.ou.edu/iroquois.html.

50. Johnny Frank, Athabascan Elder, as cited in Carrie E. Garrow and Sarah Deer, *Tribal Criminal Law and Procedure* (Walnut Creek, CA: AltaMira Press, 2004).

51. Telephone interview with Tammy Young, member Sitka Tribe of Alaska and codirector of the Alaska Native Women's Coalition, August 1999.

52. As cited by Perdue, *Cherokee Women*.

53. In 1868, the Second Treaty of Fort Laramie established the Crow Reservation and provided that the reservation "shall be . . . set apart for the absolute and undisturbed use and occupation" of the tribe, and that no non-Indians except government agents "shall ever be permitted to pass over, settle upon, or reside in" the reservation. "[T]he United States now solemnly agrees that no persons, except those herein designated and authorized to [450 U.S. 544, 554] do so, and except such officers, agents, and employees of the Government as may be authorized to enter upon Indian reservations in discharge of duties enjoined by law, shall ever be permitted to pass over, settle upon, or reside in the territory described in this article for the use

of said Indians." (Second Treaty of Fort Laramie, May 7, 1868, Art. II, 15 Stat. 650). Similarly, Article II of the Treaty of Medicine Creek, 10 Stat. 1132, provided that the Puyallup Reservation was to be "set apart, and, so far as necessary, surveyed and marked out for their exclusive use" and that no "white man [was to] be permitted to reside upon the same without permission of the tribe and the superintendent or agent."

54. *United States v. Wheeler*, 435 U.S. 313 (1978). See also President Bush, Executive Memorandum to Executive Departments and Agencies, signed September 23, 2004; President Clinton, Executive Order 13175—Consultation and Coordination with Indian Tribal Governments, November 6, 2000.

55. *Montana v. United States*, 450 U.S. at 564 (1981).

56. 450 U.S. at 565–66.

57. 25 U.S.C. 3601.

58. See *Montana v. United States*, 450 U.S. 544, 56 & n. 15 (1980).

59. Seven crimes were originally covered, but the list has been expanded to the present fourteen by a series of amendments.

60. *Major Crimes Act*, 18 U.S.C.A. 1153 (1885).

61. *United States v. Lara*, 541 U.S. 193 (2004). Because the tribe acted in its capacity as a sovereign authority, the Double Jeopardy Clause does not prohibit the federal government from proceeding with the present prosecution for a discrete federal offense. Pp. 4-16. Domestic violence case during which a federal officer was assaulted.

62. *Indian Civil Rights Act*, 25 U.S.C. 1302(7) (1968).

63. *Oliphant v. Suquamish Indian Tribe*, 435 U.S. 191 (1978).

64. Public Law 83-280, 67 Stat. 588(1953).

65. The six named states, known as the "mandatory states," are: California, Minnesota (except Red Lake Reservation), Nebraska, Oregon (except the Warm Springs Reservation), Wisconsin, and, as added in 1958, Alaska (except the Annette Islands with regard to the Metlakatla Indians).

66. PL 280 also conferred civil jurisdiction on the mandatory states, 28 U.S.C.A. 1360 (a), that is confined to adjudicatory jurisdiction only. *Bryan v. Itasca County*, 426 U.S. 373 (1976).

67. PL 280 provided that the *General Crimes Act* (18 U.S.C.A. 1152) and the *Major Crimes Act* (18 U.S.C.A. 1153) no longer applied to areas covered by PL 280 in the mandatory states (18 U.S.C.A. 1162).

68. See C. Goldberg-Ambrose and D. Champagne, "A Second Century of Dishonor: Federal Inequities and California Tribes," *Report to the Advisory Council on California Indian Policy*, (1996), pp. 47–59.

69. See Carole Goldberg-Ambrose, *Planting Tail Feathers: Tribal Survival and Public Law* (American Indian Studies Center, 1997), p. 280.

70. Not all Indian nations entered into a treaty with the United States. Further, the U.S. Congress failed to ratify hundreds of treaties negotiated with Indian nations. Vine Deloria Jr. and David E. Wilkins, *Tribes, Treaties and Constitutional Tribulations* (Austin: University of Texas Press, 1999).

71. Article 38 of the treaty with the Choctaws and Chickasaws of April 28, 1866 (14 Stat. 779).

72. Article Six, Republic of Mexico Treaty with the Navajo Chieftains, July 15, 1839. Treaty consisted of seven articles. Article stated: "In case any Navajo Indian woman succeeds in escaping by fleeing from the house of her master, on arrival of the said woman in her own land, when it is verified, that she remain free and without any obligation of the nation to give anything for her ransom." Translation from www.lapahie.com/Dinc_Treaty_1839.cfm.

73. Roe Bubar and Pamela Jumper Thurman, "Violence Against Native Women," *Social Justice* 31, no. 4 (2004): 73.

74. Vine Deloria Jr., *Custer Died for Your Sins* (Norman: University of Oklahoma Press, 1988), p. 51.

75. Indian nations within other regions of North America experienced unique circumstances in negotiating continued control of lands and territory. The relationship of the women of these nations to the land was unique according to their societies.

76. See R. Douglas Hurt, *Indian Agriculture in America: Prehistory to the Present* (Lawrence: University Press of Kansas, 1987).

77. Bethany Ruth Berger, "After Pocahontas: Indian Women and the Law, 1830 to 1934," *American Indian Law Review* 21, no.1 (1997): 7.

78. Ladiga II, 43 U.S. (2 How.) at 583.

79. Act of February 8, 1887, 24 Stat., 388.

80. *Moore v. United States*, 150 U.S. 57 (1893). Palmer's land was rented from an Indian. This land was also claimed by a full-blooded Choctaw woman named Lizzie Lishtubbi. Four days before the murder, defendant Moore married this woman. He had previously boasted that he was going to marry the woman and get the land; "that she was old and would not live long, and he would get a good stake." One of the witnesses told him that he would have trouble over it, as Charles Palmer was about the gamiest man in the territory. He replied: "I am some that way myself." As he started to leave, he said: "I may not get to marry the widow; and if I do not, if you give me away, I will kill you."

81. See Dennis McAuliffe, *Bloodland: A Family Story of Oil, Greed and Murder on the Osage Reservation* (Council Oak Books, 1999); Lawrence J. Hogan, *The Osage Indian Murders: The True Story of a 21-Murder Plot to Inherit the Headrights of Wealthy Osage Tribe Members* (AMLEX, Inc., 1988).

82. Dee Brown, *Bury My Heart at Wounded Knee: An Indian History of the American West*, 1970, p. 90 and David Stannard, *American Holocaust: Columbus and the Conquest of the New World*, 1992, p. 131.

83. Monroe E. Price, *Law and the American Indian Contemporary Legal Education Series* (1973), quoted in Lila J. George, "Why the Need for the Indian Child Welfare Act?" *Journal of Multicultural Social Work* 5 (1997): 166.

84. "School Days of an Indian Girl," *Atlantic Monthly*, 85, Issue 508 (1900).

85. Nineteen Hopi fathers were arrested and imprisoned for over a year at Alcatraz for failing to enroll their children in a government boarding school with deplorable conditions. Wendy Holliday, *Hopi History: The Story of the Alcatraz Prisoners*, available at www.nps.gov/alcatraz/tours/hopi/hopi-h1.htm.

86. U.S. Congress, Senate Committee on Indian Affairs, "Survey of the Conditions of the Indians in the United States, Hearings before a Subcommittee of the Committee on Indian Affairs," Senate, on SR 79, 70th Cong., 2nd session, 1929, 428–29, 1021–23, and 2833–35.

87. See Michael Sullivan DeFine, *A History of Governmentally Coerced Sterilization: The Plight of the Native American Woman* (University of Maine School of Law, 1997), available at www.geocities.com/CapitolHill/9118/mike2.htm; Charles R. England, *A Look at the Indian Health Service Policy of Sterilization, 1972–1976*, p. 1, available at www.dickshovel.com/IHSSterPol.html.

88. Comptroller General of the United States, B-164031(5), November 23, 1976. The regulations specified: "(1) continued a July 1973 moratorium on sterilizing persons who were under 21 years of age or mentally incompetent, (2) specified the informed consent procedure for persons legally capable of consenting to sterilization, and (3) omitted the requirement that individuals seeking sterilization be orally informed at the outset that no Pedersi benefits can be withdrawn because of failure to accept sterilization."

89. Presentation by a survivor during the Alaska Native Women's Statewide Conference (2003).

90. Bachman, *National Crime Victimization Survey Compilation*.

91. Indian tribes received initially a 4 percent set aside in VAWA 1994, a 5 percent set aside in 2000, and a 10 percent set aside in 2005.

92. H.R. 3402 (VAWA). The Acts of 1994, 2000, and 2005 required that a percentage of the total funds be set aside for Indian tribal governments to enhance their governmental response to domestic violence, sexual assault, and stalking. Further, these acts recognized and required that full faith and credit be given protections orders issued by tribal courts: "any protection order issued that is consistent with subsection (b) of this section by the court of one state or Indian tribe (the issuing state or Indian tribe) shall be accorded full faith and credit by the court of another state or Indian tribe (the enforcing state or Indian tribe) and enforced as if it were the order of the enforcing state or Indian tribe" 18 U.S.C. § 2265(a) (2000).

93. Karen Artichoker, "About Circle Sentencing," May 1996 (unpublished).

94. Joe Garcia, elected president NCAI, November 2005; Leonora Hootch, shelter director, elected Village of Emmonak Council, November 2005; Cecilia Fire Thunder, Cangleska advocate, elected president, Oglala Sioux Tribe 2004; Tex Hall, strong supporter of the safety of Indian women, re-elected president, National Congress of American Indians, November 2003. Eleanor David, co-director, Alaska Native Women's Coalition, elected to Village of Allakaket Tribal Council 2003. Wayne Taylor, public zero tolerance for domestic violence campaign, re-elected chairman of the Hopi Indian Tribe. Arlene Quetaki, specialized domestic violence prosecutor, elected governor, Pueblo of Zuni 2001; and Elmer Makua, batterer re-education provider, re-elected to Village Council 2000–present.

95. Supra note 36.

Questions

1. How is the petition that was signed by the Alaska Natives of Hydaburg an example of the subjugation of women from that community? What rights were removed from Alaska Native women? Why did the community agree to the petition?
2. Why would Nancy Ward's speech to the Treaty Commission have surprised non-Native attendees and treaty commissioners? What does it tell us about women in Cherokee society? Why were her American female counterparts unable to respond to her call for peace?
3. What does the story about Russian sailors abusing Native Alaskan women reveal about that nation's laws on violence against women? What were the repercussions for violence?
4. Why might tribes in PL-280 states have a more difficult time responding to violence against women?

In Your Community

1. Are there stories in your community that reveal the status of and teach about respect for women? How did you learn about these stories?
2. How did the General Allotment Act affect women in your community?
3. How does your tribal community work to protect women today?

4. What responsibilities do you believe the federal or state governments have in protecting the women of your community? How have they failed or made strides in keeping women and children safe?

Terms Used in Chapter 1

Common law: Unwritten law of the tribe, developed through custom and tradition.
Concurrent: Together, having the same authority; at the same time.
Covenant: A binding agreement; a promise.
Customary law: A law based on custom or tradition.
Eroded: Caused to diminish or deteriorate.
Fee lands: Land that is owned free and clear without any trust or restrictions.
Government-to-government: A relationship between equal or near-equal nations that prevents one having control over the individuals in another.
Inherent authority: An authority possessed without its being derived from another.
Mother's right: The right of a mother to her children.

Suggested Further Reading

Anderson, Karen. *Chain Her by One Foot: The Subjugation of Women in Seventeenth-Century New France.* New York: Routledge, 1991.

Berger, Bethany Ruth. "After Pocahontas: Indian Women and the Law, 1830 to 1934." *American Indian Law Review* 21, no. 1 (1997).

Bouvier, Virginia Marie. *Women and the Conquest of California, 1542-1840: Codes of Silence.* Tucson: University of Arizona Press, 2001.

Braveheart-Jordan, Maria, and Lemyra Debruyn. "So She May Walk in the Balance: Integrating the Impact of Historical Trauma in the Treatment of Native American Indian Women." In *Racism in the Lives of Women*, eds. Jeanne Adleman and Gloria M. Enguidanos. New York: Haworth Press, 1995.

Bubar, Roe, and Pamela Jumper Thurman. "Violence Against Native Women." *Social Justice* 31 (2004): 70.

Deer, Sarah. "Federal Indian Law and Violent Crime: Native Women and Children at the Mercy of the State." *Social Justice* 31 (2004): 17.

Devens, Carol. "Separate Confrontations: Gender as a Factor in Indian Adaptation to European Colonization in New France." *American Quarterly* 38 (1986): 461.

Fiske, Jo-Anne. "Colonization and the Decline of Women's Status: The Tsimshian Case." *Feminist Studies* 17 (1991): 509.

Skin on Skin

five little girls
Kiowa, Pawnee, Ojibwa, Choctaw, Crow
we were babies out of our teens
hundreds, a thousand miles
separating us from loved ones
Haskell Indian Junior College
was our home

a simple walk to the 24-hour grocery store
"Strength in numbers," Montana said
this statement was true, but not for us
Dillon's, hangout to the skinheads
they were present
as reliable as the locusts that claimed
everything in Kansas that summer

it started with taunts through the store
down one aisle then another
continued into the muggy heat
that took one's breath away
hearts racing,
we turned toward our version of home

we kept close to one another
"Stay near the houses,
they wouldn't want witnesses," Jocelyn whispered.
we could see the rooftop of our dorm,
when they made their move
then we made ours

run! Is what instinct told us
what Mother said to do in that situation
I could feel ancestors next to me
felt long black hair brushing against my sweaty face,
was it my own or someone else's?

we were caught in the tall dry grass
bordering campus

I felt dead dry stalks pushing through my t-shirt
realizing nothing thrives in this state
except the hate which was delivering
blows to my face and head

I swallowed blood, smelled the fear
coming from the skinhead
who was kicking me in the ribs
I heard cries, screams
and above everything else . . . rage

I remember a flash of black boots
I remember the words
"Dirty stupid squaws, get out of our state!"
"All you stupid squaws need haircuts!"
then I saw the flash of a switchblade
gleaming in the hot September sun

I heard my Grandmother's voice screaming,
"Move, Makoose, move!"
I felt the strength & love of my family with me
as I began to kick, scream and rage
against my attacker
my friends did the same,
I believe our helpers were with us

soon we heard screaming breaks on asphalt
I saw a flurry of Indian boys
friends on the football team
Just getting out of practice

my last image of my attacker
in his black t-shirt gleaming in the sun
as he ran with his fellow skinheads
for the high ground, like a war party
was on their trail

I felt strong arms lifting me up
holding me, trying to stop
the bleeding from my nose, lip and eye

the wounds near my ribs
these scars I still carry

they never found our attackers
I guess all skinheads look the same right?

I didn't tell my parents for two years
when I did, we had a healing ceremony
for the whole family

sometimes, late at night, nightmares haunt me
I wake up sweating, shaking & clutching my ribs
where your knife made contact

someday you, like my scars
will fade away

My Grandmother tells me this.

    Sally Brunk (Lac du Flambeau Ojibwa)

Chapter 2

Sexual Violence: An Introduction to the Social and Legal Issues for Native Women

CHARLENE ANN LAPOINTE

> *When I am gone (to the spirit world), remember to always be good to your sisters because it is through them that I will be with you.*
>
> —ADELINE STELLA BROKEN LEG-LAPOINTE
> (SPIRIT JOURNEY, FEBRUARY 3, 1999)

One night as *Ina* (my mother) lay physically weakened and her spirit began sacred preparations for her spirit journey, she spoke those words to *misuŋkala*, my precious younger brothers. The power of her message influenced me much later because, as a mere mortal being, my emotions at that very moment were a hair's width from panic! I felt a sense of myself as a small child that didn't know what to do because her mother was leaving for a different world. I could neither stop her nor figure out a way that I could go with her without violating our ancient **taboo** on suicide.

Toward the end of *Ina*'s earthly journey, I spent a lot of time with her in hospitals and was thus blessed as a witness of spiritual phenomena that we Native people speak about only in privacy with our families. Whenever I recognized that *Ina* was traveling in the spirit world, I sat reverently and respectfully in the knowledge that our ancestors were talking with her and helping her to prepare for her journey. I paid close attention to her side of the conversations because I wanted to remember her words. I wanted to take quiet time later to pray and reflect upon the spiritual meaning of her sacred talk.

Ina's advice to my brothers was powerful in its simplicity. On the surface level, her words meant just what she stated, that my brothers should be good to their sisters after she left for the spirit world. But, there was far more to it than that. Every moment of time that my sisters and I spent with our mother was unique for each of us. We each interpreted these moments differently; we each came to our own understanding; we each carry a part of her teachings with us. The more I thought about it I began to understand it as a teaching from time **immemorial** that runs through the fabric of all Native women's customs, traditions, and beliefs within the tribe.

Within my lifetime I learned through stories and subtle admonishments from my parents to the young boys and girls within our family and *ti o'spa ye* (extended families) about the sacredness of women and young girls in our tribal society. They taught by words and actions how an adolescent is no longer a child and must learn to behave respectfully toward his sisters and female cousins and vice versa. When this is learned and practiced within the family, it will show within our tribal society as a whole.

The older, more traditional-thinking Lakota talk about *Ehaŋni* (long-ago times), as I'm sure other tribal nations do in their own unique ways. As I understand *Ehaŋni*, these oral stories were told to teach and reinforce individual customs and societal standards among the people, as well as to teach listening skills and honesty in the retelling of these teachings. Women and men had their own ceremonies at different phases of their lives. Women were held in high esteem because we are the givers of life. Women were held up as sacred because for nine months we carry the spirit world within our bodies before a new spirit is born into this earthly life. We commune with and are bonded to that spirit before it makes its journey through the birth canal into this world.

Children are considered *Wakaŋ* (sacred) because they have newly arrived and are still mostly spirit. Two spirits that travel here together (twins) are even more of a gift. They are also considered a sacred burden and a teaching for the mother if she has been raised with the proper instructions in child rearing. Small children have not yet been corrupted by the burdens of the intellect, interpretations, or influences from other minds.

Some traditional elders, when they feel safe enough to do so, will still remind us, "keep a childlike quality about you." That doesn't mean that we should act like an infant into adulthood; it is meant to remind us that the innocence we see in the eyes of our children and grandchildren is the same kind of innocence that dwells within our very soul. The curiosity and awe with which a child responds to everything within the environment is how, as adults, we need to remain in our perception of the universe. In this way, we are tied to the remembrance in our daily comings and goings that the Creator gave us this quality as a compass to follow during our **sojourn** upon *Uŋci Maka* (Grandmother Earth). Our spirit is ancient; it remains the same throughout our time on earth. It is our physical bodies that grow and change and, eventually, return to the earth.

Preschool

What I share through my writing comes from my own life experiences. Since my birth as the first-born girl, all of my grandmothers and grandfathers were always nearby to provide encouragement and guidance. It came in the form of hugs; *Unci* (grandma) kisses; chokecherry patty treats; and stories about the stars, two-leggeds, four-leggeds, and *iktomi* (the trickster). Therefore, I hold these old-time *winnuh'cala* (real women) and *wicah'cala* (real men) in high esteem for their knowledge, wisdom, and gentle guidance.

As little children, my older brothers and I were free to explore our natural surroundings. We could ride in the wagon, run beside it, or jump on and off of it, as grandpa and *ah-te* (father) visited and smoked their Bull Durham roll-your-owns. All the while the ol' brown horse and the white one with one blue eye ambled their way down to the spring. The menfolk would fill up our two huge wooden barrels with water and we would have fun doing the same thing all the way back to our one-room house. We would take vegetables from the garden and pretend we were going on "expeditions" (wherever we got that word!), and spend all day on the prairies, or play down by the creek.

We lived a simple life far out in the country on the Rosebud Reservation with simple rules, loving attentive parents, grandparents, uncles, aunties, and cousins. Our little house was filled with a lot of visiting, games, humor, and laughter. The nights were intensely quiet, with only the sounds of the night creatures, and the sky seemed to always be heavy with stars. It was bliss for a child.

My father hunted and planted, always working hard at whatever job he held to provide for our family. In the winter he was the one to get up and put the wood in the cast-iron stove before we were awakened. There were those special times that I woke up early enough to watch him hook up the plow to grandpa's brown horse, hook the reins around his waist and arm, put his weight onto the plow and clack his tongue as he and the ol' brown horse worked together to turn over the soil. Wherever we lived, we always had a garden—not only for our family, but any family who needed potatoes, corn, vegetables, or melons.

My mother spent the days cooking, cleaning, and washing diapers and clothes in the tin tub that doubled as our bathtub. We played with our cousins while *Ina* picked chokecherries, buffalo berries, and plums. She also dug *timpsila* (wild turnips) with the womenfolk as they talked and laughed. She cooked special recipes of pheasant, prairie dog, deer, and other wild game. When we had the money, we ate store-bought food, too. I loved waking up to steaming hot oatmeal topped with commodity butter melting inside of fresh *aguyapi* (oven bread). We had no running water, electricity, or transportation, but that didn't matter because we were happy and well-fed.

Sometimes our Ihanktonwan relatives from the Yankton Reservation traveled a long distance in cars to visit us. It was like they were from another world. I admired the cars, but I was more interested in listening to the conversations of the womenfolk. I especially loved to hear my Ihanktonwan *Kun'si* (Ihanktonwan grandmother) laugh and talk in their dialect, because that mixture sounded like a happy song.

I will always remember how our relatives loved to sing and pray together. Lakota was the only language spoken, except when our Dakota relatives came to visit. My Sicaŋgu *Uŋci* (Sicangu grandmother), my father's aunt, was held in high esteem as a keeper of *wolakota* (the sacred teachings of the Lakota). Sometimes when she and I slept outside together, she told me about the stars and answered all my questions patiently until I fell asleep listening to her gentle voice. Our cultural and spiritual teachings were wrapped inside stories and legends that could be serious, humorous, exciting, and sometimes a bit scary. I believe that it made the teaching easier to remember.

My maternal grandfather was an herbal healer. He was old and quiet, with leather brown skin and pure white hair. Much of the time, he sat with his chair propped back against the house smoking leisurely, always watching the sky. Sometimes we would interrupt our play to sit and look at the sky with him. I didn't know what I was looking for, but it was definitely calming and sometimes made me sleepy. He knew the changing of the weather, and it seemed he knew what was coming in the wind. Grandpa paid attention to the sky. These old ones feel what is in the wind because the sacred wind knows everything.

Sometimes I wonder if he knew what was coming in the wind for me. Maybe he did. Maybe he saw a storm coming. They say it's always calm before a storm. When the thunder beings are coming, it stirs up fear among the people. When the howling and force of the wind subside, the trees straighten back up, the pelting of the rain lessens to a drizzle, and the beautiful rainbow arches across the sky. It is then that our fear subsides and we can smell the cleansed air and look to the earth to see new growth.

I didn't see or feel the change coming in the wind. I was **oblivious** to any storm so long as I was beside my family inside our cozy, kerosene-lit house. Part of the change came when my paternal grandmother moved to a nearby *wasicu* (white man) town. She lived near a park on the main street and often arranged for me to stay with her at her new home. I traveled with her in her new green convertible car with a white canvas top. Grandma always sat in the backseat passenger side while someone drove her.

At grandma's house there was a huge, tall chief-man who traveled around with a big drum and sang at *wacipis* (Lakota dances). He would come back to grandma's with other men and women who looked sleepy and talked in loud voices. Sometimes they fell down and laughed about falling or just went to sleep where they fell and snored loudly. Sometimes grandma would wake me up with a finger to her lips and a "sh-h" to be quiet. She'd slip me out the window while I was still half asleep and lead me to some bushes away from the house. There she laid me back down to sleep on a bed she made on the ground. Soon after, I suppose through the moccasin telegraph, my parents found out and would show up at any hour of the day or night to take me back out to the country. After that, my grandma wasn't allowed to take me back to her place to stay for a long time. Instead, she would come to the reservation to see me. I was the apple of grandma's eye. She was a nondrinker, nonsmoker, noncusser, nontalker, and she was painfully shy!

One day, when I was about four years old, I was at my grandmother's house in town. During the afternoon, grandma and her daughters quietly left for the store without telling me. They probably had to sneak away because I wanted to be by *Unci's* side all the time. I loved the penny candy at the store and everyone knew that *Unci* couldn't say no to me. Meanwhile, back at the house, I went inside to find grandma, but she wasn't there. The next thing I remember, I was lying in the small room on the bed and big man stepuncle was lying behind me. I remember wondering where my pants were. I remember feeling excruciating pain. To this day I believe that *Wakaŋtanka* (the Great Holy) mercifully took my spirit from my body because my mind was gone. Big man stepuncle raped and sodomized my little four-year-old body when no one was around to protect me.

> *There was this little scared rabbit hiding in the bushes quivering from fright. Whenever the wind blew and rattled the leaves her eyes darted this way and that. She sat petrified and tried to wish the leaves into staying still because when the leaves moved she felt exposed to the world. Soon daylight faded to dusk, then into night, and no one could see her. Still she sat rooted in fear that the unseen enemy was waiting to kill or do her more harm. Finally, she could see grandma's silhouette outside the kitchen door. She was peering into the night and wiping her hands with the bottom of her calico apron. Each time grandma came outside she came nearer.*

When I could hear her whisper my name, I bolted on a dead run lest the evil that befell me should grab me before I reached the safety of grandma's arms. For some reason, grandma put her apron over my head and led me inside as you would a spooked horse. On that day, in that moment of unbearable pain, my spirit journey on the good red road was detoured by a pedophile stepuncle. Through incestuous rape, this evil man forced a four-year-old girl onto the black road of alcohol, drugs, violence, suicidal ideations, suicide attempts, and a whole slough of other insane behaviors. Thus began my preschool education.

An Inside Look at War

On October 10, 1879, Colonel Richard Pratt opened the doors to the Carlisle Indian Industrial School in Carlisle, Pennsylvania. Before he opened the doors, he studied and developed his own methods to civilize and educate Indian "savages." He tested his theories on imprisoned chiefs and warriors who were incarcerated in Marion, Florida. Pratt selected several of these leaders, cut their hair in the white man's fashion of the day, bathed and shined them up, dressed them in new blue prison suits with shiny brass buttons, and shod them with new leather shoes. After Pratt outfitted his test subjects, he took them with him to Hampton Institute in Virginia to further test his theories on the socialization of Indian savages. Hampton Institute was a "Negro" industrial school where Colonel Pratt was newly employed ("Negro" being the term of the day). He wanted the heathen Indians to learn to be submissive and compliant. He wanted to prove that Indians could be civilized under the right conditions like the black man, so he used the Negro as a role model for Indians. After proving his experiment a success, Pratt began to develop Indian boarding schools.

Over the years, Colonel Pratt personally made many recruiting trips out to tribal territories and rounded up thousands of Native children five years old and up. The children were loaded onto trains and transported thousands of miles away from home. The older youth cared for the needs of the little ones as best they could during the long, cold trip to Pennsylvania. They also attempted to protect them from abuses at the boarding school. Like their tribal chiefs and warrior relatives before them, the children were also stripped of clothing and hairstyles bearing any resemblance to their particular tribe. Pratt's philosophy of "Kill the Indian, Save the Man" was evident in all aspects of America's first boarding school for Indian children. Pratt's experiment was backed by the Quakers and eventually by the U.S. government as a means of taking care of America's "Indian problem."

In 1929, fifty years after the opening of Carlisle Indian Industrial School, a five-year-old child entered a local boarding school on the Rosebud Reservation in South Dakota to begin her education. This child would later become my mother. Although the boarding school had honed the skills developed by Pratt to discourage "Indian talk" through corporal punishment, my mother was determined to keep her language and culture alive. My mother's spirit survived it all.

In 1953, at the ripe old age of five, I entered the same boarding school that my mother had attended. It had been seventy-four years after the establishment of Pratt's Pennsylvania boarding school for Indian children. By this time, Pratt's tactics were being used to not only kill the Indian, but the man as well. I became an unrecorded statistic over and over again, sexually abused by thoroughly trained, human products of Pratt's well-thought-out military system of deprivation. The war against Native children was alive and well and still churning out children conditioned to turn against their tribal culture, spirituality, and anything feminine in their **psyche**. Over the centuries, we shared the same fate as our ancestral sisters. Our men, who once were warriors of great tribal chief, warrior, and medicine societies, were changed and set loose in the homes, families, and extended families of the tribe to wreak havoc upon the ancient ways of *wolakota*.

There were no chiefs in sight when this war was being carried out upon the sacred descendants of our great chiefs and medicine people. I have read that some great chiefs volunteered their own children to attend Carlisle Indian School in order to prove their trust in the white man's education. This was done against the advice of their own people, especially the mothers. It was no different in my *Ina*'s day or my days. There were no warriors within miles when our screams died away into shocked silence. There were no medicine men with us when our Lakota spirit left our tortured little bodies.

In the wake of boarding schools came institutionalized, "once were warriors," shrewd, cunning pedophiles without a conscience. Somehow, a Native pedophile seems even more wicked (whether he is drunk or sober) because he is acting contrary to tribal teachings that women and children are sacred. Perpetrating sexual acts upon little children is an evil art of sexual violence that is being played out over and over again from generation to generation. Little girls grow into women and little boys grow into men. Without healthy guidance and direction, sexually violated girls grow into womanhood already conditioned to a high threshold of pain and suffering. Anything below that threshold is not what is normal to them. These are the ones targeted by sexual predators who prefer children and seek out ones who have already been abused.

Within a very short time of starting boarding school, I fell under the scrutiny of and received unwanted attention from both male and female pedophiles. I must have been the perfect victim, having been initiated before I got to school. The second perpetrator in my short life on this earth was my kindergarten and first grade teacher. She was a redhead who always wore her hair in a bun. She seemed to relish degrading, humiliating, and punishing me in front of my peers. Eventually, the time came that I preferred physical punishment to the ugly wrongs that she did to me and made me do to her while the rest of the class napped. If I recoiled from her touch, she punished me. If I hid from her during recess, she punished me. If I recognized and tried to help alleviate the fear and emotional pain of another student whom she focused her nasty attention upon, she punished me.

The third self-appointed sex teacher was another white female. From those particularly intrusive encounters came something dark and insidious, like memories marinating in a dark murkiness that would make me physically sick when I heard stories of women being raped with foreign objects. When young Native men disrespectfully recited sexually explicit jokes about oral sex in the presence of young women, I could not argue with them as other young women did. I usually ended up in the bathroom vomiting.

It seemed that the rapes, molestations, attempted molestations, snarling anger, and the hunter-prey stalking tactics of the predators became commonplace. The only time that I felt safe was alone or with my immediate family. It was not a foolproof defense because I grew up in boarding schools (except for a couple of semesters) and I couldn't always be with my family. I was prey just like the rest of the poor innocent little children.

Throughout my school years until my early thirties, sexual predators seemed to be everywhere! My spirit left my body many, many times. Mental health professionals have labeled this as a dissociative disorder. I believe that the ability to leave one's body is *of the spirit*. It can become a disorder, but I will go into that later in this chapter.

In boarding school, I was a chronic bed wetter and was shamed by being forced to hold up and display my soiled sheets for all the girls to see as they went by in line with their sheets. Sometimes the sheets were hung out the window for the boys to see, and they would always ask whose sheets they were. Shame and ridicule were daily lessons, as if we weren't carrying enough burdens already. When I left that particular boarding school, I went home with my family. My bed-wetting stopped because something more sinister was taking place.

Social and Legal Realities of Sexual Violence

Using my own experiences as a victim of sexual violence in childhood and young adulthood is an attempt to follow the trauma through its life cycle and to describe the unseen trash that we carry into the different phases of our life cycles, sometimes right to our very deathbed. It is meant to show that whether you were sexually traumatized once or thirty times, it is a devastation that cannot be ignored. This chapter is not a cleaned-up, sanitized storybook tale that excludes negative human aspects that we don't like to look at for very long, if at all. On the contrary, it is those very aspects that we need to identify and heal.

If reading my story brings up memories and feelings that you thought you swept deep into the recesses of your mind, please, ask for help from someone you trust. Find someone who has dealt with their own incest and/or sexual abuse issues by working their way through it in an inpatient therapeutic setting, preferably someone who has lived a continuous healthy lifestyle for more than three years. These people will help you to learn how to begin dealing with and healing your pain. We'll take a look at that as we explore the realities of sexual violence.

As an encouragement to all readers, know that when we are able to begin our own individual healing, we are able to connect the dots (so to speak). We are able to understand the "balance" that our ancestors have always encouraged us to seek, which involves our emotional, physical, mental, and spiritual selves. When our fear subsides and we are able to begin understanding and connecting the causes and effects of sexual violence, we see more clearly how centuries of sexual and other kinds of abuses against Native girls and women have brought great tribal nations to their knees.

Let's take a look at how a sexually violent act begins to devastate a person's life, whether that devastation takes decades or an entire lifetime. Why do we need to look at sexual violence against Native women? One reason is that we are the sacred bearers and givers of life. Second, we are *spiritually* stronger than our male counterparts; they are physically stronger than us. Another reason is that we Native women are the ones that hold two-thirds of our family together when the father leaves the home (mother plus children, minus father, equals two-thirds). Therefore, we are the ones who hold up the tribe. In fact, we women hold up the world! But, most important, we are ancient spirits who came to earth to learn how to use our spiritual gifts. In learning that lesson we become helpers to the spirits that we carried in our physical bodies. For me, one of the impacts of sexual violence was alcohol and drug use.

At the age of five, I was unwittingly introduced to alcohol by an aunt who tricked me. My first drink was from the "land of sky blue waters," Hamm's Beer. To this day, I still remember the feel of bubbles in my mouth after drinking this odd-tasting water. I thought it was soda pop because it was given to me with shoestrings (an old name for French fries).

I smoked my first cigarette, an unfiltered Camel, when I was nine years old. A playmate of mine found a cigarette butt where the "big boys and big girls" were smoking and talked me into trying it out with her, so I did. We went behind the laundry building and lit it up. We didn't finish smoking the rest of the cigarette because we both got really dizzy from one puff.

My next drink was as a preteen at a school for Indian girls where we were supposed to learn how to be prim-and-proper young ladies. A few girls were detailed to clean the headmaster's house where we found a gallon of church wine in the pantry. We drank it and thought we were drunk. I don't think any of us knew what it felt like to be drunk, but we sure were giggly and woozy. Nothing prim and proper about that!

By my early teens I was hanging around friends whose parents were heavy alcohol users so it was easy to sneak drinks and smoke cigarettes. The first time I really got drunk was off of bad port wine that someone bought for us for three dollars. Really bad stuff! My alcohol use escalated throughout my late teens and twenties until my early thirties. When my aunt tricked me into drinking beer when I was five years old, little did she know that booze would be the double-edged sword that would increase my vulnerability for the next twenty-nine years.

My **illicit** use and distribution of drugs began around the age of twenty-one. I used hallucinogens (acid, mescaline, psilocybin), amphetamines, marijuana, hashish, cocaine; shot up "yellow jackets" and heroin; and dropped "reds." I used whatever I got my hands on. Use of mood-altering chemicals became a very negative survival skill for me. Getting intoxicated or "high" provided only temporary relief from memories that I didn't want to remember and feelings that I didn't want to feel. I was a loner throughout childhood and college, except for family and relatives. If I isolated myself from people, I wouldn't have to deal with them. Along the way, I met many sexually violated people who also were hypervigilant and hypersensitive. I figured that since none of us trusted anyone, it would be all right to party with them. Wrong! It was the worst pit of vipers that can be imagined. It was a den of sexual predators and no female was safe—whether infant, toddler, teenager, adult, or elder. My addiction to alcohol and drugs only succeeded in making me sicker emotionally, physically, psychologically, and spiritually.

During my childhood, I became quite a talented artist. I won an award for my portraits and animal charcoals in a large county fair when I was twelve years old. When I was about fourteen or fifteen years of age, I was selected as one of four people in South Dakota to study under the tutelage of a famous Dakota artist, Oscar Howe. I had many opportunities to excel throughout my life. Still, there were things that people didn't know about me, such as my intense bouts with fear of people that kept me hidden in my room for weeks. During those times, the only person I sometimes allowed in was my mother. Sometimes I refused to eat and I let my personal hygiene go. I refer to that as my "skunk syndrome," another negative survival skill. I identified with the skunk, my four-legged relative, because it is a nocturnal and shy creature. When it becomes fearful it quickly and effectively repels humans and animals with its protective scent.

I mentioned earlier in this chapter that my bed-wetting in boarding school had stopped because something sinister was taking place. I began to harbor an intense hatred of people who terrorized and mercilessly teased the *Lakota hci* (the very Lakota) and the passive, shy, and fearful ones. This hatred gradually developed into a violent rage. I began to speak less and less and to show my rebellious stubbornness more and more, especially as I got older. I experienced my first blackout rage when I was nine years old and in the fourth grade. A girl slapped me and before I even felt the sting, my mind was gone. What brought me to my senses was pain at the top of my head. When I was fully aware of what was going on, I realized that my hair was caught in the bedsprings of the bottom bunk bed and that someone was pulling me by the ankles trying to break up the fight. I was on top of her, hitting her with my fists. I found out later that we fought until a matron came and pulled me off of her. It was a very strange experience, like being able to leave my body and watch what was happening from up above.

I began to read detective magazines and daydreamed about killing white people. Sometimes I drew detailed scenes of bloody carnage, or women being beaten and raped. I despised weakness in people, especially the women who behaved provocatively or who were sexually promiscuous. In my teenage mind, I thought they didn't know what perverts could do to them! In hindsight, I realize that it was my own self-hatred, self-loathing, and feelings of powerlessness that led me to be judgmental toward other rape victims. I became interested in the weapons section of the detective books and began saving up my babysitting money for an Uzi. As my rages became more frequent I resigned myself to the idea that I would end up in prison for the rest of my life someday for mass murder.

In 1980, I was sexually assaulted by two Indian rapists. After I got home, I went right for my little brother's room, where I knew he kept his 22-250 rifle. I asked him for the full clip, and he told me where it was—no questions asked. I locked the clip, walked next door, and demanded a neighbor woman take me to town. Again, no questions asked. She drove me all over town and out in the country looking for those perps. If I had found them, I intended to maim them and make them both **eunuchs**. I didn't care how long a prison sentence I received because rapists always got away with their crime, especially on the reservation. Moreover, the woman was always made out to look like she asked for it. I made up my mind that these rapists were not going to continue raping women and that no one was ever going to hurt me again!

When I couldn't find the rapists, I began drinking at the bar. I couldn't get drunk no matter how much I drank. Finally, at closing time I did something that I never did before. I called one of my older brothers. As soon as I heard his voice, I began to cry and told him that I had been raped. He asked me where I was, directed me to stay there and wait for him; he was on his way. He took me to his home where his wife was waiting for us. Both were comforting, nurturing, and very concerned about me. The next morning my sister-in-law talked me into going to a female physician assistant for an exam. I was shaking uncontrollably and feeling intense shame, but I went through with it. I had contracted a sexually transmitted disease (STD) from one or both of the rapists and was put on medications immediately.

Being on medication for an STD brought back memories from childhood when I had read an article in elementary school about syphilis and related it to the sexual violations perpetrated against me. As I got older, my rage began slowly consuming me. I thought that it must be the last stage of syphilis that was affecting my brain and causing me to have murderous thoughts, experience blackout rages, and be filled with so much hatred. At an early age, I was convinced that I was going insane and that I was dying.

Conclusion

One day, also in 1980, my *ate* (pronounced ah-te), my earthly father, broke a time-honored custom between father and daughter to talk directly to me about my anger. He said to me in Lakota, "My daughter, your anger is hurting a lot of people but, most of all, you are hurting yourself. It's going to be the hardest thing you ever do in your life, but when someone gets you mad I'm asking you to walk away." That was all he said, but those words gave me the courage to begin a change in my violent lifestyle. It was extremely hard to de-escalate my anger, but each time I walked away, the stronger I became. The stronger I became, the happier I was. For decades, even though I had felt intense hatred and had a hair-trigger temper, I never did like hurting anyone. When I was able to look inward and quit raging, I was able to see my life more clearly.

I began attending feminist women's conferences where women of all colors were talking openly about rape. I read and educated myself about issues of rape, but there was little talk or literature about incest. I saw that there were some tribal laws in place to protect women, but nothing specific that addressed abuses like domestic violence or marital rape. There were federal sex-offense laws but they were ineffective and rarely enforced. It was discouraging, to say the least. My thinking at that time was, if white women aren't even protected by their own nation's laws, how the heck do Native women expect to be protected under those same laws? Further, if white feminists know little or nothing about Native women on reservations, jurisdictional issues, tribal law, or tribal government, then we can't expect much help from them. We are just going to have to do our own work! If our own Native leaders are uncomfortable or hostile when it comes to talking openly about rape laws, what then about laws against incest? After more than twenty years of personal healing, I see that we still aren't much further along today in terms of strong tribal laws addressing the issues of incest and sexual violence.

I have seen many beautiful brochures, videos, curricula, and other educational material, but it is time to do more than just reading, lecturing, or listening to lectures about sexual violence. We need a mass movement of Native women to expand upon the skimpy tribal codes on sexual offenses. Yes, sex offenses are federal jurisdictional cases, but we all know that the cases that prosecutors are sure to win are the ones that are chosen to go to trial. What about those cases that are kicked back to tribal court? We have nothing meaningful in place that puts pedophiles and rapists on notice that they will be held accountable for their crimes against the humanity and sacredness of women and children. Maybe we need to banish them from our homelands for awhile (or forever) in order to make our reservations safe again. Maybe we need to talk openly about incest and the swift consequences against Native men who, in prereservation days, violated natural law. Maybe we need to dig deeper and start by talking about lifting the unwritten taboo that does not allow us to talk about incest.

We desperately need women who are in the thriving stage of their recovery from incest and sexual abuse. We need healthy Native women who can go straight into the minds, emotions, and souls of our women and children to teach them how to revive their own spirit. A spiritually wounded woman will recognize and respond to someone who has been there and back. Our spirits are unbelievably strong and our minds so sharp that we can spot an imposter (a nonthriver) in a millisecond. We will *trust* one of our own in a millisecond as well.

It is extremely difficult to report rape within the kinship system, so the family secret is kept for generations and the sexual violations continue; anger turns to rage; alcohol/drug use escalate the rage into violence; and families align against each other. More often than not the victim is drawn back into the same sick, vicious cycle. It wasn't an easy path for me to rise above the pain and hurt because toxic shame is like quicksand! Without help, my struggles only drew me deeper into the darkness. My feelings of shame, humiliation, and dirtiness kept me from reaching out for help. I felt like I was the only one that this was happening to. Emotions, like denial, are shock absorbers for the soul and can make it very difficult to think, let alone say, those three powerful words: "I NEED HELP!"

The single most powerful influence that helped me regain my sanity and sense of spirit was the *Inipi*, our purification ceremony that cleanses and renews our spirit. Everything about this simple ancient ceremony touched the deepest, darkest part of my self and melted away decades of hurt, pain, and suffering. I remember the singing of prayer-songs, the beat of the drum (heartbeat of the earth), individual prayers, spirits, gourd, steam, heat, and being cleansed from the inside outward. I listened with my spirit when I was instructed to leave all my heavy burdens inside the *Inipi* (place of purification) and to not look back. I trusted my spiritual brothers and sisters when they taught me that each time we crawl out of the *Inipi* we start life anew. I put my faith in the Great Spirit that night, and I crawled out on my hands and knees in humility, not in humiliation as I had crawled throughout my life.

Today I stand in the light of my spirit because it is a gift from the Creator. I may have crawled on my hands and knees from the onslaught of sexual predators throughout my life, but through the prayers of *ate na Ina* (father and mother) and their never-ending love, support, and firm belief in Lakota culture and spirituality, I am alive today.

Native people were all born into a simple, powerful way of life that was given to us by the Great Spirit. We have songs and ceremonies that remind us how to live as good human beings. We each have roles and responsibilities to fulfill within the family, extended family, community, tribe, nation, world, and the universe. A basic, ever-present reminder is that our actions must match our words, that we practice in our own lives what we preach, that we walk our talk.

If it is taught in Native culture that men are *protectors and providers* for the elderly, the women, and children, then Native men must begin their own healing and do just that—resume their roles as protectors and providers of their families. If it is taught that women and children are sacred, then these horrific sexual violations must STOP! If there are still real chief and warrior societies within our tribes, let them step forward and lead the fight against the incest and sexual violence that is being perpetrated upon the women and children of all red nations. If there are true medicine men in our societies, then let them know true humility and compassion for all people, especially women and children.

Within every cell of our bodies, we women carry the ancient spirit teachings of our mothers, grandmothers, and great-grandmothers, all the way back through the beginning of time. We still have our own natural tribal woman teachings intact; woman healing tears; woman ceremonies; woman touch; woman intellect; woman language; woman song; woman spirit. We can heal wounds inflicted from the sharp edges of a nontribal, linear world. We need not depend on a foreign nation's feminist movement to retake our place in tribal society.

We are the descendants of a humble and powerful way of life. We are the continuation of *wolakota*, the sacred ways of our tribes, and as such I echo my mother's words of encouragement to our Native brothers to be good to your sisters! *Mitakuye Oyasiŋ* (all my relations).

Questions

1. Why does LaPointe choose to teach about sexual violence by telling her own story? How is this style of teaching different from what you are used to reading? Why is it so effective?
2. What are some of the impacts of sexual violence identified by LaPointe? What are the individual impacts versus social or tribal impacts? Is there a difference?
3. Why is it so important to understand how sexual violence affects Native women?
4. How did Pratt's philosophy of "Kill the Indian, Save the Man" pervade the lives of Indian women and girls? Are the impacts of this still felt today?

5. What are the differences that Native women experience or face when dealing with sexual assault that non-Native women do not?
6. Why are feminist models for dealing with sexual violence inadequate for Native women?

In Your Community

1. What lessons have you been taught about how to treat women and their place within the community?
2. Does your tribe have codes addressing sexual assault? Do you feel that they are adequate? What improvements need to be made?
3. Do you agree with LaPointe's view to start discussing incest within her community even though it is viewed as taboo?
4. How do women in your community deal with sexual violence and its affects? Where can women and children go if they need help? Are the agencies run by Native women?

Terms Used in Chapter 2

Eunuch: A man whose sexual organs have been removed.
Illicit: Unlawful.
Immemorial: Reaching beyond the limits of memory, tradition, or recorded history.
Oblivious: Lacking conscious awareness.
Psyche: Spirit or soul.
Sojourn: A short stay or visit.
Taboo: A ban or an inhibition resulting from social custom or emotional aversion.

Suggested Further Reading

Baird-Olson, Karren, and Carol Ward. "Recovery and Resistance: The Renewal of Traditional Spirituality among American Indian Women." *American Indian Culture & Research Journal* 24, no. 1 (2000).

Burstow, Bonnie. "Toward a Radical Understanding of Trauma and Trauma Work." *Violence Against Women* 9 (2003): 1293, 1303.

Deer, Sarah. "Toward an Indigenous Jurisprudence of Rape." *Kansas Journal of Law and Public Policy* 14 (2004): 121.

———. "Sovereignty of the Soul: Exploring the Intersection of Rape Law Reform and Federal Indian Law." *Suffolk University Law Review* 38 (2005): 455.

Ellison, Talib. "Surviving Racism and Sexual Assault: American Indian Women Left Unprotected." *The Modern American* (Fall 2005).

Hamby, Sherry L. "Sexual Victimization in Indian Country: Barriers and Resources for Native Women Seeking Help." *National Electronic Network on Violence Against Women* 4 (May 2004).

Jaskoski, Helen. "'My Heart Will Go Out': Healing Songs of Native American Women." *International Journal of Women's Studies* 4 (1981): 118.

Rendon, Marcie R. "Facing Spiritual and Sexual Abuse in the Native Community." *The Circle* 18 (July 1997): 9.

Smith, Andrea. "Not an Indian Tradition: The Sexual Colonization of Native Peoples." *Hypatia* 18 (2003): 70.

Rape

A crime of the spirit
Like a thief
    Rapist attempting to rob
        From me what he lacks.
Shattered,
    Inside my spirit shattered
        Like Humpty Dumpty
            Like a glass Christmas tree ball
                Like me when I stood at my father's grave.
My body a shell carrying the broken pieces.

Quickly, I must put myself together,
    So that my friends will know me,
        My children will know me,
           My lover will know me,
So that I don't look at a stranger in the mirror.

Spirit (Creator),
    Sometimes you take me away from brutality.
Spirit (Creator),
    Somehow terror splits spirit and body,
        The way they talk about drowning,
           The way they talk about dying,
              With you above watching.
All that's left are bruises and a hollow shell.

Sleepwalking,
    I'm only sleepwalking,
        With my scream of terror
           Reverberating through my soul
              Like an echo in a canyon.
Sometimes I hear my scream,
    It silences the sound of my thought,
        Silences the sound of my words,
           Silences the touch of love.

        Eileen Hudon (White Earth Ojibwe)

Chapter 3

Domestic Violence: An Introduction to the Social and Legal Issues for Native Women

VICTORIA YBANEZ

Violence against Native women is an enormous problem across Indian Country. Not only does it have devastating effects on individuals and communities, it also presents some unique challenges in the work to end violence against all women. Domestic violence experienced by Native American women is a serious health threat. According to the Centers for Disease Control, intimate partner violence is one of the most serious public health problems in the United States.[1] The National Violence Against Women (NVAW) Survey indicates that American Indians/Alaska Natives are at greater risk of violent victimizations than are other Americans.[2] Findings from the NVAW Survey support findings from previous studies such as the 1999 report published by the Department of Justice stating that Native Americans were more than two times as likely to be violently victimized as blacks, whites, or Asians.[3] The survey found that about half of the violent victimizations experienced by Native Americans involved an offender with whom the victim had a prior relationship (about the same percentage as found among other victims of violence).

In our Native communities, the problem of domestic violence is complicated by struggles against institutional racism and oppression. Many solutions designed to protect women from domestic violence have been crafted by institutions that historically have been oppressive and **punitive** to Native peoples. Native women who are victims of domestic violence often find themselves being revictimized by the child protection system and the civil or criminal legal systems. While these mainstream institutions may appear supportive, historically they have minimized or ignored issues battered Native women face.

> *I can forgive but there are certain aspects of my history, whether it's solely as a Cheyenne or as an Indian person, that I cannot forget because Native Americans never want to go back and relive that horror.*
>
> —HENRIETTA MANN[4] (CHEYENNE)

The precise origins of domestic violence are often disputed by those working to end violence against Native women. However, most experts generally agree that since the arrival of colonizers, violence against Native women has become a common occurrence across Indian Country. Violence against Native women is not considered natural in indigenous societies and is a fairly new phenomenon. The most commonly held belief is that, while many Native nations had some experience with women being mistreated or battered by intimate partners, the practice was not common nor was it tolerated prior to colonization. The arrival of foreigners gave rise to the widespread crisis experienced across Indian Country today.

Our histories shape us. We will never be able to go back and be who we were prior to colonization, nor do we want to. Antiviolence work today includes identifying and centralizing our Native values and beliefs. One of the most widespread beliefs is that *women are sacred*, which grows out of our stories and teachings. When something is considered sacred, it is to be respected, honored, and regarded as powerful. Women have been historically viewed as the backbone of indigenous society.[5] We must acknowledge our past and use it as a guide to shape our future.

What Is Domestic Violence?

Domestic violence refers to a pattern of physical and/or sexual violence committed by a current or former intimate partner. Domestic violence can occur in both male–female and same-sex partner relationships. The most recognized form of domestic violence is physical violence, which may include hitting, slapping, strangling, kicking, and other violent acts. Extreme forms of physical violence include sexual violence. Indicative of all forms of domestic violence is the intent to control the victims by using various tactics. These tactics include unnatural forms of power and control:[6] isolation, intimidation, using children, emotional abuse, economic abuse, coercion and threats, minimizing, denying and blaming, cultural abuse, ritual abuse, and male privilege. The following paragraphs will describe these tactics in detail.

Isolation is a common tactic used by batterers to separate a woman from her support system. Behaviors include preventing a woman from leaving the house and interfering with her relationships with family and friends. Some women indicate that batterers isolate them by intercepting mail or phone calls, so that they gradually lose touch with friends and family.[7] Preventing her from going to school or working can also be forms of isolation.

Using intimidation includes gestures, movements, or statements that create fear in the victim. This can include body language or statements that only the victim understands. To the unknowing person, the action or gesture might seem insignificant. For example, a batterer may tell his partner, "Be careful today." On the surface, the statement seems benign. However, placing that statement in context might reveal a threat connected to a previous conversation or expectation. Many women have reported that their batterer threatened or harmed pets as a form of intimidation.

Using the children is another tactic of power and control. Batterers may tell the children negative things in order to damage the relationship between mother and child. Often, the perpetrator will threaten to leave her and take the children away. Some batterers will use the children as a form of access to her after the couple has separated.

Using emotional abuse includes calling her names as well as engaging in actions that dehumanize or degrade her. Women have reported that batterers will often play mind games that convinced them that they were going crazy. For example, one woman shared that her husband would hide her shoes and other personal items from her, placing them in the freezer or the washing machine. Since there were only two adults in the house and their children were too small to do these things, she began to believe there was something wrong with her.

Economic abuse includes such things as controlling all of the household resources, requiring the victim to ask for money, and requiring her to account for all money that she spends. Other forms of economic abuse can include actions that threaten her employment or prevent her from being employed at all. Therefore, she is completely dependent on the batterer and cannot leave the relationship.

Using coercion or threats as a tactic of power and control includes actions or statements that force the victim to respond in a specific way. Some examples include the batterer threatening to commit suicide if his partner leaves him, threatening to leave her and take the children and financial resources away from her, or threatening to report her to welfare for fraud if she doesn't drop the charges for domestic violence.

A batterer will use *minimizing, denying, and blaming* as tactics of power and control. Oftentimes, the batterer will blame the woman for the violence or will make light of the violence by telling her or anyone else "it wasn't that bad" or that "she is exaggerating the whole thing." Some women have said that their batterer blatantly lied to others about the violence. For instance, one woman reported that she told her mother-in-law about the violence. When the mother-in-law approached her son, he responded that his wife "made the whole thing up" because she was mad at him.

Cultural abuse is used to diminish the victim as a Native woman. This comes in many forms, but most often is seen as judging her for not being "Indian" enough,

VIOLENCE AGAINST NATIVE WOMEN: BATTERING

MALE PRIVILEGE
Treats her like a servant. Makes all the big decisions. Acts like the "king of the castle." Defines men's and women's roles.

ISOLATION
Controls what she does, who she sees and talks to, what she reads. Limits her outside involvement. Uses jealousy to justify actions.

INTIMIDATION
Makes her afraid by using looks, actions, gestures. Smashes things. Destroys her property. Abuses pets. Displays weapons.

EMOTIONAL ABUSE
Puts her down. Makes her feel bad about herself. Calls her names. Makes her think she's crazy. Plays mind games. Humiliates her. Makes her feel guilty.

MINIMIZE, LIE AND BLAME
Makes light of the abuse and doesn't take her concerns seriously. Says the abuse didn't happen. Shifts responsibility for abusive behavior. Says she caused it.

USING CHILDREN
Makes her feel guilty about the children. Uses the children to relay messages. Uses visitation to harass her. Threatens to take away the children.

ECONOMIC ABUSE
Prevents her from working. Makes her ask for money. Gives her an allowance. Takes her money. Doesn't let her know about or access family income.

COERCION AND THREATS
Makes and/or carries out threats to do something to hurt her. Threatens to leave her, to commit suicide, to report her to welfare. Makes her drop charges. Makes her do illegal things.

CULTURAL ABUSE
Competes over "Indianness." Misinterprets culture to prove male superiority/female submission. Uses relatives to beat her up. Buys into "blood quantum" competitions.

RITUAL ABUSE
Prays against her. Defines spirituality as masculine. Stops her from practicing her ways. Uses religion as a threat. "God doesn't allow divorce." Says her period makes her "dirty."

Left side: PUNCHING · KICKING · CHOKING · PUSHING · SLAPPING · PULLING HAIR — PHYSICAL VIOLENCE
Right side: PHYSICALLY ATTACKING THE SEXUAL PARTS OF HER BODY · TREATING HER LIKE A SEX OBJECT — SEXUAL VIOLENCE

UNNATURAL POWER & CONTROL

Produced by Sacred Circle - National Resource Center to End Violence Against Native Women. Revised 5:00

Figure 3.1. Sacred Circle Unnatural Power and Control Pyramid. Source: Courtesy of Sacred Circle, National Resource Center to End Violence Against Native Women.

that she is too assimilated, or that she is "heathen." The batterer might use his cultural knowledge or cultural powers to intimidate the woman or hold himself out to be superior to her.

Ritual abuse includes drawing from spiritual and religious practices and beliefs to control the victim. This might include using interpretations of "teachings" as a threat, preventing her from practicing her own spiritual ways, using "bad medicine" against her, or praying against her. Some batterers try to prevent their partner from attending ceremonies.

Male privilege is the belief that men are superior to women. Actions associated with this tactic include making all of the decisions because he believes he is "head of the household." Some batterers may act like a "king of the castle" and expect the woman to act as a servant.

Using sexual assault as a tactic of power and control includes sexual violence and coercion. Some of these actions are not obvious, such as language that is sexually offensive to her, forcing her to watch pornography, and threatening to have sex with one of their daughters if she does not have sex with him. The batterer might also make his victim feel that she is an inadequate sexual partner.

Physical violence generally takes place when the tactics of power and control described above are not effective to achieve the batterer's desired outcome. The violence varies in frequency and severity across relationships. In order to fully understand the extent of the domestic violence, it is important to look at the big picture. In our roles as advocates, law enforcement officers, child protection workers, civil or criminal justice interveners, we must not look at just one single incident, because it does not present an accurate view of the dangerous situation.

Myths about Domestic Violence

There are many myths in our society about domestic violence. Myths are widely held beliefs that, when left unchecked, continue to perpetuate the problem of domestic violence. Myths originate from fundamental misconceptions about the nature of violence. These myths often reinforce the battering by shifting the responsibility for the violence away from the batterer to the battered woman. In addition, myths interfere with our ability as advocates, law enforcement officers, child protection workers, and civil or criminal justice interveners to effectively work with the women we see. Myths impair our judgment and create barriers to being able to fully see the reality of violence that is occurring—in one woman's life, in our communities, and in society in general. The following section describes some of the most commonly held myths about domestic violence.

Myth: A Battered Woman Can Leave the Relationship Anytime

> *If it were me, I would have left him a long time ago. . . .*

> *Why does she stay when she is being battered?*

If you have worked with battered women or have experienced domestic violence, you have probably heard one of these statements, at least a few times—or maybe you have even said them before. In reality, battered women do not have the luxury of "walking away" from domestic violence.

- The risk of **lethality** rises significantly when a woman decides to leave the relationship. Some women say that they would rather live with the violence because it is predictable versus leaving, which could be more dangerous. If she leaves, a woman may suffer another violent attack or, worse, she may be killed if she tries to leave.
- Leaving the relationship often means that the victim and her children will have to leave the community. For a Native woman, this could mean having to leave her village, pueblo, or reservation—the very place where she grew up, the place she calls home and from which she draws great support. The land she lives on may play a significant role in her social and cultural identity.
- Leaving requires resources—both emotional and material. The ability to leave is connected to her ability to access food, shelter, clothing, money, and transportation. Battered women's shelters sometimes provide these basic needs, but they are only a temporary solution.
- The emotional aspects of battering run very deep. Many battered women have reported how difficult it is to heal from the emotional and psychological trauma. Over time, surviving battering takes an enormous amount of energy. Women say they are so exhausted from the battering that they have little energy to care for themselves or their children, make decisions, plan their days, or imagine a future outside the violent relationship.
- In addition, some battered women want to believe that when he says, "I'll never do it again," he means it.

Myth: Battering Is Caused by Lack of Control

So my cousin beat up his wife, and now everyone is saying that he really lost control this time.

He just flew off the handle . . .

Many people make the mistake of thinking that battering is caused by a loss of control, when actually battering is centered around having extreme control.

- In fact, most batterers have no problem controlling their anger and behavior in situations where it is inappropriate to use violence. For

example, a batterer may become angry with a co-worker or boss, yet he does not become violent at work as he does with his partner at home. Batterers choose to use violence or control tactics to get what they want.
- Batterers use violence because they believe they have the right to use it. This belief may be tied to male privilege.

Myth: Stress, Relationship Problems, or Alcohol Abuse Causes Domestic Violence

I was so stressed over my job . . .

I think he did it because he had too much to drink.

All of us live with stress in our lives. We experience stress due to job demands, deadlines, the death of a close relative or friend, money problems, discrimination, traffic, and from many other experiences. Yet most of us do not go home and beat up our partner. Stress is not an excuse for using violence. A batterer will often use stress as an excuse for irresponsible behavior. Community members, friends, or relatives who believe stress caused the battering are also excusing his actions.

Drinking is a problem in many Native communities. However, not everyone who drinks automatically becomes a batterer. In actuality, sober people can be violent, too. While drinking can lower inhibitions and **escalate** violence, it does not cause the violence. Alcohol use is a separate issue from the use of violence to assert power over a partner. Domestic violence is rooted in a sense of entitlement—a belief that the batterer has the right to use this form of violence in this relationship. Many people believe that treating alcoholism is the solution to domestic violence. However, domestic violence must have a separate and different response.

Myth: She (the Battered Woman) Provoked the Violence

He wouldn't hit you if you would just shut up.

You should have known better than to have done that.

Lines similar to those above place the blame on the battered woman. No woman deserves to be battered no matter what she has or has not done. Remember that battering behavior is rooted in a belief that the batterer has the right to use violence as a means to control his partner. There are not necessarily any rules or logic behind the actions of batterers. A woman might be battered for a "reason" as simple as asking for money, going to the grocery store, or talking to a friend.

Myth: Law Enforcement and Civil/Criminal Interventions Will Keep Women Safe

Just call the police—they will help you.

Why don't you get an order for protection?

In some cases, law enforcement and/or legal intervention may be effective remedies to stop the violence. However, these interventions have limitations.

- Law enforcement interventions are not the same everywhere. In some remote locations, such as reservations and villages, it may take hours, or even days, for law enforcement to respond. Even when they do respond, they may not be able to make an arrest. Also, some law enforcement officials may not be trained to respond to domestic violence and may have their own biases about battering. What's more, a woman who calls the police may face **retaliation** from the batterer. In cases where there is an arrest, the batterer could be released on bond quickly—thus able to locate the victim and punish her.
- Using law enforcement systems that have been historically oppressive toward Native women (see chapter 1) can have unforeseen consequences. Recently, there has been a rise in the number of women being arrested for domestic violence while acting in self-defense. Women who have been arrested are much less likely to call police in future situations. In addition, entering the criminal justice system sometimes alerts child protection systems to the violence. While it is the batterer who creates an unsafe situation for children, many women have been held responsible for failing to protect the children. Many women are fearful of losing custody of their children and therefore avoid contacting authorities or seeking protection orders.
- Jurisdictional issues surrounding protection orders can be complex. (See chapters 14 and 16.) Enforcement of protection orders is not always a priority. In addition, sometimes one tribal government will not honor an order written in the court of another.

Myth: What about the Male Victims? Women Batter Too

Women are batterers just as much as men; men are just ashamed to admit it.

Why aren't we working just as hard to end women's abuse of men?

Domestic violence is primarily a crime against women. Men experiencing domestic violence make up a very small percentage of the population of victims.[8] (We must also consider that included in that small number are men experiencing violence in same-sex relationships.) In addition, women are more likely to suffer serious injuries resulting from violence committed by a male partner in contrast to men's injuries resulting from violence committed by a female partner.[9] Women experience violence at much higher rates and with more serious consequences.

Causes of Domestic Violence

As Native people, our traditional lifeways have been significantly eroded. According to Paula Gunn Allen, the high rate of violence against women cases is "powerful evidence that the status of women within our tribes has suffered a grievous decline since contact. That decline has intensified in recent years."[10] Wife, partner, or spouse abuse was not accepted practice in tribal belief systems. Domestic violence has become widespread in our communities due to colonization and a history of oppression that led to the erosion of our Native ways of life.

Native nations have survived many kinds of violence over the past centuries. Violence can be seen in the forced removal of Native children during the boarding school era; the multiple massacres of Native people; and the widespread rape of Native women that took place during events such as the "Trail of Tears" and "The Long Walk." The methods used by colonizers to control and address the "Indian problem" have become internalized by many Native people today. As Native lifeways have been eroded, so have the values that did not permit such control and power of a Native man over his partner.

All forms of oppression are linked to domestic violence. Examining the "isms" (such as classism, racism, and sexism) illuminates the source of power and control in many communities. As advocates, we have to work to create institutional change in those systems, work to undo and challenge the racism, sexism, and classism that exist, as well as other isms.[11]

When we examine classism, for example, we see how economic barriers limit some women's options. Women of lower socioeconomic status do not have adequate financial resources and are often placed in the position of having to choose between living in an unsafe situation or living on the streets. Generally, women who seek domestic violence services are victims with the least amount of economic resources.[12] The stigma associated with seeking public assistance resources presents an additional barrier.

Racism is another significant layer of oppression faced by Native women. The impact of institutional racism is apparent in non-Native shelters when Native women are questioned and monitored to ensure they are not stealing. In addition, Native women have reported negative experiences with law enforcement, such as being threatened with arrest for filing false reports. Consequently, Native women often have a distrust of the very system that is intended to help them. As we work to address systemic oppression rooted in sexism, we must also recognize that racism can rear its ugly head at any place and time. Native American battered women must confront racism in places like battered women's shelters, advocacy organizations, hospitals, police departments, landlords, social services, child protection agencies, and the courts.

VIOLENCE: UNNATURAL LIFEWAY

Destruction, Racism, Materialism, Rape, Murder, Fear, Sexism, Ageism, Battering, Incest, Isolation, Homophobia, Classism, Ritual Abuse, Child Abuse, Cultural Abuse

NON-VIOLENCE: NATURAL LIFEWAY

Compassion, Peace, Honoring of Relationships, Laughter, Freedom, Understanding, Humility, Love, Hope, Life, Wisdom, Health, Respect, Generosity, Sovereignty, Courage

BRANCHES: OUTGROWTH

TRUNK: CONTRIBUTORS

VIOLENCE:
- Chemical abuse
- Boarding schools
- Witnessing violence
- Stereotypes
- Confusing anger with violence

NON-VIOLENCE:
- Prayer, ceremony
- Honor the gift in others
- Ways of non-violence and respect modeled
- Mental self-discipline
- Seek advice of Women and Elders

ROOT: CAUSE OF

VIOLENCE: IS THE BELIEF SYSTEM
- Values might over right
- Power defined as violence
- Colonization
- View reality as a male dominated hierarchy
- Justifies violence and oppression
- Promotes myths of white male superiority
- Treats women and children as property of men

NON-VIOLENCE: IS THE BELIEF SYSTEM
- Understand that all things have spirits and are related
- Respect is the foundation of all relationships
- People are spirits in physical bodies on individual lifepaths
- Women are sacred
- All people and things of creation are part of the sacred circle of life

ENDING VIOLENCE AGAINST NATIVE WOMEN FROM THE ROOTS UP

Produced by Sacred Circle - National Resource Center to End Violence Against Native Women

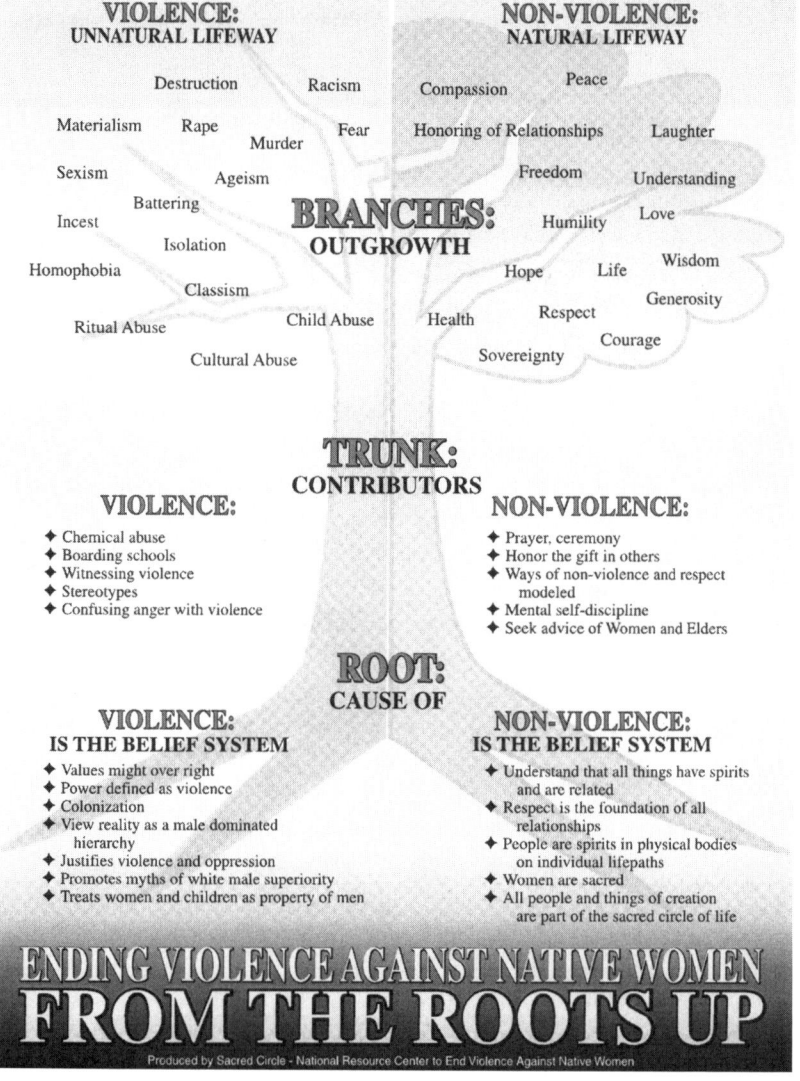

Figure 3.2. Roots of Violence. Source: Courtesy of Sacred Circle, Natural Resource Center to End Violence Against Native Women.

When examining tactics of power and control, it is important to look beyond individual acts of violence to the institutional and societal supports for domestic violence. We must ask how community institutions such as shelters, law enforcement, clergy, courts, and others reinforce the batterer's power and control tactics. How do these institutions either block or help women's efforts to deal with violence? The following are a few examples of institutional supports for domestic violence.[13]

- A county judge who refuses to enforce his own court orders requiring the batterer to seek counseling and avoid contact with the victim.
- An advocate who tells a battered woman that she has to get help from a mental health professional to "fix" herself.
- A social worker who repeatedly intrudes on a victim's life based on the batterer's false claims of welfare and child abuse.

It is essential to examine values and beliefs that support and reinforce batterers' abilities to use tactics of power and control. Are women honored or celebrated by the culture? In some of our Native communities that were originally women-centered, the contemporary governing structures exclude or marginalize the voices and roles of women. In addition, we must look at American society to identify how all women, and Native women in particular, are devalued.

Tribal Responses to Domestic Violence

Safety and accountability must be central to our work to address domestic violence as tribal nations. Safety for battered women is more than just stopping the physical violence; it also encompasses a woman's ability to be and act **sovereign**. A tribal government should foster an environment in which a battered woman is able to define and decide her own needs, free from judgment. She should be supported in understanding that the violence is not her responsibility, regardless of her actions. She needs to be treated with the respect and honor inherent in our indigenous beliefs. She should receive support and comfort from her community. In addition, the tribe must ensure that offenders are held accountable for the violence they perpetrate. Tribal civil and criminal justice systems must provide effective intervention without exceptions for relationship or community status. Above all, there must be a strong message that the community will not tolerate the use of violence.

Our work to end violence against Native women must go beyond providing direct services, such as shelter, emotional support, and legal assistance. Although direct services are critical, we must be ready to offer customized services that meet the needs of individual women. Advocacy must work to provide safety as the battered woman defines it. Mainstream ideals and models are often adopted in developing solutions to violence in Native communities. However, these Western models often compartmentalize women into fragments—forgetting that they are whole women with identities that transcend violence. They are our mothers, our sisters, our cousins, and our neighbors. They are our relatives. A woman who is being battered has a full story of her life and, in our relationship with her, we must look beyond the violence to see a whole woman.

> *When did people become more concerned with fact than with truth? The truth is the story behind the facts . . . stories are living, breathing things and that creative power that is at work between the teller and the listener is very real.*
>
> —GAYLE ROSS[14] (CHEROKEE)

Women are the backbone of indigenous societies. Native women are strong and beautiful women who have incredible strength to endure and be creative survivors. We must recognize and honor the strength of Native women and help restore their status in indigenous society. In doing so, we must work with them to respond to impacts of colonization and internalized oppression.

We are provided a window of opportunity to make a difference in a battered woman's life. We must use that time to help her understand why domestic violence exists. It is important to resist looking at domestic violence as a one-time assault and examine it as a pattern of abuse. This includes making a connection between domestic violence and a society that accepts violence against women in such epidemic proportions.

Advocacy (see chapter 12) is the cornerstone of our work to end violence against Native women. Advocates include community members who step forward to help. One challenge is finding advocates who clearly understand domestic violence and its roots in an oppressive system. Often, well-meaning advocates believe that they know what is best for the victim and do not listen to the victim's perspective. This attitude is not only disempowering to women—it can also lead to dangerous and potentially life-threatening situations. Instead, advocacy should create an environment where the realities of women's lives are allowed to be expressed even in the midst of the violence they are experiencing. An empowerment model of advocacy allows each battered woman to make choices for herself, remembering that each woman is sacred and sovereign.

Starting a battered women's shelter can establish more options for victims. Shelters provide a safe place for women and children to live while escaping the violence. In addition, shelters can also provide financial and legal assistance. Unfortunately, the development of battered women's shelters across Indian Country has been slow. This is due in part to inadequate financial resources. Most tribal governments have few resources available to dedicate to the development and operation of a shelter. Other funding sources have not always targeted the needs of Native women in these communities.[15] The geographic locations of reservations, pueblos, rancherias, and villages pose another barrier, since there are often great distances between communities, with no adequate transportation. There are also a limited number of physical structures that can be easily adapted into a shelter. Confidentiality and security become an issue when first responders may be hours or days away.

Mistakes to Avoid

Over the past three decades, as our tribal societies developed responses to domestic violence, we have become increasingly reliant on the non-Native civil and criminal justice systems. Our experience tells us that we have chosen responses from within a system that historically has been less than helpful. For many years, Native women have been raped at significantly higher rates than white women. Native women understand this reality and carry the burden of historical consequences when they call the police but are not believed; when their case is dismissed before the court because the judge is a relative of the batterer; when there is not enough evidence or resources to pursue the case. A Native woman understands this reality when she knows her mother was removed from their home and placed in a boarding school—or that her children were removed from their home and placed in a boarding school—or when her children were removed from her home because she could not stop her partner's violence against her. In addition, Native battered women understand that Native men are being incarcerated at higher rates than their white counterparts. She understands that if she calls the police, her partner may have to face federal penalties for his violence (which carry stiffer consequences than state penalties.) She also understands that if she is dealing with the law enforcement system off the reservation, her partner may find himself faced with the institutional racism inherent in mainstream communities.

Our advocacy with battered women must reflect our values. Often we find that we are adopting mainstream models that are authoritative and paternalistic. These punitive models serve to reinforce battered women as defective and fail to honor individual women for who they are.

Many domestic violence agencies and organizations view domestic violence as an individual psychological problem. This philosophy poses very serious problems and can be dangerous for Native women. Often, a battered woman is sent to a therapist or offered a support group where she can "work on her self-esteem." At the same time, batterers are sometimes sent to "batterer's treatment." While some women may find therapy helpful, and some batterers might also benefit from psychological intervention, it is important to not lose sight of the actual causes of violence against Native women. The danger in taking a psychological approach comes from introducing battered women into a mental health system because of the batterer's violence. It serves to further reinforce tactics of power and control that the batterer may already be using, such as emotional abuse, minimizing, denying, and blaming.

By defining domestic violence as a mental health issue, the system fails to recognize the larger community problem of violence against Native women. This mental health approach repositions domestic violence into an individual context of one where a batterer is not directly accountable for his choice to use violence in his relationship. Instead of a criminal act, domestic violence becomes a disease. It places responsibility on the battered woman for her victimization and further reinforces the batterer's violence.

Working to understand that different mainstream theories of domestic violence can serve to raise our ability to effectively create social change requires us to recognize that society needs to change—and to place indigenous values at the center.

> *We become activists by default. Suddenly, we're representing our tribes, the Red Race, in everything we do—whether we want to or not.*
>
> —ARIGON STARR[16] (KICKAPOO/CREEK)

Native Ways of Life

Over 560 federally recognized tribes have a commonly held traditional value of respect for women, both physical and emotional. Yet we all face the challenge of incorporating this value into our everyday lives. Our traditional lifeways worked to deter violence in our tribal communities in our past and again will serve to provide us with indigenous solutions to violence against women in our future.

If we are not actively engaged in ending violence against women, we are reinforcing the violence through **complacency**. It is important that we recognize the interconnectedness of our efforts. We have made some strides toward establishing a foundation for this work and can now see a range of responses to domestic violence across Indian Country. In addition, we are learning from each other as we develop our programs. We are also reaching out to our communities to change attitudes and beliefs that were once foreign to us but have now become common and destructive. There is still much work to be done.

Today we are being challenged to find a way to reclaim the traditional values in order to return women to their rightful status in society. We are also striving to restore balance to our communities. The very foundations of our societies depend on our success. Our work will gain strength as we incorporate a response to domestic violence that does not rely on mainstream models, but instead turns to our memories of how things worked in our tribes before colonization. We will succeed when we can design contemporary solutions with traditional values at the core.

> *I want to be remembered for emphasizing the fact that we have indigenous solutions to our problems.*
>
> —WILMA MANKILLER[17] (CHEROKEE)

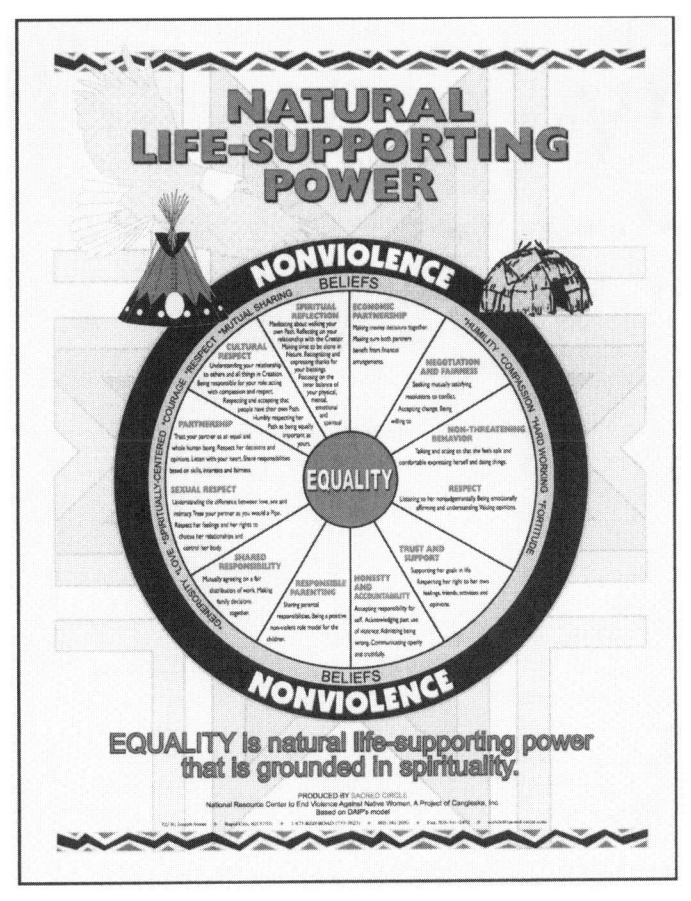

Figure 3.3. Sacred Circle Natural Worldview Wheel. Source: Courtesy of Sacred Circle, Natural Resource Center to End Violence Against Native Women.

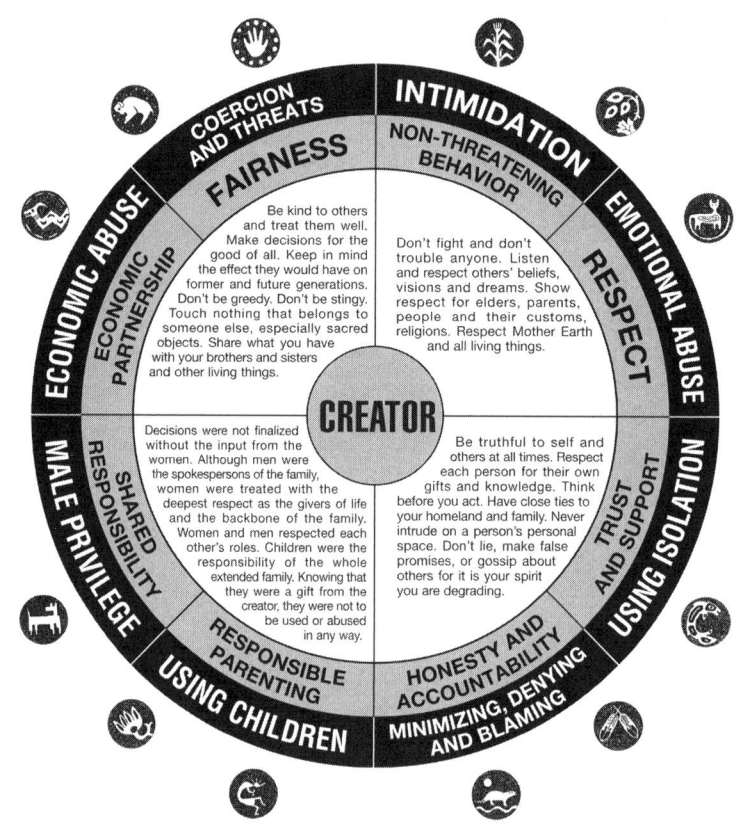

Figure 3.4. Creator Wheel. *Source*: Developed by Mending the Sacred Hoop.

Notes

1. www.cdc.gov/ncipc/factsheets/ipvoverview.htm

2. Patricia Tjaden and Nancy Thoennes, *Full Report of the Prevalence, Incidence, and Consequences of Violence Against Women: Findings from the National Violence Against Women Survey* (National Institute of Justice and Centers for Disease Control and Prevention, NCJ 183781, November 2000), pp. 21–23. American Indian/Alaska Native women were significantly more likely than white women or African American women to report they were raped. In addition, they were also significantly more likely to report they were stalked. Data from the survey by type of victimization and race reflect the following percentages: rape—American Indian/Alaska Native 34.1; white 17.1; African American 18.1; Asian/Pacific Islander 6.8; Mixed Race 24.4; physical assault—American Indian/Alaska Native women 61.4; white 51.3; African American 52.1; Asian/Pacific Islander 49.6; Mixed Race 57.7; stalking—American Indian/Alaska Native women 17.0; white 8.2; African American 6.5; Asian/Pacific Islander 4.5, Mixed race 10.6.

3. According to the Bureau of Justice Statistics Special Report, *Intimate Partner Violence and Age of Victim 1993–1999* (USDOJ, 1999).

4. Serle L. Chapman, *We, the People of Earth and Elders*, vol. 2 (Missoula, MT: Mountain Press Publishing Company, 2001), p. 314.

5. Many Native organizations working to end violence against Native women centralize the belief that women are sacred in their work. Two such organizations working on a national level influencing local work across Indian Country are Sacred Circle, located in South Dakota, and Mending the Sacred Hoop in Minnesota.

6. The Domestic Abuse Intervention Project (Duluth, Minnesota) developed a Power and Control Wheel that represented tactics of power and control. Struggling with having these unnatural beliefs incorporated into a wheel and recognizing additional tactics of power and control used against Native women, Cangleska/Sacred Circle later modified the tactics and placed them in a pyramid (see figure 3.1).

7. Through my experiences in working to end domestic violence over the past twenty years, I have talked with many battered women in many contexts. These contexts include providing advocacy, providing direct services, conducting women's educating groups, conducting focus groups, or organizing to create social change.

8. According to the Bureau of Justice Statistics Special Report, *Intimate Partner Violence and Age of Victim, 1993–1999*, intimate partner violence is primarily a crime against women. In 1999, women accounted for 85 percent of the victims of intimate partner violence (671,110 total), and men accounted for 15 percent of the victims (120,100 total).

9. Murray A. Straus and Richard J. Gelles, *Physical Violence in American Families* (New Brunswick, NJ: Transaction, 1990).

10. Paula Gunn Allen, *The Sacred Hoop: Recovering the Feminine in American Indian Traditions* (Boston: Beacon Press, 1992), p. 191. Allen continues, "The amount of violence against women, alcoholism and violence, abuse and neglect by women against children and their aged relatives have all increased. These social ills were virtually unheard of among most tribes fifty years ago."

11. Other isms may include homophobia (the expression of hatred towards or discrimination against persons of a homosexual orientation) and ageism (the expression of hatred or discrimination against persons of an older or younger age).

12. In my experience working with battered women, the vast majority of women were low-income or working-class women. I believe that women with more resources have more options available for leaving an abusive situation.

13. Some of these examples are taken from the training program *In Our Best Interest: A Process for Personal and Social Change* (Minnesota Program Development, 1987). Other examples are drawn from my experience working as an advocate for battered women.

14. Chapman, *We, The People of the Earth*, p. 114.

15. Vicki Ybanez, "The Evolution of Domestic Violence and Reform Efforts Across Indian Country," *Introductory Manual to Domestic Violence in Indian Country* (Mending the Sacred Hoop STOP Violence Against Indian Women, 2002), p. 7. Funding was slow to reach Indian Country. Advocating for change, a vocal group of Native women campaigned for VAWA "set-aside" funds to be designated for tribes and to ensure that resources reached the tribes. As a result, the STOP Violence Against Indian Women Grant Program was created to encourage tribal governments to develop and strengthen the tribal justice systems' responses (including law enforcement, prosecution, victim services, and courts) to violence against women and to improve services to victims of domestic violence, sexual assault, and stalking.

16. Chapman, *We, the People of the Earth*, p. 201.

17. Gloria Valencia-Weber and Christine P. Zuni, "Domestic Violence and Tribal Protection of Indigenous Women in the United States," *Saint John's Law Review* 69 (1994): 69.

Questions

1. Do you agree with Ybanez that respect for a woman because she is sacred is a traditional value and that those values should be used to combat domestic violence? Why does Ybanez point out that tribes do not want to return to precolonial times?
2. Why is it important for law enforcement officials and advocates to look at patterns of abuse and not individual instances when working with victims?
3. How do jurisdictional issues on reservations complicate the response of law enforcement to domestic violence cases? In PL 280 states?
4. How do Native women's current roles within tribal governments and within American society differ from their traditional roles within Native communities? How does this contribute to domestic violence?
5. How can tribal communities respond effectively to domestic violence? What are some of the difficulties tribal justice systems face that non-Native communities might not deal with?

In Your Community

1. What are some misconceptions or myths you believed true regarding domestic violence? Why is it so important to break down these myths and educate people about the reality?
2. Do you agree with Ybanez's call to traditional core values to fight domestic violence? How would you conceptualize this for your community? What are some common cultural values that could be integrated into a domestic violence response? Why might this be difficult?
3. At the end of the chapter Wilma Mankiller is quoted regarding "indigenous solutions" to contemporary problems? Can you think of any examples of this within your community? Could these be used to address domestic violence?

Terms Used in Chapter 3

Complacency: Self-satisfaction; contentment with the way things are.
Escalate: To increase in intensity or extent.
Lethality: The quality of being deadly.
Punitive: Inflicting or aiming to inflict punishment; punishing.
Retaliation: To pay back (an injury) in kind.
Sovereign: To act independently as a person or nation.

Suggested Further Reading

Brownridge, Douglas A. "Male Partner Violence Against Aboriginal Women in Canada." *Journal of Interpersonal Violence* 18 (2003): 65.

Chester, Barbara, et al. "Grandmother Dishonored: Violence Against Women by Male Partners in American Indian Communities." *Violence and Victims* 9 (1994): 249.

Fairchild, David G., et al. "Prevalence of Adult Domestic Violence Among Women Seeking Routine Care in a Native American Health Care Facility." *American Journal of Public Health* 88 (1998): 1515.

Murray, Virginia. "A Comparative Survey of the Historic Civil, Common, and American Indian Tribal Responses to Domestic Violence." *Oklahoma City University Law Review* 24 (1998): 433.

Norton, Ilene M., and Spero M. Manson. "A Silent Minority: Battered American Indian Women." *Journal of Family Violence* 10 (1995): 307.

Valencia-Weber, Gloria, and Christine P. Zuni. "Domestic Violence and Tribal Protection of Indigenous Women in the United States." *Saint John's Law Review* 69 (1995): 69.

Wahab, Stéphanie, and Lenora Olson. "Intimate Partner Violence and Sexual Assault in Native American Communities." *Trauma, Violence & Abuse* 5 (2004): 353, 357.

Zion, Jim and Elsie Zion. "'Hazho'Sokee'—Stay Together Nicely: Domestic Violence under Navajo Common Law." *Arizona State Law Journal* 25 (1993): 407, 411–413.

Run

When the morning comes
I am happy the sun is shining,
The birds are singing and I think
Of times of walks in the park
Hugging on a park bench with you.
How you loved me.
What wonderful times we had.
I come back to reality
Sitting at the kitchen table
Holding a bag of ice
To my cheek
The swelling will go down
I pray.
I have to work tomorrow
Worry about people
Hiding battle wounds.
I tell myself
I am going to leave
Had enough
There has got to be something better
The Greyhound Station has
Storage Lockers
The key is in my work locker
He won't find it there.
Little by little I stash
Jeans, shirts, toothbrush, underwear and
Money for my trip home.
What will I do when I go?
What will Mom say?
He comes home from work
Yes I am here I say happily
As not to let him know my plans
You know he can read my mind by now.
He is tired and goes to lie down in bed.
I tell him I need to go to the laundry
He doesn't want to go.
I am relieved.
I take only my clothes

He doesn't notice.
Heart beating hard
Hands shaking I go outside.
Drive to the bus station
Get my stuff
On the road I am singing a little tune
Run, Run, Run . . . Runaway.

            Lea Krmpotich Carr (White Earth Ojibwe)

Special Issues Facing Alaska Native Women Survivors of Violence

Chapter 4

ELEANOR NED-SUNNYBOY

The state of Alaska covers a region one-fifth the size of the contiguous United States. Alaska covers 586,412 square miles, with a total population of 622,000, which includes approximately 98,043 Alaska Natives. Alaska is home to 229 tribes. Of these 229 tribes, 165 are "off-road" communities, meaning that they are only accessible by air for most of the year. Ninety of these 165 off-road communities also do not have any form of contemporary law enforcement. Native people live either within 229 federally recognized tribes or in the urban areas of Alaska. When Alaska became a state in 1959, Public Law 280 (PL 280) was applied to the Native communities, meaning that tribal authority and state authority often overlap (see chapter 14). Many state and tribal officials are still not clear on exactly what this means in cases of violence against Native women. This is compounded with the fact that in *Alaska v. Native Village of Venetie Tribal Government*,[1] the U.S. Supreme Court ruled that "Indian Country" does not exist in Alaska outside of the one reservation, Metlakatla. This devastating loss of territorial **jurisdiction** has created more questions than answers for village governments. These are just some of the barriers that advocates face in their attempt to address violence against Native women in Alaska.

Alaska has one of the highest **per capita** rates of physical and sexual abuse in the nation. According to the FBI's Uniform Crime Report in 1999, Alaska reported 83.5 rapes per 100,000 females compared to a U.S. average of 31.7 per 100,000 females. In 1992, 30 percent of state child abuse, neglect, and injury reports involved Native children (94 per 1,000 Native children), with little improvement to date. Natives make up 36 percent of Alaska's inmate population. Fifty-nine percent are incarcerated for violent crimes and 38 percent for sexual offenses. Alaska also has the highest per capita rates of child sexual abuse in the nation (the official FBI data is available at www.fbi.gov/ucr/Cins_99/w99+bl05.xls).

These high rates of violence are well-documented in the larger cities. According to the 1999 Crime Report by the Anchorage Police Department, there were approximately 1,400 sexual assaults between 1995 and 1999. Six hundred (almost 42 percent) involved Alaska Native women. A majority of these cases remain unresolved today. From 1989 to 1998, reported cases of domestic violence in Anchorage alone increased by 120 percent. The percentage of Alaska Native victims in the Anchorage area was 24 percent, which is extremely high when one takes into consideration that Alaska Natives comprise only 8 percent of the Anchorage population.[2]

On October 30, 2003, it was reported that "Anchorage is expecting to be ranked No. 1 in the nation per capita on sexual assault. Statistics show that there were 374 cases of reported sexual assaults in the first six months of 2003. There are only seven detectives investigating all of them. Of the cases that are being investigated, averages of 35 are assigned to each detective." The report went on to quote a local official: "With a new sexual assault case being reported in Anchorage every day, detectives who work the front lines in these cases say they simply don't have the resources to work all of those crimes."[3]

Recent interviews with Native women indicate that violence against women and children has reached epidemic proportions. Precise statistics are unavailable for the rural communities in Alaska. Until recently, violence against Native women has been an invisible crisis with little or no studies conducted as to the scope of the problem. In informal polls taken by advocates in some off-road communities, 100 percent of the women reported that they have experienced domestic or sexual abuse.

Respect: A Traditional Foundation for Nonviolence

Historically, domestic and sexual abuse did not plague Alaska Native communities to the extent that they do today. For the most part, people lived in balance and harmony with one another and nature. This problem of abuse is a fairly new crisis that arrived with the onset of the Westernized (European) systems that interrupted our core set of values and beliefs. Our cultural systems were based on the concept of respect for all things and one another. Respect is an intricately intertwined element of the Alaska Native culture, and there is no single word in our languages that reflects this concept. It encompasses the entire way of knowing for our indigenous people. This concept of respect was deeply embedded in our lifeways. It was the focal point of all teachings and learning. This was evident in the educational, political, social, economic, and spiritual realms of our native worldview. "Most indigenous peoples' worldviews seek harmony and integration with all life, including the spiritual, natural, and human domains."[4]

With the influx of Western society came the increase in incidents of violence against women. Disruption began in the late 1800s with the arrival of the first

Russians, who came at different times throughout Alaska. The coastal communities suffered the first encounters. The early 1950s and statehood brought another influx of contradictory values and a belief system from a different society into most of our tribal communities, resulting in chaos and turmoil. The Western society carried many mixed messages for the Native people of Alaska. These messages **infiltrate**d our educational, spiritual, political, economic, and social systems. The Boarding School Era (lasting until the late 1960s and early 1970s) led to a breakdown of traditional cultural values and beliefs. The removal of children from Native villages was one of the most destructive factors in the deterioration of our social well-being and safety. Young native teens were sent off to boarding schools at a time when they should have been learning these valuable traditional life skills. The impact of this gap in traditional learning is being felt in most remote Alaskan villages to this day.

Preconstitutional Law

Up until the late 1800s, Alaska Native people lived in balance and harmony with one another and with the environment. The concept of respect was deeply embedded in our worldview—respect for oneself, for one another, for the environment, and for all living things. This was observable in the language and in our daily interactions with all living things. Respect was integrated into our creation stories, songs, and ceremonies. Children learned these lessons from a very young age and these lessons were consistently reinforced throughout the lifecycle. The most effective lesson learned was that when you disrespect anyone or anything, you bring dishonor not only to yourself, but to your ancestors and future generations. This was the biggest deterrent to violence against women and children. Indigenous scholar Tuhiwani Smith expresses this concept of respect best:

> Respect, as seen through the eyes of the indigenous people, encompasses the whole of the universe and one's relationship to it . . . [T]hrough respect the place of everyone and everything in the universe is kept in balance and harmony. Respect is reciprocal, shared, constantly interchanging principle which is expressed through all aspects of social conduct.[5]

As indigenous people of this land, we adhered to this worldview and fundamental value. Respect was the basic foundation of our traditional law. Fienup-Riordan has called Alaska Natives and other indigenous peoples the "original ecologists."

> One reason for this is that their worldviews are dependent upon reciprocity—do unto others as you would have them do unto you. All of life is considered recyclable and therefore requires certain ways of caring in order to maintain the cycle.

Native people cannot put themselves above other living things because they were all created by the Raven, and all are considered essential components of the universe.[6]

For example, in the Athabascan culture, adherence to the preconstitutional law was taught and passed on from generation to generation through the stories of creation called *K'ondonts'itnee*.

According to our elder Eliza Jones, "This is our gospel, this is what we live by."[7] Intertwined within the *K'ondonts'itnee* is the concept of respect. These legends teach about the reciprocal, shared, constantly interchanging principle to which Smith refers. As Eliza Jones says, "after listening to a story one night, we had to repeat it back to them before they told us another." Learning the *K'odonst'itnees* verbatim ensured that the stories stayed alive and retained accuracy. Effie Willams, another respected Athabascan elder, described the *K'odonst'itnees* as, "our rules—those are our rules."[8] According to Catherine Attla, "Respect is the belief that we have. It is like the Supreme Court for us. But the other cultures do not acknowledge this concept of respect in us."[9] This belief is evident in the totality of the indigenous people of Alaska. Everything has a spirit and we must acknowledge and show respect for each and every spirit.

Traditionally, each tribe depended largely on the word of the medicine people and elders for advice and intervention in a case of inappropriate behavior. Their decisions were based solely on the beliefs and values of respect. The medicine people and elders were, in essence, our traditional tribal legal system. Their words of wisdom evolved from stories of creation. The medicine people were powerful and their ways of healing were effective. Most medicine people were elders. They were approached by community or family members when things were not in balance. The medicine people listened to concerns and offered words of wisdom in addition to performing a ritual/ceremony to bring back the balance.

> To help practitioners along this reciprocal path, Native peoples developed many rituals and ceremonies with respect to motherhood and child rearing, care of animals, hunting and trapping practices, and related ceremonies for maintaining balance between the human, natural and spiritual realms.[10]

In his book *Gwitch'in Native Elders*, Shawn Wilson writes about the influential role that elders played in the community. With the onset of the Western society, their role slowly became less influential. They did not lose sight of their culture and its inherent importance, but the community did not hold them in as high esteem. Wilson stated that this is the origin of the downfall of the Native community and the wellness of its people.[11] Since tribal communities were not as dependent upon their elders as they were in the past, this resulted in the slow deterioration of indigenous traditional law.

Alaska Native people have always believed that women and children are sacred, and they have been treated accordingly. Through the teachings of respect we learned that to violate another person or any living thing was what the Athabascans called *hutlaanee*. Violation of some of these *hutlaanee* is comparable to being convicted of a felony in the Western society. At times, when someone has broken a certain *hutlaanee*, the tribe shuns that person. Allowing that person to remain in the tribe jeopardizes the well-being of all. Consequently, when a serious *hutlaanee* is broken, that person is usually banned from the tribe. This has been the ultimate deterrent to violent behavior.

Consequently, there existed little or no violence amongst tribal members. "People of one village lived as close relatives."[12] The teachings of respect and the consequences for inappropriate behavior were effective. The community took the responsibility of immediate response to violent behavior. The leaders of the tribe resorted to banishment if all else failed. Banishment is the ultimate shame that anyone can bring upon himself or herself. It brings shame to not only the individual, but also his or her ancestors and the future generations of that familial lineage. That was a very effective deterrent to inappropriate behavior and violence against women.

> Attitude was thought to be as important as action: therefore one was to be careful in thought and action so as not to injure another's mind or offend the spirits of the animals and surrounding environment. For one to have a powerful mind was to be "aware or awake to its surroundings." Their rituals and ceremonies were intended to help maintain this balance and to regain it if messages from nature and the spiritual realm so indicated. Year after year these ceremonies were performed in exactly the same way, with the idea that someone performing or observing would gain intuitive understanding of something that the person had not understood before.[13]

Unfortunately, the fundamental value of respect does not have the same power and influence that it once did. With the changes that have occurred in our political, educational, economic, spiritual, and social realms through the colonization efforts, our fundamental belief in respect for all things is eroding at a faster rate than that which we can cope with. This is evident in our Native communities in the form of high rates of alcoholism, drug abuse, suicide, and violence.

Leadership has changed very dramatically in rural Alaska. The elders are not as involved as they had been in decision making. Currently, leaders are elected (which is not traditional), and the concept of unwritten tribal law is not exercised as effectively as it was in the past. We find that in most tribal communities the change in leadership happened simultaneously with the development and implementation of the Alaska Native Land Claims Act of 1971.[14] This landmark law was the ultimate turning point for many diverse issues for the tribal communities. It was during this time that alcoholism, drug abuse, suicide, and violence reached epidemic proportions in rural Alaska. With the changes in leadership and the economic realm, village personalities began changing—and not all for the better.

Prior to this era, traditional leaders were usually people who had proven themselves to possess such leadership qualities as honesty, integrity, cooperation, and humility. Today, we find that leaders are elected officials who may or may not possess these qualities. Many times we find that our leaders are from the larger families in a community, which, at times, may not be in the best interest of the community. We also find that, in some cases, the leaders themselves are perpetrators of violence. This becomes a barrier to providing safety for women as well.

We are experiencing a very high rate of violence against women and children. Domestic violence and sexual assault are both tolerated and accepted. Violence against women and children is being perpetuated in communities where there exists no form of contemporary law enforcement and no local infrastructure to address these incidents.

In a small community, one incidence of domestic violence or sexual assault can have a very lasting negative effect on the whole village. With the slow response or lack of response by the Alaska State Troopers, abuse is both tolerated and accepted. Recently, one small community reported one sexual assault of a minor and a very violent instance of domestic abuse. Arrests are either pending or have been made in both incidents. The whole village is now divided, which sets a very unhealthy environment in which to raise our children. Many times no arrest is made, which sends the perpetrator and the whole community the message that violence against women and children is both tolerable and acceptable.

State Laws and Alaska Native Women

The response to tribal members who behave inappropriately has changed dramatically in recent years. If people do not adhere to traditional ways, we have looked to Western styles of government to address the violence. We now have nontribal members forcing nontraditional approaches on the community through such avenues as tribal court development, tribal ordinances, and tribal protective orders. These processes are alien to us. This epidemic of violence against women and children is fairly new to our tribal communities. As such, we have never been prepared to address these issues. With the approaches to these incidents being developed for us by nontribal, nonresidential individuals and entities, there is added confusion as to who is responsible for responding to these incidents and in what manner we are allowed to respond.

The state of Alaska has a mandatory arrest requirement that requires a state law enforcement officer to arrest a person if the officer has probable cause to believe that the person has, either in or outside the presence of the officer, committed domestic violence or violated a protective order within the previous twelve hours.[15] Unfortunately, the mandatory arrest law is largely ineffective in remote villages. It can take the Alaska State Troopers anywhere from a day to ten days to respond when a community reports an act of violence against a woman or child. In some cases, it may take longer depending upon weather conditions, the urgency of the other matters they are dealing with in other villages, and the apparent severity of the situation. If they do respond, it is commonly after the twelve-hour period for mandatory arrest, in which case an arrest is up to the discretion of the officer.

Many state officials have interpreted Public Law 280 to mean that the state is the only authority allowed to respond to violent incidents. This message has been conveyed to tribal communities, implying that the village government is limited in its authority to respond to violence. Consequently, many tribal communities have begun to rely solely on the state law enforcement officials to respond. Therein lies the problem. The state has discretion as to what incidents they respond to and in what time frame. Some incidents do not get any response and those that do can have a lapse in time anywhere from one to ten days. Incidents that do not result in an arrest give the community a clear message that to disclose incidents of violence will not necessarily hold the batterers accountable for their behavior. It also gives tribal communities the implicit message that violence against women is both acceptable and tolerable. Many incidents are unreported. The response by law enforcement depends largely on their training in the area of violence against women. Many times, law enforcement officers will minimize the incident and question the validity of the woman's word, especially where alcohol and/or drugs are involved.

With the application of PL 280 upon Alaska statehood, the sovereignty of our Native villages was in question. There was much confusion as to what PL 280 really meant. Recently, one such case, *Native Village of Perryville v. John W. Tague*,[16] has received national attention. Tague had perpetrated violence against several community members. These victims and other community members of the village asked the Perryville Village Council to banish Tague. The Council issued a village order and requested state assistance to enforce the order. However, some state officials were disinclined to enforce the order. The Alaska chief assistant attorney general contested the Council's action, saying that the **injunction** banishing Tague and the **writ** of assistance asking for help enforcing the injunction were improperly issued. He informed the Alaska Superior Court that his office would advise the Department of Public Safety to vacate the permanent injunction and writ of assistance. He also argued that Tague was not a member of the Native Village of Perryville and that the sole authority for state recognition and enforcement of Perryville's protection order was in PL 280. Although the state has ruled to uphold the tribal banishment order, this is an example of the confusion that exists in our state on the PL 280 status.

Frequently the only people standing up for a woman in need of protection from a batterer or rapist are members of the local community. Consequently, the life of a woman depends largely on the local community's ability to provide immediate assistance. Given the extreme danger created by abusers and the remoteness of the communities, villages must develop their own programs using existing local resources. The development of this local response is the only assurance that women and their children in rural Alaska will be provided with the very basic human right of safety.

Currently, arrests are being made, perpetrators are being court-ordered to batterers' re-education programs, and women are being sent to urban shelters, but the problem continues. Perpetrators go through the program but recidivism is still very high. This approach to domestic abuse is still new and often seems foreign. Most tribal members do not fully understand the state legal system. It is an alien response to an alien problem. We need to develop an approach that makes sense to our people. We need programs that are culturally and community specific and within the tribal legal realm that we are familiar with: our tribal sovereignty.

Barriers

Many communities are beginning to develop their own local responses to these incidents, but many are left without resources to develop a basic infrastructure. In many small communities, 100 percent of all women have at one time or another been victims of domestic and/or sexual abuse. For a community with a population of approximately 170, the rate of domestic violence and sexual assault is usually two or three per week. Many of the incidents are not reported for a variety of reasons. During recent workshops conducted in one of these off-road communities, village residents reported that the number one barrier to reporting is that the perpetrators' family members become involved. If the perpetrator has a large volatile family, this adds to the danger. Often, an incident will set one family against another family. Many communities are currently torn apart with this type of reaction to violence against women. When an arrest is made, the victim, her advocate, and her family are usually blamed and become the target for retaliation. Victim blaming is still a significant problem.

In some cases, the perpetrator and/or his family threaten to commit future acts of violence. This is compounded by the slow or nonexistent response by the Alaska State Troopers. The lack of immediate response from law enforcement further endangers not only the victim and her family, but also advocates for the victims. This is the dangerous reality of women who are being abused in rural isolated Alaska where no form of law enforcement or no basic infrastructure exists to address violence against women. Because most communities are accessible only by air, endangered women cannot leave the community until a scheduled flight, which might be days later and can depend upon the weather.

In the interior region of Alaska, winter temperatures can drop to -40 degrees Fahrenheit, with average daylight lasting only three to four hours. The closest home might be anywhere from a mile to several miles away. Many times, seeking refuge at a neighbor's home is not an option, especially in situations where infants or small children are involved. Also, many people are not very familiar with full faith and credit (see chapter 16) and may not want to become involved with a case coming from a different village.

Women and children are not safe in these communities. The traditional attitude that women and children are sacred needs to be reintroduced and relearned through the traditional teachings of our people. Each community needs to be responsible for teaching nonviolent living by reintroducing the cultural concept of respect for all things and one another. Many of the domestic violence and sexual assault workshops that have been held in these villages are based on the Western (Anglo-American) feminist model, which has little or no effect on the abusers. The residents of these communities need to take ownership of the problem and develop their own solutions. This needs to happen now. We cannot depend on outsiders to tell us what the problem is or how to address it. It needs to come from the residents themselves. The only method that can work is our traditional method of teaching and learning. We know of no other technique that even stands a chance of working.

The core value of respect, which provided our people with checks and balances on appropriate behavior, is no longer as effective as it once was. As this concept of respect was eroded so was the well-being and safety of our people. Violence has become an everyday event. There is not a day that goes by when the Alaska Native Women's Coalition does not hear of a women being beaten or raped. There continues to be a very high tolerance for domestic abuse. Young girls are being violated sexually, and the perpetrators are not held accountable. Arrests are infrequent. Women are being beaten and abused, and the perpetrators are not held accountable. The victim's safety is jeopardized. The victim is often blamed.

Tribes are now beginning to realize that they have jurisdiction over their tribal members and that incidents happening in their community are as much their responsibility as they are the state's. Through tribal court training and workshops, they are beginning to exercise their jurisdictional muscle. Many were provided with generic domestic relation ordinances and sample tribal protective orders. A few have issued them. The fact remains that if there is no form of law enforcement in the community and the tribal courts and councils have not received training in just what constitutes these acts of violence or have not taken the time to organize a team to enforce the orders and keep the women safe, then these protective orders are ineffective and further burden the victim.

At the village level, many people still do not understand the process and the idea of protection orders. The only people who are very familiar with the orders and the state judicial system are the ones who have experienced them. Unfortunately, they are the perpetrators. They become well-versed in the legal system and use it to their benefit, going so far as to challenge the tribal orders. Controversial cases can arise if there are allegations that the tribe did not provide due process. Tribes need to realize that the safest way to avoid challenges from the state government is to provide notice, an opportunity to be heard, and fair hearings. Impartiality is still a problem in many communities where tribal leaders are related to the perpetrators.

Small airline companies ("bush pilots") play a significant role in Alaska because they are the only form of transportation for many villages. Since a banished perpetrator can only return to the village if he can purchase an airline ticket, these air carriers are a critical link in providing safety to women. Air carrier recognition of tribal protective orders and cooperation has been occurring in Alaska, but not consistently. A handful of air carriers serving tribal communities were familiar with the state protective orders but not many with tribal protective orders. A majority of these air carriers did not seem to realize that tribes have the authority to issue protective orders. Here, then, is another area in which training needs to be done relative to tribal protective orders in rural Alaska.

Some of our tribal communities have issued tribal protective orders and have successfully used the central registry system, which is part of the Alaska Public Safety Information Network (APSIN). Inclusion in the state registry system increases the likelihood that a protection order will be enforced. Currently, state law only allows protective orders issued by or filed with a court of this state to be placed into the APSIN.

Additionally, some tribes have issued a tribal protection order in which the petitioner is the whole community. Since the central registry system is set up to accommodate only orders that contain seven required elements and in which the petitioner is one person, these types of tribal protection orders could not be entered into the system. Fortunately, some tribal protection orders are now being issued and enforced in a large part by some community members themselves. Other tribal villages have issued protective orders that mirrored the state's. These were entered into the APSIN system with little or no difficulty and enforced by both the state and tribal officials. The problem remains, however, with perpetrators who are related to tribal leaders. In these cases, we find that there is no tribal enforcement of protection orders.

In my prior capacity as the STOP Violence Against Indian Women coordinator for one of the regional nonprofits, we purported to provide services to forty-three of the villages in Alaska. Realistically, this was not happening and could not happen. Although women were calling on a daily basis for advocacy assistance, we were not successful in organizing efforts at the local level for these villages to address violence perpetuated against women and children. Our efforts to develop a local Community Response Plan to Address Domestic Violence and Sexual Assault were not successful. We found that there was a very high burnout rate among village advocates as well as tribal staff. Additionally, village leadership changes every two years. Consequently, continuity as to who, at the village level, is addressing violence against women and children was almost nonexistent.

Vision of Hope

The Alaska Native Women's Coalition (ANWC) was developed in 2001. The need for this coalition arose out of continued concern about the safety of Native women in Alaska. Formed by and for Native women, the Coalition seeks to work toward the elimination of personal and societal violence in the lives of women and children. Survivors' voices have brought to the forefront an invaluable expression of the Alaska Native women's realities. Through these voices, the current challenges and barriers to the safety of women and children living in remote, isolated villages have been identified and documented. Consistent dialogue with tribes has resulted in the development of community-based, culturally responsive projects currently being piloted in selected tribal communities. ANWC continues to focus on reclaiming customary values and beliefs that prohibited violence against Native women and children. The tribal communities are provided with the opportunity to take ownership of the problem and its solutions. Many are concluding that strengthening sovereignty seems to be a realistic goal.

With urban resources many miles away, tribal residents are beginning to realize that the solution to these problems lies within the community. Some communities are beginning to take ownership of the problem of violence against women and children. Villages are beginning to develop an effective, community-specific approach to addressing violence against women and children through the revitalization of the cultural values and beliefs. Additionally, we are working to reestablish the role of our respected elders as teachers. For example, in one of our smaller tribal communities the residents are working hard to implement projects that occur in a cultural setting, such as a fish camp. With the elders as teachers, residents are actively pursuing projects that focus on nonviolent lifestyles. Curricula are being developed stressing the indigenous concept of respect for all things. The traditional message that to violate another brings shame not only to self, but to the family, ancestors, and the future familial lineage is being reinforced. More tribal members are intertwining contemporary judicial approaches with their traditional, indigenous beliefs.

Many tribal councils are taking a more active role in providing safety for women and children. Village service providers are being trained to intervene in incidents of violence with the safety of women and children as their highest priority. An influential component of the development of the community response is that tribal residents are realizing and articulating that violence against women and children will no longer be tolerated and accepted. In that lies the hope for building a safer more respectful tribal community.

Notes

1. 522 U.S. 520 (1998).
2. *1999 Annual Statistical Report* (Anchorage Police Department, 1999), available at http://www.muni.org/iceimages/APD1/99UCR.pdf.
3. See http://groups.yahoo.com/group/CAVNET_IW/message/1598.
4. J. Burger, *Gaia Atlas of First Peoples* (New York: Anchor Doubleday, 1990); P. Knudtson and D. Suzuki, *Wisdom of the Elders* (Toronto: Stoddard, 1992).
5. L.T. Smith, *Decolonizing Methodologies: Research and Indigenous People* (London, New York: Zed Books, 1999).
6. Milton M.R. Freeman and Ludwig N. Carbyn, *Traditional Knowledge and Renewable Resource Management in Northern Region* (Edmonton: IUCN Commission on Ecology and the Boreal Institute for Northern Studies, 1988).
7. Personal interview with Eleanor David, Koyukuk, Alaska, June 2000. Eliza Jones is a very well-respected elder with many years of teaching, documenting, and researching the Koyukon Athabascan language.
8. Personal interview with Eleanor David, Allakaket, Alaska, February 2000. Effie Williams was eighty years old at the time and still upholds these traditional values and beliefs.
9. Catherine Attla, *Make Prayers to the Raven* (video, 1987). Catherine Attla, a respected elder from Huslia, Alaska, is very well known for her contribution to the teachings of the traditional Athabascan lifeways.
10. Oscar A. Kawagley, *A Yupiaq Worldview: Pathway to Ecology and Spirit* (Prospect Heights, IL: Waveland Press, 1995).
11. Shawn Wilson, *Gwitch'in Native Elders* (Alaska Native Knowledge Network, University of Alaska, Fairbanks, 1996).
12. M. Muktoyuk, *Inupiaq Rules For Living* (Anchorage: Alaska Methodist University Press, 1988).
13. Kawagley, *Yupiaq Worldview*, 74.
14. ANCSA 43 USC Sec. 1601.
15. AS 18.65.530.
16. Case No. 3AN-00-12245 CI.

Questions

1. What are barriers that Alaska Native people face when dealing with violence against women that are unique to their state and people?
2. What are some of Ned-Sunnyboy's suggestions for fighting these barriers? Do you agree?
3. How do the Venetie decision and Public Law 280 complicate domestic violence and sexual assault issues in Alaska? Who has jurisdiction over these crimes occurring in Native villages in Alaska?
4. What does Ned-Sunnyboy mean when she says that boarding schools led to a "gap in traditional learning that is being felt in most remote Alaskan Villages to this day"? How does this relate to domestic violence and sexual assault?
5. Why does the author consult with elders and make a point about *K'ondonsts'itnee*?
6. How do state laws discriminate against remote Alaska Native villages and women?
7. What are some internal community problems that Ned-Sunnyboy addresses that present barriers to dealing with violence against women at a community level?

In Your Community

1. Do you agree with Ned-Sunnyboy's call to traditional values of respect and tribal responsibility in combating violence against women? What are some local responses and ideas for these issues in your community?
2. Is it difficult for women in your community to obtain protective orders? Do police respond to domestic violence calls in a timely manner?
3. Are there Native advocates for women in your community? What challenges do they face?
4. How is the situation in Alaska similar or different to what your community faces when dealing with violence against women?

Terms Used in Chapter 4

Infiltrate: To penetrate, especially with hostile intent.
Injunction: A court order prohibiting a party from a specific course of action.
Jurisdiction: The area in which a government has the right and power to make decisions.
Per capita: "By heads"; by the number of individual persons.

Writ: A written order issued by a court, commanding the party to whom it is addressed to perform or cease performing a specified act.

Suggested Further Reading

Magen, Randy H., and Darryl S. Wood. *Intimate Partner Violence Against AHTNA (Alaska Native) Women in the Copper River Basin.* University of Alaska Anchorage, July 2006, available at http://www.ncjrs.gov/pdffiles1/nij/grants/215350.pdf.

Nella, Lee. "Scattered Like Reindeer: Alaska Natives and the Loss of Autonomy." In *Native Americans and the Criminal Justice System,* Jeffery Ian Ross and Larry Gould, eds., p. 217. Boulder, CO: Paradigm, 2006.

Rosay, André, and Robert H. Langworthy. *Descriptive Analysis of Sexual Assaults in Anchorage, Alaska.* Justice Center, University of Alaska, 2003.

Segal, Bernard. "Responding to Victimized Alaska Native Women in Treatment for Substance Use." *Substance Use & Misuse* 36 (2001): 845, 851.

Shephard, Judy. "Where Do You Go When It's 40 Below? Domestic Violence Among Rural Alaska Native Women." *Affilia* 16 (2001): 488.

Kitchen Table Wisdom

Afterwards I sat alone
By the kitchen table
Listening to the same wind
Batter the same wood
Holding our little house together
But nothing
Held me together
Or so I thought.

Years later
Grown daughters say
They hid at the top of the stairs
Watching me cry quietly
Shoulders bent under the weight
Of all village women
I would suddenly hush
If they showed themselves
So they left in the comfort of the table
Knowing I needed
Warm tears
To sooth purple cheeks.

The curled column of blue smoke
Off the end of my pipe
My swollen eyes followed
As the memory of stinging slaps
Etched deeper in my wrinkled brain
Imprinting forever the sickening feel of soft flesh
Pummeled by familiar fists
Again and again.

Clock ticking away hours
Into minutes before the kids would get up
And I was caught in the act
Of pretending
Nothing happened
While I cooked breakfast
And smiled.

People talk about shelters
But in the village
Shelter came after he left the house
Freeing the kitchen table
In the warm sunlight.

Didn't dare
Cry to anyone
Because if they helped
They might also get beat
For seeing the truth.

Told the magistrate one time
He laughed
Told me to leave
Smoked pot at our wedding
So his lips were forever sealed
With the 'good old boy' kiss.

Years later
After many dark nights of the soul
Sitting at the kitchen table
I realized there are no victims
Only volunteers
Keep leaving and
Trust the wisdom
Gleaned from the kitchen table
As the clock ticks away
Remember the pain
Someday you'll decide not to go back.

        Margaret "Augie" Kochuten (Quinault)

Overview of Issues Facing Native Women Who Are Survivors of Violence in Urban Communities

Chapter 5

ROSE L. CLARK AND CARRIE L. JOHNSON

Native women in urban communities are challenged with many risks and barriers. Historically, violence against Native women was not common. Women were valued in the culture. Today Native women are victims of violence at a higher rate than any other ethnic group. Forms of violence against Native women include physical, economic, verbal, and sexual, as well as **stalking**. The physical, environmental, social, and psychological conditions that confront Native women are well documented. Factors that have contributed to the high rates of violence include multigenerational trauma, poverty, high rates of unemployment, survivors exposed to violence as children, as well as alcohol and substance abuse.

Although the majority of Natives live in urban areas, there is often a serious lack of culturally appropriate resources or services in urban areas for Native women who are victims of violence. This lack of culturally appropriate services or resources includes service providers not having an understanding of the culture and traditions of Native people. Due to the lack of cultural competence and awareness among some service providers, Native women may be hesitant to disclose the violence. Other culturally appropriate services or resources that may be lacking include incorporating the traditions and values of the individual in the services such as incorporating traditional healing, if appropriate. Native women living in urban areas often face unique legal, social, and economic challenges. Urban Native survivors of domestic violence are further challenged by language barriers, lack of necessary skills to navigate the health and social systems, and competing cultural practices that constrict choices in seeking safety from violence. Because urban Native women tend to reside near and blend in with other ethnic groups, they are often overshadowed by other more highly visible and identifiable groups, which contributes to the lack of services targeted for and delivered to urban Native women.

Prevalence and Incidence of Violence among Native Women in Urban Areas

Despite an outpouring of research over the past twenty years, many serious gaps exist in the understanding of violence against women, particularly among urban Native women. There is very little information on the extent and prevalence of domestic violence among urban Native women. The data that has been gathered is based in large part on reservation samples. Contributing to the lack of data available on urban Native women are racial misclassification, collapsing urban Native women into an "other" category; poor and inconsistent data reporting methods; and a lack of centralized data collection within the urban social and health systems.[1] These issues only compound the barriers that exist for Native women living in urban environments and often render them invisible to the general public.

The rates of violence among urban Native women, who are far from a homogenous group, vary markedly within the Native population. Some regions of tribes and urban Natives have been affected by violence to a much greater extent than others. There is also a significant correlation between substance abuse and violence.[2] What we do not know is the interpretation of this correlation. It is not clear whether domestic violence causes substance abuse or whether substance abuse causes domestic violence. In addition, substance abuse is neither necessary nor a sufficient explanation for violent behavior because its influence is dependent on several contextual factors, such as history of victimization. When reviewing the literature and research regarding the relationship between domestic violence and substance abuse, it is particularly important to avoid its victim-blaming potential. The intent of the authors is to bring awareness to the relationship between domestic violence and substance abuse so that a coordinated system of care may be developed to address Native women's needs.

In a recent study on domestic violence and substance use among Native women living in rural and urban nonreservation sites in California, there were three main predictors that emerged for recent violence for these women.[3] These included severe childhood violent victimization, low-income status, and problem drinking. One of the strongest predictors was severe childhood violence. Native women with experiences of severe childhood violence were 6.5 times as likely to report recent violence than those who did not have such experiences. Similarly, Native women identified as problem drinkers were 5.5 times more likely to experience recent violence. Native women having an income under $20,000 a year were 4.9 times more likely to be victims of violence in the past twelve months. Other predictors emerged as well. Not surprisingly, Native women whose attitudes reflected tolerance of physical fighting and violence were 6.6 times more likely to experience recent violent victimization. Finally, Native women who reported more experiences of prejudice and racism from non-Indians were 4.4 times more likely to report being victimized in the past twelve months.

The study "Pregnant and Parenting American Indian Needs" included 290 respondents in one urban and one rural area in California. This study found many Native women reported personal experiences of lifetime victimization, with higher rates found among the alcohol- or drug-involved group. In fact, 43 percent of the alcohol- or drug-involved group reported being attacked with a gun, knife, or other weapon. Even more (64 percent) reported that they had been attacked with the intent to seriously injure them without a weapon being involved. Finally, 36 percent reported they had been forced into a sexual act through force or threat of force.[4]

According to the Bureau of Justice Statistics, in their report *American Indians and Crime*, Natives have a violent crime victimization rate that is 2.5 times higher than the national rate (101 violent crimes per 1,000 vs. 41 per 1,000, respectively). Further, the violent crime rate was highest for Natives living in urban rather than rural areas (130 per 1,000 for urban and 81 per 1,000 for rural). While Natives experienced higher rates of violent victimization than persons of other races at every income level, Natives with an annual income of less than $10,000 reported the highest rate of violent victimization (182 per 1,000). Of particular note is that more than half the violent victimization of Natives involved offenders with whom the victim had a prior relationship, and about one in five violent acts against Natives involved an offender who was an intimate family member. While violent crime against whites and blacks is primarily intraracial, the majority of Native victims reported their offender as white (57 percent) and black (9 percent), while almost a third (30 percent) were victimized by other Natives. Such statistics illustrate that Natives who are living in urban areas and who are struggling with severe poverty—increasingly, Native women—are among the highest at risk for violent criminal victimization.[5]

Native women report rape and sexual assault at a rate two times greater than the overall population (5 per 1,000 for Native compared to 2 per 1,000 for all races). Native victims of rape or sexual assault most often reported that their offender was of a different race, with about nine in ten victims estimated to have assailants who were white or black. Native women were significantly more likely than white women, African American women, or mixed race women to report they were raped. They were also significantly more likely than white or African American women to report that they were stalked.[6]

Native women who are at highest risk for violence are those who have interracial marriages or relationships—women who are more likely to live in urban centers than reservations or rural areas. In metropolitan areas, these women may be at a greater risk of violence because they may be increasingly isolated from their extended family or cultural group, which might otherwise serve as a protective factor against violence.

Alcohol and drug use is significantly positively correlated with intimate and family violence among all racial groups, and substance abuse has long been a major social problem among Natives. Nearly 62 percent of Native victims of violence reported that their offender had been drinking at the time of the offense compared to 42 percent for all races.[7] The risk associated with Native women is compelling when examining the issue of substance abuse and its relationship with violence. Alcohol-related death rates for Native women are significantly higher than the rate for women of all racial groups. A popular explanation for such high rates of alcohol and substance use among Native women is the notion of self-medication in the attempt to cope with prior victimization (including incest, rape, and sexual assault)—a cycle that contributes to higher rates of mortality and increased risk of revictimization.

The rates of violence among Native women have also had a significant impact on the rates of child abuse and neglect of Native children. In the United States from 1992 to 1995, Natives and Asians were the only racial or ethnic groups to experience increases in the rate of abuse or neglect of children under age fifteen, as measured by incidents recorded by Child Protective Services agencies.[8] The increase in reported incidents involving Native children was more than three times as large as that for Asian children. The per capita rate for Native children was seven times that of Asian children. These Native children that are victims of child abuse will most likely continue to have problems in adulthood, because the trauma continues to be passed down to subsequent generations, becoming a part of the multigenerational trauma.[9]

Risk and Vulnerability Factors Associated with Violence Against Native Women

There are multiple factors that are associated with violence toward Native women; some of these factors are unique to Native women in urban communities. Foremost is the effect of the Multigenerational Trauma Cycle.[10] This cycle is the effect of **colonization** on Natives. Colonization resulted in the systematic destruction of the culture and lifeways of indigenous people around the world. Historically, the indigenous individual, family, and community were intact and spiritually connected to their surroundings. With the arrival of the Europeans, Natives were faced with the destruction of traditional cultural values, practices, and beliefs. Other effects of colonization were epidemic disease, massacres, slavery, **relocation** to reservations, destructive federal policies, and broken treaties.

Residential schools were set up ostensibly to educate Native children, but in reality they kept them from practicing their traditions, language, and culture. While in the residential schools, Native children did not learn traditional parenting skills; often what they did learn was harsh punishment and abuse. Although there are differences between tribes, traditional parenting skills usually include the belief that harsh discipline should be avoided, that noninterference is the best way to correct behavior, and that children should learn through observation.[11] Residential schools for some Native children affected their ability to parent later in life. **Assimilation** was not limited to residential schools but was evident in the public school system as well. The public school system and mission schools were also set up as a way to assimilate Native children. Native children often faced prejudice and racism from administration, teachers, and non-Indian students.

Relocation to urban areas was another factor adding to the problems Natives faced. After World War II, the federal government adopted a program of relocation as another tool to assimilate Natives. Because of this relocation policy a steady stream of Indians migrated to various cities across the nation to improve their economic and social situations.[12] For these people life and work among non-Indians was their first urban experience. The relocation caused stress and anxiety. Insecurity and fear ruled many Natives, making them feel lost and inferior to the majority population of white Americans. They encountered unemployment, poverty, and crime in urban mainstream culture and felt social alienation, community prejudice, and racism. They faced isolation, loneliness, broken marriages, crime, alcoholism, school dropouts, and suicide. Urban culture left many Native people feeling socially and psychologically alienated. Assimilation meant that they became strangers to their own families, communities, and tribes.

The impact of colonization has had a significant impact on Natives. The influence of boarding schools, relocation, and other historical factors contributed to many problems such as post-traumatic stress disorder (PTSD), depression and other mental health problems, and substance abuse, all of which contribute to the high rates of violence so prevalent in the Native community. A study in 1992 reported that Native adults and children appear to suffer commonly from depression.[13] Depressed feelings are frequently complicated by anxiety and the use of alcohol and other drugs. Low self-esteem, depression, substance abuse, and life frustrations contribute to an increase in violent behaviors, which include physical and sexual abuse of children, child neglect, spouse and elder abuse, assault, homicide, and suicide.

Other studies have examined PTSD in Native communities. PTSD has been associated with substance abuse, anxiety, and depression. Many Natives have turned to alcohol and drugs to deal with problems caused by their loss of dignity; negative self-perception; discrimination; estrangement; and economic, social, and cultural stress as a way to self-medicate mental health problems. There is a high level of co-occurring disorders in Native communities.[14]

The effects of alcohol and drugs on the Native family are devastating. The family and community closeness have deteriorated and resulted in an increase of family violence. Research suggests that the abuse of Native women and children by Native men can be traced to the introduction of alcohol.[15] Native programs also point to the cultural genocide of Native people as contributing to the violence against Native women.[16] A common result of family violence and alcoholism is child neglect and abuse. Child abuse and neglect in Native children is a serious problem. According to the U.S. Bureau of Justice statistics, in 1995 there was one substantiated report of a child victim of abuse or neglect for every thirty Native children ages fourteen or younger compared to one report for every fifty-eight children of any race.

Parental alcohol abuse has been associated with child abuse. One study attributed chaotic family situations and other problems such as alcoholism and depression to child abuse and neglect.[17] Native children who were victims of child abuse are prone to a Multigenerational Trauma Cycle. The literature reports that problems in adulthood were due to being a victim of child abuse. A study found that child abuse and both physical and sexual abuse were risk factors for conduct disorders and that both child abuse and conduct disorders were risk factors for alcohol dependence. Alcohol dependency was a risk factor for physical intimate partner violence. Thus, a history of physical abuse in childhood was a significant predictor of being a victim and a perpetrator of physical partner violence.[18] The Multigenerational Trauma Cycle contributes to the high rates of violence in our community. As survivors of violence have children of their own, the cycle will most likely continue if coordinated culturally appropriate services are not provided.

Disharmony and imbalance are created by the Multigenerational Trauma Cycle. When harmony and balance are broken, the spiritual self is weak and one is more vulnerable to the effects of the cycle. Restoring harmony and balance is needed in order to break the Multigenerational Trauma Cycle so that the trauma is not passed on to our children and future generations. For our future generations we have to restore the harmony and balance that has been lost in so many Native families and communities.

When identifying risk and vulnerability factors among urban Native women who are victims of violence it is important to recognize the effects of the historical trauma and the Multigenerational Trauma Cycle. These include past victimization, growing up in a violent home, exposure to chronic trauma, substance abuse, poverty, poor self-image, and shame. For urban Native women it also includes being away from their community, the loss of family and cultural support, and being in a new environment. Therefore, when examining violence in Native women, particularly in an urban area, it is important to understand and emphasize the importance of the perpetuation of violence due to the Multigenerational Trauma Cycle.

Effects of Violence on Native Women

Often, urban Native women are not the only victims of the violence—other family members, the community, social systems, and children who are exposed to the violence will often suffer from the effects as well. Frustrations and anger about unjust social conditions combine with depression; alcohol abuse and the social acceptance of acting out behaviors contribute to violence being a major problem in many Native communities. Families where violence is common tend to share an unspoken belief that violence is normal and inescapable. Violence in Native communities, like other destructive and self-destructive behaviors, tends to be associated with low self-esteem, frustration, and alcohol and substance abuse. Negative social conditions like poverty and discrimination create anger and frustration.

There has been an abundance of research documenting the consequences for children exposed to violence.[19] Not only does domestic violence affect children who witness it, but also its effects are exacerbated when children are themselves victims of child battering. An estimated three million children witness acts of violence against their mothers every year, and many come to believe that violent behavior is an acceptable way to express anger, frustration, or a will to control. Abuse and neglect are associated with both short- and long-term negative consequences for a child's physical and mental health, cognitive skills and educational attainment, and social and behavioral development. Children of survivor parents typically display strong feelings of grief and loss, abandonment, betrayal, rage, and guilt. Older children may also have feelings of shame. Children have issues around abandonment and separation and some may become parentified. Children's responses to family violence vary according to temperament and their age at the time the violence occurred. Children who experience or witness domestic violence are at increased risk of adopting these same strategies in their interactions with their partners and children.[20]

Barriers to Services in Urban Communities

Native women in urban communities are faced with many barriers when seeking services for victims of violence. These barriers are often related to the risk factors mentioned previously. It is also important to take into consideration historical events, multigenerational trauma, and culture when working with urban Native women in both intervention and prevention.

Moving from a reservation or a rural area to an urban community can be difficult. There are many reasons why Native women may move to an urban area. These include: to find employment, education, or health resources; or to visit or move closer to a family member. In a new urban environment, there is a different system of care to navigate. Many of the women who come to an urban area are unaware of the services available to them, transportation to the services can be challenging, and by leaving their reservation they no longer have family and cultural support. Native women in an urban environment often feel invisible, alone, and isolated. So being in a violent relationship will make life even more difficult. Once the urban Native woman starts to realize that she should leave a violent relationship, she often will not know to whom she can turn for help. If she does decide to leave the violent relationship, her first concern is most often her safety and often the safety of her children. She will be afraid of another beating or being murdered. This can be an extremely difficult decision for a Native woman who does not have support and does not know where to seek support. These women often do not have income or food. Many Native women are below the poverty level in urban environments. They do not have transportation or a safe place to go, and they do not know how to seek services for themselves. As a result, Native women in urban communities who are victims of violence may stay in a violent relationship longer, risking their safety and their children's safety.

Another important barrier Native women with children encounter is the fear of losing their children. If there is violence in the home, mothers are afraid to seek help from social service agencies who may report them to child protection services agencies, which may in turn remove the children. If the children are removed, many times urban Native women face unrealistic demands to regain custody in a system that virtually sets them up for failure and does not recognize their culturally specific needs. Again, there is a lack of support in obtaining all the services needed to get their children back. Within such a bind, Native women often give up and continue to medicate themselves with alcohol and drugs, increasing their mental health problems, and continuing to be revictimized.

Another barrier in an urban area is misidentification. Natives are often misidentified as another race, which contributes to their reluctance to seek services. If they are misidentified, then the Indian Child Welfare Act (ICWA) may not be followed. Their tribes may not be contacted, and their children may be placed in nonrelative or non-Indian homes. In fact, the parents often do not know their rights concerning ICWA.

Native women with children also often encounter additional barriers to services in an urban area. It is more difficult to find a shelter that takes children, more than one child, or older children. If they are trying to flee a violent relationship in order to protect themselves and their children and cannot find a shelter, they are often left homeless.

Identity problems in an urban community are another difficulty for women and their children. Many Native people often feel invisible, isolated, and do not feel they belong. For example, a Native child may be the only Native student in the entire school. In addition, they experience discrimination and prejudice from non-Indians, making them feel inferior. There are not as many opportunities to participate in cultural events or activities in an urban environment. In urban areas there is such a large number of different tribal groups that there may not be any cultural activities for their particular tribe. As a result there is a loss of cultural identity, which contributes to the depression, other mental health problems, substance abuse, and behavioral problems for children.

Many urban Native women do not possess the support or ability to acquire services to assist themselves. Native women are often not aware of their rights or feel intimated by the system. They often do not know how to obtain a restraining order or custody orders. They do know where the services are, how to get there, or may have to go to multiple locations for a variety of services. Transportation is a huge problem for Native women in an urban environment. In addition, Native women who are just arriving from the reservation where the violence occurred may also have to work with the tribal courts on their reservation.

Substance abuse is also a barrier to urban Native women seeking services and compounds the other barriers mentioned. A study done at an urban Indian health center showed that most of the women who were being counseled for domestic violence were not married, had low family incomes, and both the women and their partners abused drugs. All the women experienced increased depression and stress due to battering. The battered women reported more problems with alcohol than women with no history of domestic violence.[21] Due to historical trauma, as mentioned earlier, many of these women are also experiencing mental health problems such as depression, anxiety, and post-traumatic stress disorder. Substance abuse and mental health problems will only add to the many barriers they are already challenged with in an urban environment. The lack of coordination of services that the women may need, such as domestic violence services, substance abuse services, and mental health services, further impedes Native women's ability to access services.

Although there are many specialized services for women victims of violence in urban areas such as rape centers; shelters; and advocacy, medical, law enforcement, mental health, and children's services, many of these services are not sensitive to the needs of urban Native women. Therefore, urban Native women may find it difficult to leave their family to enter into a shelter that is not aware of the needs or importance of extended family and the traditional significance of family and culture. Urban Native women have difficulty trusting and expressing their feelings, so communication and language can be a barrier. The difficulty in trusting and expressing their feelings may come from the collective past of Native people,[22] as well as discrimination and oppression from mainstream society and lack of a provider's awareness of Native people. These different services often play different roles and can make navigating services very cumbersome for many urban Native women. These systems often do not understand or recognize the impact of colonization and multigenerational trauma on Native families and, therefore, are not sensitive to the unique needs of urban Native women.

Working with Native Women in Urban Communities

We need to train more service providers in urban areas to deal with the unique challenges faced by Native women victims of violence. Training should be geared to police, court personnel, social workers and other mental health providers, hotlines, shelters, medical personnel, and teachers.

There is a need for more Native advocates and providers in urban areas so that these services designed to assist Native women draw on the culture and implement the traditions. The first priority for a victim of violence is safety. After the woman is in a safe situation, then the substance abuse and mental health problems have to be addressed, as they have a profound affect on their road to recovery and self-sufficiency. Having Native women who have experienced violence be mentors, advocates, and counselors for other Native women is extremely important.

It is important to educate Native women on their rights pertaining to domestic violence, marital rape, and stalking, as well as Indian child welfare issues. Outreach to Native women in the urban environment is necessary to let them know what services and supports are available to them. For Native women in large urban communities, home visits, if safety is not compromised, are extremely helpful, as is providing transportation for them to get to services.

Vocational training programs would assist Native women to learn job skills in order to become financially independent and stable so that they can live in a non-violent environment.

Conclusion

Native women victims of violence who live in urban areas experience a unique set of circumstances. They face invisibility, isolation, discrimination, as well as a host of social problems such as poverty, unemployment, homelessness, and substance abuse. Urban Native women experience disproportionately high rates of violence, which affect them, their families, their communities, and their children. This cycle of violence is passed on from generation to generation. This Multigenerational Trauma Cycle contributes to the unresolved grief experienced as a result of historical trauma. Urban Native women face a number of barriers when navigating social service systems in urban areas, including the lack of culturally appropriate services and a lack of service providers who are knowledgeable of the community and cultural needs.

The individual needs of each Native woman who is a victim of violence must be examined to determine what services she needs, and the woman must have a voice in what treatment or services she needs and wants. These treatments could be a combination of evidence-based treatments with traditional Native treatments. Evidence-based treatments are the traditional Western treatments (cognitive-behavioral, psychoanalytic, and so forth). These treatments can often be integrated with or adapted to Native values and traditions to better assist Native women in healing.

Restoring harmony and balance through the use of traditional methods in conjunction with evidenced-based interventions is needed in order to break out of the Multigenerational Trauma Cycle so that future generations are not lost in a cycle of violence.

Notes

1. R. Clark, "Healing the Generations: Urban American Indians in Recovery," in *Mental Health Care for Urban Indians: Clinical Insights from Native Practitioners*, T. Witko, ed. (Washington, DC: American Psychological Association, 2006).

2. Steven W. Perry, *American Indians and Crime: A BJS Statistical Profile 1992–2002* (Washington, DC: Bureau of Justice Statistics, U.S. Department of Justice, December 2004, NCJ 203097), available at /www.ojp.usdoj.gov/bjs/pubalp2.htm#aic.

3. E. Zahnd, S. Holtby, D. Klein, and C. McCain, *American Indian Women: Preventing Violence and Drinking Project Final Report* (National Institute on Alcohol Abuse and Alcoholism and the Office for Research on Women's Health, 2002).

4. D. Klein, E. Zahnd, B. Kolody, S. Holtby, and L. Midanik, *Final Report of the Pregnant and Parenting American Indian Study* (Western Consortium for Public Health and San Diego State University Foundation, 1995); E. Zahnd and D. Klein, "The Needs of Pregnant and Parenting American Indian Women at Risk for Problem Alcohol or Drug Use," *American Indian Culture and Research Journal* 21, no. 3 (1997): 119–44.

5. Perry, *American Indians and Crime*.

6. Patricia Tjaden and Nancy Thoennes, *Full Report of the Prevalence, Incidence, and Consequences of Violence Against Women: Findings from the National Violence Against Women Survey* (National Institute of Justice and Centers for Disease Control and Prevention, NCJ 183781, November 2000).

7. Perry, *American Indians and Crime*.

8. Lawrence A. Greenfeld and Steven K. Smith, *American Indians and Crime* (Washington, DC: Bureau of Justice Statistics, U.S. Department of Justice, February 1999, NCJ 173386), available at http://www.ojp.usdoj.gov/bjs/pub/pdf/aic.pdf.

9. C. L. Johnson, "An Innovative Healing Model: Empowering Urban Native Americans," in *Mental Health Care for Urban Indians: Clinical Insights from Native Practitioners*, T. Witko, ed. (Washington, DC: American Psychological Association, 2006).

10. Johnson, "Innovative Healing Model."

11. Johnson, "Innovative Healing Model."

12. D. L. Fixico, *The Urban Indian Experience in America* (Albuquerque, NM: University of New Mexico Press, 2000).

13. Scott H. Nelson, George F. McCoy, Maria Stetter, and Craig Vanderwagen, "An Overview of Mental Health Services for American Indians and Alaska Natives in the 1990s," *Hospital and Community Psychiatry* 43 (1992): 257–61.

14. See www.ajph.org/cgi/reprint/92/4/520, last accessed on July 11, 2007.

15. L. Groginsky and C. Freeman, "Domestic Violence in Native American Indian and Alaskan Native Communities," *Protecting Children* 11, no. 3 (1995): 13–16.

16. Johnson, "Innovative Healing Model."

17. J. M. Piasecki, S. M. Manson, M. P. Barnoff, A. B. Hiat, S. S. Taylor, and D. W. Bechtold, "Abuse and Neglect of American Indian Children: Findings from a Survey of Providers," *American Indian and Alaska Native Mental Health Research* 3 (1989): 43–62.

18. S. J. Kunitz, J. E. Levy, J. McCloskey, and K. R. Gabriel, "Alcohol Dependence and Domestic Violence as Sequel of Abuse and Conduct Disorder in Childhood," *Child Abuse and Neglect* 22 (1998): 11.

19. See, for example, R. A. Geffner, P. G. Jaffe, and M. Sudermann, eds., *Children Exposed to Domestic Violence: Current Issues in Research, Intervention, Prevention, and Policy Development* (New York: Haworth Maltreatment & Trauma Press, 2000).

20. Geffner et al., *Children Exposed*.

21. I. M. Norton and S. M. Manson, "Silent Minority: Battered American Indian Women," *Journal of Family Violence* 10 (1995): 307–18.

22. Johnson, "Innovative Healing Model."

Questions

1. What is the relationship between severe childhood violence and adult violence?
2. Why do you think Native women who identified as problem drinkers were 5.5 times more likely to be victims of violence?
3. Why do you think Native women are significantly more likely to be raped or stalked than women of other races?
4. What is meant by the term Multigenerational Trauma Cycle? What is its relationship to violence?

In Your Community

1. How can urban communities with small numbers of Native women reach out to Native women?
2. What are some of the barriers to services Native women find in the urban area closest to you? What can be done to remove those barriers?

Terms Used in Chapter 5

Assimilation: Refers to the process of becoming a part of or more like another.

Colonization: The act of establishing colonies, where one dominant culture settles an area generally inhabited by another culture.

Relocation: Refers to the U.S. policy of moving large numbers of Natives from reservations to urban areas.

Stalking: Behavior where an individual repeatedly engages in harassing, unwanted conduct directed at another. It could include phoning, following, e-mailing, threatening to harm an individual or his or her family members, or many other types of actions.

Suggested Further Reading

Evans-Campbell, Teresa, et al. "Interpersonal Violence in the Lives of Urban American Indian and Alaska Native Women." *American Journal of Public Health* 96 (2006): 1416.

Fixico, D.L. *The Urban Indian Experience in America.* Albuquerque, NM: University of New Mexico Press, 2000.

Norton, Ilena M., and Spero M. Manson. "Domestic Violence Intervention in an Urban Indian Health Center." *Community Mental Health Journal* 33 (1997): 331.

STORIES OF SURVIVAL   II

The Dance of Violence

Pulling the blanket up
Hiding
her eyes
She screamed silent
To her own
mother's cries

the words got lost
in what is good
what is not
she can only know
what she sees
what she's got

and on the week end
she is a jingle dancer

mama says
don't let this
happen to you
love should not hurt
she does not know
if it's true

and on the week end
she is a pow wow princess

little girl scared
she can not run
can not hide
she wonders how this
can be
Native Pride

and on the week end
she wears her beaded crown

mama stands bruised
preaches

her word
convincing herself
the child's
not hurt

*and on the week end
she watches her girl dance*

locked in the violence
of distorted
tradition
the old way is lost
by the choice of
omission

carnage revealed
in denial
is cloaked
the cycle continues
on the truth
we have choked

*and on the week ends
We Dance*

we nod at each other
like this is
the way it should be
ignoring the sound
of a jingle dance
plea

*and on the week ends
we are Indians*

jingle girl grows
continues to dance
she loves
a grass dancer

she takes a
love chance

and on the week ends
they owl dance

married traditional
she wears
her white skins
it was not long after
the hurting
begins

and on the week end
she watches her tiny tot

pulling the blanket up
hiding
her eyes
she screams silent
to her own mother's
cries

                Tracie Jones Myrick Meyer (Kalapuya)

Chapter 6

From a Woman Who Experienced Violence

ANONYMOUS

The New Family in Town

The kerosene light glowed its warm yellow softness against the red-and-white checked oilcloth. Supper was finished and each family member had completed evening chores. My dad let me help him shovel the ash into a bucket from our wood cooking stove. It was dark outside and the flashing northern lights could be seen from our kitchen window as my little brother and I climbed onto our grandpa's lap. His chair was off-limits to everyone, except us when he was sitting in it! Most nights the women gathered to talk after dinner dishes were done. The men, including my grandpa, dad, and uncles, went to their favorite chairs at the perimeter of the kitchen as the women gathered around the kitchen table.

My brother and I knew that when the grandmas, aunties, and our mom completed their evening discussion that it would be time for card-playing, jokes, and stories. My uncle Walter would cook fudge as my uncle Alan would pop popcorn. My brother and I played our usual evening games. As we played, we would listen to the grown-ups and argue about who would be the one to scrape fudge from the side of the pan!

The women had been talking for a short time when my little brother and I were called to the kitchen table. They looked stern. We wondered if we had misbehaved in some way. As we stood by the table we were asked if we knew the family that had just recently moved to town and were now living at the end of our street. We answered that we had met Patty, the girl our age, but we hadn't met her older teenage brothers. Patty's family wasn't very friendly. Their mother was cranky and she looked mean with dark circles around her eyes. Their family had a mom and kids but no dad or other family members in their home.

The women in our family instructed us to take food to them the next day and to continue to do this until they told us to stop. Each of them would cook something. We followed their instructions. On the first day, the mom reluctantly took our gift of food. We could barely hear her when she thanked us.

Taking food to a family is a custom commonly practiced when someone dies. Other people in the town weren't taking food to the family, so we wondered why we were treating the family as though someone had died. What was important to us was that our family was asking us to help. We were being treated like big kids and not babies!

Over the next several days as we heard the women in our family talking, we learned that most of the townspeople wanted nothing to do with the new family. Other children were told not to play with them. Others wanted them to be told to leave our town. The reason why the family was not welcome in our community was very serious. We learned that the mom had shot and killed the dad. During a fight they struggled over a gun, and she shot him.

The second day, when we were bringing food, we saw two women from our family go to the new neighbor's home. They brought the mom to our house. We were instructed to play outside while they talked to her. She left with puffy eyes and a red face. The women gave her hugs as she left our house. Eventually, the new family moved to another town. My family befriended them for the brief time they lived near us. My brother and I learned our first responsibilities to neighbors. I was four and he was two.

Running a Train

A group of boys at school had lied about "running a train"[1] on me. They threatened to tell that lie throughout school if I refused to be a "girlfriend" to one of them. I laughed at them because I didn't expect that anyone would believe them. I had often been teased about being one of the last virgins in my class. I was into books—not boys! I was wrong because everyone at school believed them. My friends' parents didn't want them hanging out with me because of their lies! Eventually, I sought out new friends and became involved with a boyfriend that would become my husband. He was fifteen. I was sixteen. Our relationship was cemented because he believed my side of the story. We married when he turned eighteen.

The first years of our marriage included some minor violence. I didn't fear him and I didn't believe him to be a violent person because of a slap or a push. I slapped him back. I played football as a teenager and wasn't fearful of physical aggression. I wasn't easily intimidated. I was accustomed to fighting with my brother and his friends as we were growing up.

My husband grew more muscular with age. I, on the other hand, grew into my nurturing role as a mother to our daughter. As I became economically dependent by being a mother, he became increasingly disrespectful and demanding. By the time our daughter was two, he was even more violent. I left him and enrolled in college. He took my act of emancipation as a personal insult and retaliated by making me a target for more violence. Unfortunately, I could not afford a divorce at the time and was worried about dooming myself to hell for an eternity just to divorce him!

Although my family knew about some of the violence, they were willing to let me make my own decisions about my life. They wouldn't interfere! In the midst of the divorce dilemma, I knew I needed economic freedom and I couldn't get that without an education. Working for minimum wage would keep me at a dead-end job or in poverty. Neither one would provide me with an escape from him.

Trapped

The snowplows provided a road lined on both sides with six-foot-high snow piles. Even though the wind was blowing coldly, it didn't swoop down into the roadway. I walked a mile down the road to his house to get my daughter. I was in school, so weekends were really the only opportunity that I had to be with her. During the week, I needed to study each night. As I arrived at the house my husband shared with his sister, I was anxious to pick up and leave with our four-year-old daughter. However, she was having a good time and didn't want to leave her new toys or kitten. So I sat down to visit with my sister-in-law while she played. After half an hour, she left for the evening. As soon as she left, he was on top of me! I was five months pregnant and unusually big! I didn't want to be intimate with him. He became extremely angry about the rejection and dragged me into his bedroom, beating me severely, stripping my clothes, and raping me. I was concerned about my unborn child, because he punched me in the stomach repeatedly. I was so badly bruised that I was unable to move. After raping me, he hid my clothes at his mother's house; boots, coat, keys, everything! He locked me in his room for several days. Our daughter was taken to his mother's house.

I wondered what his family thought as day after day he brought food to me and I stayed in his room. A few times a day he would escort me to the bathroom. He would stand guard outside the bathroom, then escort me back to his room. Wrapped in a sheet, I considered jumping out the window, but I was on the second floor and was uncertain about what harm that would bring to my unborn child. I realized that he was waiting for the visible bruises to disappear before he finally let me go. His final remark to me as he handed me my clothes was the threat, "Don't forget, we're still married! You are still my wife and have to behave like one!"

Walking back home, I thought of the coldness of this freedom. Each week I would be expected to bring our daughter to him. If I didn't, he would come to my place and break in. The police would back him up even if he came to "visit" in the middle of the night because we were married and our daughter was his child.

This was not the first time he raped me. My unborn child's very existence came from his rape. A few short months after I tried to separate from my husband, he came to my place around midnight on the pretense of visiting "his" daughter. After threatening to break down the door if I didn't let him in, I opened it to appease him. He assaulted me for not letting him in immediately. He dragged me up the staircase to my bedroom where I was brutally raped. Throughout the rape a pillow was held over my face as I fought and tried to scream for help. No one heard me, and no one came to help. After the rape, I was kicked and punched until he lost his energy to continue.

The following day I couldn't walk and was in extreme pain when I moved. My fifteen-year-old brother-in-law stopped by to visit my daughter and me as he usually did on Saturdays. He played with her for a few hours. Every so often, he would call to me and ask if I was coming down. Eventually, he came upstairs and knocked on my partially open bedroom door. I asked what he wanted. He asked if he could come in. I told him no. He stepped into my room anyway. Shocked and silent as he looked at me, he walked over and gently kissed me on the cheek. He left angrily saying, "He did this to you! I know what he did!"

After two years of extreme hardship, I went back to my husband. I knew that it was safer to be with him than without him. I knew he wouldn't rape me if I lived with him. I would experience less violence and less severe violence.

Whenever I would try to leave him or when I lived away from him for a few years, I experienced attacks that included him breaking into my home during the middle of the night, raping me when he claimed to come to the house to visit our children, or abducting me as I visited friends or family. After so much abuse, his direct threats meant little to me, so he began to threaten me with violence against my sisters if I didn't return to him or if I threatened to leave him.

When I reported the violence to the police, I was told that there was nothing that could be done since there were no witnesses. It would just be my word against his. Eventually, when I became frustrated with the police, I went to the prosecutor's office for help. He told me that as long as I was married there was nothing I could do. After all, "You can't testify against your husband. However, if you insist, I will consider pressing charges if you initiate a divorce within two weeks."

I was sent to a police photographer who instructed me to strip nude. He proceeded to take at least thirty pictures of my body from all angles. All my bruises were below the neck. This experience was both degrading and humiliating. I was further humiliated when I returned to the prosecutor with the sealed envelope of my pictures. He leered at them for at least ten minutes with a grin on his face. He reminded me of my two-week deadline for initiating a divorce and said he might consider pressing charges then.

No one would stop his violence. The police gave him a green light by giving him permission to keep acting violent. Only one of numerous protection orders was ever enforced. Even when a violation included an assault, I was given lame excuses by law enforcement like, "You let him in!" or "He was just visiting his children!" or "Why don't you divorce him instead of calling us!" and "We can't do anything!"

My femaleness was often targeted in one form or another, including the numerous rapes. Most of his assaults didn't involve outright violence but did involve sexual assault because I was in too much physical pain to fight back, resist, or take any other action. When I was raped, I would include a description in a protection order. No one in the legal system ever said anything about it. Eventually, I stopped telling them. I was invisible to the legal system. Their protections were not for me. It didn't matter if I called the police or if my neighbors called the police. If I had visible injuries, if he used weapons, or if I was raped, none of it mattered to them. I believe that I was invisible to them because I am an Indian woman. The legal system wasn't designed to protect me, or anyone like me.

His family gave him a green light, too, except for one brother. His mother refused to believe that her favorite son could be violent. He was the one that was always there for her offering help and support. He painted her house, took her shopping, and called her every day. He was a good friend, a thoughtful brother, and he showed love and affection to his children. Who could ask for more? He was the dependable family man. No one as good as him could perpetrate the violence I described.

My family gave him a green light through their value system. They didn't believe in divorce. No one on either side of the family had divorced. They believed in raising children with their father. They believed in a family staying together. They believed in forgiveness. They believed that prayer would bring about a change in his violent behavior! He knew my love for my family and the values that bound us would tie me to him. All their beliefs and kindness inadvertently provided him permission to continue his violence. He knew that everyone was on his side because of their beliefs about marriage, children, and women. Ultimately, it was his violence that was treated as sacred. None of the authority that surrounded, guided, and counseled me would place limits on his violence.

Sometimes the emotional pain was so intense that it was difficult to relate to others or even acknowledge their presence. I was trapped in the relationship because of practical things like income, childcare, and housing. The dilemmas that bound me were values like "no one in my family had divorced"; "if I gave up this marriage, I also would have to give up my religion"; and "children need their father." All were powerful restraints on my seesaw of hope and hopelessness.

In order to cope, I needed to separate his two personalities. He seemed to be two different people, the one I married and the one I hated. The violent person could appear at any moment. There was no pattern to it. I would sometimes awaken in the middle of the night to an assault. No warning! No pattern! No reason! I thought he was crazy and needed psychiatric care. There was no way that I was able to make that happen. I had tried.

My mother told me, "You made your bed, now lie in it!" My father was different, and he was there to help and support me whenever I asked. However, I could not bring myself to tell him of the despicable attacks against my body and soul. I wanted to remain valued in his eyes.

The Tube

I could hear the voices far away. Their tempo was reassuring. I drifted back to sleep. Again, I heard the reassuring voices and opened my eyes. The room was unfamiliar. I fell back asleep. Later, I awakened and tried to call for someone. I didn't know where I was. I felt calm, rested, and at peace. Where was I and where were my children? Again I fell asleep. Drowsily awakening yet again, I heard voices near me. This time I opened my eyes to see my mother and my sister Julie standing over me talking. I couldn't stay awake. I awoke and they were gone. Again, I fell asleep. I heard their voices and wondered if I was dreaming. I opened my eyes and this time they were looking at me. My mom began to cry. My sister held her hands over her mouth. I tried to talk to them but couldn't. I didn't know what was wrong. I fell asleep. Finally, when I heard them talking, I concentrated on staying awake. I saw them again and tried to talk to them. I noticed my throat was dry. As I raised my hand to my mouth, I realized there were tubes down my nose and throat. I tried to pull them out so I could talk to my mother and sister. I wanted to know if my children were okay and if my husband was in jail. I was overjoyed to think he might finally be in jail. I must have drifted back to sleep because there was a lot of excitement around me and I was being given a shot. This continued until one day I woke up and didn't go back to sleep. I was told that I was in intensive care and that I had suffered a fractured skull and had been in a coma. I asked if my husband was in jail. No one would answer me.

My mom and sister returned. I discovered that nothing had happened to my husband because we were married. I still couldn't testify against him. He was my guardian because we were married. Only he could sign me out of the hospital. I was told that he hadn't decided if he was going to sign me out since he wasn't sure that he wanted me back! I wasn't healthy enough to sign myself out! He talked to the nurses regularly and they liked him.

Surprisingly, my mind was clear at that time. I knew that I was trapped by circumstances. I also knew that I would leave him when my babies became school age, when I could work and be independent. I knew that once I had a job, I could save money for a divorce. The police and courts had never proved helpful to me. I knew that my safety depended on having a plan that required me to help myself.

I left when my children were in school. I experienced more assaults, including rape. Although I had obtained protection orders, he never abided by them. The police and the courts always seemed to reinforce his point of view, as if he had done nothing wrong!

No More

The night I ended up in the hospital again with a second skull fracture and a broken nose, I decided that I would work in a shelter for battered women. I had been repeatedly humiliated by having to tell my story over and over while talking to crisis line advocates as I lay on a gurney with an audience of over twenty people in the emergency room. I had been denied shelter at each one I called because I had too many children. I was also denied assistance for the next day's court appearance. I vowed that I would work in one of those places and learn everything that I could to help other women experiencing violence.

In this assault he had a knife and was pressing it into my throat when the police walked in, but they never found it! My long hair cut with his knife was scattered in thick bunches about the bedroom as well as my nightgown that he cut off me. Blood splattered the kitchen walls, the stairwell, and my bedroom. It is amazing to me that a knife was never found!

I left the hospital and went to work to ask my co-worker in Indian Education to accompany me to court. She was a social worker and I thought she might be able to help me. She was the first person outside family and the legal system who knew about the violence. The other office workers were horrified when they saw me. Blood was still caked to my face and hair as we went to court. He pled "not guilty"!

I sold my car and bought a one-way family train ticket to another state. My plan was to stay away until his trial. Several months went by. He was granted several continuances. I was notified by the prosecutor that a trial date was finally set. As I arrived at court with my social worker friend, Ellen, and the arresting officer, I looked across the room at my husband. He looked quite confident. He had an attorney friend representing him, about four friends, and two of his brothers sitting in the courtroom with him. They were all relaxed and confident. When it came time to testify, my husband looked at me and the arresting police officer and pled guilty. He was sentenced to ninety days in jail. He was sent to jail directly from the courtroom.

After all the assaults, all of the rapes, he would spend only one summer in jail! He was only sentenced to ninety days! Although his time in jail was short, it was the only consequence he ever received to stop his violence. He called me from jail saying that now that we had this behind us could we get back together!

Over the next several years I experienced threats and a kidnapping at gunpoint. When I reported the kidnapping to the police, they laughed at me. Even though I was divorced from him when this occurred, they told me a husband can't kidnap his wife. One officer said, "Stop being vindictive. He was just picking up the kids."

Nearly two years later, I was working in a shelter for battered women. A few months after I started work as an advocate, I joined in with three other women to co-found the first Native women's shelter in Minnesota. My commitment to this work is a commitment to my children, who didn't have a choice. I have been an advocate for other battered women and their children since 1982. I believe in making a difference for women experiencing violence.

Today I live free of immediate violence. Momentous occasions like weddings, funerals, or the birth of a new baby in the family bring reminders of the past. When two people become parents they are tied throughout their lifetimes to the children that connect them. The children carry the burden of deciding how to include both parents in these milestones. As I approach my sixties, the assaults I experienced in my twenties and thirties are becoming medical problems today.

My ex-husband continued to be violent in his later relationships, which ended due to his behavior. Eventually, he became violent toward his brothers, and once toward his mother. Today, he is pitiful, sick, and helpless. Our children have learned compassion and treat him kindly. They each have drawn a line with his abusiveness, and he has come to respect that with them. The children had to do this in their own way and in their own time.

My life has been enriched by the advocates I have met and worked with, both women and men, Native and non-Native. The family life I experienced as a child is what I see when I walk into a shelter for battered women. The same potential for helping and sharing is evident at the kitchen table where women are talking to one another. The men who support this work in numerous ways are like my uncles, my grandpa, and my father who supported the women in my childhood home.

My children are still the stars that guide me. I have never forgotten that they are my teachers. I would live my life over in just the same way to have the children I am blessed with! They bring joy and laughter to the world.

It is the beauty of my childhood that has sustained me and nurtured me through the harshest moments. Shortly before my mother died a few years ago, she told me the story of being raped and getting pregnant with me at age seventeen. The conclusion to her story was, "I found you a good family, didn't I, my girl?"

Note
1. "Running a train" is a euphemism for gang rape or rape by several individuals in a group.

Questions
1. What aspects of the author's experiences with her husband are indicative of what we learned about the cycle of domestic violence and control in chapter 3? What barriers prevented her from leaving him sooner?
2. Why did the protection orders and laws against domestic abuse not serve their purpose in shielding the author from sexual assault and violence? Why did police ignore the victim's accusations against her husband?
3. Why do you think the husband resorted to sexual assault to gain power and control over the author?
4. Why is it important for the author to make the connection between her early family experiences and her current work as an advocate?

In Your Community
1. How can families of victims and perpetrators work to support the victim instead of acting as barriers to her receipt of assistance and access to healing? How do you visualize this in your community?
2. The author feels let down and ignored by the police, the legal system, and women's shelters in her community due in a large part to the fact that she is Indian. What can be done at a local level so that victims do not have to relive her experiences?
3. What types of partnerships would benefit Indian women victims in your community? Resources?
4. The author is a survivor. Do you know strong women like her in your community who work at the grassroots level to keep Indian women and children safe?

Suggested Further Reading
Bergen, Raquel Kennedy. *Wife Rape: Understanding the Response of Survivors and Service Providers.* Thousand Oaks, CA: Sage Publications, 1996.

Mahoney, Patricia. "High Rape Chronicity and Low Rates of Help-Seeking Among Wife Rape Survivors in a Nonclinical Sample: Implications for Research and Practice." *Violence Against Women* 5, no. 9 (1999): 993.

Bouncy, Lively

Bouncy, lively
bouncy, lively
up to the ceiling and
down to the floor
bouncy against the window
and bouncy against the door
bouncy, lively. . .
bouncing endlessly
dreamlike and surreal
in an inanimate
faraway absence from pain

The voice of a child
interrupted the rhythm,
the bouncing ball rolled
to an abrupt stop.

I was no longer a red rubber ball
I was a woman—a battered woman
grabbed, punched, thrown in a car,
kicked, thumped, clutched, beaten
lengths of my hair
lay on the floor.

Years have passed,
yet I remember so vividly
the shock, the unreality and
the violence of that day.
But mostly, I remember
that even a strong, educated
competent, Comanche woman;
I—an advisor to other women
in similar situations,
could be so classic
in my reactions.

    Juanita Pahdopony (Comanche)

Walking in the Darkness, Then Finding the Light

Chapter 7

LISA FRANK

Seven years ago, I traveled thousands of miles from a small Alaska village to go to a tribal university in Lawrence, Kansas. I was an immature young college student who never thought about issues like domestic violence and sexual assault. Although I grew up witnessing domestic violence, I would try to ignore it and forget it ever happened. Where I am from, violence was never discussed. I was also under the impression that violent acts were never going to happen to me. I was really naive. My point of view on these issues changed drastically when I was raped on October 8, 1996.

During the past ten years, I have gradually become an advocate for sexual assault survivors based on my experience of the effects of rape. It took me years to gather up the courage to share my story without crying or triggering memories of that horrible night. Dealing with the eighteen-month process of the court system, the lack of response from the school I was attending, the emotional effects from rape, and the healing was exhausting and complicated. Having to face the fact that I was raped was also very intense. I did not know what to do, expect, or think. It felt like the **perpetrator** stole a part of my heart and spirit.

For an Indian person, to have one's spirit abused or stolen is as good as being dead. After I was raped, nothing in my life was ever the same. My life was shaped by this traumatic experience. As I worked with my emotions and accepted the fact that I was raped, I became spiritually stronger and had the will to go on. Yet I had to accept the fact that nothing in my life would ever be the same. It took me seven years to regain all that was stolen from me on that horrible night. Going through this ordeal has taken thousands of tears, pounds of heartache, and a world of love from my friends and family to recover my spirit. My spirit will never be the same as it was before being raped. I am still in the process of healing, as I will be forever. I will try to help anyone I can because these feelings are embedded in my memory. As victims, many are scarred for life. Nothing in this world will ever completely take the feeling, memory, and the victimization away. My advice to other victims is, "Don't dwell on the past, but look to the future for the good things in life."

I grew up in a small and trusting community where everybody knew each other and trusted each other. I was related to everyone, so I never thought any type of violence could happen to me. This is the main reason I was so naive when I traveled away from my home to another state. After the rape, I was shaken up and I could not function mentally. All I wanted was to go home to my family to regain the little strength I had left and to heal my broken spirit. Prior to the rape, I purchased a ticket to return home for Christmas break. After I was raped, my family didn't have the money to purchase another ticket to return home sooner. So, I had to wait in Lawrence, Kansas, two and a half months before going home. That was the longest two and a half months of my life.

Impact of Sexual Assault

It was difficult for me to try to live a normal life again after the rape. There are simple daily routines people do that I was terrified to do. For example, I didn't feel safe walking anywhere, whether it was day or night. I found it difficult to be in a room with a male or to be touched by anyone. I didn't want to be alone, but I also felt uncomfortable surrounded by a lot of people. I was robbed of my trust for everyone and everything—even myself. I would have anxiety attacks, but I didn't know back then what they were called. I always looked over my shoulder to make sure no one was there to hurt me again. I was paranoid about everything to the point I couldn't live a normal life. These are the few things I had to cope with. A person does not necessarily "get over" the trauma of rape, but one has to understand why these feelings are happening and how to cope with them. I still have problems with some simple daily routines, but it is not as bad as it used to be. There are still the internal triggers that stay with me, such as the smell of grass, the sight of the stars, and the sounds of crickets or locusts. These are specific things I remember from when I was raped. Each time I encounter these triggers, my thoughts are always redirected to my memory of that horrible night, bringing back the feeling of violation. The disgusted feelings I had that night and thereafter will never completely go away. The only thing I have control over is to find ways to cope with them.

Before I was raped, I was already a "statistic" by being an Alaska Native woman, a middle-class citizen, and witnessing domestic violence at a young age. Then I added another statistic by being raped. Becoming another damn statistic, I didn't know how to deal with the new emotions I was feeling due to being raped.

So I turned to the only thing I knew to cope with it—alcohol. I used alcohol to numb the pain I was feeling. I didn't want to close my eyes and have the image of that night return to haunt me. For years, there were many times I cried myself to sleep. I drank practically every night for the two and a half months I had to wait in Lawrence just to get through it, trying to erase my visions of that horrid night. The few times I didn't drink, I stayed up all night and slept all day because I was afraid of having a **flashback**. I was lucky to have good friends in college. They stood by me every day and made sure I was never alone. My friends believed me the moment I told them what happened. They were so angry at my perpetrator that they wanted to hurt him more than he hurt me. They never left my side, for which I will be forever grateful. Out of my friends, Calvin was the one who made the biggest difference to my well-being. He was there for me when I needed to talk, laugh, cry, or just hang out. I can only imagine how my life would have turned out if he had not been there.

A couple of days after the assault, the perpetrator posted bail. He was not only free to walk the streets, he was allowed back on campus, even though they knew he was arrested for sexual assault. I was informed of his presence on campus by the county victim-witness specialist. She was the one who handled my case when I went to court. She worked with the district attorney who was assigned to **prosecute** the crime. The university did not have the decency of informing me he was back as a student, thereby neglecting the importance of my safety. I did not know what the perpetrator was capable of because he warned me not to report what happened. I was very scared for my life. From the time I had reported the rape, it was clear to me that everything was always about his rights and not mine. I thought the laws were made to protect the victim, not the perpetrator! I did everything correctly from the beginning: I reported the rape, was examined at the hospital for evidence, and went to court to testify. Everything seemed to backfire on me, and I felt that he got away with raping me. This made me want to drink more because I was so angry, and I wanted to drink that feeling away. The drinking didn't make my situation better—it made it worse. I felt as if my mind was clouded and I couldn't think straight. I was counting down the days to go home to start the healing process since I had numbed myself with alcohol.

The Hospital

After I reported the rape, I was transferred to the hospital to be examined by a nurse to collect evidence for the prosecution. Being examined was like being violated again, but I knew it was something I had to do in order to help my case. I felt like a little kid again because all I wanted to do was cry and go home where I felt safe. The officer who transported me asked if I would like to have a local advocate to meet me at the hospital. I was still in shock, so I just nodded my head. The advocate I met at the hospital, Sarah, became a lifelong friend. Without this lady I don't know if I would have made it this far. She has been by my side since day one. Both Sarah and my mother, Jean, made a big impact on my life. My mother was there for me every time I called home during those two months. There were countless times I called her crying, and just hearing her voice soothed me. She blamed herself because her baby, thousands of miles away, had been raped, and she felt powerless to make me feel better. But hearing her voice gave me the strength I needed to keep sane. My mother and Sarah have helped in so many ways that I cannot attempt to explain, and I don't think there are any words to thank them enough. These two ladies are among the strongest women I know. They influenced me to help others who are in need. I truly believe my grandfathers are watching over me from above by sending the love and support of my mother and Sarah to me. They were there for me in the most crucial point in my life by making me laugh when I need to laugh, giving me a shoulder to cry on, keeping me company, and listening when I needed to talk. I don't know how to repay them. My mother and Sarah both have good hearts, great personalities, and the friendship we have will never die.

Campus Administration

I was very disappointed by the university administration's response to my assault. I had anticipated that the school would have supported me, as the victim, and taken some kind of action against the perpetrator. This did not happen at all! The school did not do anything to ensure my safety or my well-being after I was raped on their campus by one of their students. What really angered me was that the administration accepted the perpetrator back into school as a student as though he didn't do anything wrong. Since the university had recently been expanded and remodeled, I expected their school policies would have improved also, especially in their response to sexual assault against Native women. The message I received through their actions was that they didn't care, nor did they want to face the fact that students were being raped on their campus.

Since the university is a school for Native students, I assumed they would do everything in their power to protect Native victims. Their inaction made me feel angrier and more depressed. The school should have suspended the perpetrator and notified me as to what actions were taken. Other helpful steps would have been to offer some type of security to make me feel more secure, and counseling. I should have received information on what to expect after being raped, both emotionally and physically. Also, I would have appreciated having a person to talk to twenty-four hours a day and a support group established on campus. In my case, anything would have been better than nothing. If these steps were taken, I'm sure my point of view on everything would be different. I was very fortunate to meet Sarah. She was the one who gave me all of the support described above. I thought it was sad no one from the school could provide these basic services to their own students.

When I first arrived at the university, I heard rumors about a couple of rapes that occurred in the men's dorms. For example, people would say "there is a girl from this dorm or that dorm was raped last Friday." Names were never mentioned, but people could usually identify the victim. It was very common for the perpetrator to have his friends harass and intimidate the victim. After I was raped, I knew that there were rumors about me. People even knew which dorm I lived in. I realized I needed to act as if nothing happened so people in the dorms would not spread even more rumors about me.

Later I met one of the girls who was raped in the men's dorms a couple of weeks before me. She told me her story and it was very violent. I honestly don't know how she survived after hearing her experience. The difference between her story and mine was that I reported my rape. Not only did she not report the rape, she didn't have the heart to tell her parents. She had no support and she mentally blocked it out because she didn't want to deal with it. She also saw her perpetrator around campus a lot. Both of our perpetrators probably assaulted other women during the time they attended that university. I discovered that there were numerous unreported assaults on campus. Unfortunately, this is a common problem at other colleges, universities, and institutions in the United States. One would think something would be done to prevent the enormous rate of sexual assault, but the statistics are not improving.

The way I was treated by the university administration after I was raped was disturbing and unjust. I was not able to concentrate on my academics, so I withdrew from my classes because I was failing. I then discussed my situation with the residential director and received permission to stay in the dorms until my family purchased a ticket to go home. Yet two days later, I received a letter underneath my door stating if I didn't leave the dorm by 5:00 p.m. that day, I would be escorted out by campus security. I panicked because I had no money and I didn't know anyone in Lawrence. Luckily, since I met Sarah at the hospital and had her phone number, I gave her a call and told her my situation. She did not even hesitate before offering me a place to stay until I could get a plane ticket home. I always look back and wonder what would have happened to me if I didn't know Sarah. Would the university have thrown me out without a place to stay? I highly doubt they would have helped me because they didn't even acknowledge my situation in the first place. Universities need to make new and improved policies to help the victims in these types of situations, especially if they are from out-of-state and do not have money.

The one and only thing the university provided was a counselor at the hospital who stayed with me for a couple of hours. Unfortunately, she was no help at all. She was with me in at the hospital, but she did not counsel me as to what to expect of my feelings or what to expect in the examination. I was very scared and I was lucky Sarah was with me to inform me of what to expect. When I was done at the hospital, the counselor gave me a ride back to my dorm, and I never heard from her again. It would have been helpful to have some type of follow-up. The university should feel embarrassed if they call that providing help. Universities are sending a message to victims that they condone sexual assault. I needed someone to tell me it was normal to feel the way I felt, what to expect, and to assure me that I would be safe. I needed someone who actually cared and wanted to help me, not a disconnected and impersonal employee who had to "take another call." University counselors can learn a lot from local advocacy programs, such as Rape Victim-Survivor Services (RVSS). Information and training on sexual assault is easily accessible.

When a campus counselor responds to a rape call, they need to be educated and informed on what rape victims experience. They need to be there for the victims in every aspect from counseling to helping victims find a way home. These simple gestures from the university would have made an impact. I have become frustrated by the high rate of sexual assault because there are a lot of Native people, young and old, who are going through this trauma, which can be prevented! The universities not only need to educate their staff on sexual assault, but the students as well. The most important thing is for universities to actually take action to ensure the safety of the student when there is a rape call.

When I finally went home, I wrote a letter to the university administration, explaining what happened to me. I expressed my dissatisfaction with their response to my rape on their campus. I hoped my letter would make a difference, but apparently it didn't. Not only did I not receive an apology, they did not even have the decency to respond to my letter. I should have known not to expect a response from the start.

The Court System

The inaction of the university in my situation was disappointing and depressing. However, dealing with the court system was even more complicated. During the eighteen months I dealt with the court system, two trial dates were scheduled. On the first scheduled trial date, the perpetrator failed to appear. The second trial date was canceled due to a **plea bargain**. I lived with a lot of stress during those eighteen months waiting for the conviction. All the while, the perpetrator spent only a total of nine months in the Douglas County Jail.

When the first trial date was set, my mother and I traveled from Alaska in order for me to testify. It was emotionally exhausting preparing to testify and thinking about being in the witness stand. I didn't want to be questioned by the defense lawyer because I was scared he would try to prove I was lying or blame me for the rape. I was not ready to be interrogated. On the day of the first trial, we received word that the perpetrator left Lawrence. The trial was postponed until the perpetrator was caught. I was told that bounty hunters would be sent to track him.

I felt scared because I didn't know where he was or what he was capable of doing. My mother and I returned to Alaska where all we could do was wait until the bounty hunters caught him. Months later, I was informed the perpetrator was caught in the state of Washington, on a reservation, drinking in a bar. He was extradited back to Lawrence, and the second trial date was set. I was relieved because I knew he was back in custody and we could get the trial over with. Sarah received money donated from a local church in Kansas for my mother to accompany me to the second trial. As the date came closer, the prosecutor called me at home in Alaska to inform me they made a "plea bargain" and lowered the crime from a **felony** to a **misdemeanor**. The decision was based on a lack of evidence to convince a jury and convict my violator of rape. I was so distraught! I felt like all the work I had done was for nothing. I felt like I was raped all over again—this time, by the system. Justice did not prevail in my case.

Sentencing Hearing

I wasn't required by the state of Kansas to attend the **sentencing hearing**, and they didn't have the budget to buy a plane ticket for me. However, I was given the opportunity to by Sarah because she still had the money that was supposed to pay for my mother's airfare for the second trial. This would give me an opportunity to speak to the judge. At first, I declined the offer because I did not want to see the perpetrator ever again. Then I reconsidered because of everything I had been through. There was no reason for me to stop trying to get back at him for what HE had stolen from me. I told Sarah I wanted to take her up on her offer. I needed to do this for my personal closure! The best thing was that no one knew I was going to attend the sentencing hearing except for the people on the prosecution side—not even the judge himself!

Back in Lawrence, I was on my way to the court building looking forward to seeing what kind of reaction my presence would have on the perpetrator and his lawyer. I remember walking toward the courtroom feeling really nervous, but I was so deep in thought that I didn't notice HE was also walking toward the courtroom in handcuffs. He saw me and he looked scared and pathetic. He quickly looked down because he knew he was guilty. During the hearing, we each had a turn to speak to the judge. The perpetrator stated that he was a "changed" man and he was fit to live in "society" again. He also informed the judge that some church in Lawrence was going to take him in while he was on probation. From the time the perpetrator was caught in Washington until the end of the plea bargain process, he had only served a total of nine months in the county jail. It was infuriating for me to sit back and listen to his plea without screaming objections.

When it was my turn to speak, I had a lot going through my mind and I did not know when to start. I stood beside the podium, opposite of where HE was sitting, to speak directly to the judge. As soon as I opened my mouth, I started crying and could not stop. I don't know if anyone understood me because I was crying so hard. It seemed as if all the pain I had felt the previous months caught up with me at that moment. I walked directly to the perpetrator and asked him if it was worth it, hurting me this much. All the while, he was looking at the floor and did not look at me. People in the courtroom thought I was going to attack him. Deep down I wish I had, but it would not have solved any of my problems. I truly believe that if you do bad to others, bad will come back three times fold. I know the man above has a plan for rapists. When I finished speaking, I thanked the judge for listening to what I had to say and went outside to calm down. The look on people's faces in the courtroom made me feel as if I had made no impression at all and this made me more upset. However, when the hearing was over, I was told I did a great job and I did make an impact on the judge. The judge expressed his wish to send the perpetrator back to jail for the maximum sentence, but the laws only allowed him to sentence an extra month. I believe the law should allow judges to sentence the perpetrators of sexual assault to longer sentences if he or she feels there is enough evidence to do so. The extra month was included in the nine months he spent in Douglas County Jail. If I hadn't spoken at the hearing that day, the perpetrator may have been released.

Truthfully, looking back now, I probably would not have reported the crime if I knew the amount of pain it would cause me. In some ways, though, it was worth it because the perpetrator has "Attempted Aggravated Sexual Battery" on his criminal record for the rest of his worthless life and I finally found the closure I needed.

After the sentencing, I made a deal with Sarah. We both decided to get a tattoo to symbolize all the work and pain we endured dealing with the university, the courts, and the related emotions. We went downtown to the tattoo parlor. I decided on a rose and Sarah decided on a ring of daisies. While I was getting my tattoo, I was thinking of all I had experienced in the previous eighteen months and I didn't feel any pain. These flowered tattoos also represented closure for Sarah and me. Now was the time to move on and start the long healing process.

Healing

After I was raped, I went through a period of self-blame, like most rape victims. If it wasn't for my friends and family telling me over and over it was not my fault for being raped, I would probably still be blaming myself now. During this time, I thought, "Why did I let this happen to me?" "What if I did this . . . ? "What if . . . ? What if . . . ?" I know now I was blaming myself for nothing because I couldn't control his actions. I was torturing myself because there was nothing I could have done to prevent the rape from happening. All women have the right to say "yes" or "no," and I said "NO!" He was the one who made the choice to rape. One of the reasons I think guys rape is because they see a lot of rapists avoid conviction. They may take this as a message that it's okay to hurt another human being. The United States government should take action against all sexual assault cases by sentencing with harsher punishments. Right now, the court system is sending the message to all the rapists and potential rapists that they will not spend time in jail. I am very thankful to the man above that I am still here today and strong enough to share my story with other victims.

In the past ten years, I never thought about how my situation of being raped affected my family because I was too busy trying to heal myself. I realized, years later, they are still hurting. I have accepted the fact that I was raped, but I don't think my family has yet. They need to find their own peace, like I did. I think they blamed themselves because none of them could be with me after I told them I was raped, but they supported me in my time of need and I survived—that's all that is important. Following the assault, I asked my mother if she had told my grandmother, her mother, Annie. She said she was on her way to tell her one day. When she arrived, my grandmother already knew. That would have been impossible because at that time no one else knew. My grandmother is one of those powerful people who can see things in her dreams, and her dreams often come true. She calmly told my mother, "Don't worry about Lisa, she is strong, and she will get through this," in our language. After hearing this, I felt the darkness and the heavy weight I had been carrying all that time lifted away from me. This was exactly what I needed to hear to give me more strength to go on. This was probably the first time I felt at peace with myself in a very long time.

Today, there are a lot of people who choose not to think of issues of violence, especially rape, because they are uncomfortable discussing the issue. Most likely they grew up thinking it is wrong to speak of such an issue. That may change one day when this issue becomes personal when a loved one is raped, such as a mother, sister, cousin, daughter, niece, or friend. This is possible due to the high statistics indicating that over one-third of all Native women will be raped in their lifetime. In many Native cultures, it is considered wrong to speak of sexual violence and that is part of the reason it still exists today. This is where things need to change, to break that cycle of violence. We all can make this happen if we join together and fight for the future generations. Not all rape victims have a strong support system—that is why a lot of Native women who are raped become alcoholics, drug users, and many commit suicide. I know how easy it is to fall into that trap of drinking to try to take the pain away. But I am lucky I didn't choose to stay on that road; I had family and friends who loved me. They are the ones who saved me and gave me purpose, so I could stop abusing alcohol. I wanted to be a role model for my younger cousins—I don't want them to look down on me. I want to show them they can do anything they want and that they can be strong too, because the strength is in our blood.

It is important for someone going through an emotional or tragic episode in their lives to have family and friends to rely on for love and support. I am fortunate to have people like this in my life. In addition to the support I received, I needed another cure, which was to go home! This was the medicine I needed from the beginning to get better. My home comforted me because this is where I belong with my people. I thank God for giving my people such a blessed place to live.

During my healing process, it was easy to slip back into abusing alcohol. It took me years to realize I turned to alcohol every time I had a problem, or if I got mad. This is not a healthy lifestyle, so I am trying to find other productive ways to deal with my problems. One way I blow off steam when I feel down is to go shopping. I feel that I am letting go of the bad feeling and replacing it with something new. However, I do need to find a less expensive way to feel better. Each person has to find their own remedy of dealing with their troubles, so that they do not turn to alcohol and drugs. As I found out, alcohol only makes it worse! I abused alcohol during my painful process of trying to convict the guy who raped me. When a person is going through such an ordeal, it seems easier to try to drink the pain away. However, that person is only hurting herself and the people who love her. This type of abuse can easily lead to addiction. I think this is the reason there is an alarming rate of young Native alcoholics.

Speaking Out

Four years after I was assaulted, I truly began my healing process. I found the courage and strength to finally speak about my story. First, I slowly shared my story with the people I cared about because I knew they would not be judgmental. I remember how much it would hurt when I talked about what had happened, and I would always end up crying. Then one summer I was asked to speak on a youth panel at home. I was obligated to speak because all of my cousins my age were speaking too. I had no clue of what I should talk about. As my turn was approaching, the rape came to mind. There were over a hundred people in the Community Hall, including village residents, all of whom are my relatives, reporters, visitors, and tourists.

I was never as nervous as I was when it was my turn to speak. I was self-conscious about what people were thinking of me bringing up this type of issue. Then I told myself, "I shouldn't be feeling like this. This issue needs to be addressed everywhere. Why shouldn't I start in my hometown?" So, I kept talking. When the youth panel was finished, a lot of people congratulated me for being so strong to speak out. This was the first time I felt really happy in a long time, maybe in years. I knew then this was what I wanted to do to help others who were victimized. People I didn't even know well started telling me their personal stories, and I felt honored because they trusted and respected me.

I used to compare my story with others who have been raped. But I was told that we each experience violence in different ways and not to compare anymore because it is not fair to say I didn't suffer as much as the other person did. So, I quit doing that to myself. As rape victims, we all experience pain and we all struggle to try to get our lives back together. The only thing that makes us different is which path we choose in recovery. A lot of people have been victimized and have kept it a secret due to personal reasons or because they thought it was the norm in their own cultures. Hearing stories such as that made me feel more confident to continue to speak up. In a way, I feel as though I am not only speaking for myself, but for the people who don't have the strength yet, and for the people who aren't with us anymore due to violence.

I was invited to a youth conference a year later. I was on a panel with two very powerful and well-known Native men speakers. After I spoke, the eldest of the two openly admitted he was abused as a child. It takes great courage for a Native man to confess he was abused in front of a lot of people. He was actually acknowledging me for speaking. I was in such awe of his strength!

My first college experience is not going to hold me back from continuing my education. If I let it, then it would be like letting him win. I am much too strong to quit everything I have worked so hard for these past seven years. My advice is— don't let the bad things get in your way of pursuing your dream. If you do, you will never go anywhere because there are always downfalls in everything we do. Just keep looking at the positive side and things will pay off at the end.

It gives me great pleasure to help someone open up and start the healing process by telling my story and what I've gone through. I can give them some options of what they can do to express their repressed feelings, such as writing down their thoughts, joining a support group, or even joining an exercise class. Or I can let them know that being raped was not their fault and listen to their story. These simple gestures mean so much to a person when they feel down and out. They will soon find their own strength to keep living life. We each have a strength deep inside us, but we have to be patient to explore it. I keep thinking if my ancestors survived for thousands of years through a lot of rough times, I could get through this too.

This cycle of violence needs to be broken. We, as Native American and Alaska Native women, need to acknowledge the fact that domestic violence and sexual assault exist in our communities. We need to deal with the effects of these issues, individually and as a culture. Once we are individually healthy, we need to stop accepting this violence, as a tribe. Tolerance is the reason why violence against women still exists today.

Abuse will continue to exist in our communities if people don't do anything about it. I have been told that I am strong for surviving what I've been through. I don't feel as strong as they say. The reason I've made it this far is because of the support I received. I am very blessed to have the courage, energy, and the will to go on and speak openly to try to make a difference in at least one person's life. I hope my story will encourage more victims to speak up and to discover their own strength.

In all cultures and religions there is a higher power that comes in many shapes and forms. I believe that the higher power has a plan for each of us, whether it results in a good or bad situation. How we, individually, deal with these situations is our test in life. In my situation, it would be easy for me to give up on life by ending it with drugs and alcohol or by my own actions, but I have chosen to deal with my situation and learn from it. I responded by healing myself and helping other victims. I personally feel this is my calling because nothing gives me the happiness I feel when I reach someone by telling my story. In these past ten years, I have met so many strong, spirited survivors. These women have overcome so much, and yet they still have a smile on their faces helping others who are in the place they once were. These are the people I truly envy because they have courage, willpower, and knowledge to help victims. I have heard many speakers who have these qualities, and I hope one day I will be like them.

In the summer of 2003, I learned that my perpetrator was picked up in California for a probation violation. He had two counts against him since the time my case went to court in the summer of 1996. The two counts were Attempted Aggravated Sexual Battery and Aggravated Failure to Appear. He was extradited back to Lawrence, Kansas, to appear in court. I was not sorry to hear that he cried in court during his appearance and was sentenced to a year in prison. This outcome is better than the nine months he served in Douglas County Jail for my rape. I am very happy that he spent more time in jail, where he belongs forever. Knowing he was finally held accountable for his actions is helping me to see the light!

Questions
1. What are some of the effects of sexual assault or rape that Frank identifies? Why is it impossible for the victim to just "get over" these feelings? Why is it so important for first responders, such as advocates, police, nurses, and lawmakers, to understand these feelings and stages?
2. What is the process that a victim of sexual assault has to go through if he or she decides to report the crime? Why does this often feel like a revictimization?
3. Why do so many women fail to report sexual assaults?
4. Why is it so important to have emotional, physical, spiritual, and legal support throughout the process? What are some of the consequences of not having that type of support?
5. Why does Frank point out that every rape or sexual assault survivor's feelings are valid no matter how seriously others interpret the assault?
6. How did the university fail the victim? What can college campuses, particularly tribal colleges, do to be more supportive of victims? How can they make their programs sensitive to the needs of American Indian women and men?

In Your Community
1. What can people in your community do to assist a victim of sexual assault through the process and lessen the unknown?
2. If you could design a Sexual Assault Response Team on your campus, what would it look like? What would the composition of your team be? What professions or students would be represented?
3. What should colleges do to sexual assault perpetrators who are students?
4. What does healing mean for you and your community?

Terms Used in Chapter 7
Felony: A crime carrying a minimum term of one year or more in state prison.
Flashback: A recurring, intensely vivid mental image of a past traumatic experience.
Misdemeanor: A lesser crime punishable by a fine and/or county jail time for up to one year.
Perpetrator: The person responsible for a crime.
Plea bargain: In criminal procedure, a negotiation between the defendant and his or her attorney on one side and the prosecutor on the other, in which the defendant agrees to plead "guilty" or "no contest" to some

crimes in return for reduction of the severity of the charges, dismissal of some of the charges, the prosecutor's willingness to recommend a particular sentence, or some other benefit to the defendant.

Prosecute: In criminal law, to charge a person with a crime and thereafter pursue the case through trial on behalf of the government.

Sentencing hearing: The period in a criminal case devoted to determining the sanctions to be imposed on the defendant.

Suggested Further Reading

Anderson, Michelle J. "The Legacy of the Prompt Complaint Requirement, Corroboration Requirement, and Cautionary Instructions on Campus Sexual Assault." Villanova University School of Law, Paper 20 (2004).

Holtfreter, Kristy, and Jennifer Boyd. "A Coordinated Community Response to Intimate Partner Violence on the College Campus." *Victims and Offenders* 1 (2006): 141.

Sanday, Peggy Reeves. "Rape-Prone Versus Rape-Free Campus Cultures." *Violence Against Women* 2 (1996): 191.

Intimate Disfigurement

Lying in a dark pool at the bottom of the shower
I see myself
Tied with sinew
Gagged by my pride
And struggling, dragging my body
Across the hot floor
Cold thick liquid beats me down
The more I drag myself the stronger the torrent
It sticks to my skin
Adheres my skin to the tile
My hair clumps in knots
Ripping away from my head
Like survivors of a sinking ship
Jumping overboard in one last effort to
free themselves from disaster
I give in, I cry out
Except no one is there to listen

   Amanda D. Faircloth (Lumbee)

Violence across the Lifecycle

Chapter 8

DIANE E. BENSON

It might have been the first time I was hit, but I could not say for sure. I remember it well, even now; because it seemed to be the first time I was convinced that a violent act against me was unwarranted. A keen awareness had swept over me—I knew no safe place to be. I was in another foster home then, my young life welted by a society and a system that provided no justice. But on that day, home from my sixth-grade schooling, I ran in the door, proud artwork in hand, only to be greeted by a fist that knocked me near unconscious straight across the small living room. Apparently, I startled my foster mother's son visiting from logging camp. Some things, no matter how normal, you never get used to.

A tiny hut of a home in Ketchikan, Alaska, nestled in a cove occupied by a mammoth pulp mill, kept my two brothers and I captive a good part of the 1960s. It wasn't that our foster mother was a bad person, she wasn't. She was an elderly widow, raised in Forks, Washington, and accustomed to the logging life, who felt sorry for my brothers and me. My father, a logger at the time, could not manage the care of three little ones and travel to the remote campsites at the same time. Dad approached other family members for help, but they felt unable or unprepared to take on more children. We arrived at our new foster home in Ward Cove when I was five, my brother Chuck four, and my brother Dennis three. We were all together and that seemed like a good idea from dad's point of view. We were safe, so he thought. We missed our mother.

Our mother achieved only fifth grade in the missionary school in Sitka, Sheldon Jackson, where most of our tribal members were eventually confined for American schooling. A family member says our mother was withdrawn from school because she contracted tuberculosis. She was physically beautiful, too beautiful some would say, and jealousy seemed to cause others to avoid her so I am told. Always dressed up, she played in her own big doll house in a backyard in the modest village of Sitka, alone. I was an adult when I learned from my father that she had been sexually abused as a child. This spoke to why this hardheaded, unemotional, yet curiously sympathetic man tolerated her many inconsistencies. My father, a bit of a happy drunk, a cynical intellectual, and a gambler, was no saint either, but he was our father. It was our deepest desire to be with our parents and with our older half brother. We wanted our family.

Prior to the time we were dropped off at Ward Cove, my brothers and I had moved often from home to home. Alaskan Territorial Court records reveal that my mother did not show up at divorce court to argue custody or notions of child neglect. It was the late 1950s; my mother was Indian, uneducated, and had no court representation. Alaska was about to be the forty-ninth state. Laws were still forming. Issues of alcohol abuse and infidelity remained unsettled in court and unsettling for us as we again unpacked bags.

Mom left Alaska in shame and never came back after the divorce. Her absence left a hole, but in some ways, we never knew her anyway. She was just a beautiful sad face in my memory. But dad, he had taken me hunting from the time I could walk. He took us down to the beaches under the light of an early morning moon to dig clams. He showed us the trees and the waters. During the divorce period, Dad took us kids around from house to house looking for safe places. He didn't find any.

It happened that as toddlers we would find ourselves homeless, and not by anyone's intent. Even prior to divorce, we three kids were frequently left behind in our parents' drama. Once, a local tribal woman in Ketchikan recognized us three children sitting in the airport, alone for some time, and took us to her home. She returned us to our feuding parents, but we were eventually shuffled off to another home. We stayed in a wonderful home in Juneau. I remember the man was a fireman and his wife smiled a lot. I rode the fire truck in the parade, and it was the happiest day. Maybe it was Alaska Day. When I had a birthday, she made a cake, and I wanted to stay with them forever. Soon after, we were sent to another home. It was never clear how much these placements were my dad's effort, and how much were the State's effort. A few months here and a few months there, in one home after another, began to create furrowed brows on the foreheads of three little children. We even have pictures to prove it. Then we were dropped at a home in downtown Ketchikan that would burn down.

Like most of the homes where we were placed, the family was white and this was true of the home below the boardwalk in Ketchikan. Our memories bring forth the images of well-fed older kids with lots of red hair and freckles, and a slightly rotund woman with a loud voice who was terribly stingy with bread and food in general. It seemed to amuse her to throw a piece of bread on the floor and watch us go for it. We were constantly hungry there, and our beds provided no comfort to these pains. She kept us in the attic, my youngest brother sleeping on a piece of plywood, and usually me with him, wrapped in an Army blanket. My other brother was kept in a crib with no mattress, only bare springs and a sheet. We were dirty and I can still feel it, and had no shoes. Her children tormented us, and I would hide my brothers behind me trying to protect them from the pinches and slaps and taunting. As winter went on, and Christmas got closer, I dreamed of owning a gun. Dad came once to visit and asked me what I wanted from Santa. I told him—a machine gun and food. I only got a fake gun with caps. I was a disappointed and angry little five-year-old girl. But I did get a candy bar.

The house enveloped in smoke and flames one night. I remember looking out the small window of the attic. People were running around outside. A fire truck came. The family was out of the house. They never came to get us. A fireman found us after fear had time to torture me, and I had screamed to them to get my brother, the one in the crib, and thereafter I remember holding the hand of a fireman, who was holding my youngest brother, running through the stinging slushy snow in bare feet. The house burned completely to the ground. How we ever ended up in this home, we don't know, but we were so glad to be away from it.

We stayed briefly with some people in a very small apartment, and then Dad picked us up. We thought we were going to stay with him now. He bought me some things and packed a little suitcase, and took us to Ward Cove. I waited for months in that tiny shack at the window for his return. It would be a long time before he came back.

In Ward Cove, we bathed in water pumped from a rain barrel, swam in the bay polluted by the mill, and picked buckets of blueberries and caught fish upstream with our hands and **ingenuity**. We dug clams, and caught crabs, and sometimes my brothers went out on the boat with our foster parent's son-in-law and fished or hunted deer. Her son would come back from logging camp sometimes, and he would drink a lot. She had two older grandsons, and one of them went to jail for stabbing his girlfriend to death. The other would "babysit" us at his parents' home, and while doing so would torment my brothers and I, taking us down and tickling us until we cried, or blowing his breath in our face, filling our mouths and nose until we could no longer breathe. He thought it was funny. One day he started taking me into another room, in the dark, and put his weight on me, his hands between my legs. Each time he took me in the dark room, he was more invading. I was maybe six or seven when it began. Our foster mother let me have a cat around that time, and the cat was my best friend in the world. Her grandson told me he would kill my cat if I ever told anyone. It is too hard for my brothers to even think about it all because they couldn't protect me. I can't discuss it with them still, because the pain in their eyes clouds my recollections. Through those years, I often hid from morning to sundown in the woods, roaming about, much more afraid of home than of any four-legged animals.

My foster parent's older grandson who killed his girlfriend was released one time, apparently in-between prison and institutionalization for the criminally insane. He showed up at the house, and time seemed forever, as the drinking went on, and everyone began the usual crying or screaming or drunken laughter. I felt his hands crawl up my young forming legs, and my shaking and gripping fear was only ended by another threat, from the brother who didn't seem to care to have "his girl" messed with by his brother. I often slept with my back against the wall.

The world seemed insane. We went to church, because the church picked us up. Our foster mother had little or no money and so a drive to town seven miles away for church was out of the question. The poverty also forced us to obtain necessities from things people threw away at the dump or to buy rejected hand-me-downs from others for a quarter. Church usually followed a night of alcoholic horror. Nothing seemed consistent. The church told us to turn the other cheek, that God was coming back, and that with Jesus our lives would be happy. And the church told us we couldn't wear any Native symbols. They were seen as heathen.

Shame about our tribal ethnicity grew. Kids on the school buses would pull my ears, hit me in the face, shove me on the floor, and push me out of my seat. I would turn the other cheek. Going home, or going to school, with a bloody nose was not unusual. The bus driver sometimes became angry with me for not being seated. We were called "siwash," and "salmon cruncher," and "dirty Indians." I must have been in third grade when actually thinking that "dirty Indian" was my nickname. Then a principal would call me Pocahontas because of my long hair, and he would smile. The white kids laughed. Fellow students often knocked my lunch to the floor or shoved me into the wall. I would sometimes soil my pants in class rather than draw attention or go to the restroom where I was sure to meet more aggravation. These incidents were rarely discussed. I was too afraid to say anything, although teachers sometimes complained to my foster mother that I was slow and shy. It was all just part of going to public school in Ketchikan.

Sometimes our foster mother would send me down the road to take pies she made out of the blueberries us kids picked, to an old man who lived in the tiniest of shacks by the old run-down mill by the river's mouth. Each trip I became more resistant to going, and my bare feet would kick up the dust in steps that became shorter and shorter. Why couldn't my brothers take the pies? He would bounce me up and down on his knee and then his lap, until I knew it was a wrong and ugly thing that he was doing. The last time I was there, I pushed him away and ran.

The best part of those early years was when we were sent to stay with dad at logging camp. We lived at Freshwater Bay for a spell, or at Twelve Mile Arm, and even at a floating camp off Prince of Wales Island. We would race out of the one-room school at lunch time and put a **skiff** in the water and paddle around, or chase the bears or camp foreman's horse away from the tiny travel-trailer we lived in, or run through the woods and climb trees. We smelled the cedar and the spruce and felt their limbs embrace us. It was our country. It didn't last long and we were hauled away back to Ward Cove.

Our foster mother was a sad woman who smoked incessantly. I sometimes felt she knew that odd and awful things were going on but she would shake her head and say nothing. She did decide that I should have my own room rather than sleep on the sofa, so she boarded up the old porch and it became my very own room. I once found the nerve, in a fit of rage, to tell her that her grandson had been molesting me but she wouldn't hear of it. By that time, he had left for Germany as a serviceman. I hid in my room. Shame consumed me. At church, I began to distrust everyone. The minister had his body so close against mine one day that I trembled uncontrollably. He would say he was filled with the spirit as he delivered the message of God. At the church, rumors about in-church sexual misconduct were spreading, and I felt compelled to leave church behind. I was twelve years old and alone. I would make my own rules.

One night, with two new friends from school, one Tlingit like me, and the other white, but poor like me, I stole a bottle of Calvert's Extra whiskey and smuggled it into my room. A white girl at school had told me that she couldn't be my lockermate anymore because her boyfriend didn't like Indians. I had gone on the attack that very day and burst into houses of two white girls from school, letting them know my hate and rage. I was no longer turning the other cheek. We mulled over these things as that southern bourbon went down our twelve-year-old throats like water. Over half that bottle saturated my ninety-pound body and I went into blackout. I woke up hours later in a pool of vomit. Fortunately, I guess one of the girls had moved my head to avoid asphyxiation. For three days I vomited, sweated, and ached, unable to eat or function from this obvious alcohol overdose. Some school official inquired about my condition, but the girls just told her I had the flu. The police came to my home, searched my room, and found the empty bottle. They said booze had been stolen from the liquor store up the way. I was never again able to drink bourbon after that, but I managed to consume many other things. But the good news was, other students were now afraid of me. The bad news was, I got charged for stealing.

So, my new friends and I began a gang. I went to jail for running away and for stealing a blanket to keep warm and to wrap tightly around me to keep the rats away. I slept that way under some stranger's house. When the police arrested me, cold and hungry, they asked me why I ran away. I sat silent, in stubborn refusal of emotion. I wondered why they didn't get my real mother now. Didn't they have to find her? Instead, I was sent to jail. Being the youngest in the jail cell, since the juvenile facility at the time also housed adult women, I pretended to be crazy and capable of anything. It seemed necessary, given the stabbing in the cell the night before. The other inmates left me alone, and it was like I found my calling. I could act like anything. The gang, "The Charity Cats," a name in celebration of our impoverished but resourceful ways, pranced through the streets in stolen green wool jackets and newly found identity and freedom. I got out of jail, released to my foster mother, and thereafter committed myself to the gang.

The Charity Cats grew rapidly in numbers, and crews of ten- to fourteen-year-old girls roamed the streets and schools with the commitment of protecting one another and punishing anyone who got in the way. We practiced running from cops by baiting them with curfew violations, and throwing booze bottles at cop cars. We had escape practice sessions, as we proudly knew the city's boardwalks, trap doors, stairwells, and a multitude of hiding places. Typical tensions caused a few light rumbles on the docks with others who felt slighted by us. We began to pack weapons. We stole No-Doze pills from the drugstore and hung out all night, wired, looking for more things to "catch a buzz." We began sniffing gas, cooking spray, paint, glue, anything. At thirteen, I organized another run-away plan, and the story ended up in the newspaper.

Eighth-grade teachers at the school were probably tortured by the endless taunting and mean pranks of classrooms mixed with Native and primarily white students full of 1960s rebellion and race-based animosities. After being pumped full of power from successfully harassing a math teacher to tears, we ran into the woods and smoked our cigarettes—daring the world to do anything about it. I told some other "Charity Cats" I was running away and showed them my packed bag. My plan was to catch the ferryboat to Seattle. I just needed to take some time to scrounge some money. After school, word had gotten around, and several of the Charity Cats and "J.D.'s" decided to join me. The J.D.'s (acronym for juvenile delinquents) were our newly organized male counterpart. In total fourteen of us kids, all Native except for the two white girls, hid in the boiler room of the old abandoned Ketchikan hospital. For a week we fed each other from bomb shelter rations, food bought with stolen money from rolling drunks, robbing citizens, and from flirting shamelessly with sailors. It ended with gunned police and a paddy wagon.

I was sitting on an oil drum, sharing some bite to eat with the other kids in our dungeon-like shelter when the police burst through the door and chaos erupted. I jumped so hard from the fright, an officer stuck a gun straight in my face and told me not to make "a f—ing move or I'll blow your head off." Other than a liquor-store owner charging out with a gun and firing (after we stole a couple bottles), I had never had a gun aimed at me, let alone in my face. I was stunned. All I could think was that I was thirteen years old and I had a ten-year-old boy beside me, and we were going to die. The officers put handcuffs on the guys and since they wouldn't stay on us girls, tied us together with ropes. We were loaded into vans. Us girls kicked our shoes out the back door of our van, flirted with the drivers, and basically did anything in an attempt to get them to stop in hopes of escaping. It didn't work, and a couple of us lost our shoes, and most of us were booked on charges of breaking and entering, minors in possession, and illegal weapon possessions. Thereafter police would stop me whenever anything occurred, since I was now referred to as a "ringleader." We all went to jail.

I ran away several times after that. One time me and two Charity Cats caught a fishing boat to Metlakatla, the only official Indian reservation in Alaska so it was said, twenty miles away, and got into mischief over there. It was great being there. All Indians, feeling welcome, and not feeling afraid all the time—it was a great place to be. But, the State Troopers caught up with us, and threw us all in the City Jail. I spent the Easter of 1968 in jail there, spending hours sitting with my skinny legs through the bars, wishing I were home, at my foster mother's house. She would leave an Easter basket at the end of my bed for me to wake up and find each year before church, and I ached to be home. I didn't let on much to the others. My foster mother did care for us I realized, but her miserable family was so troublesome for us. I wished I had the warmth of my own bed. Instead of dwelling on it, I helped the others flood the toilet and set the mattress on fire. It got us some attention anyway.

Other kids on the reservation felt the injustice of our expulsion from the community and when the State Troopers were hauling us down to the floatplane to fly us back to Ketchikan, they lined the streets and pounded on the car. We were so jazzed by the sight of it all, that one of the Charity Cats hurled herself off the dock, into the water, to keep us from having to get on the plane, prolonging our departure. Nevertheless, we were sent back to our dark and private hells. Jail was often a reprieve.

In jail, we played chicken, a game where you wrap a towel around your neck and choke yourself until you black out, and if you did it right, went into a kind of convulsion. We called it the funky chicken. It caused one of the Charity Cats to be institutionalized. Brain damage or something we were told. Cynically, I wondered if she faked it, just to get out of jail. One of the kids, a twelve-year-old boy from Metlakatla that hung out with us sometimes, died from sniffing gas. Nothing stopped us from killing the unspoken pain however. If it was death, so be it.

One of those trips to jail cost me my boyfriend at the time, a nice slightly older student, Tlingit, and someone who really tried to keep me out of trouble until he finally gave up and went out with a white girl. Stinging from the insult, I decided to date my first white boy. He was the president of the senior class or something, and his father owned a contracting service. He invited me out one day, and I agreed. We would go to a movie and a school dance. My foster mother made me a cute dress out of a pink stretchy material. Early on in the evening, he said he had to stop by his parents' place first to check on something. He invited me in, I went in, and he shut the door. He offered me a drink. I said no. In no time, he was throwing me onto the bed in the apartment, and I was kicking him off, and we struggled back and forth until we heard a knock on the door. A couple other white guys came in, with tequila. It was clear that we weren't going to any movie, and that I was intended for their evening's amusement. I made the decision to drink hard. I would drink until I felt nothing, determined that if I was to be gang-raped, I would not feel it, or, I would drink them under the table. We drank and drank, and they eventually passed out. Bruised and sore from the assaults, I walked the seven miles back home through the wet night, and upon arriving home at sun up, took off my dress and burned it in the burn barrel. The next morning my foster mother asked me how my date was, and I didn't have the heart or soul to tell her. I said it was fine.

One day, Charity Cats 1, 2, and 3—me, Margaret, and Veronica—took some spray paint to the high school our first year there. We painted Brown Power, and Black Power (just to confuse things), and other markings all over the school walls, covering the halls, the stairwells, and even bathrooms while conducting other vandalism. In the process, I threw some item at the back of the principal's head, catching him as he was getting up. I was hauled by force and physically thrown out the door of the school in front of a crowd of students. That and some other pranks through the glue-sniffing day caused us girls to be arrested and jailed again. The principal said I was the worst student he had ever seen in nineteen years of being around public schools. With a dark smirk, I expressed my pride for it to the others. The school counselor had once told me that I would probably end up pregnant and a dropout like most Native girls, and having been reduced to low-level classes, I thought what did I give a damn about school. I had wanted to be in Color Guard and be part of the basketball games. I even went to a couple of practices, but the rage, the alcohol, the drugs, and that counselor's words, erased those ideas away. That day's activities caused me to be kicked out of school permanently until some curious lawyer or someone found the law that required me to go to school and that meant the school had to take me back. But that took a year and, in the interim, I was sent to Sitka to live with my maternal grandparents.

I liked Sitka. At least I was with my own people. Grandma and Grandpa spoke Tlingit quietly around the house, told stories about our family, and it felt good. But I was the problem child, lest anyone should forget, and I was not allowed to leave the top of the stairs when company was over, and I was not allowed to step on the carpet, only walk on the plastic, or allowed to sit on any furniture in the living room. I sat on a stool at my grandmother's feet. I cleaned things up as requested and spoke politely. It was my desire to belong and to somehow be worthy. But old habits called me to sneak out of the house from time to time, hang with my new friends, drink into oblivion in the Russian graveyard, and try new highs. It was a pretty good year, and I wasn't arrested for anything. I went back to Ketchikan and to Kay-Hi and tried to start over. Life and its demons wouldn't allow it.

Even though I wasn't up to the same mischief and was studying at school, I was still angry and resistant with authority, and that included my foster mother. I also enjoyed stealing and managed to acquire an entire wardrobe out of it. The more I acted out, the harder it was to look into the ever-growing sad eyes of my foster mother. I was making her life terribly unpleasant and I knew it, yet I could do nothing. I had an ever-smoldering rage. To worsen the situation, her grandson had returned from Germany and one night had forced me down to the bed in his mother's house, determined to resume the violations. This time I fought hard—I was bigger, and I was angry. In the struggle, I bit his lip clean through and blood shot everywhere. In a fury, he grabbed for me as I ran, knocking into things, and I ran. Even though I was in a skirt, I ran out of sight of him and walked the few miles, crying hopelessly in the rain, to the police station. In a tired and helpless state, I told the police officer what had happened and how this man had been molesting me. The middle-aged officer, looking hard at my thin cold legs, replied in a whispering voice that he wouldn't mind "having some too." My heart squeezing, I got up slowly and moved carefully to the door. And I ran. I ran screaming, screaming in the rain, until my throat stung and I felt I'd vomit. I wanted to slam my head into a rock. Instead, I took stock of my soaking wet, childlike body, and I went to the hotel downtown where my boyfriend from Metlakatla was staying, and I had sex with him. I decided everything, from that point, would be on my terms. I would take what I had to take, and do whatever I had to do. I would have the power. I was fourteen years old.

One morning towards the end of that wet, dark winter, I awoke from a bad dream and set about to make breakfast, cooking up some fried potatoes like my brothers and I liked, like our foster mother made for us. She was sleeping on the couch and I heard her sigh when I began to drop the peeled potatoes into the hot cast-iron pan. My brothers got up with the smell and sat at the tiny kitchen table. We were visiting with one another, and it was nice. I was troubled by the dream I had had. I now had a full pan of potatoes and onions going and our mouths began to water. While talking to my brothers, I happened to look at our foster mother lying on the couch. She looked peculiar. She was too still. I went to her, and felt her. She was cold, not moving. I saw the dream, and I knew this was not good. I ran and woke her son Scott who was snoring away and told him that something was wrong with her. As I heard him say, "Mom, Mom, wake up," and the change in his voice, choking, I ran in the bathroom and stood in the tiny rusted shower and prayed. I prayed hard, and I told God that he must wake her right now, because it was important, even if it was just for a minute, it was important. I had to tell her that I did love her. I would be willing to do anything. He had to make it happen. It didn't happen, and as the hearse came, and of all things, it was a hearse, I took a cigarette from my abuser who stood there, pale and shaking, and watched them drive away—with her and with every shred of my hope or faith. I sucked on the cigarette and turned towards the darkness of my soul.

"It's your fault, Diane, that she's dead," said her daughter and someone else. I figured they spoke the truth and why not. A few short hours later, the house was full of people trying to decide what to do with her stuff, us kids, and the house, sometimes crying, and their cigarette smoke everywhere. The scene was baffling and my head was swimming. I overheard her daughter say that us kids would have to be taken to the Children's Home or somewhere. I didn't want to go. I'd heard about the place and we weren't going. I talked quietly to my brothers. I was running away to Metlakatla and they should go with me.

That afternoon we were all at her daughter's house in Ketchikan, with our dog Lady, dazed by the change, and us kids schemed to run away as alcohol cast its spell on the household, and angry outbursts made us twitch. One brother was thrown against the wall at one point, and I grabbed the youngest brother and ran. We ran until our lungs ached to one of the Charity Cats' house. We hid in her bedroom closet away from her mother until we could make a boat to Metlakatla. In Metlakatla we went straight away to my boyfriend's parents' house, where we settled in for the night. Quiet was not to be ours, as the evening turned into a blur of alcoholic confusion and the parents began to fight. My boyfriend and his dad turned scuffling quickly into blows of ugly violence. My boyfriend's hand and arm went through some glass, and blood sprayed everywhere, even a piece of his flesh lying in a pool of red. I was in one of his white T-shirts, and as I tried to calm down the household, me almost in a serene state with the utter chaos, his mother screaming and crying, kids hysterical, I mechanically called the base hospital and whoever I could reach and then mopped blood. As my boyfriend left for treatment, and me covered in a seriously blood-soaked T-shirt, I put the little ones to bed, and then told the parents to stop blaming each other and stop scaring their children. I tucked everyone into bed as if it was my duty, and then I opened a bottle of whiskey, sat on the couch and read *Romeo and Juliet* and drank until my boyfriend came back late that night.

My boyfriend tossed and turned in sweat-soaked pain as I watched the sun come up. In the still morning light, I heard a gunshot. My heart skipped as my eyes closed and I slipped unwillingly into sleep's fearful darkness. Apparently, the neighbor killed himself in front of his wife and kids. I no longer felt a thing about anything. Life was nothing but a sentence born on the unworthy.

Although the night had been what it had been, we did not want to leave my boyfriend's family. When the State Troopers finally showed up some days later to take my brother and I away back to Ketchikan, my tall and fierce boyfriend and his large stocky father made it clear that they would not get past the door to take us away. It took a few more days but the Troopers finally had their way. We were hauled back to Ketchikan.

My brothers were placed in a home with a Christian couple from the church we had attended. The couple had decided it was best that I not be allowed to see my brothers, since I was "a bad influence." When it came to my brothers I only wanted them safe and near. They were all that mattered. Still hopeful I would see my brothers, I was put into a State-sanctioned foster home where the adults of the household were prone to drink. It wasn't long before I understood I would not be living with my brothers again. I cried quietly into my pillow most every night. I wanted the nerve to cut my wrists clean through, but could only muster a few light cuts with razors on my wrists and hands. I hated my weakness.

In this new foster home, I was separated from the family at dinnertime. I loved the smell of pork chop suey that she cooked several times during my stay, but never allowed me to eat. Instead, my new foster mother would place a tin TV tray in the living room with a plate of pasta noodles and a can of chili on top as my dinner. I learned to hate that combination of tastes and craved their meals, particularly all that pork, celery, onion, and soy sauce over rice. I cleaned their house, sometimes hand-scrubbing the kitchen floor, even while their own kids went out, and tried to be a good kid. I was too lost and empty to be that rebellious. I would go out sometimes and meet my Metlakatla boyfriend, and one time he bought me shoes. My foster mother, enraged upon seeing the shoes, accused me of being a whore. I was not allowed to visit my boyfriend thereafter, even though my dad had let them know in a rare call that he approved.

My foster parents received a State check for caring for me, but they never managed to buy me clothes or shoes for school or anything else. I would walk out into the cold wet mornings to retrieve their mail from the mailbox so I knew the checks came. I sometimes borrowed their daughter's clothes. All the clothes I had acquired at Wards Cove, albeit by stealing, were long gone, stolen away from me by an even greedier bunch. I wore cowboy boots, because that's all I had left. At a school that required girls to wear dresses, this didn't fit too well. That's why my boyfriend bought me shoes. Receipt of a check usually meant drinking would follow. A number of times the foster parents would wake me in the wee hours to watch them dance as they drunkenly swayed to Ink Spots songs like "Smoke Gets in Your Eyes." I would sit there, sleepy-eyed but anxious, knowing in a few short hours I'd have to be up for school. I willingly watched them dance because I was afraid if I didn't, I would be evicted from the home. The more I tried to be "good" the more I really began to resent the situation. What was the point in trying to do the right thing if this was the payoff?

Due to the historical problems with Native students like myself, Ketchikan High School saw fit to hire a Native counselor. We were excited about that, and we all lined up to see him. He was a Vietnam veteran, a Tlingit and Filipino man, who did not pretend with us. He talked straight to us about not only drugs, but also about life, our lives, and acknowledged our pain, even if we wouldn't. We liked him. He inspired our Native pride, and feeling such pride one day, we organized in an unusual rebellious act. Rather than wear the hippie fashions of 1970, we wore Native attire to school. We followed the dress code with our skirts to our knees, and blouses buttoned, but wore Native necklaces, beaded vests, and whatever any gang member's family would loan. These were things many of us never saw in public, ever. It was probably the most frightening but strangely liberating thing we had ever done. Especially when we had to separate to go to our individual classes and sit with the stares from teachers and snickers from students. And we did it. Our counselor was proud, but the school seemed to think maybe he was causing a problem stirring up Native students. It was always something. But we held our heads up in a new way for a whole day. It was a great feeling, even if short-lived.

During that year, the Charity Cats began to spar with one another, and power struggles stressed the unity. While I was in Sitka things had changed. Most of the J.D.'s were in jail, and the addition of new Charity Cat members confused the leadership. Eventually I was at odds with other members and faced off with them in halls. I had written a letter to my dad telling him how horrible it was at the new foster home. He showed it to the State people and the foster home license was taken away, I was told. After the letter, I was sent to the dreaded Children's Home, and it wasn't so bad, just crammed and lonely. The foster parents' daughter wanted revenge and some members of the Charity Cats were going to oblige. I received death threats by phone at the Children's Home. I told my PO (probation officer). He showed me a stack of files about six, seven inches high and asked me if I knew what it was. I said no. He said all of it was about me. We starting talking about youth halls, and places for teenagers to go, and that there were little activities or resources for impoverished kids and kids on the streets. I would walk through town thinking about it. I ended up going to a school dance supposedly with police protection at his urging. I was out of the gang. Gangs, I found out, take on a deadly life of their own making.

Police protection felt like an oxymoron, since we hated the police. We hated them for harassing us, picking us up for no reason, even holding us up to seventy-two hours, and for offering us Native girls the option of providing them sexual favors rather than jail. Once, upon such an offer, I told the officer, in certain expletives, where he could go. Then I ran for my life. That incident involved my arrest for assaulting a white girl with a deadly weapon. I had a switchblade that I had proudly obtained from burglarizing a store a couple years' previous with another Charity Cat. He told me I would get ten years if I didn't "go out the road with him." Instead, I went to court and received more **probation** time, but this time with the promise that anything more would send me to McLaughlin in Anchorage. Hard time. Now I was to rely on police to protect me from my own gang. It seemed inconceivable, and I got drunk at the dance, and from there disappeared into drug and alcohol oblivion. I was tired of police, of gangs, of everybody. I had a bullet go through my hair and hit the wall behind me at a drug party, seen blood after blood all over walls, fists smashing faces, walked in drug paranoia often, and once passed out drunk in a muddy ditch. A couple of drug dealers apparently killed the friend who had rescued me from the ditch not long after, but no one was charged for it. Nothing was worse than being a "narc" and to tell was to be a "narc," so no one told, and no one was arrested. Besides, the drug dealers were white, and no one expected them to do time anyway. But I missed my friend terribly. He cared. And a Charity Cat's old boyfriend hung himself. I was simply tired of it all. To worsen my despair, I was trash that couldn't see my brothers. Midsummer I was sent to Sitka to my grandparents only to end up in jail.

My grandparents did their best, but I was so removed from notions of family, obligation, or normalcy that I sought instant gratification—adhering to the philosophy, in a destructive way, that one only has today. I did not expect to live beyond my teenage years. I made a grand plan with some friends to run away to Australia and build a commune—a community of our own. I made it as far as the ferry terminal with stolen money and a criminal boyfriend waiting on board. My girlfriend and I were hauled to the City Jail where she spent three days and I spent two weeks, apparently due to my probation status and criminal record. The police immediately took all my belongings, including the leather string that held my shirt together, as well as the jail mattress, blanket, toothbrush, and anything moveable. I attempted to use my cowboy boots to lay my head on while curled up on the freezing concrete floor, but they promptly seized those as well. My grandmother came to visit once, staring at me through the bars, and cried how I shamed our family. I felt sorry for her, but numb to life. My uncle, back from Vietnam, told me I wasn't the first one to be in jail. The future didn't interest me, nor did the past.

My Sitka probation officer informed me I would be attending Mt. Edgecumbe Indian Boarding School. Even though it was just a two-minute ride by boat from Sitka, it seemed a lifetime away. It was the best curve life had thrown my way, as it would turn out, even though on registration day I was police-escorted to school in handcuffs and released to the administration. I eventually made good grades, got into some mischief, but I was never arrested again. The next year I followed a boyfriend to Fairbanks and entered a boarding home to complete my senior year of high school. I made a new start.

The boarding home parents, although Indian, were removed from the life of the village. In awkward attempts to make me feel welcomed, they inadvertently overcooked fish eggs and then seemed offended when I could not eat them. I was not accustomed to salad and dressings, and some other foods, and this caused immediate friction. I kept to myself, became involved in school activities, and began speaking out on current issues in classes. Although academically it was a good year, the home life was stressful. The day after graduation, the family told me their job was done and I had one hour to pack and get out. With no place to go, other than a Bureau of Indian Affairs (BIA) plane ticket back to Sitka, I visited my grandparents for a couple of weeks, then left for Ketchikan to find my brothers. I was broke, and I was seventeen years old and homeless.

Back in Ketchikan, I hung out with one brother and we lived off things we hocked or sold, even camping out at Wards Cove in a tent. I ended up at the hospital suffering from malnutrition, they told me. Did we have a place to go so I could recover? I lied, said we did, but we didn't. I was afraid they would try to do something with me if I said I had no place to go. We decided to go to Seattle and visit our father's mother and at least eat, have a bed to sleep in, and then just go from there. We went hungry often and found ourselves rationing bread and sandwich meat for meals, standing in soup lines, or going to churches to get free food, or simply begging on the street. Once we were arrested in Seattle because my brother had a knife strapped on his belt. We didn't know that was against the law in the city. They tried to find out from where we had run away. We told them we were not runaways. They called places in Alaska for an hour or so. We were not reported missing from anywhere. We had no place to go back to and, scratching their heads, they let us go. We hitchhiked around the country and eventually went our separate ways. In the worst days alone, I slept in trees, along side roads, or under discarded plastic in rain, and ate out of garbage cans. In the best days, I begged enough money to eat real meals, get a bed in a hostel, or meet up with generous people. At eighteen, I settled in Portland, got a couple of jobs with my BIA school typing training, got an efficiency apartment, and made a couple of friends. It seemed life wasn't too bad, but demons in my head wouldn't let me sleep or sit still, and I missed the mountains and skies of my homeland, and so I finally worked my way back to Alaska. I settled in Fairbanks and within months was so brutalized by a white man that belonged to some militia group that I spent the summer hiding in someone's cabin out of sheer and total fear.

This sixty-year-old heavyset white man I met because my car ran out of gas said he had a bad heart, was alone, and needed help, and so, naively seeing this as an opportunity, I moved into his home and worked off rent by cleaning and cooking, as well as working during the week at the Native community center in Fairbanks. There, I heard stories of Native women murdered and dumped along the roadside and no one arrested for it. I listened to families cry, hopeless for justice. One night, the heavyset white man came into my room and raped me. He fell asleep in his room afterwards, and I crept into his room with a gun and held it to his head. I stood there and, with a profound realization, put the gun away, and stole away into the night, running down the road in my bare feet, carrying my boots. If I killed that white man, I would be hung for it or worse. I was a Native in a white man's house. I ran hard.

Just as I crossed a road into the woods, his truck came screeching to a halt nearby, and he swung his shotgun around and fired. I ran to a house terrified, but no answer. I ran north through the woods, the birch trees too slim to hide me like the spruce or cedar trees of home. Hearing the gun, I dove into a ditch. I felt pain sear through my leg, but I dared not move. I pressed my face down into the earth, hoping the steam from my breath would not betray me. I felt the wetness of blood while I lay there.

Morning light began to break and I worked my way through the woods to my old boarding home parents' house, and knocked on their daughter's window. She pulled me into the house and cleaned my wound. I told her I landed on a nail. I really don't know why I told her that. Later that morning, she urged me to tell her parents, but they immediately demanded that I leave and not jeopardize their family. That man would be hunting for me, and they didn't want any trouble. Their fears were justified as it would turn out—I was unaware at the time that this same white man had raped six other Native women under similar conditions. The family was just as concerned about, as I was terrified of, the militia group that he belonged to as well. To add insult to injury, the police had thought to arrest me, at his request, for breaking and entering his house. I felt attacked on all fronts and terribly alone. I spent the summer hiding, going to work, and withdrawn from everything. I pretended things were fine, and quietly drank away pain. One day, during work, I saw a wino sitting on the riverbank and I went out and joined him.

I soon went to work on the pipeline, where I worked for three years, drank and drugged my way along, was raped in Arizona at knifepoint, the guy charged with a misdemeanor, and I eventually attempted suicide by overdose. By this point, I felt I had a sign tattooed onto my forehead that said, "Beat me—I'm a Victim." No one ever came to my defense, I reflected, and I accepted in my demoralization that I was not worthy, that I deserved it somehow, and that I was simply marked. I nearly drank myself to death on a couple of occasions, played Russian roulette with a handgun, and fumbled through some attempts at relationships, while jumping from job to job. Upon the birth of my son, I felt the stirring to change my situation. I spent the first six years of his life seeking counseling and finally drug and alcohol treatment. During that time, I hit an emotional bottom, when a man I had dated over a couple years got drunk and committed suicide.

I was thirty-two when I finally got clean and sober. I spent the first two years of my sobriety suffering from what a therapist called post-traumatic stress disorder. I was lucky to stumble upon this therapist and, with hospitalization, and her treatment, I found life again. Unlike other therapists, she did not seek to medicate me. I believe my son was the sole reason I lived. It was love for him that moved me to clean up, go to school, and return to my culture.

On rare occasions, I still have nightmares and require more quiet space and privacy than maybe the average person, even though now I can enjoy people, enjoy the well-being of others, and rejoice in the camaraderie of tribal gatherings. In the effort to overcome, I may have overachieved, having run for the highest office in Alaska as a third-party candidate, fought at very public levels of controversy defending basic human and tribal rights, and graduated first in my family with a post-graduate degree. People wonder what motivates me, and all I can say is, a little kindness goes a long way, and tapping into the strength of my ancestors guided my sense of worth and value, and carries me today.

Furthermore, in my life, it was those little moments of someone extending a hand of love and kindness that touched my heart. It was the smiles and acceptance of some elders who took the time to talk to me and tell me I could lift myself up, and especially the elder who told me, "you're not crazy, you're hurt." Somehow, the acknowledgment was overwhelming. I believe not only individuals, but the judicial system, and society, must show compassion while demanding, and rightly so, accountability. I believe truth combined with compassion saves lives.

Questions

1. How did the foster care system fail Benson and her brothers? How did this contribute to the violence she experienced throughout her life?
2. What recommendations do you have for the foster care system in its service to Native children? What can be done to make them safe within their foster homes?
3. What are signs of sexual abuse in children that Benson exhibited throughout her childhood? What are interventions that can be taken for children who are being abused or have experienced abuse?
4. Why was it so important for the elder to acknowledge Benson's pain and attribute her behavior to the abuses she experienced? How can this help in the healing process? Why did community members not realize that her behavior was a reflection of her experiences?

5. How did the police contribute to her abuse and mistreatment?
6. What did she do or abuse to kill the pain of what she was experiencing?
7. In the end of the chapter Benson refers to the Native women who have gone missing in Alaska and the lack of justice for them. Do you think this is still going on today? Why do the murders of Native women receive so little attention? What can be done to combat this?

In Your Community
1. Is there a support system for children and teenagers in your community? Do they interact with elders?
2. What types of programs are there for women who have experienced violence such as that experienced by Benson?

Terms Used in Chapter 8
Ingenuity: Inventive skill or imagination; cleverness.
Probation: The act of suspending the sentence of a person convicted of a criminal offense and granting that person provisional freedom on the promise of good behavior.
Skiff: A flat-bottom open boat of shallow draft, having a pointed bow and a square stern.

Suggested Further Reading
Bohn, Diane K. "Lifetime Physical and Sexual Abuse, Substance Abuse, Depression, and Suicide Attempts Among Native American Women." *Issues in Mental Health Nursing* 24 (2003): 333.
DeBruyn, Lemyra, et al. "Child Maltreatment in American Indian and Alaska Native Communities: Integrating Culture, History, and Public Health for Intervention and Prevention." *Child Maltreatment* 6 (2001): 89.
EchoHawk, Larry. "Child Sexual Abuse in Indian Country: Is the Guardian Keeping in Mind the Seventh Generation?" *New York University Journal of Legislative and Public Policy* 5 (2001): 83, 107.
Gray, Norma. "Addressing Trauma in Substance Abuse Treatment with American Indian Adolescents." *Journal of Substance Abuse Treatment* 15 (1998): 393.
Hopfoll, Stevan E., et al. "The Impact of Perceived Child Physical and Sexual Abuse History on Native American Women's Psychological Well-Being and AIDS Risk." *Journal of Consulting and Clinical Psychology* 70 (2002): 252.
Koss, Mary P., et al. "Adverse Childhood Exposures and Alcohol Dependence Among Seven Native American Tribes." *American Journal of Preventive Medicine* 25 (2003): 238.

WRONG!!!

When I was five years old, I saw my Dad slap my Mom
No one told her it was wrong

As I was growing up my brother disrespected my Mom
No one said it was wrong

When I was fifteen, my brother beat me
No one told him it was wrong

When my friend told me that a tribal elder molested her
No one told her it was wrong

When my cousin was killed by her husband
No one told the community it was wrong

When I was sexually harassed on the job
No one told my co-workers it was wrong

When I went to the Family Services Office and was treated unfairly
No one told them it was wrong

When the police asked me, "What did you do to make him hit you?"
Someone should have told them they were wrong

When he stood in front of the judge
They told him it was wrong

When my son mistreats his girlfriend
I will tell him it's wrong

When my daughter becomes afraid of her boyfriend
I will tell her it's wrong

Someday, my grandchildren will live in a world
Where they won't have to be told "it's wrong!"

        Frances M. Blackburn (Northern Arapahoe)

Prisoner W-20170/Other

Chapter 9

STORMY OGDEN

> *According to the California Department of Corrections this was who I was for eight years of my life. For the first five years, I was locked behind their prison walls; the last three years I was under the supervision of the state parole office. However, there is more to me than that.*

I write this chapter as a California Indian woman, a recognized member of the Tule River Yokuts tribe, my grandmother's people. I am also Kashaya and Lake County Pomo, my grandfather's people. I also write as an ex-prisoner of the state of California, housed at the California Rehabilitation Center (CRC) located in the southern part of the state. I am also a survivor of colonization.

The colonizers brought with them two tools of mass destruction—the Bible and the bottle, which were both forced upon Native people. In addition to using these tools of genocide, the colonizers criminalized the traditional ways of behavior and conduct of Native people and sought to control indigenous people through their laws. Enforcement of these foreign laws meant Native people were locked up in a spectrum of punishing institutions, including military forts, missions, reservations, boarding schools, and, more recently, the state and federal prisons.[1] In North America, the groups that are most likely to be sent to jail and prison are the poor and people of color. A large proportion of these people who end up behind bars are indigenous. On any given day, one in twenty-five American Indians is under the jurisdiction of the criminal justice system, a rate that is 2.4 times that of whites.[2] American Indian women are particularly targeted for punishment. During 1988 in South Dakota, almost half of the women imprisoned (44 percent) were American Indian, yet they comprised only 7 percent of the state's population according to the 1990 census.[3]

Angela Davis and Cassandra Shaylor describe the prison industrial complex (PIC) as an intricate web of racism, social control, and profit.[4] The experience of racial subordination, repression, and economic exploitation is not new to the Native people of these lands. From the missions to the reservations, the Indians of California have struggled for survival in the face of an array of brutal mechanisms designed to control and eliminate the region's first peoples.

Built on the ancestral lands of indigenous people, the U.S. prison industrial complex has contributed to the devastating process of colonization. It is essential for scholars and activists to understand the colonial roots of the PIC and to make visible the stories of Native prisoners.

My People/Our Lands

My Indian heritage is Yokuts and Pomo. We have creation stories that will always connect us to these lands of our ancestors, and we continue to live on these lands today. The Yokuts inhabited a three-hundred-mile-wide range, which included the San Joaquin Valley and adjoining foothills.[5] The Yokuts were agriculturalists and held the most fertile land in California. The Yokuts people retain our history and maintain there were at least seventy tribal communities before contact with Europeans. The Pomo people occupied approximately seven widely separated localities in the coastal ranges north of the San Francisco Bay. The hallmark of our tribal identity is the Pomo language, which has connected these geographically divided communities.

Prior to the arrival of Europeans, the area that became known as California had the largest and most diverse indigenous populations of any area in North America. Native California was perhaps the most diverse in ecology, social structure, and history. According to Rupert and Jeanette Costo, California Indians were highly skilled explorers of North America and enjoyed a sophisticated knowledge of their environment, which they had developed over thousands of years.[6]

Our elders tell us that the Natives of California lived in well-ordered societies. Every part of their tribal society was enriched and maintained through religious and traditional laws. Religion was the primary method of social control, with conflicts handled mainly through sanctions, not confrontation and warfare.[7] The indigenous nations of California were governed by their own laws. The laws were established over hundreds of years; our oral histories and songs teach us this.[8] Individuals accepted these laws because they ensured collective survival. When violations occurred, the rule was restitution instead of retribution. Exile from the tribe was an extreme penalty.

In Utmost of Good Faith

The UTMOST GOOD FAITH shall always be observed towards the Indians; their land and property shall never be taken from them without their consent; and in their property, rights and liberty, they shall never be invaded or disturbed, unless in justified and lawful wars authorized by Congress; but laws founded in justice and humanity shall from time to time be made, for preventing wrongs being done to them, and for preserving peace and friendship with them.[9]

Tribal nations have always had strong legal systems. Through storytelling, song, and dance, rules and laws were passed from generation to generation. The laws became customs that were ingrained in the very lifeblood of the people. Everyday behavior had its own rules of conduct, which the people understood and embraced.

In contrast, the U.S. criminal justice system in Indian Country is overly complex and difficult to understand. Its governing principles are contained in hundreds of statutes and court decisions. Due to these laws, almost every aspect of the internal and external relations of Indian people became the target of control by the U.S. government. As a result, American Indians are more likely to come into conflict with the criminal justice system at an earlier age. This early involvement in the criminal justice system is an outcome of colonization. Native offenders are often incarcerated in federal prisons instead of state or local facilities because of federal criminal jurisdiction over many Indian lands.

There were no prisons in North America before the arrival of the Euro-Americans. Prisons were created for people who broke the European laws. White European Puritans created prisons and the laws that put people in them. As institutions of social control, prisons should be viewed in context with the policy of assimilation and the lack of acceptance of Native spiritual and cultural ways.

The U.S. government began to interfere with traditional tribal justice systems in 1885, when Congress passed the Major Crimes Act, 18 U.S.C.A. 1153. This act gave federal courts jurisdiction over crimes committed by Indians against Indians in Indian Country, in complete disregard for international law, treaty law, and Article VI of the U.S. Constitution. The effect of this has been to diminish tribal sovereignty. Many other legal intrusions followed. Nearly every form of Indian religion was banned on the reservations by the mid-1800s, and extreme measures were taken to discourage Indians from maintaining their tribal customs.[10] Control and destruction of our lands and culture continued for generations.

In January 1895, a large group of Indian prisoners was confined in Alcatraz, a military installation on a harsh island of rock in San Francisco Harbor. These prisoners were nineteen Hopi "hostiles" who opposed the forced education of their children in the government boarding schools. As late as the 1930s, the Bureau of Indian Affairs enforced the "Indian Offenses Act," which forbade Indian religion, assigned English names to replace Indian ones, and even outlawed Indian hairstyles. As the criminal jurisdiction of the United States increasingly imposed itself on Indian nations, the government relied on three arguments to support its jurisdiction over Indian Country without the consent of Indian nations:

1. The Plenary Power Doctrine, which asserted that Congress had absolute power to assert authority over Indian nations. This clearly contradicted internal law, as well as Article VI of the U.S. Constitution, which expressly states that all treaties between Indian nations and the U.S. government have supremacy over any law Congress might enact. Congress has asserted that it may unilaterally abrogate a treaty without the consent of the nations—parties to the treaties.[11]
2. The Federal-Indian Trust Doctrine, which is defined as being a unique moral and legal duty of the United States to assist Indians in the protection of their property and rights. This doctrine is supposed to work in the best interest of the Indian nations. However, this is where the concept of the **paternalistic** "Great White Father" in Washington comes into play. In this regard, we have been treated as children, unable to make our own decisions. This has been devastating for Indian nations.
3. The Doctrine of Geographical Incorporation, which claims that since Indian lands (such as reservations) are located within the boundaries of the United States, the United States holds title to all of the land and they also have the absolute right to assert legal jurisdiction over this land.[12]

These three arguments can be seen as being instruments of racism and forms of social control. The continuing role of the U.S. justice system in colonizing Indian people is visible in the large numbers of Native Americans, Native Hawaiians, and Alaska Natives who have been convicted in the white man's courts for hunting, fishing, and subsistence gathering in accordance with their customs. Those laws often violate indigenous treaties and rights. According to Luana Ross, "Native worlds were devastated by the course of their forced relationship with Euro-Americans and their laws."[13]

Many Native Americans have also been targeted because of their political activism. More recently, Native youth activists and warriors in the United States and Canada have been imprisoned because of their involvement in defending Native burial grounds and sacred sites, because they try to defend fishing and hunting rights, or because they oppose corporate exploitation of their lands.[14]

The Colonial Roots of Prison Labor

For five years, I worked as a clerk in the California prison system. Like a slave, I had no choice about the work I did, nor was I paid fully for my labor. The thirty-two dollars a month that I earned had to pay for overpriced feminine products, soap, shampoo, and toothpaste in the prison commissary. Prison labor, rooted in the history of slavery and colonization, plays an important role in the economics of incarceration. The prison industrial complex has a twofold purpose: social control and profit. Like the military industrial complex, the prison industrial complex interweaves government agencies with business interests who seek to make a profit from imprisoning the poor and people of color. Like any industry, the prison economy needs raw material. In this case, the raw materials are people—prisoners. Prisoners generate profits for the companies that build and house prisons. They also generate profits by providing a cheap, plentiful, and easily controlled workforce.

In the past two decades, prisons in California have shed the pretense of rehabilitation in favor of large warehouse-style prisons that provide few opportunities for education or training. Instead, prisoners are exploited as a cheap source of labor, both to maintain the prison itself and to bring in income through prison industries. In fact, they often keep prisoners in their cells for twenty-three hours a day. Prison wardens are clear that they are not here to **rehabilitate**, but only to punish. Clearly, history is repeating itself.

While researchers have identified the origins of prison labor in the enslavement of African Americans in the southern states, the history of Indian slavery has been overlooked. Economic exploitation and forced slave labor are not new to Native peoples, especially the indigenous people of early California. If we are to map the origins of the prison industrial complex in California accurately, we must look at the history of forced labor in the Golden State. When the colonizers arrived in eighteenth-century California, they stereotyped Native people and assumed that they were weak and only useful for labor. The Spanish and Mexican invaders valued the Indian people as an essential workforce necessary to build their missions, presidios, and pueblos and to work in the fields.

The American system continued these policies. In 1850, the California legislature passed a law called the Government and Protection of the Indians Act, which can be described as legalized slavery. This act provided for the indenture of loitering, intoxicated, and orphaned Indians, and the forced regulation of their employment. It also defined a special class of crimes and punishment for these Indians. The law, enacted on April 22, 1850, established within its twenty various sections the mechanism whereby Indians of all ages could be indentured to any white citizen.[15] A white man could pay the fine and costs of any Indian convicted of an offense punishable before a justice of the peace. Then, the Indian person was required to work for the white man until the fine was paid off.

The act also gave local justices of the peace jurisdiction over all Indians within their districts and allowed the Indians to be punished with up to twenty-five lashes for stealing. According to Sidney L. Harring, "[t]he same Act also made provision for **indenturing** Indian children as servants and curtailed tribal land rights."[16] Under the apprenticeship provisions of the laws of 1850 and 1860, the abduction and sale of Indians, especially young women and children, was a regular business in California.[17] These provisions in the state law resulted in the institution of a slave mart in Los Angeles where captives were auctioned off to the highest bidder for "private service."[18] Although the slave mart has since disappeared, UNICOR, the California prison industry authority, continues to sell captive labor to the highest bidder.

The Little Girl That Became a Prisoner

The journey began for me at the age of five, when my mother put me into the backseat of our car and drove us away from our home and my father. She was driving away from a marriage consumed by alcoholism and domestic violence. Mom thought we would be safe somewhere else. Little did she know that she was driving me towards a life of sexual abuse and violence at the hands of people that were supposed to love the little girl with big, dark Indian eyes.

The abuse started as soon as we relocated, when the next-door neighbor's son started putting his hands down my panties. I remember telling my grandmother what was going on. She responded, "Don't you tell anyone about this or it will cause problems." I did tell and she was right—it did cause problems. It opened the door for my new stepfather and my grandmother's husband to start grooming me for sexual abuse when I was seven years old. Both men introduced me to adult comic books. My grandfather also started giving me alcohol. My stepfather would bathe me and put me to bed. Over time, he began to fondle me. One night, he was caught outside my bedroom window watching me undress for bed. I remember seeing him through the window, his face all distorted. It was not until recently that I realized that he was "jacking-off" while watching me. His abuse did not stop with me; he also fought violently with my mother.

By the age of ten, I was well on my way to becoming an alcoholic. Also at this time, my mother began to abuse me. Her words still ring in my head: "You are just a dirty Indian like your dad. You are a no good half-breed, and you will grow up to be a drunken Indian, just like your dad."

> *Half Breed*
> *a word that has made me*
> *a stranger in my own land.*

She would frequently throw hot coffee in my face, or take her long nails and dig them into my flesh, trying to draw blood.

From the ages of eleven through thirteen, the verbal and sexual abuse elevated. I was not allowed to go back to live with my dad, even though I cried and begged my mother to allow me. Sometimes I was able to spend summers with him, but never the entire summer, just a few weeks at a time. It was always hard on me when I had to return to my mother's house.

> *All my women role models were white*
> *They did not know how to deal with this Indian child*
> *Who grew so dark in the summer*
> *During the school year they would cut and perm that Injun hair*
> *putting me in pretty dresses and*
> *then telling me in soft hushed voices,*
> *Your dad is just a dirty drunk Indian and you will be just like him.*

I never told my dad what was going on at home because things at my dad's house were not much better. He was still drinking and abusing his new wife.

It was during this time that I started to abuse drugs and alcohol on my own. My home life was pure hell and that extended to school. When I was twelve, I was raped by four boys who went to school with me. My best girlfriend watched as these boys tore off my jeans and menstrual napkin, and proceeded to rape me one after the other. Later, I remember sitting in the bathtub in the cold water crying. No one was there for me, so I cleaned myself up and went to bed. After that happened, I started running away from home and skipping school. I ended up in juvenile hall three times before I left home for good. I thought if I ran away, that all the abuse would stop. However, I ultimately ran to another life that was just as violent, if not more so.

From the ages of fourteen through nineteen, I lived with a man who became my first husband. He was thirteen years older than I was. He was verbally, sexually, and physically abusive to me during our years together. I stayed with him because I had no place to go. I could not return home. I finally gathered the courage to run away from him, but what I ran to was even worse. Alcohol, drugs, bars, backseats of cars, rapes, and beatings consumed my days and nights. I spent a lot of time in the hospital, once for a broken arm, another time for a gunshot wound, and a third time to have an **IUD** surgically removed because I was raped with a cane. There were too many different men, too many empty bottles, and too many suicide attempts.

> *In my past I laid upon a strange bed in a hotel*
> *Praying that I would not wake up in the morning.*
> *At these times it was done as a ritual*
> *Long hot showers, purifying my body,*
> *Combing my long dark hair, wrapping it into neat braids,*
> *Singing my own death song.*

> Other times I would be sitting on the side of an empty bed,
> Around me would be empty whisky bottles
> And a shiny new razor blade in my hand.

At the age of twenty-two, I was sentenced to five years in the California Rehabilitation Center at Norco. By then, imprisonment was just a new phase in the cycle of abuse.

Women at Risk

The majority of women defendants in the criminal justice system have extensive histories of childhood and adult abuse that may result in homelessness, substance abuse, and economic marginality that forces them to survive by illegal means. The systems that place victims under correctional control include the criminalization of women's survival strategies.[19]

Moreover, many incarcerated women were exposed to violence that began early in their lives. American Indian women are the victims of crime at a rate that is nearly 50 percent higher than that reported by black males.[20] Women are also affected by their socioeconomic status, as low-income women of color have the greatest abuse risk. This leaves them vulnerable to being criminally entrapped and forced by abusive policies into the corrections systems. Violence perpetrated against women and girls can put them at risk for incarceration by forcing abused girls and women into the criminal justice system where they are not seen as victims, but as offenders in the eyes of the state.[21]

The female population in the prison system is dominated by drug offenders. The actual offenses vary—from possession or minor involvement to more large-scale drug sales and distribution. The offenses also include prostitution performed for drug money or holding small amounts of drugs for their male partners. The "war on drugs" is sometimes called the "war on women" because it has brought proportionately more women than men into the prison settings.[22] Racial discrimination in the criminal justice system has a devastating effect on women of color. According to Mary E. Gilfus, "[w]omen of color are more likely than white women to be arrested and charged with more serious offenses, to be prosecuted, to be convicted and to serve prison time."[23]

Ross notes that "[t]he violence experienced by women prior to incarceration continues inside the prison in a variety of forms including sexual intimidation, the overuse of mind-altering drugs, lengthy stays in lockup, and the denial of cultural activities for Native Americans."[24] We lose our dignity as soon as we enter the criminal justice center. It starts with a strip search—vaginal searches are particularly humiliating, but also painful. We are told to shower with a de-lousing soap, given state-issued clothes that are either too big or too small, and then we are given a prison number. The reality of the nightmare begins to set in the first time we hear the sound of the door closing and the turn of the key.

Out of Sight/Out of Mind

In the warmth of my fantasy
I awake to the cold gray walls
Of my reality.

These words thundered in my mind as the judge read my sentence: "Ms. Ogden, you are sentenced to five years, which will be served at the California Rehabilitation Center in Norco."

My reality is becoming more common for women in the United States, especially for American Indian women. Our Native women face overwhelming odds at every stage of the criminal justice system.[25] Yet, when I was trying to gather information on the number of American Indian women in prison, I found that it was almost impossible to find any accurate numbers. To quote the late American Indian activist Little Rock Reed, "the American Indian segment of the population of people is the forgotten segment; the segment that is so small in other racial and ethnic groups warehoused in America's prison that it is insignificant."[26] The few articles that are available on this topic are either generic, lump both men and women together, or they focus solely on Indian men.

Native American women are lost in the system because race classification systems in most prisons only allow for identities of White, Black, Hispanic, or "Other." Ross explains that "[p]risoners are ritualistically dehumanized, regulated, and reduced to numbers."[27]

> Located outside the door to my cell was a small, white, 3 x 5 card that listed my last name, my state number, and my racial classification—"Other." Every morning as I left for my job assignment, I would cross out "Other" and write "American Indian," but each afternoon when I returned for noon count, there would be a new card with "Other" written on it. This went on for a few days when finally the correctional officer approached me, and said, "Next time, Ogden, it will be a write up and a loss of good time." The next morning, before work, I found a permanent laundry marker, tore the card off the wall, and wrote "American Indian" on the wall.

All women in prison are fighting to maintain a sense of self within a system that isolates, degrades, and punishes. But, as American Indians, we must also fight for our identity on the very lands of our ancestors.

Women are the fastest-growing segment of the prison population. Today, there are over 140,000 women incarcerated in prisons and jails (nearly triple the number since 1985), and nearly one million under criminal justice control. California now has the distinction of having the most women prisoners in the nation, as well as the world's largest prison. There are over 11,000 women in prison in California. The two largest women's prisons in the world are located outside of Chowchilla, California, and imprison almost 8,000 women. The combined population at Valley State Prison and the Central California Women's Facility is higher than the city of Chowchilla where they are located. The majority of women are in prison for economic and nonviolent crimes, namely, drug offenses. As the number of women behind bars grows, the detrimental effects are felt by a whole generation of children, since a high percent of the women are mothers.

We Are Losing Our Children

It is impossible to explain to your three year old, over the phone, that you love her and that you will be home soon. Afterwards, you go back to your cell and cry yourself to sleep because "soon" is five or more years. The children, also known as the "hidden victims of incarceration" also suffer due to their mothers' absence.[28]

The growth of the prison system has dramatically affected the lives of millions of children. Although children whose parents are incarcerated do not automatically enter the foster care system, there is an increasing number of children who are entering it. In 1999, U.S. prisons held the parents of over 1.5 million children, an increase of over 500,000 since 1991.[29]

The incarceration of women uniquely influences families and communities because women are often the primary caregivers of children. Additionally, black, Latino, and Native children are at a greater risk for losing a parent to incarceration. When a woman goes to prison and there is no one able to care for her child, she runs the risk of losing her legal parental rights. Thousands of children end up as wards of the state and are shuffled through the foster care system while their mothers are incarcerated. Still more are adopted out, never to see their incarcerated mother again.

In California, 195,000 children have a parent in state prison and another 97,000 children have parents in county jail. Many women feel guilty and shameful about having to leave their children. Reunification is a desired goal, but women prisoners need various resources and assistance to accomplish this. Children separated from their mothers by incarceration also exhibit emotional and health problems, such as nightmares, bedwetting, withdrawal, and fear of darkness.[30] The negative consequences of having a mother in jail could assist in funneling these children into the criminal justice system, failing to break to the cycle of oppression.

The courts should be obligated to ensure that Native mothers who are criminally charged are made aware of their tribal nation's rights under the Indian Child Welfare Act (ICWA). Every measure should be taken by criminal justice workers both in and out of the prisons to assist the incarcerated Indian mothers in maintaining as much contact with their children as possible during incarceration to diminish the effect of losing their parent.

What We Face Inside

Incarcerated women suffer different traumas than men in prison. The needs and the problems that women face in prison are much different than those of men, and our emotional reactions are quite different. In order to understand the emotional difficulties that affect many women prisoners, one needs to consider their backgrounds and the obstacles they face as mothers in prison. Women prisoners suffer from harsh discipline and sexual harassment. Women also have unique medical and mental needs, which are difficult to address in the harsh environment of prisons. Access to reliable health or mental health care is a major concern for all female prisoners. Women are afraid that incompetent medical attention, more than the illness itself, will lead to death.[31]

My last roommate at CRC was a soft-spoken, middle-aged Mexican woman from Los Angeles. Like many other women, Rita was doing time because she was addicted to drugs. The last few months before her release she had terrible stomach pains. Rita begged for a doctor to take a serious look at her pains. Prison staff refused to listen to her, accusing her of trying to get free drugs. Many nights I would sit up with her as she cried because the pain was unbearable. It got to a point where Rita was unable to eat because she would throw it back up. We tried to get her some extra milk when we could. Rita's parole date came, and she was able to go back home. We got word a few weeks after her release that Rita was taken to the hospital, where she died on the operating table. The cancer had spread like wildfire; there was nothing they could do.

Medication is used as a way to control women in prison. Studies in the United States indicate that incarcerated women are more heavily medicated than incarcerated men.[32] Most psychiatry in prison has everything to do with control and management and nothing to do with holistic, effective treatment.

> *I was medicated the entire time I was in county jail. Before I was sentenced, the doctor prescribed me Elavil twice daily and Mellaril three times daily. These medications made me sleep most of the day and night. I would wake only to go to "chow-hall" and to take a shower. These meds were given to me throughout my nine-month incarceration. By the time I left for state prison,*

> the pills had affected my speech. The thoughts were there but I had a difficult time getting the words out. My mouth and skin were dry and I was weak from constant sleep. Upon arriving at the prison I was given Thorazine for two weeks; it made me a walking zombie. The other Indian women there told me that many of them were also medicated. After being sentenced to five years at the California Rehabilitation Center and returning to jail I was given a med packet with a small pill inside. "What is this for?" I asked the guard as she locked my cell door. "It came from the doctor this morning when he found out that you were being sentenced. Take it Stormy—it's just to calm down," she told me. The next thing I remember was my cellmate shaking me as I sat on the floor, watching my cigarette burn a hole into my nightgown. "What did they give you Storm?" "I am not sure what it was," I said to her with slurred speech, "all I know is that it was small." "Must have been Thorazine," was her reply, "the doctor gives that to all of us women, especially the Sisters that get sentenced to prison."

Inadequate medical care is one of the most pressing problems facing women prisoners. Women in custody have an increased incidence of chronic health problems, including asthma, gynecological disease, nutrition problems, and convulsive seizure disorders, often due to their exposure to violence. Moreover, care is provided with an eye toward reducing costs and is often based upon the military model, which assumes a healthy male. Consequently, medical care for women in California prisons is woefully inadequate. In addition, increasing numbers of women arrive at prison malnourished, with sexually transmitted diseases and untreated gynecological problems. Many scholars and activists have argued that the poor medical care in prisons is a violation of the 8th Amendment prohibition against cruel and unusual punishment.

Sexual Abuse

Many women in prison were victimized by sexual violence and abuse before incarceration. It is estimated that 43 percent to 57 percent of women in state and federal prisons have been physically abused at some time in their lives.[33] Any experience of sexual abuse in prison compounds their suffering. Privacy violations are an unpleasant fact of prison life. Historically, incarcerated women in the United States have experienced sexual advances, coercion, and harassment by the staff.[34] Guards observe female inmates at all times, while taking showers, dressing, and going to the bathroom. Women are searched continuously, from pat downs after meals to complete strip and body searches after family visits. Many women are victims of sexual abuse by staff (both male and female). The abuse includes sexually offensive language and inappropriate touching of their breasts and genitals when conducting searches.

Conclusion

The one thing that prisons do well is punish prisoners. Prisons strip people of their dignity, their health, and whatever self-esteem and self-respect they once had. Prisons also punish the children and families of prisoners. Prisons do not stop crimes.

Just as alcoholism has touched the life of every Native person, so has the U.S. criminal justice system—in particular, the prison system. As Luana Ross points out, most Native people have been incarcerated or they have a relative who is currently in prison.[35] In my family, it was my great-grandfather, then me, then my brother, and then my baby sister. The high rate of imprisonment can only be described as genocidal. Foreign laws that were forced upon us have devastated the Native world and the number of jailed Natives is a chilling reminder of this fact. Native people are being locked up at alarming numbers in their own ancestral homeland. Our struggle has been threefold: for our ancestral land, our religious rights, and, simply, our right to live.

For Native women the struggle has also been about the right to freedom from sexual assault, which often leads us to prison. As Andrea Smith demonstrates, colonists depicted Native women as impure and, therefore, inherently "rapable." Colonization is inextricable from the sexual violation of Native women: "As long as Native people continue to live on the lands rich in energy resources that government or corporate interests want, the sexual colonization of Native people will continue. Native bodies will continue to be depicted as expendable and inherently violable as long as they continue to stand in the way of the theft of Native lands."[36]

For the Native women of North America, sexual assault and imprisonment are two interlocking, violent colonial mechanisms. The criminalization and imprisonment of Native women can be interpreted as yet another attempt to control indigenous lands and as part of the ongoing effort to deny Native sovereignty.

The criminal justice system can be seen as an institution of formal social control used by the dominant society to enforce its own cultural values, social order, and economic system on Native people. This is evident, based on the fact that racial and ethnic minorities are disproportionately incarcerated. The laws and policies that govern the criminal justice system today are rooted in the laws and policies that were created to massacre and exterminate people native to this land. The philosophies that allowed people to use slaves to build this country and to use immigrant labor for the purpose of industrialization are the same as the philosophies used today to justify using sweatshop and prison labor for the capitalist system.

Our women and girls under correctional control are among the country's most impoverished and vulnerable population, yet they have very few advocates. Services must be designed to be accessible, culturally appropriate, respectful, and useful. We need to remember that these women are grandmothers, mothers, sisters, aunties, and daughters; they are us and we are them.

> *What was my crime, why five years in prison?*
> *Less than $2,000 of welfare fraud*
> *What was my crime?*
> *Being a survivor of molestation and rape*
> *What was my crime?*
> *Being addicted to alcohol and drugs*
> *What was my crime?*
> *Being a survivor of domestic violence*
> *What was my crime?*
> *Being an America Indian woman.*

Notes

1. Luana Ross, *Inventing the Savage: The Social Construction of Native American Criminality* (Austin: University of Texas Press, 1998), p. 5.
2. Lawrence A. Greenfeld and Steven K. Smith, *American Indians and Crime* (Washington, DC: Bureau of Justice Statistics, U.S. Department of Justice, February 1999).
3. Carol C. Lujan, "Women Warriors: American Indian Women, Crime and Alcohol," *Women and Crime* 7 (1995): 91.
4. Angela Davis and Cassandra Shaylor, "Race, Gender and the Prison Industrial Complex: California and Beyond," *Meridians* 2 (2001): 1.
5. F. Frank Latta, *Handbook of Yokuts Indians* (Bakersfield, CA: Bear State Books, 1949), p. v.
6. Rupert Costo and H. Jeannette Costo, *Natives of the Golden State: The California Indians* (San Francisco: Indian Historian Press, 1987), p. 3.
7. The Advisory Council on California Indian Policy, *The Special Circumstances of California Indians* (1997).
8. Costo and Costo, *Natives of the Golden State*, p. 17.
9. Ordinance for the Government of the Territory of the United States Northwest of the River Ohio, 1789.
10. Little Rock Reed, *The American Indian in the White Man's Prisons: A Story of Genocide* (Taos, NM: Uncompromising Books, 1993), p. 2.
11. Reed, *American Indian*, p. 25.
12. Reed, *American Indian*, p. 25.
13. Ross, *Inventing the Savage*, p. 89.
14. Reed, *American Indian*, p. 31.

15. Jack Norton, *Genocide in Northwestern California: When Our World Cried* (San Francisco: The Indian Historian Press, 1997), p. 44.
16. Sidney L. Harring, *Crow Dog's Case: American Indian Sovereignty, Tribal Law, and United States Law in the Nineteenth Century* (New York: Cambridge University Press, 1994), p. 45.
17. Norton, *Genocide*, p. 44.
18. Norton, *Genocide*, p. 207.
19. See Mary E. Gilfus, *Women's Experiences of Abuse as a Risk Factor for Incarceration* (National Electronic Network on Violence Against Women, December 2002), available at www.vawnet.org.
20. William G. Archambeault, "The Web of Steel and the Heart of the Eagle: The Contextual Interface of American Corrections and Native Americans," *Prison Journal* 83 (2003): 51.
21. Gilfus, *Women's Experiences*, p. 2.
22. Merry Morash and Pamela Schram, *The Prison Experience: Special Issues of Women in Prison* (Prospect Heights, IL: Waveland Press, 2002).
23. Gilfus, *Women's Experiences*, p. 7.
24. Ross, *Inventing the Savage*, p. 6.
25. Ross, *Inventing the Savage*, p. 78.
26. Reed, *American Indian*, p. vii.
27. Ross, *Inventing the Savage*, p. 115.
28. Kathryn Watterson, *Women in Prison: Inside the Concrete Womb* (Boston: Northeastern University Press, 1996), p. 99.
29. See Christopher J. Mumola, *Incarcerated Parents and Their Children* (Washington, DC: Bureau of Justice Statistics, USDOJ, 2000).
30. Morash and Schram, *Prison Experience*, p. 78.
31. Watterson, *Women in Prison*, p. 25.
32. Watterson, *Women in Prison*, p. 118.
33. Gilfus, *Women's Experiences*, p. 2.
34. Morash and Schram, *Prison Experience*, p. 120.
35. Ross, *Inventing the Savage*, p. 1.
36. Andrea Smith, "Not an Indian Tradition: The Sexual Colonization of Native Peoples," *Hypatia* 18, no. 2 (2003): 13.

Questions

1. What are the colonial roots of the prison system and prison labor in California? What early California legal policies affect how California Indian women are treated today?
2. How did the abuse that Ogden experienced as a child and young adult put her at risk for ending up in the prison system?
3. Why are the numbers of Indian women in the prison system so high as compared to the population of Indian people? As compared to non-Indian people?
4. Why are Indian women held for such minor violations? Is it hypocritical that Indian women are fighting for their identity within prisons on their ancestral lands?

5. What can be done to prevent Indian women from entering the prison system? How does the incarceration of Indian women affect their children and tribal communities?
6. Why is it important for Indian women to understand the Indian Child Welfare Act?
7. Do you agree with Ogden that the experiences of Indian women in prison and the numbers of Native women imprisoned represent an extension of colonialism? Why?

In Your Community
1. How does the prison system affect your community? Are there unusually high numbers of your tribe's members who have been in prison?
2. After reading this chapter, do you see any connections between personal history, the history of relations between colonial powers and your tribal community, and the people you know in the prison system?
3. What interventions can be performed in your community to assist women victims of sexual assault and domestic violence so they do not end up on the path towards prison?
4. What can be done at the community level when women are in prison to ensure a connection to their children and culture?

Terms Used in Chapter 9
Indenturing: Binding one person to work for another.
IUD: Intrauterine device—a form of birth control.
Paternalistic: Like a father; benevolent but intrusive.
Rehabilitate: To restore someone to a useful place in society.

Suggested Further Reading
Abril, Julie C. "Native American Identities among Women Prisoners." *Prison Journal* 83, no. 1 (2003): 38.
Archambeault, William G. "Imprisonment and American Indian Medicine Ways." In *Native Americans and the Criminal Justice System*, Jeffery Ian Ross and Larry Gould, eds., p. 143. Boulder, CO: Paradigm Publishers, 2006.
Luna-Firebaugh, Eileen M. "Incarcerating Ourselves." *Prison Journal* 83, no. 1 (2003): 51.

Lecturing in Indian Studies on the Eve of the Millennium

Floored by the student's question,
I try to see myself through His eyes
But cannot get past the woman in the mirror.
Scarred lip and eyebrow
Remnant, overly casual
Stance and drawl of an
Ex-bar fighter.
I clear my throat,
"I can tell you
How to get good at nine ball,
What bars in North Eastern Oklahoma
Offer you a glass with your beer,
Or I could talk about weaving, today's lecture topic.
But if you want Indian wisdom
About peace
You should avoid asking those
With scars on their knuckles."

        Kim Shuck (Tsalagi, Sauk/Fox)

Living in Fear

Chapter 10

KARLENE

Writing this chapter is terrifying for many reasons. First and foremost, I have not been totally "out" since I moved back to my hometown, which is small (approximately 35,000 people). There is a mixture of conservatism and liberalism in my hometown. Many people, including former co-workers, friends, and acquaintances, have not been very accepting and have often been hostile to me because of their own fear, ignorance, and hatred caused by homophobia. I lost so many friends after I told them that I am two-spirited. It was painful to lose them because my friendships are an important aspect of my life. Some of my family members who know are accepting, and some don't want to talk about it.

Another reason why writing this chapter is terrifying is because I am sharing some of my experiences from when I was in a violent relationship with another woman. Although this happened years ago, it is hard to talk about it today. I am still afraid of her. For this reason I will not disclose her name or share the name of the city where we lived. Furthermore, I will write not only about my personal experiences, but I will try to give objective information regarding this issue. By sharing my personal experiences, I hope readers will come away with the understanding that we must accept everyone regardless of their sexual orientation. It is equally crucial to hold abusers accountable for their actions and provide a safe place for their partners.

The following important definitions will be helpful for the reader:

Sexual orientation: How a person identifies sexually, physically, and emotionally in the way he or she is attracted to someone of the same gender, another gender, or both genders.
Lesbian: A woman who is gay; loving other women.

Gay: A term for someone who forms physical and emotional relationships with a person of the same gender. Gay can be used to talk about both men and women, but commonly refers to men.

Bisexual: Someone who is physically, sexually, and emotionally attracted to persons of the same and different genders.

Queer: "Umbrella term" for the social/political/intellectual movement that seeks to encompass a broad range of sexual identities, behaviors, and expressions.

LGBTTQQ: Acronym for lesbian, gay, bisexual, transgender, two-spirited, queer, and "questioning" folks.

Questioning: Someone who is questioning his or her sexual orientation. This can often be an exciting and terrifying time because often we thought we were heterosexual and then we notice certain feelings have surfaced for another from the same gender, which sometimes causes confusion.

Coming out: Coming out of the "closet," acknowledging who we are as LGBTTQQ individuals. Coming out is a form of being true to ourselves and is often terrifying because of rejection from those biased and phobic against LGBTTQQs. It can also be exhilarating to accept oneself.

Out: To "out" someone, to tell others about their sexual minority status—to bring that information out into the world without the individual wanting it known. Although "coming out" usually involves voluntarily doing so, "outing" someone is generally not done in a positive way.

Homo/Bi/Trans/Queer-phobia: Fear and hatred of gays, lesbians, bisexuals, and the transgender and queer community. The fear and hatred usually comes in forms of prejudice, discrimination, harassment, threats, and acts of violence.

Heterosexism: The assumption that everyone is, or should be, heterosexual and that heterosexuality is the only normal, natural expression of sexuality. It implies that heterosexuality is superior and, therefore, preferable.

Transgender: Self-identifying term for someone whose gender identity or expression differs from "traditional roles."

Two-spirited: A term sometimes used to identify First Nations/Native Americans/Alaska Natives who are lesbian, gay, bisexual, or transgender. Before white European intrusion, many tribes treated two-spirited folks with respect. The term "two-spirit" evolved out of a Native American gay/lesbian international gathering in Minneapolis in 1988. Today, many LGBTTQQ First Nations/Native Americans/Alaska Natives use the term "two-spirited" to identify their sexuality/gender.

Intimate partner violence revolves around power and control and is one form of oppression. Other forms of oppression (such as racism, homo/bi/trans-phobia, heterosexism, ageism, sexism, ableism, anti-Semitism, or misogyny) are all connected, because they involve fear, ignorance, hatred, and threats of or actual violence.

I first began to realize I was lesbian/two-spirited when I was fifteen, but I think I always knew. I used to wonder why I was "different" from others; why I wasn't attracted to boys when so many of my girlfriends were discovering that part of themselves. I kept waiting and waiting but realized the excitement wasn't about discovering attraction to boys but to *girls*. It was terrifying yet exciting to me.

I was around twenty when I had my first relationship with JT. I felt so excited to know that there was a mutual attraction between us. I always looked up to her because she took care of me when I was younger and living on the streets because of certain conditions in my home. The emotional abuse started almost immediately after I moved in with JT. We used to go out partying a lot to get away from her parents who disapproved of our relationship. When we went out, she would become angry and accuse me of paying more attention to friends than I did her. She would yell, scream, and call me names. I remember thinking that her rage scared me but that it meant that she must really love me. I thought jealousy was a part of loving someone. Because of JT's jealousy, I started to distance myself from my friends and family. She made sure that my world centered on her and only her. I was still caught up in the excitement of my first relationship with a woman.

The emotional abuse included putting me down for being Indian, which always surprised me since she was part Indian herself. The abuse also included name-calling, insults, criticism, and withholding medication. She threatened me and my family. She would often say I could never do anything right. Her hateful words ate away at my self-esteem and self-worth.

I don't know exactly when the abuse crossed over from emotional to physical and sexual violence. I do remember one of the earliest times. I was sleeping, when suddenly she slugged me in the face, then threw me off the bed and started kicking me. The physical violence escalated in severity and frequency, including hitting, punching, kicking, choking, pulling my hair, and other forms of violence. Often she would withhold affection or accuse me of sleeping around with both men and women. She would force me to have sex with her even when I said, "no." One of the most painful, humiliating, and degrading incidents was when she let one of her male friends rape me. She was paid cash and drugs for it. Afterwards, we went home and she beat me up, accusing me *of actually liking it and then she raped me too.*

I felt trapped in the relationship. I was so ashamed. Often I would think about getting away but didn't know where to go. I was isolated from family and friends.

There wasn't a battered women's shelter in my town at the time. I had nowhere to go. The police weren't helpful. Most Alaska towns and villages are surrounded by mountains and/or water, and the only way out is usually by boat or air (and, of course, you need money to be able to do so). And, in spite of the emotional, physical, and sexual violence, I still loved her. She had a tender, charismatic side that was attractive to me in the first place.

I finally fled the relationship when she tried to kill me. She severely beat me and shot at me with a gun. The bullet missed me by inches. I was bruised and bloody. As I ran outside I could barely walk and was gasping for breath. Later I found out I had broken ribs, a shattered eardrum, internal injuries, and a hairline fracture under my eye. I often looked behind me when I was walking to see if she was nearby, afraid that she was stalking me. To this day I still get severe headaches from the trauma.

It was painful for me to accept that I was in a violent relationship. I thought I deserved it or that I must have caused it. I felt so much shame and guilt. Because of my internalized homophobia, the shame was deep and profound. This was my first lesbian relationship, and I was shocked to find out women could hurt other women that way. I struggled with the fact that I fought back in self-defense, because I thought that meant I was equally violent. I tried talking to some of my friends, but for the most part they didn't want to hear it—or they blamed me for the abuse. I felt totally alone, so I numbed myself with drugs and alcohol.

Statistics about same-gender intimate partner abuse are difficult to find, but many believe it occurs in similar frequency and severity as it does in heterosexual relationships. The Los Angeles STOP Partner Abuse/Domestic Violence Program states that:

> Partner abuse/domestic violence is not a matter of losing control or managing anger. It is not a communication problem or relationship issue and is not caused by stress. Rather, partner abuse/domestic violence is a deliberate and systematic pattern of physical, sexual, psychological, financial, and/or verbally abusive behaviors used by one person in an intimate relationship to gain and maintain power and control over the thoughts, beliefs and/or actions of the other. It may include threats, intimidation and covert harm as well as life threatening acts of violence. The pattern of abusive behavior usually occurs within a cycle that escalates and grows in severity over time.

Partner abuse/domestic violence/abuse occurs in same-sex couples in much the same way as it does male-female couples. However, in LGBTTQQ relationships, the abusive partner will often threaten to "out" their partner if they aren't already out to friends, family, and co-workers. If you come from a small community, it is hard to find support, especially if you share mutual friends. If the nonabusive partner has children, there is fear that Children's Protective Services will take them away because of not only of being LGBTTQQ, but also because of the violence.

Although the majority of LGBTTQQ relationships are healthy, safe, and nurturing, it is important for the LGBTTQQ communities to accept the reality that abuse does occur in same-sex relationships as it does in heterosexual relationships. We need to overcome our denial in order to help people in need.

What can be done to provide outreach and advocacy? The following suggestions may be helpful:

- Each community, city, reservation, pueblo, village, and county needs to provide community outreach, advocacy, and awareness, through newspapers, media, and trainings on intimate partner violence in same-sex relationships.
- Provide training on the various types of oppression—racism, homo/bi/trans-phobia, anti-Semitism, ageism, misogyny, and intimate partner violence—and how they are connected and affect us all. We cannot end oppression without making the connection between violence and attitudes about different groups of people.
- Provide oppression training in battered women's shelters and safe homes. In addition, provide outreach to the queer communities, letting them know which shelter programs and safe homes are LGBTTQQ inclusive and sensitive.
- Establish support groups for LGBTTQQ communities. It is also important to provide counseling and outreach to our queer Native youth. Today there are thousands of our Native youth living on the streets who are rejected from family because of their queer status or because of violence in the home. We are taught that Native youth are our future, yet many of these youth are treated as "throw-away" kids.
- It is not uncommon for children to witness violence. We need to provide advocacy and counseling for them in order to hopefully stop the vicious cycle. State agencies, tribes, and tribal courts need to understand how violence affects the kids.
- In various Native cultures, family/extended family/clan members/elders/youth are an important part of us and our survival as First Nations/Native Americans/Alaska Natives. It is imperative for us not to exclude our LGBTTQQ folks. We as Native people understand how it is to be oppressed through racism, classism, and ageism. Why should we turn around and oppress a tribal member because of their sexual orientation/lifestyle?

- Tribal courts need extensive training on violence in same-sex relationships and how to hold the batterer accountable. In addition, rural and urban legal systems need extensive training programs.
- Crisis intervention and advocacy for the victim of abuse/violence is needed. This may include taking the victim to another reservation, pueblo, village, or to an urban location to provide safety.
- Often in abusive relationships, the abuser has control of finances. It is important to provide emergency funds for the nonabusive partner to relocate and/or start over.
- Included in outreach and advocacy, it is necessary to provide assessments for those who may be at risk, to find out who is the primary aggressor and for whom to provide safety.
- Hate crimes, which include gay bashing, threats of violence or actual violence, and murder of LGBTTQQs, continue to rise at an alarming rate. It is so important for us to provide community education and awareness about these acts of terror/hate and how they affect us all as Native people.

Often we may be asked why we need to be inclusive of the LGBTTQQ community. The most obvious reason is because those of us in the LGBTTQQ community are someone's mother, father, daughter, son, and friend. It is hard enough to survive in a world that is hateful and racist. We need our allies, our tribal nations. We should not stand alone.

My healing journey has been a struggle and often painful; however, I am seventeen years clean and sober. I have regained my sense of pride as a Tlingit and two-spirited woman. I've regained the inherent belief that women are sacred to our First Nations/Native American/Alaska Native people. My journey includes working for social change through training and activism on the different types of oppression, sharing my experiences, and ensuring that the voices of LGBTTQQ aren't silenced.

As mentioned in the beginning of this article, writing this is terrifying for me because I am outing myself. I know I will be faced with rejection and hostility, but I am hoping I will also gain allies and friendships will become stronger. It is important for me to be true to myself. And even though this is terrifying for me to share about being two-spirited, I feel an overwhelming sense of freedom.

Questions

1. What issues do two-spirited women have to deal with surrounding a violent relationship that may not be issues for heterosexual women?

2. How is intimate partner violence in same-sex partnerships similar to heterosexual relationships? Are the feelings that the victim experiences the same?
3. Do you agree with Karlene's suggestions regarding outreach and advocacy for the LGBTTQQ community? Which one do you think is the most important to address or the most needed?
4. Why is it important to include children and youth in LGBTTQQ training, education, and outreach?

In Your Community
1. How would you implement one of Karlene's strategies in your community? How do you think your community would respond to it?
2. How are two-spirited women treated within your community? Do oral stories or written documents reveal how they were treated historically? Did they hold any special status within your community?

Suggested Further Reading

Balsam, Kimberly F., et al. "Culture, Trauma, and Wellness: A Comparison of Heterosexual and Lesbian, Gay, Bisexual, and Two-Spirit Native Americans." *Cultural Diversity & Ethnic Minority Psychology* 10 (2004): 287.

Brown, Lester B., ed. *Two Spirit People: American Indian Lesbian Women and Gay Men.* New York: Haworth Press, 1997.

Jacobs, Sue-Ellen, et al., eds. *Two-Spirit People: Native American Gender Identity, Sexuality and Spirituality.* Urbana: University of Illinois Press, 1997.

Wolf

Naked, lying in the snow waiting to die
Not a book beginning
A moment exhaustion lets her believe
This is enough
Here is where she will die

As she waits and fades
Mind wandering
Body cold, stiff
Exhaling her dreams
Seeing them float away with her breath

She hears a voice
"Come on sister, get up"
"Now is not the time, get up"
Eyes shifting, pupils narrowing
Searching for unseen voices

There stands a wolf
looking at her, yellow eyes peering
"Come on sister, get up"
"Let's walk"
"Come on, I'll walk with you"

Cold joints protest movement
white snow cuts dry brown skin
slowly rising against a winter sky
not believing what she is seeing/hearing
but she knows *mitakuye oyasin*

Her relative has come for her
To take her to the other side
"Come on sister, come with me"
She follows, she's going to go home
Ready for the journey that hasn't come

"Come on sister, walk with me"
Three steps behind she stumbles

Walking is not helping
The cold added to the pain
Already embedded between her legs

She wanted sleep
Allow darkness to surround her
Let herself drown in the sea of stars above
To erase everything she remembers
About how she got here

How she came to be naked in the snow
Her cousin tricked her
Stuck in a truck moving too fast to jump
Taken to a remote area too far too scream
Abused and raped amid fresh snow

That is when she ran
He got up for just a second
It was all she needed
Bare feet running through crunching snow

That is how this wolf found her
A tired escapee
She falters again
"Come on sister, come with me"
Wolf knows she is not done

"Come on sister, run with me"
"I'll stay with you, run with me"
Legs moving faster
Lungs expand and oxygen breathes new life
And she wants to live

Then it was enough,
Too tired to continue
She laid down again
"Sister, I'll stay with you"
Wolf stayed until the lights hit their bodies

Last seen standing near her
"I am with you" as wolf backs away
A forest ranger has found her on a road they never use
Running towards her with a blanket
Thankful, *mitakuye oyasin*, for his decision to check this road, this night

        Coya Hope White Hat-Artichoker (Lakota)

ADVOCACY III

How Madwomen Survive

I come from a long line of madwomen and of this, I am proud.

Strong women
with determined resiliency,
open minds, and hands that knew no idleness.

A great grandmother who became accustomed
to the whiskey-colored breath of strangers
in order that her children be fed.

A grandmother who captured and killed
the white chickens of neighbors
for the same reason.

And a mother who tried and failed
and tried and failed
and tried and failed

and tried and failed to understand the reasoning
behind the lies of men
who said they were her lovers.

I come from a long line of madwomen and of this, I am proud.

There is a difference in madness and craziness:
Craziness causes one to twirl and twirl until a great breath sucks
her spirit home leaving her mind and body to laugh on their own.

Madness allows the mind and body to function
while the spirit dances
to the heartbeat of the stars.

I come from a long line of madwomen and of this, I am proud.

Women who folded their shame
into the gathers of their pride
wrapped them both around their ankles

and continued to dance, letting everyone know
they were not afraid to dance backward
if it meant survival.

I come from a long line of madwomen and of this, I am proud.

    MariJo Moore (Cherokee)

Introduction to Advocacy for Native Women Who Have Been Raped

Chapter 11

BONNIE CLAIRMONT AND SARAH DEER

There is no single word for rape in any Native language. Many historians, elders, and researchers believe that rape was either nonexistent or very rare prior to colonization. For this reason, there has been no traditional response to rape within Native communities. Regardless, many Native traditions include values such as helping others through crisis situations and hard times in a good, **holistic** way. It is important to incorporate these traditional beliefs and inborn intuitions into the response to contemporary sexual violence. However, working as a sexual assault advocate is not something one is merely born into—it takes study, practice, and prayer to become an effective advocate. This article is not a substitute for training (in some locations, persons working as sexual assault advocates must participate in at least forty hours of training), but provides an overview of some of the basic skills that are helpful in responding to Native women who have been raped.

Rape and sexual violence have reached epidemic levels in Indian Country. Without effective and compassionate people who are willing to bring comfort and understanding, many survivors of sexual assault can be left with feelings of hopelessness and unresolved loss. Working with Native women who have been sexually assaulted can be a powerful and rewarding experience. Advocates can help a woman who has been raped find a sense of justice, and finding justice may facilitate healing. Often that justice is not always found within either traditional or contemporary criminal justice systems because the majority of rapes are either not reported or not prosecuted. That is where the role of the advocate becomes very important. Sometimes, for a survivor of sexual violence, the sense of justice might be realizing they "survived" the rape. Advocates can serve as a type of companion, friend, listener, sister, and teacher all wrapped into one. In addition, advocates are often agents of social change who promote a community of nonviolence and peace.

There are certain skills that can be developed and honed to be a more effective advocate, but we should never lose the foundation of our work, which is grounded in ancient and traditional belief systems and structures. This chapter presents an overview of some basic skills that many advocates have found helpful in responding to sexual assault, but it is by no means an exhaustive checklist. In fact, many advocates find that the development of these skills is a lifelong process.

Educating Yourself about Sexual Assault

Federal, state, and tribal laws each have their own definition of rape and sexual assault. Most often, sexual assault is defined as any sexual behavior that takes place without **consent** of one person. Often, "rape" is defined more narrowly, requiring sexual intercourse (penetration) without consent. Nationwide and in Indian communities, most victims of sexual assault are female. While it is important to acknowledge the existence and needs of male sexual assault victims, this chapter focuses on the unique needs of Native women who have been sexually assaulted.

One of the ways to define sexual violence is to develop an understanding of what it is *not*. There are a number of myths about sexual violence in the dominant culture, many of which are also commonly held myths in Indian communities. It is important to address these myths, because they can lead to victim blaming. A few of the most common myths are addressed below.

MYTH: Women who are raped deserve it because they have been drinking and/or using drugs.
FACT: Consenting to the use of alcohol or drugs is not the same as consenting to sexual activities. A person who uses alcohol or drugs does not cause someone to assault her; rather the perpetrator chooses to take advantage of a person who is vulnerable due to the alcohol or drugs. In many instances, the perpetrator may have drugged the victim or coerced her into drinking in order to make her defenseless and vulnerable.

MYTH: Most rapes are committed by strangers.
FACT: The vast majority of sexual assaults are committed by someone the victim already knows. The National Crime Victimization Survey indicates that 59 percent of Native victims indicated they knew their assailant.[1] Sexual assault is often a factor in domestic violence, though victims seldom report this type of violence. Unwanted sexual activity is always a crime.

MYTH: Rape can be avoided if women avoid unsafe areas or other "dangerous places" where people might be hiding or lurking.

FACT: Rape can happen anywhere, but the majority occur in places that are familiar to the victim, such as in the victim's car, her home, or an acquaintance's home. Even though rapes can occur in deserted areas such as parks, alleys, roadways, it is important to remember that no one knows ahead of time that a rape is going to occur. The bottom line is that women have the right to go where they want to go and not be raped.

MYTH: A person who has experienced a "real rape" will be sobbing and should have visible injuries.
FACT: There is a **continuum** of response to sexual violence, ranging from a very expressed response to a very controlled response. How a person responds to a traumatic event such as rape depends on many variables such as her socialization, how she generally handles crisis situations, the type of support she's receiving, the length of time that has elapsed since the rape, and other factors. There is no right or wrong way to respond to such a violent assault as rape. The fact that a survivor does not have visible injuries may be due to the fact that she cooperated with the perpetrator in order to minimize the physical trauma or the possibility of being killed. Whatever the victim did in order to survive the rape was the right thing to do. Cooperation in order to survive is not the same as consent. Consent is not possible when there is fear, force, or coercion.

MYTH: True sexual assault victims will report the crime immediately to the police.
FACT: There are many reasons why a victim may choose to not report her assault to the police or to anyone. A few of these reasons are listed below.

- **Need to protect family honor in Indian culture:** There is often a belief that whatever you do in life affects the clan/family system, which often numbers in the hundreds. If the victim is already feeling guilty about the incident, she may not want to subject her "family" to further humiliation due to the gossip and negative backlash from misconceptions about rape.
- **Fear of retaliation by perpetrator or by perpetrator's family:** The perpetrator may have directly threatened the victim with further harm in order to prevent her from reporting to law enforcement. There can also be an implied threat that is not directly conveyed, but arises from fear of the power the perpetrator used in the assault. The fear can be greater if the perpetrator has relatives who are in key positions of power in the community (such as the police force, tribal council, or tribal courts). There are increased reports of sexual assault by Indian spiritual leaders and medicine men across Indian Country (see chapter 13). These men are

often seen as omnipotent, well-respected in their communities, and very powerful.
- **Fear and distrust of systems:** Many times, survivors and their families may distrust the contemporary criminal justice systems for valid reasons. Both anecdotal evidence and documented cases indicate that Indian people have experienced maltreatment by law enforcement, courts, hospitals, and welfare systems. Incidents range from victim blaming/racist attitudes to removal of children from their homes to physical brutality/excessive force. In many instances, victims believe that even if they report their assault to police, nothing will be done. This belief may be even stronger if the perpetrator was non-Indian. They may also be concerned that they will be arrested for something they did in the past and fear that the perpetrator will disclose this if they report.

Developing Basic Crisis Intervention Skills

In some communities, advocates become involved in cases that have happened just a few hours or days ago. Working with women who have been raped in the immediate aftermath of the incident can be challenging. Each case is different, and each woman's response to the crime is unique. Usually, a woman's immediate needs fall into one or more of the following categories:

1. I want to contact medical personnel.
2. I want to contact a friend or family member.
3. I do not want anyone to know what has happened.
4. I do not know what to do.
5. I want to be alone.
6. I want to do something to the perpetrator(s).
7. I want to contact law enforcement.

After a rape, many victims feel unsafe. To a bystander, those fears may appear to be unrealistic or irrational. It is extremely important to find out what those fears are, to normalize those fears as part of the trauma of rape, to affirm that this is a terrifying time, and to aid the victim by brainstorming protective measures to take in order to minimize the threat and imposing harm that any one of the fears may cause.

Common fears:

1. The perpetrator knows where she lives and might return
2. The perpetrator may harm a family member
3. Being alone
4. Going out of the house

5. Retaliation by perpetrator's family

Some of the protective measures may include:

1. Assisting the victim with having her locks changed
2. Reminding the victim that it is okay to call 911
3. Informing the victim of her right to file for restraining order or order for protection
4. Informing the victim that if the perpetrator is arrested, the court can order the perpetrator to stay away from the victim through a "no-contact" order
5. Helping the victim identify someone such as a friend or relative who can stay with her or who she can stay with until she feels safer
6. Providing the victim with other options such as informing trusted neighbors/coworkers if they see the perpetrator around the victim's home/work that they should call the police or inform the victim immediately

The trauma of rape usually impacts a victim in a holistic way. The rape or sexual assault may also be thought of as sexuality assault because as human beings, our sexuality is our whole person: physical, mental, emotional, and spiritual. When rape occurs, a victim is left with an overwhelming sense of powerlessness because the perpetrator's primary motive for the rape is for power and control. One of the most important things that advocates can do is provide survivors with information and options.

In a crisis situation, it is sometimes difficult to identify all possible choices and actions. If we can help the survivor weigh the "pros" and "cons" of different possibilities, our service will be incredibly helpful. The human brain and human spirit go through dramatic changes after an event such as sexual assault. This may make it difficult for a survivor to analyze all of her options. It is also important to remember that rape is a common occurrence in the lives of many Native women. Often, women may experience multiple incidents of sexual violence throughout the course of their lives (see chapter 8). For example, it is possible that a woman who reports a rape today may have experienced childhood sexual abuse many years ago. These prior experiences may influence her feelings about the current situation.

Needs after Assault
PHYSICAL—There are a variety of reasons that a victim may need medical attention after a sexual assault. The most obvious reason is to address any physical injuries. Medical attention is also needed to gather and document forensic evidence in the event the victim seeks to have the crime prosecuted. Survivors who

seek medical attention can also receive antibiotics for the prophylactic (preventive) treatment of sexually transmitted infections and receive emergency contraception to prevent pregnancy due to the rape. It is important to understand that, historically, many Native women have experienced negative treatment by medical professionals. Many have experienced forced sterilization or have been given poor medical attention (especially on reservations by unskilled medical staff). Therefore, advocates and other service providers need to be mindful of the victim's reluctance to seek medical attention and that her **stoic** affect may be more about distrust and fear than any other reason. If this reaction is misinterpreted and the victim is treated as though she is ignorant, the victim will be even more reluctant to report the crime. Advocates can assist the victim in making choices by providing her with good information about what she can expect should she decide to seek medical attention and by offering and providing support as needed.

EMOTIONAL—A survivor may also need some counseling and/or emotional support for her feelings. She may choose to receive this emotional support from a rape crisis counselor (not necessarily someone from her race or community, in order to protect her confidentiality and anonymity) or address her emotional pain through traditional ceremonies. In addition, the survivor may need help identifying a trusted person within her immediate family or extended family system. As service providers and first responders, we can also aid the survivor's emotional healing by **validating** her feelings. Validating feelings requires active listening and withholding judgment. It is important to provide accurate, thorough information about options so she can begin to reclaim her right to make choices for herself. An effective counselor will support the choices that the survivor makes, even if they are not the choices she would make herself.

MENTAL—Service providers also need to address the mental aspect of the victim's assault. The aftermath of sexual assault can be a very confusing time. Victims often say that they are "feeling really crazy trying to make sense of what happened." A survivor may be confused about the exact sequence of events of the incident, which often diminishes her credibility. She may also believe all the myths about sexual assault and may not even believe this to be a "real rape." As service providers, it is important to assure the survivor that her experience is legitimate. We can point her to places where she can understand more about why rape happens (rape crisis centers, books, and brochures), which can help her begin to realize that she is not responsible for the rape. At minimum, we should say the words, "You didn't deserve this. It wasn't your fault."

SPIRITUAL—At some point in time, the spiritual aspect of this violation may need to be addressed in order for full healing to occur. Because sexual assault can have such a profound impact on the spirit, it may be important to contact a traditional healer or medicine person to respond to the survivor. It is important to understand that spiritual healing is not limited to attending worship services in an organized religious denomination but can include options such as meditation, solitude, and prayer. While many people desire to have such intervention early in the process, each survivor is different. Be sure to respect the wishes and needs of the victim as she identifies them. When referring a woman to a traditional healer, ensure that this person is a reputable healer.

Advocates might also be called upon to assist survivors of sexual assault in the criminal justice system. From the forensic exam to the law enforcement interview to the courtroom, survivors often need support and explanations. For this reason, it is important that advocates are educated about the various components of the criminal justice system. The entire system can be very complex and confusing. Victims find themselves navigating through a criminal justice system marked by a complex maze of laws, jurisdictional boundaries, and authority. Victims are sometimes met with insensitive, uninformed services providers. There can be long delays in the investigative and prosecution process and lack of coordination between all service providers, where communication breaks down, resulting in information not reaching the victim in a timely fashion. The resulting confusion and frustration can leave the victim in fear for her safety, frustrated with the criminal justice process and feeling retraumatized by the entire process. An important role of advocacy is to offer and provide support to the victim as she navigates through this maze, intervene as needed, be a voice when she requests, ensure that her rights are protected and that her safety and confidentiality are a first priority.

Cultivating Skills to Offer Long-Term Support

It is not uncommon for women to seek assistance and support for a sexual assault that happened many years ago. For many women, keeping the sexual assault a "secret" has taken a great deal of energy and stamina. When responding, advocates may want to express understanding and praise for the survivor's ability to stay so strong. Some survivors find that their lives subsequent to the sexual assault "were never the same" again. They may seek help months or years after the assault because the memories and emotional pain have become overwhelming. Survivors may also experience **trigger**s of past events—such as a smell, sight, taste, or sound that reminds them of the event. Even with the passage of time, survivors may still experience the assault as though it just happened yesterday, particularly if the perpetrator was never brought to justice and she continues to see him in the community.

As with a recent assault, advocates can offer holistic support by addressing the four needs: physical, mental, emotional, and spiritual. Even if the assault happened weeks, months, or even years ago, there may still be lasting physical effects. Her body may still carry the pain, tension, and rage that came with the assault. In addition, she may have contracted a sexually transmitted infection (STI) or incurred injuries that have stayed with her. Encouraging the survivor to seek medical attention is one avenue for addressing the physical needs. Other ways to address physical needs may include massages, cedar baths, relaxation exercises—activities that soothe and care for the body. Advocates can encourage survivors to listen to their own bodies and respond accordingly to what is needed.

If the survivor never reported the assault to law enforcement, she may be feeling guilty or frustrated with herself. She may worry that the perpetrator is still walking free or that he got away with the crime. Healing from sexual assault almost always includes a component of finding justice. Even without the contemporary criminal justice system, there may be other ways in which a survivor can find a form of justice. Each survivor has a unique path and journey to finding justice for herself. Justice can be achieved in a variety of contexts, including ceremonies. For some survivors, living a good life can be a form of justice and finding outlets for their anger and feelings of injustice can also be liberating. In this regard, many victims find a sense of justice by working with other victims or by volunteering their time working for social change.

Engaging the System Response

In addition to working with brave and courageous survivors, advocates have the opportunity to work for social change. Social change work requires addressing the societal, cultural, and legal issues that survivors of sexual assault encounter. It means taking risks and speaking out about sexual violence and the root causes of sexual violence. In many communities, there has been extended silence and shame around the issues of sexual abuse. Advocates can help break the silence in many different ways, including community education, outreach, and training.

Community education is a basic skill that advocates should develop in order to address the many myths about sexual assault. There are a variety of methods to educate a community. The following are just a few examples:

- Publish brochures and leaflets to distribute at a pow-wow or other community event where many people are gathered.
- Be a guest on the local radio station.
- Offer to do education in the local schools.
- Write letters and articles for the local newspaper.
- Organize a march or vigil to honor survivors.

Outreach is another important skill for advocates working on social change. Outreach is slightly different than community education because it specifically targets survivors. Survivors need to know that there is help available in the community. Therefore, advocates may choose to develop specific brochures and business cards that explain the services available and encourage people to call. These should be distributed anywhere survivors might be (which is everywhere)—including health clinics, beauty parlors, community centers, women's restrooms, tribally owned businesses, and so forth.

Training is the third component of social change. Many times, those in professional positions are not sensitive to the needs of sexual assault survivors. For example, an uneducated law enforcement officer might be gruff or indifferent during an interview with a survivor. An untrained prosecutor might become easily frustrated by a survivor who doesn't want to testify. A medical doctor might rush through an exam without explaining the various procedures. It is not uncommon for survivors to encounter untrained professionals in an attempt to heal and to find justice from the assault. Advocacy organizations can be called upon to provide training to law enforcement, prosecutors, judges, and medical and mental health professionals. In some communities, it might take a lot of effort on the part of advocates to convince the various entities that they need training. A good training program will address myths and misconceptions about sexual assault and explain how different service providers can improve their response to sexual assault. Additionally, advocates can encourage a coordinated community response to rape by helping establish **protocol** and procedure for the different service providers.

Ultimately, social change requires advocates to constantly challenge the systems that ignore or silence survivors of sexual assault. This element of social change is not easy. Many people are very uncomfortable with discussions about sexual assault. Oftentimes, there is tremendous denial that the crime even occurs in the community. Rape and sexual assault are painful topics, and it can be exhausting work to convince a community that things need to change. Advocates should support one another and take care of themselves to avoid burnout. Advocacy programs need to create protocols and procedures that ensure the safety and well-being of advocates. In their role of helpers, advocates need community-wide support for the work they do to help victims of sexual assault.

Note

1. Steven W. Perry, *American Indians and Crime: A BJS Statistical Profile 1992–2002* (Washington, DC: Bureau of Justice Statistics, USDOJ, December 2004, NCJ 203097), available at /www.ojp.usdoj.gov/bjs/pubalp2.htm#aic.

Questions

1. Name some of the ways in which survivors are impacted by sexual assault.

2. What are three common myths about sexual assault? Did you believe any of the myths to be true? Which ones? Can you identify additional myths about sexual assault not mentioned in this chapter?
3. What are some common fears of sexual assault victims? What can an advocate do to help alleviate these fears?
4. What is meant by a holistic approach to healing from sexual assault? Why is a holistic approach important?
5. Why do you think that it is common for women to seek assistance and support from a sexual assault weeks, months, or years after the assault? What are the differences and similarities in advocating for a recent victim and one raped long ago?
6. Do you agree that tribal traditions can be helpful in developing a contemporary response to sexual assault? Why or why not?

In Your Community

1. Is there silence in your community surrounding sexual violence? If so, why do you think there is silence?
2. How would you implement some of the social change components in your community? Do you think people would be receptive?

Terms Used in Chapter 11

Consent: To voluntarily agree to an act.
Continuum: A spectrum; succession.
Holistic: Refers to a method of healing that focuses on the whole person (physical, mental, emotional, and spiritual aspects), not just one aspect.
Protocol: An accepted system of behavior or procedure.
Stoic: Seemingly indifferent to or unaffected by joy, grief, pleasure, or pain.
Trigger: Something (smell, sight, action, noise) that causes a sexual assault victim to remember the experience.
Validating: Confirming and strengthening.

Suggested Further Reading

Buchwald, Emilie, et al., eds. *Transforming a Rape Culture.* Minneapolis, MN: Milkweed, 1993.
Oden, Mary E., and Jody Clay-Warner, eds. *Confronting Rape and Sexual Assault.* Wilmington, DE: Scholarly Resources, 1998.

Conversations Between Here and Home

Emma Lee's husband beat her up
this weekend,
his government check was held up
and he borrowed the money
to drink on.
Anna had to miss one week of work
because her youngest child
got sick
she says, "It's hard sometime, but
easier than with a man."
"I haven't seen Jim for two weeks
now," his wife tells me on the phone.
(I saw him Saturday with that Anadarko
woman.)

Angry women are building
houses of stones.
They are grinding the mortar
between straw-thin teeth
and broken families.

        Joy Harjo (Mvskoke)

The Role of Advocates in the Tribal Legal System: Context Is Everything

Chapter 12

BRENDA HILL

The influx of money, resources, and attention to violence against women since the enactment of the Violence Against Women Act of 1994 (VAWA) is indeed historic, or "herstoric," if you will. The dominant American culture, for the first time, sent a powerful message that battering women is an unacceptable, violent crime that deserves a societal response.

VAWA defines domestic violence against adult women as a violent crime. Framing battering as a violent crime is appropriate. This perspective has reinforced the need for legal advocacy for women who have been battered and for their children. As women who have been battered have always known, the criminal justice system is limited in what and how it can respond. There is a sense of **futility** and exasperation among Native women because we continue to suffer the highest rates of domestic violence, sexual assault, and murder in America, even given the resources of VAWA. Controversy continues about the ability of criminal justice systems, especially underfunded tribal systems, to hold offenders accountable, much less make significant changes in their behaviors and attitudes toward women. This reality warrants a critical analysis of the assumptions and expectations surrounding the current societal response to violence against women.

Legal advocacy is necessary, but it is only effective if contextualized within the history and dynamics of violence against Native women. Legal advocacy for Native women who are battered must be founded upon an understanding of the root causes of violence against Native women. The dynamics of battering and the role of advocates in the lives of women who have been battered must be understood from the perspective of Native peoples.

Native advocates, whether working with rancherias, pueblos, villages, or PL 280 tribes or "treaty tribes," know that tribal courts are still in the early stages of development. Both the criminal justice and law enforcement systems are underresourced.

It is imperative for legal advocates to understand the dynamics of those systems and the struggles they face in order to accurately perceive their roles and perform their work. All advocates need to free themselves from the strictures of "systems thinking" and think outside the box. Critical and creative thinking that considers the needs of both Native women and their tribes, yet maintains focus on the overall status of Native women, will establish the basis for advocates' vision, leadership, and solutions to ending the violence. That is the context of our work with individual, unique Native women who are battered, and the status of Native women as a group. As in all things influencing women's lives, context is everything.

The History and Root Causes of Violence Against Native Women

The history of Native women is often distorted or absent because colonization has caused our memories and stories to be filtered through an unnatural belief system that ignores and devalues women. Femicide (killing women) is an untold part of the **genocide** of Native people. Colonizers targeted Native women for torture, rape, and murder for two reasons: first, because they were Native, and, second, because they were women. The colonizers understood on some level that to destroy Native culture, Native women must be destroyed. Attempts to destroy tribal sovereignty began with the destruction of women's sovereignty.

Before colonization, the vast majority of tribal peoples had nonviolent lifeways based on the natural belief system, usually represented by a circle (see figure 3.3 in chapter 3). The natural belief system is based on nonviolence, the relationships between all things, respect, and compassion. Battering does not occur within a belief system that acknowledges and honors the power, role, and sovereignty of women.

> "Where are your women?"
>
> The speaker is Attakullakulla, a Cherokee chief renowned for his shrewd and effective diplomacy. He has come to negotiate a treaty with the whites. Among his delegation are women "as famous in war, as powerful in the council." Their presence also has ceremonial significance: it is meant to show honor to the other delegation . . . Implicit in their chief's question, "Where are your women?" the Cherokee hear, "Where is your balance? What is your intent?" They see the balance is absent and are wary of the white man's motives. They intuit the power of destruction.
>
> —from the work of Marilou Awiakta, Cherokee[1]

The imposition of an unnatural belief system through colonization denies Native women the right to control their own bodies and lives. The unnatural belief system condones and encourages violence against women by endorsing the misperceptions of male superiority, ownership and control of women and children, and men's rights to control the environment. Domestic terrorism cannot occur without these unnatural beliefs that objectify women and justify violence against them.

The unnatural belief system is internalized in most Native communities and takes the form of a hierarchy. Hierarchy, represented by a triangle (see figure 3.1 in chapter 3), is a theory that people have a right to control or be dominant over others based on status or physical and/or economic strength. The colonizing culture created institutions, including governments and nuclear families, to justify, support, and enforce relationships based upon dominance. Hierarchies are built and maintained by violence. It's like playing "King of the Hill." People push, kick, punch, pinch, and act violently to get to the top of the hill and must continue to be violent to stay there. Since this is a male-dominated hierarchy, there is no "Queen of the Hill" game.

Colonization is **oppression**. Internalized oppression is a weapon and consequence of oppression. Oppression becomes internalized when Native people believe and act according to the oppressor's belief system, values, and lifeways as if they were their own. One result of internalized oppression is shame, which can result in Native people disowning their individual and cultural reality. Increased levels of violence, especially against women and children, are the products of internalized oppression. The oppressor doesn't have to exert any more pressure, because the oppressed now do it to each other and themselves.

The systemic oppression of people through racism, sexism, classism, ableism, and heterosexism is a result of this hierarchy. Native women are harmed by multiple forms of oppression, diminishing their ability to live safely and autonomously. From this perspective, advocacy, safety, and accountability are framed as civil and human rights issues. Identifying the root cause of violence against women as culturally based expands our work to proactive social change with the aim of sovereignty of women throughout society.

> Indian tribes must act like Indians. That's the only justification for preserving internal sovereignty . . . So if we're going to have internal sovereignty, we're going to have to bring back the majority of social traditions . . . if we don't bring those traditions back, then the problems those traditions solved are going to continue to grow. Then we'll have to get funding to set up programs to deal with those issues . . . When you set up programs, you are exercising your internal sovereignty, but the funding sources determine how the program is going to operate and then the funding source defines internal sovereignty.
> —Vine Deloria, Jr., American Indian Research and Policy Institute[2]

Be clear. Alcohol contributes to, but does not cause, violence against women. Witnessing violence in childhood contributes to, but does not cause violence. Everybody feels stressed, depressed, or angry at some time; not everybody chooses to act violently. Just like childhood abuse and witnessing violence, alcohol is a contributor to violence that intensifies and increases its frequency. These issues must be confronted. But that alone will not end violence.

The Dynamics of Battering

First and foremost, battering is a crime. Therefore, it is also a criminal justice and human rights issue. Battering and the other forms of violence are tactics of terror. The destruction of a person's or nation's sovereign rights through acts of terrorism is the destruction of the very essence of who we are as individuals and nations. Amnesty International's *Report of Torture* includes Biderman's "Chart of Coercion," which describes techniques used to torture and brainwash prisoners of war: isolation, monopolization of perception, induced debility and exhaustion, threats, occasional indulgences, demonstrating "omnipotence," degradation, and enforcing trivial demands.[3] These are the same tactics batterers use to maintain control over their partners. It is no coincidence that they are the same tactics used in the colonization of Native people.

It is imperative that advocates have an intimate understanding of the tactics of battering, especially how tactics interact and overlap in a continuous pattern of behavior. Advocates must remember that when a battered woman seeks the assistance of advocates, this signals to the batterer that he is losing control, which can result in an escalation of physical and sexual violence.

The best source of information on the use of battering tactics is the woman who is being battered. She has expertise about the response of the many programs and institutions from which she has attempted to get help. An advocate needs to look to the woman she is working with for information and often guidance to figure out how to assist her in reestablishing power and control over her life.

Advocacy

Advocates are the **biased** supporters of women who have been battered. There is no other job or position that allows for this stance. Advocates are 100 percent of the time about the sovereignty of women. We are accountable to the women with whom we work, and there should be no conflict of interest.

Being an advocate is powerful in the best sense of the word. Advocates are afforded the challenge and opportunity to make a difference in the lives of our sisters, other relatives, and societies. This work provides an opportunity to reclaim the connections and relationships devastated by colonization and oppression. Advocacy includes providing the following services to individual women:

- Twenty-four-hour crisis line
- Shelter
- Food and clothing
- Transportation and accompaniment to court and other services
- General, legal, and medical advocacy
- Consciousness-raising/support groups
- Information and referrals
- Assistance with rent and utilities
- Childcare and crisis intervention
- Men's reeducation groups
- Probation departments
- Children's programming

Advocacy also includes being an agent of social change and providing leadership for coordinated community responses and national initiatives to end violence against women. The list above can be lengthened to include anything a woman needs to be safe and get her life back. The list can be restricted by victim blaming and lack of funds and support. In addition, advocacy programs might suffer due to a lack of creativity or energy, program politics, or barriers imposed from outside agencies.

As Native advocates, we can use our knowledge about kinship and relations as a model for our work with women. We can take the time to visit with our relatives who have been battered or raped, respectfully listen and believe what we are told, validate their expertise, and then take action. Advocates assist sisters and other relatives to accurately define their experiences and **proactive**ly work to end violence in individual women's lives and in our communities and society. Advocates focus on women's safety, accountability, and social change—not the faults of women.

Our relationships with individual women are the fabric of social change. Advocates work side-by-side with our sisters, trust that women know what they need, and prioritize their safety, integrity, and autonomy. The major elements of these relationships include:

- Validating of the voice, expertise, and leadership of women who are battered
- Modeling respect, compassion, and nonviolence
- Holding ourselves personally accountable for our internalized oppression and behavior

- Believing and nonjudgmentally supporting women as whole human beings
- Working for women's sovereignty

Advocacy for Social Change

Advocacy is often inappropriately defined in the context of only responding to the individual crises of women who are battered or raped. This type of emergency response is necessary, though reactive; it is waiting until the violence occurs to jump into action. Advocacy requires us to work toward respectful systems that effectively respond to women who are battered. However, systems reform can also be reactive and will not end the violence against women—it doesn't confront the root cause of the violence. Ending violence against women requires transforming belief systems—social change. Social change to transform belief systems requires working in the political, economic, institutional, and cultural arenas of society.

Tribal nations have the potential to reclaim their natural belief systems and lifeways. The reclamation of tribal culture and ending violence against Native women are interdependent. One cannot happen without the other. Native advocates are blessed with a vision of women and our communities created by our ancestors.

Social Change, Not Social Services!

Advocacy requires clarity about the differences between social change work and the social service model that we are often taught to accept as the norm. Social change is distinct from social service. The typical social service model requires little analysis outside of the individual experiences. The focus is on individual victimization or "dysfunction," often resulting in victim blaming. The social service model requires separation and detachment from relationships, from other institutions, and from anything deemed political. The social change perspective, however, requires making connections and relationships between individual experiences, oppression, culture, and history. Social change is political; it requires critical analysis of power and control, oppression, and human rights. Social change is a grassroots, collective effort.

Social change requires a proactive stance that brings change to system structures and cultural beliefs. Social service, in contrast, maintains the status quo; it assumes the current functioning of political, medical, and social systems is "natural." Social service tends to encourage individuals to adapt to the needs of the established political, medical, and economic systems. Social service is an institutional reaction by people in power and requires accountability to funding institutions. Social change to end violence against women, on the other hand, requires accountability to women who are battered.

A social change or grassroots model of advocacy validates the sovereignty of women in all aspects of the work. Our work should move beyond the limitations of a "direct services" approach of mental health or social services. Our work is advocacy and social change.

Would We Be Talking about "Her" If His Violence Was Stopped?

Advocacy should not attempt to analyze or "fix" women. That is victim blaming and does not acknowledge a woman's sovereignty and ability to make decisions about her life. Focusing solely on women's behaviors demonstrates that we have not held the batterer accountable and that his violence is allowed to continue. Unfortunately, mental health approaches to domestic violence are still common. Mental health practice is largely based on the American medical model, which does not make connections between individual experiences, culture, history, politics, or spirituality. Mental health approaches do not address the existence of racism, sexism, classism, homophobia, ageism, and other forms of oppression as outgrowths of the unnatural belief system. Consequently, a mental health approach can be ineffective and revictimizing. For Native women, it often works to minimize battering and "treats" individuals rather than addressing the root cause of violence or offender accountability.

Confidentiality

A major responsibility of advocates is to protect and defend the confidentiality of women who are battered. Confidentiality is the cornerstone of safety and can be a matter of life or death. Confidentiality respects the personal sovereignty of the woman who is battered. Betrayal of trust and confidence is an extremely powerful and dangerous tactic of battering and is also a method of colluding with the batterer. If confidentiality cannot be guaranteed, women who are battered have no logical reason to risk trusting anyone with their story or lives. Therefore, advocates must have the ability to maintain the confidentiality of women who are battered.

Problems arise when advocates are **subpoena**ed to testify in court. There are two main reasons that advocates are subpoenaed. First, an advocate may be subpoenaed to testify about something confided to her, something she heard, or something she saw while working with a specific woman. A second reason an advocate might be subpoenaed is to provide expert testimony.

Testifying as a direct witness is a clear conflict of interest for an advocate; as a biased supporter of women who are battered, confidentiality must be maintained. It is best to avoid these situations. Once on the stand, an advocate has little control over what will happen or what will be asked. However, there are times that testifying may be possible without compromising the woman's safety if the situation is discussed with the woman and her attorney. In those rare cases, the woman herself should sign a release of information authorizing the testimony. Proceed with caution. Advocates and advocacy programs are watched by all the women in the community who are being battered (and their relatives) to see if advocates keep their word and can be trusted to protect them. Even the perception of impropriety or breach of confidentiality will become known in the community and can devastate an advocacy program. If women feel that the advocacy program cannot be trusted, more women will be battered and murdered.

Privileged communication is a legal status that usually exists between doctors and patients or attorneys and clients. This means that information shared within the working relationship cannot be disclosed in court. The vast majority of jurisdictions, including tribal, do not have victim-advocate privileged communication. As sovereign nations, however, tribes can pass laws to recognize victim-advocate privileged communication. Such laws help protect confidentiality. Often, advocacy programs are the catalyst for developing and lobbying tribal councils to pass victim-advocate privileged communication (and other domestic violence) laws. If the tribe codifies victim-advocate privilege, state and federal jurisdictions must honor the privilege because state or federal courts cannot compel an advocate to testify in violation of tribal law. Be aware that any information shared with a third party may negate this privilege.

An advocate may also be called to testify as an expert witness. This requires no knowledge of the particular court case or connection to any of the people involved with the case. Domestic violence expert witnesses can provide foundational information about domestic violence in general. They can testify about such topics as the dynamics of domestic violence and why women recant (change their story) or refuse to testify. The court must qualify expert witnesses to prove they actually do have expertise in the field. Since there is no degree in "advocacy," most legal advocates refer to their years of experience, the number of battered women they have worked with, attendance at workshops, the books and studies they have read, and membership with domestic violence associations to prove their expertise.

Providing expert testimony as an advocate is not without controversy. For example, if the woman in a particular case does not want the case to go forward, testifying as an expert witness may challenge the stance of advocates as the biased supporter of women who are battered. Each advocacy program should have thoughtful discussions about this dilemma, perhaps on a case-by-case basis. Certainly if the woman wants an expert witness in her case, the legal advocate should support her decision. However, consider the possibility of finding expert witnesses from neighboring communities or forming coalitions to meet this need in order to avoid the perception that local advocates breech confidentiality or are biased.

Tribal Program or Nonprofit?

One of the challenges faced by advocate programs is the overarching agency under which they operate. Many times, the supervising agency may present a barrier for providing effective and comprehensive advocacy and maintaining confidentiality. Many domestic violence programs in Indian Country consist of one or two women operating under the umbrella of a tribal social service or mental health agency or criminal justice department. Often these advocates have dual roles such as "child protection worker/domestic violence advocate, or "social worker/domestic violence advocate." This creates a dangerous and precarious situation for all involved by making conflicts of interest an inherent aspect of the work. For example, it is impossible for someone to be a child protection worker (responsible for reuniting families) and simultaneously be a biased supporter of women who are battered.

If advocates are tribal employees, they operate under tribal personnel policies and procedures that usually reflect little history or experience with advocacy programs, or safety and accountability issues. Additionally, tribal programs are often fraught with the negative effects of tribal politics. Under tribal government programs, advocates are often expected to act as emissaries for the employer's program or systems and are often charged with the responsibility of getting women to cooperate with those systems, rather than the other way around. For example, it is impossible to work for the tribal police department and also claim to protect women's confidentiality. It is the role of law enforcement to be objective and provide evidence to aide in prosecution. An advocate working under the auspices of tribal prosecution has the same problem. It is the role of prosecution to get convictions, and an advocate working for the prosecutor might be expected to pressure a woman to testify. Prosecution may or may not be in the best interest of the woman who is battered. Safety might mean leaving rather than testifying.

Oftentimes, advocates working for tribal government programs face conflicts of interest. Here are some things to consider:

- What happens when women are charged with crimes as a result of the batterer's tactics or an inappropriate response by law enforcement?
- What happens if a tribal council wants the names of women in shelter?
- What happens if a council member or relative is arrested for domestic violence?

In all of these scenarios, whom will women trust? How can advocates act on behalf of women who are battered without being insubordinate? It is important to find a way for domestic violence programs to operate independently.

Developing an advocacy program is a process. If that process begins within a tribal governmental agency, consider the following:

> It is the responsibility of the tribal domestic violence shelter/program to create space within the tribal structure that reflects and honors the experience of the native woman who is battered. It is also the responsibility of the tribal program to ensure that a woman seeking advocacy and related services will receive confidentiality and immunity from a tribal government structure that can be fraught with politics . . . In some tribal communities, native women have incorporated their shelter/advocacy program with the state and become a 501 (c) (3) private, nonprofit and/or a tribally incorporated/chartered organization. Just like the federal government or state government, Tribes can enter into a sub-grant relationship with the incorporated domestic violence shelter/program. In this relationship, the Tribe is the grantee and a legal document known as a Memorandum of Agreement, contract, etc., outlines the program and financial responsibilities of the Tribe and the sub-grantee.[4]

Legal Advocates

The title of "legal advocate" is relatively new. In the beginning of the movement to end violence against Native women, before there was funding available, battered and formerly battered women worked as advocates on a grassroots level. There was no distinction between "types" of advocates. The recent institutionalization of advocacy has resulted in specialization for many advocates. Though this may have its benefits, it may also re-create barriers that social change work attempts to overcome. Specialization can be dangerous if it leads to a "case management approach" that responds to parts of women and pieces or incidences in their lives rather than creating a relationship and responding with the woman to the whole of her life.

Advocates must be aware of the potential for splintering their relationships with women and weakening their advocacy if they do not consciously attempt to make connections with all aspects of a woman's life when working with her. Solely concentrating on the legal process is contrary to the holistic response to domestic violence. Advocacy is largely about making connections. In order to create social change and undo internalized oppression, ending violence against Native women and reclaiming the natural, Native belief system/lifeways must happen simultaneously. They are integral parts of each other. Making connections is "thinking Indian," thinking as Native women.

When advocates work collectively, individual areas of expertise and skill are acknowledged and used as the situation requires. No specialization is designated.

Many programs might officially use only the title "advocate," although individual advocates may be informally considered the program's "legal advocate," "shelter advocate," "housing advocate," and so forth. The difference between this approach and a specialized approach is that each advocate, regardless of special skills, is expected to willingly and knowledgeably work with any woman on any issue. That said, legal advocacy is an extremely powerful aspect of assisting women in regaining control over their lives and that of their children. Legal advocacy occurs on three levels: individual, systems, and societal.

Individual Advocacy

Individual legal advocacy can include (but is not limited to) the following:

- Individualized support
- Providing accurate information about the operation of the court system(s)
- Transportation
- Accompaniment through the court system
- Paying filing fees for protection orders, divorce, and so forth.
- Assistance in completing necessary documents

Advocates cannot provide legal advice unless they are attorneys. However, advocates can offer basic information, refer to attorneys, and assist women in filing protection orders and other court-related paperwork. Advocates can act (with the woman's permission) as the contact person for law enforcement, attorneys, and others involved in her legal situation. Legal advocates commonly help women with or find available resources to deal with divorces, child custody and visitation, and even things like taxes and bankruptcy. Legal advocacy also includes tracking paperwork through the system, making sure papers get served, and keeping contact with law enforcement officials and attorneys to assure a woman's case is not lost in the system or mishandled.

At the same time, legal advocates must be aware of and respond to other crises and concerns affecting the women with whom they work. Women can be unsafe due to hunger, homelessness, exhaustion, constant worry about the children, and concussion syndrome (the usually short-term effects of a concussion, including confusion, difficulty in concentrating, blurred vision, headaches, and so forth) that can last for months or years. Juggling these concerns is the challenge for women and advocates. Legal advocates must focus on the priorities of the woman, not those of the program or the system. Many women simply want the resources to get on with their lives. If advocates do not listen to women about what they know about their batterer and his response to her actions, or to what she really wants, it can result in further victimization. Programs of all kinds are known to impose a maze of hoops and barriers, further victimizing women. By definition, women who are battered have had power and control taken from them. Our job as advocates is to step up, with the woman's permission, and act as equalizers in those situations.

Protection Orders

Advocates routinely help women write protection orders and make sure they are served (see chapter 15). Women must learn how to obtain a permanent protection order and know about its enforcement and limitations. Protection orders are not bulletproof. Is child custody an issue for the victim? Is filing for emergency child custody at the same time as filing a protection order necessary? Throughout the process, advocates must visit with women to learn about the tactics their batterers use against them and the potential for escalation of the violence. Together, an advocate and a woman can develop a comprehensive safety plan. As far as the protection order, a legal advocate should listen to the woman and ask her exactly what she wants. She might also need to ask how her batterer might manipulate the system. An advocate should also ask the woman about her specific expectations. The advocate can then work with her to individually tailor her protection order petition.

A woman may need to have some contact with her batterer for several reasons, including the exchange of children or to get money (alimony or support) from him. Visit with her ahead of time to discuss ways to safely accomplish those meetings and detail the process in the protection order. This way, she can have minimal contact with him (or none at all). Be creative when filling out the protection order. Ask for everything—a judge cannot order things not requested.

Most protection orders require the removal of firearms from the batterer. Legal advocates can make sure this requirement is specifically addressed by the court and enforced by law enforcement. A woman should be given information about what constitutes a violation of the protection order, including phone calls and third-party contacts. A legal advocate can tell a woman how to report and how to document violations so that law enforcement and courts can enforce the protection order.

Women who are battered often drop protection orders or have contact with their batterers while a protection order is in place. This aggravates a lot of people who do not understand the dynamics of battering. This occurs for a variety or reasons, including:

- She simply wants the violence to stop and to have an opportunity to make the relationship work.
- She may be "guilted" about their children not having a father.
- She just wants a few more days to get it together.
- She is too scared to testify in court at the permanent protection order hearing.
- She knows law enforcement is understaffed, the court overwhelmed, and so enforcement of protection orders is minimal at best.

Whatever the case, dropping a protection order is her right. Advocates should support the decisions and autonomy of women in making these kinds of decisions about protection orders.

Children

Legal advocates must also be prepared to handle multiple issues involving children of a woman who has been battered. Custody, visitation, and child support issues can compromise the woman's (and children's) safety. Ignorance and misunderstanding of the dynamics of battering have led to removal of children by child protection agencies under an inappropriate charge of "failure to protect." Judges have also been known to give custody to batterers. The legal advocate must establish priorities for the agencies involved—first the safety of the women and their children, then offender accountability The message must consistently be "Woman abuse is child abuse." Work from the perspective that, if a woman is safe and has sufficient resources, her children will be safe and provided for as well.

"Using the children," perhaps one of the most powerful tactics of battering, is complicated and intensified by the collusion of social services agencies. The success of this tactic is a major reason women return to their batterers, because they fear losing their children. Access to the woman is often achieved through court-ordered visitation, where children are just as vulnerable as their mothers. Ideally, legal advocates will proactively provide education in the form of model policies and procedures and codes. Legal advocates must continually remind law enforcement, criminal justice systems, and child protection programs that the majority of women who are murdered by their batterers have done everything the legal system suggests they do (protection orders, divorce, moving away, and so forth). One of the most dangerous times for a woman and her children is when they have to meet with the batterer for visitation.

The **ambiguity** and confusion surrounding custody awarded in protection orders is one of the major challenges when helping women be safe and keep custody of their children. When a woman flees to another jurisdiction for safety, her protection order is enforceable, no matter where she goes (see chapter 16). The one exception is the custody and support provisions of that protection order. Since the original federal law (VAWA) did not specifically mention custody and support, enforcing jurisdictions sometimes treat safety and custody as two separate issues. Consequently, efforts to have custody provisions enforced can result in a separate court action, which requires notice to the father, alerting him to the location of the woman and her children. Although a few jurisdictions are considering expanding their laws to give custody provisions full faith and credit, this will take time. The legal advocate should research the court history and laws where the woman is relocating to determine options. Related challenges may include tribal enrollment issues, conflicting custody orders from different tribal courts, and possible attempts to gain custody by other family members. Legal advocates must be prepared to work with individual women for long periods of time (often years) to resolve these issues.

Privileged Communication

Generally, legal advocates are not recognized as having any legal privilege protecting the content of victim-advocate communication (like an attorney would have with a client). As stated earlier in this chapter, a tribe could adopt such a statute. Regardless of any existing victim-advocate privilege, legal advocates can and should develop policies, procedures, and protocols for their programs honoring both confidentiality and privileged communication. These would afford the program some protection and give direction to legal and other advocates should a subpoena or court order for information be served. Another common and potentially devastating challenge to confidentiality or privileged communication includes child custody orders naming women assumed to be in shelter. The court may try to name the advocate as a co-respondent in such orders, trying to compel the advocate to surrender the children. Generally, policies should place the response to these situations in the hands of the advocacy program director. The program attorney (usually acting pro bono) can apply to the court to quash subpoenas and take other needed legal action to protect women, their children, and the program.

In Court

Preparing for court appearances is another important aspect of legal advocacy. Educating a woman about the process through role-playing, visiting the courtroom, and meeting court staff can make her less fearful of the experience. A police escort to and from the court may be a needed safety consideration and the advocate should ask her whether she thinks it will be necessary. It is also the responsibility of the advocate to think ahead about the layout of the courthouse. Is there a safe waiting room? Or can she (and the legal advocate) be cornered by the batterer or his family? Do you need to request a police presence before, during, and/or after court? Does she need childcare and transportation? All of these issues present safety concerns for women and their advocates. Legal advocates rarely worry about their own safety, but their vulnerability is also an indication of a heightened level of danger for the woman and other court staff. The court system should have written policies to address these safety issues. Helping the court write these policies is an excellent opportunity to make the staff and justices aware of the extraordinary dangers battered women face.

It is not the job of advocates to force women to cooperate with law enforcement or the criminal justice system. Both law enforcement and the criminal justice system have specific responsibilities that do not include the safety and sovereignty of women. Even successful prosecutions do not always ensure safety for women. It is the advocate's job to ensure women are not used by the legal system as tools to obtain convictions without regard to overall safety. Certainly convictions can be an important aspect of offender accountability. But convictions are never a guarantee, and the chronic lack of jail space and underresourced probation departments may mean the batterer is back out on the street. Moreover, cooperation with the legal system can, in some cases, inflame the batterer and escalate the danger for the woman.

Legal advocates often work with women who are battered and accused of crimes ranging from failure to protect her children, drunk and disorderly conduct, assault, and sometimes murder of their batterer. Regardless of guilt or innocence, advocates maintain their relationship with the woman, while assuring her legal representation in court. If advocates are proactively educating the court and law enforcement on issues of collusion, self-defense, and batterer tactics to control his partner, fewer women will end up in court on trumped-up or legitimate charges.

Documentation and Evidence

A legal advocate must be careful when documenting interactions with a woman who is battered because documents could potentially be accessed by the batterer. Anything written by an advocate is considered program property and can be subpoenaed if not protected by the tribal code. When it comes to writing things down, the general rule is "less is better." Since a case management approach is inappropriate and disrespectful, advocates should not be writing anything similar to progress notes, opinions, observations, or treatment planning. This approach is unethical and potentially dangerous. A woman's file can include basic contact information, documentation of resource referrals, referral agency response (as a basis for doing systems work), and demographic information. Documentation of threats, violence, and injuries inflicted by the batterer may be kept to hold him accountable. Law enforcement, medical, and other reports can be included in women's files as they are often a matter of public record and usually document the history of the batterers' violence. Generally, do not include any information that could be construed to reflect anything negative concerning the woman.

Some advocates recommend taking pictures of injuries and obtaining copies of official reports because they work in systems where such documentation has been known to disappear. That type of situation requires legal advocates to work toward systems accountability. Find out the source of gaps in the system. Visit with the prosecutor and see what information he or she needs. Establishing written agreements, policies, procedures, and protocols regarding evidence is important to ensure consistency. This is particularly important when personnel changes are frequent. The work is difficult enough without establishing operating policies with each new staff person or manager.

Legal Advocates as Paralegals?

Currently, tribal councils are hearing that legal advocates could work as tribal attorneys or paralegals. This is controversial because it moves away from the grassroots nature of advocacy and brings up issues of accountability. Becoming an arm of the court may compromise a legal advocate's biased stance towards the women. As an arm of the court, who is the legal advocate accountable to? Every step and change made in how the work is done must take into consideration the impact on the safety and status of women who are battered.

Because legal advocates need to be accountable only to the women they serve, there is a need to recruit and train attorneys. It is important for women who are battered to have attorneys who are sympathetic to their issues. Domestic violence is certainly a legal specialty. Advocates can provide basic "DV 101" training for attorneys and also refer them to organizations like the Battered Women's Justice Project (BWJP). BWJP can provide the consultation, research, and case law necessary for local attorneys to do their work effectively.

System Legal Advocacy

The role of legal advocates within the tribal criminal justice system is multifaceted. Most of the work is done on an individual basis with women. Advocates are often overwhelmed by this part of the work. However, it is important to step outside the crisis management mode and build working relationships with court system personnel. The context of these relationships is influenced by the history of tribal justice systems. Over time, federal laws and policies have resulted in fragmented tribal systems that often lack infrastructure, resources, and experienced personnel. Unstable political environments, poverty, and geographic distances complicate the work of everyone on tribal lands. Tribal courts aren't immune to these difficulties.

Acknowledging these shared challenges as well as the shared goals of women's safety and offender accountability creates common ground for advocates and court personnel. A legal advocate's job is to earn the respect of the court, so that they see legal advocates as assets, not liabilities. Having conversations under non-threatening circumstances about each other's work responsibilities, roles, and priorities sets the stage for arranging cross-training and policy development and resolving future conflicts.

One consequence of the historic problems of tribal court systems is a general feeling of negativity. Politics, rumors, favoritism, and unprofessionalism can be issues in every tribal community. That's not to say these phenomena don't exist in non-Native communities. However, these issues can be labeled an "Indian problem" due to internalized oppression. All tribal entities can relate to this situation. But many questions need critical examination: Is this about lack of character? Internalized oppression? The imposition of an unworkable system? Or all of the above? Where do traditional methods fit into the court system? Regardless of the situation, how can the safety of women and offender accountability be top priorities?

If advocates seek to make alliances with the system, those questions need to be honestly considered. The dynamics of hierarchy require analysis from the perspective of power and control: who has it, how they use it, and what influences them. Advocates must be proactive in these situations rather than waiting for permission or approval from the "powers that be." As women and community members, advocates have the right and responsibility to speak out. Advocates have the ability and status to act on issues concerning character, internalized oppression, and systems problems. Making allies and resolving problems involves strategy, conversation, and education.

For example, it's cliché to say that Indian programs and court systems do not work because people favor their relatives or let them off the hook. We see this played out when our relatives are involved in domestic violence. How do we hold ourselves accountable as relatives? Is bailing out or justifying the violence of our son, father, nephew, or uncle helpful to them? Certainly we have not made the woman safer in doing this. As Native people, we know that when our relatives act badly, condoning their behavior does not help them in their life—mentally, emotionally, or spiritually. Legal advocates need to model how to hold relatives accountable and help them make the personal transformations necessary so they can also be good relatives. Legal advocates need to have difficult conversations with grandmas, mothers, and friends who act out of concern yet in ways that endanger everybody—endanger the woman's health and endanger the man's freedom. It is better to deal with the problem honestly now then to let it get worse by hiding behind an argument.

Legal advocates, as experts on the dynamics of battering and collusion, are usually the ones to write policies, procedures, and protocols for agencies detailing the response to these situations. Legal advocates should educate court staff about the dynamics of domestic violence, the reality of fear and danger women face, and the physical injuries and exhaustion women experience. Emphasize that women's safety and offender accountability must be prioritized. Training is more effective if you can bring in a co-facilitator who has worked in the legal system (for example, another tribal court judge or clerk of court), and who also has experience in the effort to end violence against women. Those folks may not yet exist in your community, so educating or mentoring with allies from your programs is a way to create this resource.

Many women deal with the court system on their own. Ideally, they should be able to move through the system and be treated respectfully and effectively without an advocate, but we know this is not how the court often operates. That is why training and education is so important, especially for clerks of the court. They are often the "gatekeepers" for the system. Their response to women can very often determine whether or not a woman will continue to use the court or give up on the prosecution or protection order case.

Laws, Policy, and Jurisdiction

Tribal jurisdictions vary across the nation, and often women end up dealing with multiple jurisdictions: tribal, state, and federal. Knowledge of the formal and informal operations of these systems is important. Legal advocacy includes familiarity with existing codes, policy, procedure, and protocol within the criminal justice system. Many times, documentation of policies is either nonexistent or inadequate. It is then the job of advocates to write or revise the code, policy, procedure, or protocol. Find out what the process is for implementing a code or policy. This task does not have to be as difficult as it sounds.

The first step, as in almost all aspects of advocacy, is to create a relationship with people in the system. Visit informally. Have coffee or lunch. The purpose is to create a relationship that serves as the foundation for the more difficult work ahead. Build trust and rapport by learning about one another's work routine, responsibilities, and environment. What are their concerns and struggles? How can advocates support their work? Advocates should emphasize common goals and concerns, but maintain their stance as the biased supporters of women who are battered.

> I was a pretty inexperienced advocate, but had a lot of energy and commitment. I'd gone to court with a woman to get a protection order, saw the judge sign it even. But after 3 days it still hadn't been served. I was righteously steamed! Marched over to law enforcement. To make a long story short, the cops hadn't

even seen the protection order yet. Marched to the clerk of courts office where I was informed that the form was on the bottom of a pile. They were short-staffed, had no policy prioritizing dv stuff . . . and they were out of paper . . . ! So I brought them paper. Learned to call first, make no assumptions about other people's work and ask how I can help them get their work done . . . Big waste of time and energy . . . and worse, the woman needing protection could have been hurt because we weren't talking to each other and priorities were messed up.
—(oral account shared by author)

Legal advocates will not actually have legal standing in court unless the tribal code or a judge allows it. As advocates, it's our job to "act as if," not wait for permission to challenge policy or write a needed code. As community members and relatives, we have the responsibility and right to respectfully work on behalf of women, ourselves, and the community. Just as tribes have the right to exercise their sovereignty in the creation of codes addressing violence against women, advocates have the right to exercise their sovereignty as individuals.

Lack of criminal jurisdiction over non-Natives is a huge gap in the sovereignty of tribes and the protection of Native women (see chapter 14). However, federal law allows tribes to detain non-Native offenders until the state or federal officials pick them up. Until tribes regain the right to jurisdiction over non-Natives, tribes can find ways to exercise their sovereignty and protect women using exclusion and banishment.

On issues of jurisdiction and sovereignty, legal advocacy extends to the national level. Sections of VAWA and other national domestic violence legislation that address the special circumstances and needs of Native women are the result of decades of advocacy by Native women. They are advocates in their homelands who also work with national Native and anti-domestic violence organizations to change federal policy in addition to tribal and state policies.

Societal Change through a Coordinated Community Response

A coordinated community response to end violence against women encompasses a broad range of initiatives, based upon system and societal change. Advocates usually provide leadership, strategies, and vision for this effort—a vision of safety for women. Other players are people within law enforcement, the criminal justice system, and men's programs who have authority to establish policy, procedure, and protocol. Of all the players, advocates are the only ones able to maintain biased support of women who are battered.

The goal of a coordinated community response (CCR) is safety for women and accountability for offenders. This is accomplished by education, dialogue, policy, and legislation. A major objective of a CCR is accountability of law enforcement, the criminal justice system, men's programs, and shelter/advocacy programs. Leadership of advocates and women who have been battered is key to that objective. It is inappropriate and revictimizing to use CCR meetings for "staffing" of women, discussion of women's behavior, or as a mental health or social services task force. A CCR may involve other programs such as child protection, social services, medical personnel, and housing agencies. However, battering must be clearly acknowledged as a violent crime, and the CCR as a criminal justice initiative.

Conclusion

This chapter has attempted to provide the highlights and key issues of legal advocacy. Given the limitations of space and the endless legal matters women who are battered face, legal advocates must be prepared to face (and hopefully learn to enjoy) the challenge. They must also trust their instincts, think critically, be creative, continuously ask questions, and learn. The lives of women and their children often depend on the commitment of advocates. So, for advocates, women who are battered, and their allies, this quote is offered to maintain context of the struggle and for inspiration:

> The development of this work is founded in the creation of a social movement for change. Implementing this initiative in Indian Country is different than for the rest of the country because we, as Indian people, have access to our traditions and customs. Our task is to unravel all the imported attitudes from the fabric of our tribal societies and emerge as the dream we were to our ancestors seven generations ago.
> —Terri L. Henry, member of the Eastern Band of Cherokee[5]

Note

1. Marilou Awiakta, "Amazons in Appalachia" in *A Gathering of Spirit: Writing and Art by North American Indian Women*, ed. Beth Brant (Montpelier, VT: Sinister Wisdom Books, 1982) p. 125.

2. See www.airpi.org/projects/tribsov.html.

3. Biderman's "Chart of Coercion," in Amnesty International's *Report on Torture* (London: Gerald Duckworth & Co., 1975): 53.

4. "From the Roots Up: An Overview of Shelter and Advocacy Program Development Supporting Women's Sovereignty," Sacred Circle, National Resource Center to End Violence Against Native Women.

5. Unpublished. On file with author.

Questions

1. Describe the tactics used by colonizers to destroy Native culture. What forced beliefs or systems contributed to violence against Native women?
2. Compare and contrast tribal sovereignty to Native women's sovereignty. What place does a land base hold in each? What is the significance of land and women's bodies in the struggle for respect for Native women?

3. How do advocates empower the women they work with instead of telling them what to do? Describe the ideal relationship between advocate and the individual woman.
4. Describe the similarities and differences between the medical/social work approach with the grassroots/social change approach in advocating on behalf of women. How can people in these different fields work together to assist survivors? Which model do you think works better for tribal communities? Why?
5. How does confidentiality conflict with evidence collection in courts? Why is it important for tribes to have laws concerning privileged communication to help in the protection of women?
6. How can specializations within the field of advocacy work against the advocates serving women?
7. What are some causes of the negativity seen in tribal courts?

In Your Community
1. What difficulties and challenges does your tribal court face? How does this interfere with your advocate's job to protect women who are battered or assaulted? What improvements can be made to protect the safety of women within your community?
2. How does your community overcome nepotism or the protection of perpetrators who are family members? What ideas do you have to combat this problem?
3. How does individual sovereignty conflict with tribal sovereignty in your community surrounding violence against women? Do you think there is a distinction between the two?

Terms Used in Chapter 12
Ambiguity: A situation or expression that can be understood in more than one way, and the meaning may be unclear.
Biased: Unable or unwilling to form an objective opinion about something.
Futility: Lack of usefulness or effectiveness.
Genocide: The systematic killing or attempted killing of all people from a national, ethnic, or religious group.
Oppression: The act of subjecting a person or a people to a harsh or cruel form of domination.
Proactive: Taking the initiative by acting rather than reacting to events.
Subpoena: A written legal order summoning a witness or requiring evidence to be submitted to a court.

the house of comfort

the blonde with the dark roots says
call it the 'house of comfort' instead
of the battered women's shelter
the ex-crack head with pierced tongue says
call it the 'house of inspiration' instead
of a group home for abused women
the hispanic says
'mi casa, su casa'
& though it is not my house
it is my home for awhile
though i can't find the broom
or toilet paper
it is my haven for awhile
& where so many bottles &
packages have names & initials
of women who are no longer here
leave a legacy of possibilities

the 'tracy' on a peanut butter jar
the 'm. j.' on a coffee creamer
the 'don't eat' on susan's soups
petroglyphic histories etched on
food stamp purchased goods
& they are gone

gone on to what?
back to homes that weren't refuges?
back to addresses where they were assaulted?
or gone to unknown futures
spare rooms at friend's trailers
subsidized apartments in
noisy neighborhoods
struggling
struggling with freedom
struggling with choices
given by the 'house of comfort'.

Nila NorthSun (Shoshone/Chippewa)

Chapter 13

Overview of Sexual Violence Perpetrated by Purported Indian Medicine Men

BONNIE CLAIRMONT

The elders have told us, "The wisdom and vision you are seeking is within you." Despite this advice, Indian people have sought help, wisdom, renewed health, and guidance through spiritual journeys with tribal spiritual leaders and medicine men. Within Native communities, there are those who appear to be gifted at helping people through their spiritual journeys. They are the "chosen ones," the spiritual guides chosen by the Great Spirit to help their people. These "chosen ones" live a life of personal self-sacrifice while attending to the spiritual needs of their people, often living a life of modest means and humility. Unfortunately, there are others who are misusing their positions of power along with growing accounts of "self-proclaimed/instant spiritual leaders" and "false/plastic medicine men" in Indian Country. These individuals are misrepresenting themselves and misusing and abusing the power they have been given for their own benefit.

If anything is sacred to Indian people, it is our spirituality. Indian people did not traditionally regard their spiritual beliefs and practices as a "religion," practiced once a week, as some Christians do. Old-time spiritual people/elders referred to spirituality as "a way of life." The term "religion" does not accurately describe spirituality as practiced by Indian people because it doesn't accurately describe the deeper search for meaning and the belief in the interconnectedness and relationship between all living things. Indian people recognized the importance of respecting all living things as being part of the circle of life. We accepted the circle of life as an interdependent and **egalitarian** system. It is for this reason that violence, particularly violence against women, was once virtually nonexistent. Indian people believed that causing harm to any part of this circle would cause harm to oneself; thus we upheld the sanctity and sovereignty of the women.

Being the original inhabitants of this continent, Indian people have always had spiritual practices to sustain them and guide their everyday lives. Native spiritual ceremonies are guided by nature, the seasons, and other natural occurrences. These practices were woven into the fabric of our everyday lives. From sunrise to sunset we offer thanksgiving for living another day in this creation. Our spirituality was inherent during food gathering ceremonies to make offerings of gratitude to mother earth for that which was taken; asking for success during hunts in order that the people would have adequate **sustenance**; to ask for protection during warfare for the warriors who were protecting their villages, their traditions, the women, and children; for special occasions such as the celebration of accomplishments, **rites** of passage, name-giving ceremonies for children, "making of relatives/adoption" ceremonies in order to provide extended family, caregivers, and protectors for children; for the celebration of life; for healing sicknesses; and ceremonies to guide departed loved ones to the spirit world upon their passing from this life. All of these spiritual ceremonies and more were done with prayer in the Native languages, accompanied by appropriate songs, rituals, and oral traditions that were handed down from one generation to the next.

Learning about spirits and the interconnectedness between all living things began at an early age. In the Ho-Chunk Nation, for example, boys as young as twelve had their faces painted black and were sent out into the woods alone for several days on spiritual quests, where they fasted and prayed. A young man would pray, seeking a deeper understanding of life. If he was a "chosen one," chosen by the Creator and the spirits, this young man was blessed with a vision, a profound understanding, a revelation that would benefit their people for generations to come.

The life of a true spiritual leader was one of complete self-sacrifice, always tending to the spiritual healing needs of their people. The old-time medicine men and prayer people were very humble, lived very modestly and rarely traveled outside of their communities. They remained close to home in the event someone would need their help. They were individuals who married and kept their sacred unions intact, often over a course of four generations. They maintained the sanctity of their marriages by respecting their partners, remaining monogamous, and refraining from any form of violence or abuse toward their partners. They also lived in accordance with the practices they **proselytize**d in order that future generations could come to rely on the steadfastness of their beliefs. Their female partners would help in the ceremonies in accordance with their respective roles. These roles were held very sacred and intrinsic to the wholeness and the successful outcome of that ceremony. Female partners assisted with female patients in order to maintain appropriate boundaries during healing ceremonies. They created safety for the patient by either being present when the medicine man had to touch the woman or by administering the medicine to the female patient themselves. As

Paula Gunn Allen points out, *Irriaku* (Corn Mother) is present at every ceremony. "Without the presence of her power, no ceremony can produce the power it is designed to create or release. These uses of the feminine testify that primary power, the power to make and to relate, belongs to the preponderantly feminine powers of the universe."[1] If the couple was blessed with children, they raised the children around the spiritual ceremonies so they in turn could learn the appropriate protocols and pass those traditions on to their children.

Native spiritual practices include medicines and herbs and sacred objects to be used in concert with the sacred ceremonies. Many nations possess inherent beliefs that it was a woman who originally brought their sacred medicines, sacred bundles, and instruments along with instructions on the proper use and care of these sacred objects. The White Buffalo Calf Maiden, a sacred woman, brought the Sacred Pipe of the Nation to the Lakota people and instructed the people in regard to the sacred seven rites and ceremonies. According to legend, she appeared before two scouts. One had bad thoughts, but the other said, "That is a sacred woman. Throw all bad thoughts away." She approached the man who did not have bad thoughts with a Sacred Pipe and said, "Behold, with this you shall multiply and be a good nation. Nothing but good shall come from it. Only the hands of the good shall take care of it and the bad shall not even see it."[2] As evidenced in this legend, only those individuals who follow the unwritten rules of the Sacred Pipe and do not have bad thoughts toward women shall take care of it. Others shall not even see it.

Pre-Christian Natives followed many spiritual traditions. There is evidence that most tribal societies were matrilineal, matrilocal, and matriarchal and that spiritual practices were women-centered and women-based. Within these societies, Indian women served as spiritual leaders, tribal leaders, and as military leaders. The men had profound respect for the opinions of the women in the village—particularly during wartimes. A Dakota legend states that "if the women did not agree with a decision to go to war, the Tiyospaye mothers would paint a rock red and throw it in the middle of the men's council meeting. When this happened there was no more discussion on the issue, the women's resolution was final."

The arrival of Europeans marked a major change in Native society. European Christian missionaries looked upon Native spirituality as pagan superstition inspired by Satan. Native American religious practices were misunderstood, forbidden, and even outlawed. Religious offenses on the reservations were codified by the commissioner of Indian Affairs, Thomas J. Morgan, in 1892 in his "Rules for Indian Courts," whereby he established a series of criminal offenses aimed at Native American religious practices.[3] Native people were imprisoned for simply practicing their spirituality in the traditional ways that their ancestors had used since time immemorial. Many Native spiritual ceremonies and practices were nearly destroyed and had to go underground in order to survive the genocide. Many of these practices nearly disappeared, but Indian people believe the Creator protected their sacred ceremonies from complete destruction. Spiritual leaders, in particular, fought to keep their practices from being totally destroyed by European genocide. "In many cases, a significant number of prophetic spiritual leaders were forced to advocate a militant resistance and a strategy of complex alliances, often turning hostile in the face of non-Native aggression while also rejecting any form of unilateral, submissive accommodation."[4]

Genocide is more than the killing of the physical body—it also includes the destruction of cultural traditions and spirituality. To ensure complete **subjugation** of Indian nations, the colonizers realized that they would have to subjugate Indian women as well. In that effort, the federal Bureau of Indian Affairs began opening boarding schools in the 1870s. In 1879, Colonel Henry Pratt founded the Carlisle Indian Industrial School, with his well-known philosophy being "Kill the Indian, Save the Man." His idea was to destroy the inherent values of Indian people in order to maintain the European paternal stronghold. Carlisle and the Indian boarding schools that followed were set up to break spirits and destroy traditional extended families and cultures. Indian children were forcibly shipped to either government-controlled or Christian missionary schools where they were denied the right to speak Native languages, to wear Native clothing, or to practice any form of Native spirituality.[5] They received Judeo-Christian indoctrination from the priests and nuns through the types of chores they performed and the biblical training they received while attending the boarding schools. The boys learned agricultural lessons, and the girls received instruction in "ironing, sewing, washing, serving raw oysters at cocktail parties and making attractive flower arrangements in order to transform them into middle class housewives."[6]

In these schools, Indian children received Bible lessons and were indoctrinated to Judeo-Christian traditions where they learned about patriarchal, misogynistic belief systems. This indoctrination was based on biblical passages that seemed to justify the subordination of women and contributed to violence against women. For example, Genesis 2:24: "Therefore a man leaves his father and mother and cleaves to his wife and they become one flesh." During marriage, the wife forfeited her identity in order to become the property of her husband. Such an interpretation led to a disregard for the woman as a person in her own right. The husband was then given the right to do as he chose with his "property," as evidenced in Ephesians 5:22: "Wives be subject to your husband."

Other theological ideas have justified treating women violently, such as the male being identified with the spirit and the female identified with the body, an entity that needed to be controlled, and the sanctioning of violence to accomplish that goal.[7] Children in boarding schools ultimately learned that violence is acceptable due to the many abuses they suffered at the hands of Catholic priests and nuns. Randy Fred (Tseshaht), a former boarding school student, says that "children in his school began to mimic the abuse they were experiencing."[8] Paula Gunn Allen affirms that colonizers felt that Native people needed to learn the value of hierarchy, the role of physical abuse in maintaining that hierarchy, and the importance of women remaining submissive to their men. "They had to convince both men and women that a woman's proper place was under the authority of her husband and that a man's proper place was under the authority of the priests."[9]

Colonization failed in its attempts to completely annihilate Indian culture and spirituality, but it was successful in causing long-term damage to Native culture and family and social systems. The legacy of the Boarding School Era and the long-term traumatic effects on the children who attended the schools continues to reverberate in subsequent generations. Depriving Indian people the right to parent their children in the natural belief systems of their people became the colonizers' most powerful weapon of oppression. Over time, many Indian people gradually succumbed to the oppression and internalized it by adopting unnatural belief systems. The internalized oppression resulted in the destruction of some of Indian peoples' most sacred values.

One of the long-term effects of this internalized oppression is the problem of sexual assault perpetrated by Native spiritual leaders/medicine men. Until recently, this problem has been a well-kept secret because victims were too terrified to disclose abuse perpetrated by someone who seems to be so omnipotent, so godlike. There are no statistics, no studies, and no research on this horrendous act of betrayed trust. The little research available focuses solely on Christian denominations and is either years old or statistically "soft."[10] Authentic, nonviolent spiritual leaders teach people because it is their responsibility to pass what they have learned from their elders to younger generations. The role of a true spiritual leader is to provide spiritual direction and assist individuals in developing a relationship with the Creator. Legitimate spiritual leaders help people identify their own internal source of power, wisdom, and understanding that was placed there by the Creator. Often they are called upon to do more and be more for their people. The real problem begins when a spiritual leader begins to believe he is all-knowing and the person who needs help also starts to believe that he is all-knowing. This leads to a person trusting the spiritual leader and allowing him to not only guide her spiritual process but every aspect of her life.

The spiritual leader may begin to see himself as holy and omnipotent. He may become so narcissistic that he believes he possesses the power to heal and may dismiss the fact that he is only the instrument of a power far greater than himself. In the words of Black Elk, "I cured with the power that came through me. Of course, it was not I who cured, it was the power from the Outer World, the visions and the ceremonies had only made me like a hole through which the power could come to the two-leggeds. If I thought that I was doing it myself, the hole would close up and no power could come through. Then everything I could do would be foolish."[11] Jim Clairmont, a Sicangu Lakota and recognized spiritual helper, when referred to as a spiritual leader, responds, "I am only an *Ikce Wicasa*, a common man."

The exploitation and abuse perpetrated by these "false medicine men" ranges from financial exploitation, sexual advances, propositions, and inappropriate touching (e.g., groping, fondling during ceremonies) to physical assault, battering, and rape. These spiritual leaders convince those they are helping that they are powerful and must be obeyed. There are even accounts of women saying that they were extremely fearful of the unseen, mystical powers that this man possessed. They feared what he was capable of doing with that mystical power if she were to resist his sexual advances, sexual favors, or his demand for total obedience and financial sacrifice.

There are many warning signs that a "medicine man" may not be genuine or is driven by his own need for power, control, or financial gain. Some of the warning signs that deserve particular attention include the following:

1. *The Instant/Self-Proclaimed Medicine Man*—Unfortunately, there are numerous people (both Native and non-Native) who are self-proclaimed "instant" medicine men. They have not engaged in a lifelong process of learning the unwritten rules of their traditions and spiritual practice through oral tradition or actual participation. In all likelihood they haven't received the proper admonishments from their spiritual mentors and gatekeepers about what could befall a medicine man who doesn't adhere to the unwritten rules and who uses their power to exploit others. There is a mistaken belief that one can become a medicine man overnight, as though all that is required is a sacred pipe or participation in a sweat lodge. "One Sunday mass does not make a pope. One sweat lodge does not a medicine man make."[12]
2. *The Profiteering Medicine Man*—There are many reports of false medicine men who are receiving monetary payment for their work by charging on a per person basis, with prices ranging upwards of $1,000 for anyone wanting to attend a sweat lodge or needing help. Many of these false medicine men are advertising their services on the Internet and are offering "tutorials" in spirituality. True spiritual leaders do not make a profit from their teachings, whether from selling books or holding workshops or sweat lodges. They do not charge for their services.[13] No one who truly believes in American Indian spirituality would ever offer to tutor total strangers in religious matters online, much less charge anyone

money. So, the people who are pilfering in the name of spirituality are not genuine spiritual leaders.

Native spirituality has also been exploited for financial gain through appropriation of our culture and traditions. Andrea Smith describes this phenomenon:

> A variety of Indian medicine men and purported medicine men moved into white society where there were easy pickings. Whites would pay hundred of dollars for the privilege of sitting on the ground, having corn flour thrown in their faces, and being told that the earth was round and all things lived in circles. The next step was performing sweat lodges for non-Indians. Another step was to cut out the best-looking blonde for a "special ceremony" in which she would play Mother Earth while the medicine man, or whoever had conned the blonde, would be Father Sky. They would couple to preserve the life on the planet. In short, the arena between cultures became a scene of intense exploitation.[14]

Some additional warning signs that a medicine man could be dangerous include, but are not limited to:

- Prefers to meet with you privately
- Prefers to meet with you in inappropriate places (e.g., hotels)
- Legitimizes his inappropriate behavior as being ordered by the "spirits"
- Makes you believe that he is powerful and must be obeyed
- Makes you feel special with his flirtatiousness
- Has a history of "womanizing," infidelity, and battering
- Has a history of fathering children that he has abandoned
- Makes you pay for expenses, fees, ceremonies
- Has a history of untreated alcohol/drug abuse
- Fosters incestuous feelings of secrecy, fear, shame, and confusion
- Makes you begin to feel his needs are more important than yours
- Advertises himself on the Internet
- Encourages the relationship to become sexualized through looks, language, touches, and rape
- Makes you believe that you must give up everything
- Makes you feel inadequate, even evil

The ultimate goal for the "false medicine man" is the sexual abuse or assault of vulnerable women and children in order to satisfy his own need for power, control, and sexual gratification. He lures victims, grooming them and eventually seducing them or inducing them to have sexual intercourse by making them believe that they can only achieve enlightenment by serving his sexual needs.

The effects of this type of abuse run deep and affect every fiber of a victim's being. Women who have experienced this type of abuse have reported extreme losses, including loss of their spirituality; loss of faith in the Great Spirit; loss of feelings of safety from the perpetrator, the perpetrator's family, and from the community due to the backlash of people defending the perpetrator, by either blaming the victim or not believing her; loss of learning healthy intimacy and sexuality; and loss of trust. These are only a few examples of the effects. There is nothing more harmful than breaking a person's spirit, and when it is perpetrated by someone who is held in high esteem, someone who is revered and trusted, the effects can be devastating.

The problem of sexual assault/exploitation by spiritual leaders has been a slow evolution starting with the European invasion, followed by a long history of colonization and genocide and the subsequent acculturation of Indian people into white mainstream submission. It is also clear that Indian women's sovereignty and status in tribal communities was compromised for the benefit of elevating the status of Indian men in accordance with the Eurocentric and Christian hierarchical system. Cultural subjugation was successful because Indian women and children were the primary targets of that subjugation.

This problem has many contributing factors. As discussed earlier, sexual assault by spiritual leaders stems from the systematic dissolution of tradition and destruction of inherent values whereby Indian women's status in tribal societies was compromised due to Judeo-Christian indoctrination. The lack of accountability and the silence and secrecy that surrounds this problem has caused it to reach epidemic proportions. Indian people must be ready to hear disclosures from victims and demand that tribal leaders and legal systems hold these false medicine men and their peers accountable through criminal prosecution. We must avoid blaming the victim and hold the perpetrator accountable for his actions. A conviction sends a resounding message to the community and particularly to the perpetrator that a crime has been committed against the tribal, state, or federal government. There are reported cases of false medicine men who have been charged and convicted of criminal sexual conduct that have drawn national media attention.

In the case of *United States v. Dale Johns*, a practitioner of traditional Indian spirituality was convicted in September 29, 1992, of three counts of rape and five counts of sexually abusing his stepdaughter when she was between the ages of fifteen and twenty-one. Johns, thirty-nine, a former social services director on a reservation in northern Minnesota, was sentenced to nine years in prison by Judge Harry McLaughlin. In sentencing Johns, McLaughlin admonished him by saying, "You have betrayed your standing in the community, your role as a religious leader and your role as stepfather to the victim."[15]

In a 1996 case, *State of Minnesota v. Jeffrey David Wall*, a thirty-one-year-old Kiowa Indian received twelve years in prison for three counts of third-degree criminal sexual conduct. Wall represented himself as an American Indian spiritual advisor and operated an Indian art gallery. He held art classes in his home and would often invite schoolchildren into his home to learn about American Indian culture and art. After he gained their confidence, prosecutors said, he had sex with three girls, two of whom were then thirteen and one of whom was fourteen, under the guise of American Indian "spiritual rituals." Days before his court appearance, Wall told the *Pioneer Press* newspaper that authorities were mistaking time-honored Indian spiritualistic traditions for cult activity. Al Zdrazil, the assistant Ramsey County attorney who prosecuted the case, said, "Wall is a manipulator who put on a good show. This was not a racist prosecution. He claimed that what he was teaching was American Indian spirituality. We claimed it was not." Zdrazil continued, "Wall told one of the girls that God told him she was supposed to have his children. That's not American Indian. He also advertised as a shaman. American Indian healers don't advertise."[16]

Community members can demand increased penalties for convicted perpetrators. In the case of Jeffrey Wall, a group of Indian people called Strong Hearts of the Circle, who were organized to address violence in the Indian community, wrote a letter to the judge admonishing Wall for misrepresenting Native culture. They protested his attempts to justify his abuse and to circumvent the charges by claiming religious persecution. The Strong Hearts asserted that "there is no aspect of their culture that would excuse such behavior." Their letter helped in securing a longer sentence for the defendant in this case.

In other cases, spiritual leaders/medicine men are often asked to perform healing rituals to help people suffering from a variety of physical ailments. In a more recent case, *United States v. Hebert Yazzie*, a Navajo medicine man was charged and convicted of false imprisonment, criminal sexual penetration, and intimidation. He was sentenced to eighteen years in prison in May 2003. Yazzie had been asked to perform a healing ceremony to ensure the safe delivery of a couple's baby that was turned in an odd position in the mother's womb. The woman testified that Yazzie told her to wear a dress and then during the ceremony told her to take off her underwear and spread her legs. She said she knew something was wrong, and she refused. Instead, he offered to pay for sex, the woman testified. She refused, and said he pushed her into the car and raped her. Because he held her against her will, Yazzie was convicted of false imprisonment. Yazzie was also charged and convicted of an intimidation of a witness charge because he threatened that he would destroy her family if she told anyone about the rape.[17]

Although these cases represent successful prosecutions, there are many unreported cases of medicine men who continue to exploit, abuse, and rape in the name of tradition and spirituality. Additional contributing factors include, but are not limited to:

1. Having private or intimate access to patients such as hospital rooms and bedrooms
2. Being glorified and sanctified. Many Indian people tend to put false medicine men on pedestals and forget that they are human and are capable of hurting others by not following the unwritten rules that guide their roles.
3. Operating in isolation without supervision
4. Serving multiple roles, which results in boundaries becoming blurred and possibly violated
5. Denying the power (whether real or perceived) that medicine men possess. Medicine men do wield power due to the positions they hold in the community and are capable of misusing that power.
6. Appealing to the benevolence of those they are helping by appearing to be burned out and needy. A medicine man who does not take care of his own spiritual, physical, and emotional needs may turn to those he is supposed to be helping to satisfy his own needs. Those individuals may feel indebted to him and may want to reciprocate by putting the needs of the medicine man first. Women who have been abused may be more apt to fall into this trap due to Christian indoctrination inherited from our ancestors who are boarding school survivors. The tendency to glorify suffering is consistently reinforced by images of the Crucifixion, which "encourages women to be more concerned about their victimizer than about themselves."[18]

There are many options for communities to stop this kind of violence against women. Some of those responses include, but are not limited to:

- Removing perpetrator from community (banishment)
- Boycotting him/his ceremonies
  - Don't refer people to him
  - Don't utilize him for spiritual purposes
- Don't attend his ceremonies
- Warning people about him
- Creating a list of reputable spiritual leaders
- Demanding accountability
- Demanding increased penalties
- Incorporating this violation into tribal codes

- Imposing traditional sanctions
- Creating awareness by addressing the problem
  - Tribal newspaper
  - Incorporate into program brochures, materials
- Creating website of convicted spiritual leaders
- Referring to/utilizing medicine women
- Validating victims of sexual assault
- Educating children about sexual abuse
- Consulting with local shelter program before utilizing medicine men
- Removing barriers that prevent victims from reporting

Most importantly, call upon the medicine men association in the community and insist that peers hold one another accountable. An example of this would be the Traditional Elder's Circle declaration of October 1980, where they issued this warning:

> It has been brought to the attention of the Elders and their representatives in Council that various individuals are moving about this Great Turtle Island and across the great waters to foreign soil, purporting to be spiritual leaders. They carry pipes and other objects sacred to the Red Nations, the indigenous people of the western hemisphere. These individuals are gathering non-Indian people as followers who believe they are receiving instructions of the original people. We, the Elders and our representatives sitting in Council, give warning to these non-Indian followers that it is in our understanding this is not a proper process, that the authority to carry these sacred objects is given by the people, and the purpose and procedure is specific to time and the needs of the people. The medicine people are chosen by the medicine and long instruction and discipline is necessary before ceremonies and healing can be done. These procedures are always in the Native tongue; there are no exceptions and profit is not the motivation. There are many Nations with many and varied procedures specifically for the welfare of their people. These processes and ceremonies are of the most Sacred Nature.[19]

Community response necessitates a return to our traditional beliefs, which uphold the sanctity and sovereignty of Indian women. Communities must safeguard the old beliefs and unwritten rules that remind Indian people of what could befall someone who violates the most sacred laws of Indian people. Indian communities have seen many false medicine men fall from their pinnacles by encountering severe hardships (e.g., loss of their partner/family, contracting serious illness, loss of face and dignity). As affirmed by Winona LaDuke, "White man's law was all paper," yet Indians possessed some of the most effective consequences for violations of traditional values and unwritten rules. A traditional sanction for a "false medicine man" who chose to misuse his position to abuse women and children was banishment, which historically was one of those "unwritten rules." With tribes taking back their sovereign rights to define their own criminal jurisdiction and refining their tribal codes, this penalty can be included in tribal codes, and this is being done by a few tribal communities. The Grand Portage Band of Ojibwe in Minnesota approved a banishment law in October 2003.[20] There is no consequence more serious than to be expelled by your own people. It sends a resounding message that violence against women will not be tolerated.

Additionally, tribal community members can organize their communities to create broader, more collective responses. In 1997, in Minneapolis, Minnesota, a group of concerned Indian people joined together to address the problem of spirituality abuse as a response to several well-known spiritual leaders who were convicted of sexual assault. This group wrote grants and held a conference called "Strengthening the Circle of Trust." Over the course of five years, the conference grew to encompass a national perspective, generating widespread attention to this well-kept secret. The conference has given many survivors a voice and encouraged Indian people to confront this issue.

Indian people can no longer participate in their own subjugation. Violence against Indian women and children has been a powerful tool of that subjugation, oppression, and cultural genocide. Sexual exploitation, assault, and rape perpetrated by anyone tears at the very center of an Indian person's very being because it is there where the spirit resides. Sexual exploitation and rape in the name of spirituality is a complete and total mockery of Indian traditions, defiling the sanctity of precious and cherished spiritual ceremonies. It is the very people who are the keepers of those traditions and medicines who are committing these atrocities. Indian people must rely on the wisdom within them to confront and end this assault on our spirituality and preserve and protect the sovereignty of Indian women from those who attempt to destroy it. Women's sovereignty is central to Indian sovereignty because nations cannot be free if their Indian women are not free.

Notes

1. Paula Gunn Allen, *The Sacred Hoop: Recovering the Feminine in American Indian Traditions* (Boston: Beacon Press, 1992), p. 17.

2. Black Elk and John G. Neihardt, *Black Elk Speaks* (Lincoln: University of Nebraska Press, 1972), pp. 4–5.

3. Lee Irwin, "Freedom, Law and Prophecy: A Brief History of Native American Religious Resistance," in *Native American Spirituality: A Critical Reader* (Lincoln: University of Nebraska Press, 2000), p. 2.

4. Gregory Evans Dowd, *A Spirited Resistance: The North American Indian Struggle for Unity 1775–1815* (Baltimore, MD: Johns Hopkins University Press, 1992).

5. Francis Prucha, *Documents of United States Indian Policy*, 2nd ed. (Lincoln: University of Nebraska Press, 1990).

6. Robert A. Trennert, "Educating Indian Girls at Non-Reservation Boarding Schools, 1878–1920," *The Western Historical Quarterly* 13, no. 3 (July 1982): 271–90.
7. See Genesis 2:22, 3:16, 19:1-8; Exodus 20:17, 21:7-11, 22:18.
8. Celia Haig-Brown, *Resistance and Renewal: Surviving the Indian Residential School* (Vancouver, BC: Tillacum Library, 1988), pp. 14–15.
9. Allen, *The Sacred Hoop*, p. 38.
10. Anne A. Simpkinson, "Soul Betrayal," *Common Boundary* (November/December 1996).
11. Black Elk and Neihardt, *Black Elk Speaks*, p. 204.
12. Becky Blanton, quoting John Gisselbrecht in, "Beware: False Medicine Men," Sierra Times.com (January 13, 2004).
13. Vine Deloria, Jr., *God Is Red: A Native View of Religion*, 3rd ed. (Golden, CO: Fulcrum, 2003), p. 39.
14. Vine Deloria, Jr. *God is Red*, p. 39.
15. Donna Halversen, "Indian Medicine Practitioner Gets 9 Years for Abuse," *Star Tribune*, December 20, 1992.
16. Ben Chanco, "Indian Shaman Pleads Guilty to Having Sex with Teenagers," *Pioneer Press*, May 16, 1996.
17. "Poser Medicine Man Convicted in Rape Gets 18 Years," *Gallup Independent*, January 2003.
18. Joanne Carlson Browne and Rebecca Parker, "For God So Loved the World," in *Violence Against Women and Children: A Christian Theological Sourcebook*, Carol J. Adams and Marie M. Fortune, eds. (New York: Continuum, 1995).
19. Communique No. 1 (Northern Cheyenne Nation Rosebud Creek Two Moons Camp, Montana, October 5, 1980), available at http://www.twocircles.org/comque_01.html.
20. *Grand Forks News*, December 6, 2003.

Questions

1. What are some general traits or values that precolonial medicine people displayed? How can you use these indicators to tell if someone is not a real medicine man?
2. How did the history of colonization and boarding schools effect the role of Native spiritual leaders within their communities? What attitudes have changed as far as how the spiritual leader views himself?
3. Why do you think there is such a prevalence of "instant" or self-proclaimed medicine men, both Native and non-Native? What is their effect on Native communities?
4. Why are the warning signs of sexual assault by a medicine man so difficult to identify?
5. How can tribes hold medicine men perpetrators of sexual assault accountable for their crimes? How can they assist in the prevention of assaults? What about in urban settings versus reservations?
6. Why do you think women who have been previously abused are more apt to be abused by false medicine men?

In Your Community

1. What is the role of women in healing ceremonies and spiritual guidance in your community? Are there any stories or anecdotes that you have heard that demonstrate this?
2. What point of view is Clairmont writing from? How are her descriptions of medicine men similar or different from what you know of medicine people in your community?
3. What has your community done to support victims of sexual assault by medicine men? If there are no examples from your community, what do you think are effective steps a tribal government can take to show that it takes these issues seriously?

Terms Used in Chapter 13

Egalitarian: Promoting equal political, economic, social, and civil rights for all people.
Proselytize: To induce someone to convert to one's own religious faith.
Rites: A ceremonial act or series of acts.
Subjugation: The act of bringing under control; conquering.
Sustenance: Something, especially food, that sustains life or health.

Suggested Further Reading

Smith, Andrea. *Conquest: Sexual Violence and American Indian Genocide* (Cambridge, MA: South End Press, 2005).

Did I Know Your Dad?

Ponytail, brown wide eyes, muscles tensing, you ask,
"Did you know my dad?" I do not respond, mind flexing,
I remember what I don't want to see—his stocky short body,
beer in hand, full wavy hair, like yours, dull probing stare . . .

Brown veiny hands, held me tight one night, on the office floor,
eighteen years old, squirming youth's confusion, hardened and numb,
he ripped at me, stale breath sucking trust through a hole in my universe—
piercing Christmas Eve's to come. My boyfriend joking uncomfortably
in the next room at a party he never wanted to attend, me, fitting in,
employed insecurity, gasping for pride, fighting insides, thrusts that
pinned me raw against my boss's desk, and out of upper-hand desperation,
I ask for more.

Your pained youthful face studies my deadened look, asking again,
Did I know your dad? And I say, "I remember him," and your slightly relieved
smile lifts your doleful eyes to mine, and I look away, mumbling, "How is he?"
But I don't hear your response in that eternal second. My conscience falling,
I hear "mother" and nausea building I query, "Where is she?" You reply,
"She moved back to the village"—my body soaring through memory, of bizarre
misgivings, my abused youth seeking familiar in a mind rape of lust,
with your dad.

A six-year-old girl's sprawling passage on dirty carpets and stained
sheets of a neighbor's bedroom—my continual journey—when I met your dad,
when I met your dad, looking at me in the same graspable way. It was familiar.
His gross clumsy efforts, loose belly bumping me, mouth tearing blood from
Me. I knew your dad. And, you tell me "He died." Strangely, I cried. Not in
front
of you. I just went home. And I cried.

      Diane E. Benson (Tlingit)

TRIBAL LEGAL SYSTEMS   IV

Survival

The ghosts haunt me
Spirits taken, souls removed
—Culture, families, beliefs—
We are a nation within a nation

Beaten down, forced to submission
Children cry out in the night, unheard
—Education, knowledge, power—
We have risen to a new level of strength

We are a nation within a nation
Souls restored, spirits renewed
No longer taking the back seat
Knowledge is power, and now we know

Our voices will be heard—We are women
A force with the ability to give life
The ability to make a difference
For ourselves, for our children
For our people

    Venus St. Martin (Colville/Nez Perce)

Jurisdiction and Violence Against Native Women

Chapter 14

B. J. JONES

One of the most effective ways to prevent future violence against Native women is to hold offenders accountable through the various criminal justice systems that exist in Indian communities. Tribal, state, and sometimes even federal courts play various roles in assuring that those persons who perpetrate violence against Native women are prosecuted, punished, and reformed in accordance with the law. When the law is blurred as to who has the responsibility and authority to prosecute and punish perpetrators of domestic violence against Native women, the security of women is compromised and the legal system is diminished in the eyes of both victims and offenders. This chapter is an attempt to explain what role the federal, state, and tribal justice systems play in protecting Native women who are the victims of domestic violence and sexual assault.

Unfortunately, many of the rules described in this chapter will appear complicated and legalistic, and sometimes void of common sense. However, having a basic understanding of them is critical to assuring safety for victims of domestic violence and sexual assault and holding perpetrators of domestic violence accountable.

Jurisdiction in General Terms

What Is "Jurisdiction"?

The authority of a government to prosecute and punish a person who commits domestic violence depends upon which government has "jurisdiction" over the act of domestic violence. Jurisdiction is a simple concept that Indian tribes recognized from time immemorial: when a person lives or travels within a community, that person is subject to the laws of that community and will be punished for violating those laws in accordance with the values of that community. A person cannot, for example, claim that he or she is not subject to the laws of a particular community by asserting that he or she had no voice in deciding what particular laws should be upheld. Therefore, an Indian from the Blackfeet reservation in Montana who marries a Navajo wife and lives among the Navajo should, it would seem, be subject to the values and community norms of the Navajo people and should not be able to claim that he is not because he has no right to vote for the leaders of the Navajo nation. This would also seem to be a fair proposition for a non-Indian who marries a Navajo woman and lives in the Navajo community. Unfortunately, as this chapter will demonstrate, because Indian tribal courts have been stripped of authority over certain persons, the basic rule that a person who lives within a community is subject to that community's values and punishments does not accurately describe jurisdiction in Indian Country. This makes it both confounding and potentially dangerous for victims of domestic violence when it is unclear who has the authority to arrest and punish a perpetrator of domestic violence.

Types of Jurisdiction: Personal, Subject Matter, and Territorial
The authority to impose laws upon persons within a certain territory and the right to punish those persons who violate those laws is referred to as "jurisdiction." Jurisdiction may refer to authority over a particular type of violation—such as murder, rape, or an assault—and also refers to the authority over a person who commits the offense. The first type of jurisdiction is referred to as "subject matter jurisdiction," and the second type of jurisdiction is referred to as "personal jurisdiction." The last element of jurisdiction is called "territorial jurisdiction" and refers to authority over the geographic area where the crime occurred.

Traditional Concepts of Jurisdiction
Jurisdictional concepts are not foreign to Indian tribes because tribes utilized these core principles among themselves for centuries prior to the arrival of the Europeans. For example, it was common among the Lakota for a man who married into another band to go and live among that band with his wife and her family. By his actions, he became subject to the laws of that band or the "jurisdiction" of that band and could be punished by them if he mistreated his wife. If his behavior became so intolerable that it threatened the welfare of the entire community, he could be banished from that community. The notion of respect for the laws and customs of other peoples was also a common denominator amongst Indian tribes. So, if we go back to the example of the Lakota man marrying into another band,

if the band of his wife banished him for mistreating her in some way, they would oftentimes punish him in a manner so that other communities would recognize his inappropriate behavior, such as cutting his nose. When he returned to his band or went to another Indian nation that stigma would go with him and the other bands would acknowledge the wrongfulness of this behavior. This was the Lakota notion of "full faith and credit" (see chapter 16).

If Indian tribes were permitted by the U.S. government to apply their traditional concepts of "jurisdiction" to the problem of domestic violence within their communities, the result would be that Indian communities would be vested with their **inherent rights**. This includes the right to impose their values in order to protect Native women within their territories, without regard to the race of the perpetrator or type of crime he committed. This is not the rule, however. Instead, jurisdiction in Indian communities is too often based upon the type of crime committed, the racial identity of the perpetrator or victim, and whether any federal laws restrict tribal or state authority. Tribes are permitted to impose their laws upon perpetrators of domestic violence in some situations, while in others they are absolutely barred. In some situations, both the federal and tribal governments may have jurisdiction to punish offenders, while in others only the state courts may punish offenders. This mishmash of jurisdictional rules is confusing even for the lawyers and judges who are charged with confronting domestic violence. So, it is understandable that victims of crime and their advocates become confounded about which court can provide protection and redress for a victim of domestic violence.

Civil Versus Criminal Jurisdiction

In domestic violence and sexual assault cases, courts may become involved in several different ways. When a perpetrator of domestic violence or sexual assault is charged with a crime, the court exercises criminal jurisdiction over the prosecution of that offender. Criminal jurisdiction involves a tribal, state, or federal government filing a criminal charge against an offender and the respective government prosecutor trying the case to either a judge or jury. In almost all tribal, state, and federal jurisdictions, the government must establish the offender's guilt beyond a reasonable doubt. The offender (defendant) also has certain rights granted him by the federal Constitution (in federal prosecutions), a state constitution (in a state prosecution), or the tribal constitution and federal Indian Civil Rights Act[1] (in a tribal prosecution). The victim is not responsible for bringing the case to trial or procuring witnesses, but her cooperation is often important to the government in successfully prosecuting the offender.

The recent Kobe Bryant case in Colorado illustrates the differences in criminal and civil cases. In that case the State of Colorado was prosecuting Bryant for the charge of rape, while the victim of that rape filed her own civil suit against him and asked for money damages to compensate her for his actions. When the criminal case was dismissed by the state, the victim continued to pursue her civil claim against him.

Civil jurisdiction refers to a suit between two private persons or parties where the government is not involved. In domestic violence and sexual assault cases, the civil jurisdiction of a court is used, for example, by a victim to obtain a domestic violence protection order or to sue her offender for money damages. Even when the prosecutor declines to prosecute a case, the victim herself can file her own civil suit. The burden of proving that the domestic violence or sexual assault has occurred is different in civil cases because the victim need only show that the act occurred by a **preponderance** of the evidence. Such evidence is established when the victim can show that it is more likely than not that the domestic violence occurred.

This chapter is an attempt to clarify some of the confusing rules regarding jurisdiction over domestic violence in Indian Country so that victims, advocates, and others who deal with this serious problem will understand who has the authority to hold offenders accountable and to provide safety for victims. This chapter is not a substitute for a thorough review of tribal, state, and federal laws regarding domestic violence that may apply to your communities. However, it does discuss some of the general principles that govern this issue and will aid the reader in identifying which government has the authority to arrest, prosecute, and punish offenders and to issue civil protection orders to Native women who are victims of domestic violence.

Federal Jurisdiction over Domestic Violence Committed Against Native Women

Why Do the Federal Courts Have Authority over Some Indian Reservations to Respond to Domestic Violence and Sexual Assault?

In most non-Native communities, the U.S. (federal) government and its court system are rarely involved in responding to domestic violence. This is because the U.S. government has very limited criminal jurisdiction and the problems associated with domestic violence are generally left to local, state, and tribal governments to combat. The federal government does provide substantial funding for states and tribes to develop and enact laws, provide protection for victims of domestic violence, and arrest and hold offenders accountable. This funding is intended to strengthen tribal and state responses, not to substitute for local community responses.

In some Indian communities, however, the U.S. government, through its prosecutors (U.S. attorneys) and court systems, does have some authority to directly intervene to prosecute domestic violence offenses. This is due to the special relationship between Indian tribes and the U.S. government. This special relationship, oftentimes referred to as a **trust relationship**, allows the U.S. government to assist Indian tribes in providing law and order on certain Indian reservations. Federal authority over domestic violence crimes committed on some Indian reservations is derived from three principal federal statutes that grant to the U.S. government criminal jurisdiction over certain types of crime. These laws apply on those reservations that are in states that have not been given jurisdiction over crimes in Indian Country and when the crime has occurred in Indian Country. "Indian Country" is a legal term defined in federal law, 18 U.S.C. § 1151, to include all lands within Indian reservations, trust lands that lie outside of Indian reservations, and "dependent Indian communities," which are lands where the U.S. government has a requirement to supervise the area where substantial populations of Native people live. If the state has been given jurisdiction through PL 280, the rules that follow involving federal criminal jurisdiction may not apply.

Federal Laws That Protect Women Against Domestic Violence and Sexual Assault in Indian Country

The principal federal law that gives the U.S. courts certain jurisdiction over crimes committed on Indian lands is called the Major Crimes Act.[2] This federal law was enacted after the U.S. Supreme Court declared in the late 1800s that Indian tribes had the exclusive authority to punish Indians who committed crimes against other Indians within the tribe's lands.[3] That case involved Crow Dog and a murder committed on what is now the Rosebud Sioux Indian Reservation. When the tribe imposed a traditional sanction of **restitution** on Crow Dog, the U.S. court stepped in and prosecuted Crow Dog for murder. Crow Dog, however, successfully argued to the U.S. Supreme Court that the federal court had no "subject matter" jurisdiction over the crime because the tribe retained its right to punish its own members for crimes and Congress had not given the federal courts any authority.[4]

Congress then passed a law that permits the federal government to prosecute any Indian who commits one of fourteen **enumerate**d crimes within an Indian community against any person, Indian or non-Indian.[5] There is no definition of "Indian" under this federal law, or any other federal law pertaining to criminal conduct on Indian reservations. Therefore, the U.S. Supreme Court has adopted a definition of Indian that requires proof that the person has some degree of Indian blood and is considered by the community as an Indian.[6] The specific crimes that the United States may prosecute under the Major Crimes Act that relate to domestic violence include murder, manslaughter, kidnapping, maiming, rape, assault with a deadly weapon, and assault resulting in serious bodily injury.

Many acts of domestic violence do not fit within the definitions of these crimes, because they often involve relatively "less serious" kinds of violence. For example, it is very unlikely that the United States would prosecute an assault where a man strikes a woman breaking her nose because such a crime does not rise to the legal level of "serious bodily injury." In that situation, it is up to the Indian tribe where that crime occurred to prosecute the defendant if he is an Indian person. However, advocates and others who are concerned about assuring prosecutions of those persons who commit domestic violence against Native women should familiarize themselves with the definitions of the crimes covered by the Major Crimes Act because many times the conduct reported could be prosecuted by the United States.

Rape, for example, can be prosecuted under the federal system if sexual relations are forced or the victim is too impaired by mental or physical incapacity to consent. Rape is an extremely underprosecuted crime in many Indian communities because of the low incidences of reporting, and also because it generally does not involve independent witnesses and sometimes involves intoxicated victims, which make the cases difficult to prove "beyond a reasonable doubt." The mere fact that a woman was intoxicated when the crime occurred should not preclude a prosecution in the federal system, because intoxication can be used to show that the victim was incapable of consenting. There are numerous court cases involving intoxicated victims where the courts have upheld convictions.

Another federal law, the General Crimes Act[7] (also referred to as the Indian Country Crimes Act) gives the United States jurisdiction over other types of domestic violence in Indian Country. This law applies all the United States criminal laws to interracial crimes in Indian Country, including the crimes of murder, manslaughter, rape, assault, and other serious crimes. It applies when a non-Indian commits a crime against an Indian or when an Indian commits a crime against a non-Indian and the crime is not enumerated in the Major Crimes Act. The only exception to the United States prosecuting an Indian under the General Crimes Act for committing a crime against a non-Indian is that the United States may not have jurisdiction if the tribe has already punished the Indian for the offense.[8] Congress by statute restricted U.S. courts' jurisdiction over non-Major Crimes Act violations where the tribe has already punished an Indian offender.

Impact of Federal Prosecution on Tribal Court Action

Even if a crime of domestic violence appears to be serious enough to be prosecuted by the United States, an Indian tribe should continue to prosecute the case. In many situations, the United States delays prosecution. The tribal system is often the first criminal justice system to respond to the violence. An offender should not be released from the tribal jail to await a federal charge merely because the offense is serious enough to warrant federal charges. This endangers a victim's safety and may result in further victimization. In addition, there is no guarantee that the United States will prosecute an offender, even if the crime seems to meet the definition of one of the offenses under the Major Crimes Act. The tribe should pursue the domestic violence charge even if it may eventually be prosecuted in the federal system. An Indian tribe can prosecute an Indian offender for a crime covered by the Major Crimes Act and the United States can prosecute the same offender. Double jeopardy prevents one government from prosecuting or punishing a person twice for the same conduct. However, double jeopardy does not apply to separate governments (state and tribe or federal government and tribe) prosecuting the same offender for the same conduct. The Supreme Court in *U.S. v. Lara*[9] recently upheld the authority of tribes to prosecute nonmember Indians and held that such prosecutions do not violate the Double Jeopardy Clause, even though the United States may also prosecute.

Table 14.1. Criminal Jurisdictional Chart

	Criminal Jurisdictional Chart in Areas Where Jurisdiction Not Conferred to State	
Offender	Victim	Jurisdiction
Non-Indian	Non-Indian	State jurisdiction is exclusive of federal and tribal jurisdiction.
Non-Indian	Indian	Federal jurisdiction under 18 U.S.C. § 1152 is exclusive of state and tribal jurisdiction.
Indian	Non-Indian	If listed in 18 U.S.C. § 1153, there is federal jurisdiction, exclusive of the state, but probably not of the tribe. If the listed offense is not otherwise defined and punished by federal law applicable in the special maritime and territorial jurisdiction of the United States, state law is assimilated. If not listed in 18 U.S.C. § 1153, there is federal jurisdiction, exclusive of the state, but not of the tribe, under 18 U.S.C. § 1152. If the offense is not defined and punished by a statute applicable within the special maritime and territorial jurisdiction of the United States, state law is assimilated under 18 U.S.C. § 13.
Indian	Indian	If the offense is listed in 18 U.S.C. § 1153, there is federal jurisdiction, exclusive of the state, but probably not of the tribe. If the listed offense is not otherwise defined and punished by federal law applicable in the special maritime and territorial jurisdiction of the United States, state law is assimilated. See section 1153(b). If not listed in 18 U.S.C. § 1153, tribal jurisdiction is exclusive.

Source: U.S. Department of Justice, U.S. Attorneys, "Jurisdictional Summary," *Criminal Resource Manual*, Title 9, p. 689.

If the crime of domestic violence is not serious enough to be included under the Major Crimes Act, and it is committed by one Indian against another Indian on an Indian reservation, the tribal courts have exclusive jurisdiction to prosecute the offender, unless the state has been given jurisdiction under PL 280, which is discussed later in this chapter.

Domestic Violence and Sexual Assault by Non-Indians Against Indians: Who Has Jurisdiction?

The General Crimes Act[10] is extremely important for holding non-Indians who commit domestic violence against Native women legally accountable for their actions. According to a 1999 Department of Justice report,[11] 70 percent of the domestic violence committed against Native women was committed by non-Indians. Although this statistic may not be true for all Indian reservations, it does indicate that many Native women face great danger in interracial relationships and the legal system must be prepared to respond when such violence occurs. The obligation of the federal and state governments is especially pertinent because of a U.S. Supreme Court decision *Oliphant v. Suquamish Tribe*,[12] which prohibits tribal criminal jurisdiction over non-Indians. In the absence of any criminal jurisdiction over non-Indians, tribes must rely upon their counterparts in the federal and state justice systems to assure protection for their members and accountability for non-Indian offenders. For example, if a non-Indian assaults a Native woman and seriously injures her on a reservation, the United States can prosecute the non-Indian under the General Crimes Act and use any federal law that exists that defines assault. Even if no federal law exists defining the crime, the United States could prosecute the non-Indian using state law under another federal law called the Assimilative Crimes Act.[13]

State law could be used by the federal government to prosecute violations of protection orders involving non-Indian offenders. The federal full faith and credit provision, passed as part of the Violence Against Women Act (see chapter 16), compels both states and tribes to punish persons who violate other court's protection orders within their jurisdictions in the same manner as they would deal with a violation of their own protection orders. Because of the *Oliphant* decision, however, tribes cannot fully comply with this law, as they do not have the power to criminally prosecute non-Indians. However, the United States, through the General Crimes Act and Assimilative Crimes Act, could prosecute the non-Indian offender using state law relating to violation of protection orders. Similarly, if a non-Indian commits a crime such as simple assault against an Indian woman on a reservation, the United States should prosecute the case under the General Crimes Act. Even though the crime may appear minor to the United States, no crime of domestic violence is minor in the eyes of a victim who faces the daily perils of being in a violent relationship.

If a case is covered by the General Crimes Act, the state courts most likely lack the authority to prosecute the crime. This is especially true if the perpetrator is an Indian. If the perpetrator is a non-Indian and the victim is Indian, federal law seems to bar state court authority over that non-Indian, but many state criminal justice systems continue to punish non-Indians who commit domestic violence against Indian women on reservations. Although this practice is questionable, it should not be discouraged if the federal system is not responding to the types of crimes the state is prosecuting. There must be some blanket of security for a victim of domestic violence. The defendant who is prosecuted in state court can raise any defense he has through his attorney. Law enforcement officers, advocates, and others who strive to protect women from domestic violence in Indian Country should not be charged with resolving all the complicated jurisdictional scenarios that may arise in prosecuting domestic violence cases.

Domestic Violence and Sexual Assault Crimes Involving Crossing Indian Country Borders

Another type of case where the United States has jurisdiction over domestic violence crimes that occur on Indian reservations are those crimes that concern crossing Indian reservation borders with the intent to commit domestic violence or violate a domestic violence protection order. This category of crime was created as part of the Violence Against Women Act[14] to deal with domestic violence offenders who cross from one state to another or from state to reservation to commit crimes of violence or to violate an existing protection order. Since these crimes involve more than one jurisdiction, the states and tribes could have problems apprehending the perpetrators or bringing them to justice. For example, if a tribal member of the Navajo nation receives a domestic violence protection order against her boyfriend in a state court in Tucson, Arizona, and returns to the Navajo reservation and then her former boyfriend follows her from Tucson to the Navajo reservation and violates the protection order, this would be a federal crime. However, advocates and others should be aware that these laws are rarely used because they require the United States to show that the person had the "intent" to commit acts of domestic violence or violate a protection order at the time that he crossed the reservation or state boundary. Although this may be difficult to prove, this should not deter an advocate from referring a case to the United States if the offender crosses a boundary. Unlike the Major Crimes Act and General Crimes Act, which do not apply in those states that were given jurisdiction over the Indian reservations, the Interstate

Domestic Violence and Interstate Violation of Protection Order federal laws apply in all states and on all Indian reservations.

The United States may also have authority to prosecute firearms violations on Indian reservations. Firearms laws prevent any person who has been convicted of a misdemeanor (state or tribal) crime of domestic violence or who has a protection order in place against him that expressly prevents acts of violence, from possessing a firearm.[15] However, the language of the protection order must comply with the federal law (showing that the person represents a threat of harm to the victim or the order explicitly prohibits the use of force). Again, just as with the interstate laws, the firearms laws apply on all Indian reservations regardless of whether the state has been given jurisdiction over the particular reservation.

State Court Jurisdiction

Understanding Public Law 280

The federal laws giving the United States jurisdiction over certain crimes that occur on Indian reservations do not apply to all Indian reservations in this country. In 1953, Congress passed a law called Public Law 280 (PL 280) that gave certain states criminal jurisdiction over Indian reservations. Those states include: Minnesota (except the Red Lake Reservation and Bois Forte Reservation), Wisconsin (except the Menominee Reservation), California, Alaska, Oregon (except the Warm Springs Reservation), and Nebraska. (The Omaha, Winnebago, and Santee Sioux reservations have regained their criminal jurisdiction in Nebraska.) Other states were given the option to assume jurisdiction over reservations within their borders and many states have done so, including Montana (over the Flathead Reservation) and Washington (over certain types of offenses). In those states where PL 280 applies, state domestic violence laws apply to Indian reservations and the state courts have jurisdiction over all offenders, Indian and non-Indian. Just as it is important for tribes to develop a positive relationship with federal law enforcement and federal courts on reservations where federal jurisdiction may exist, it is equally important for state and tribal officials on reservations to collaborate where states can prosecute domestic violence crimes.

Can Tribal Courts Exercise Jurisdiction Over Domestic Violence Crimes and Civil Remedies in PL 280 States?

The fact that an Indian tribe is located in a PL 280 state does not prevent the tribe from developing its own justice system to combat domestic violence within its community. So, for example, if a member of a tribe in California needs a domestic violence protection order for her own safety against another tribal member, she may file in either the state or tribal court. The tribe may also exercise criminal jurisdiction over Indians who commit domestic violence within their reservations, although the state may also prosecute the crime. Most tribes rely upon state courts to prosecute most domestic violence violations within their reservations, especially when the violation is serious and warrants a jail or prison sentence. Some tribes in these states have developed their own law enforcement departments and tribal courts to collaborate with state and county officials to patrol and regulate criminal activity within their reservations. The important thing to remember about domestic violence under PL 280 is that both the state government and the tribal government can exert authority over offenders.

On PL 280 reservations both tribes and states can use civil jurisdiction to protect victims of domestic violence. A civil case is one filed by a private person or entity against another person or entity that does not involve an allegation of a crime. For example, a domestic violence protection order is a type of civil proceeding because the victim of domestic violence files her action against the perpetrator. The perpetrator does not face the possibility of a jail sentence in a civil protection order hearing, although he may be subject to a criminal prosecution if he violates a civil protection order. An Indian tribal court has the authority to issue a civil protection order against a person, even a non-Indian, although it may not have the criminal jurisdiction to put a non-Indian in jail if he violates the order. Obviously, a civil protection order that does not have the backing of a criminal justice system to prosecute violations is not going to deter a person from continuing to harass or annoy a partner. Therefore, it is extremely important for an Indian tribe that issues civil protection orders on PL 280 reservations to assure that the state will enforce protection orders and prosecute those persons who do violate these orders. This requires effective state-tribal collaboration to provide a necessary safety net for victims.

Tribal Authority over Domestic Violence

Tribal governments are restricted in their authority over persons within their territories. If these restrictions did not exist, the simple solution to domestic violence in Indian Country would be to support and strengthen the over 260 tribal criminal justice systems that exist in this country to bolster their efforts to protect the women within their communities. Due to the restrictions on tribal authority, tribes must use creative methods to protect women within their communities from both Indians and non-Indians. At present, Indian tribes have authority to criminally prosecute any Indian that commits domestic violence within Indian Country. The U.S. Supreme Court has declared that no Indian Country exists in Alaska, except the Metlakatla Indian community,[16] and therefore it is very unlikely that Alaska tribes can exercise criminal jurisdiction even over their own community members. This does not prevent them from granting civil protection orders to their own members against other members. A recent case from Alaska also demonstrates that these tribes can banish persons from their communities who represent a danger to the community (see chapter 4).

The U.S. Supreme Court has decided two cases that have restricted tribal court criminal jurisdiction over nonmembers of an Indian tribe. In *Oliphant v. Suquamish Tribe* the Supreme Court declared in 1978 that Indian tribes could not criminally prosecute non-Indians because such authority was inconsistent with their status in the American legal system. The court seemed concerned that non-Indians have no political voice in the tribal political systems and believed that tribes did not need to have authority over non-Indians to preserve the peace of their communities. This decision does not prevent Indian tribes from using other, noncriminal, methods to prevent non-Indians from committing domestic violence within their communities. When the full faith and credit provisions of the Violence Against Women Act were amended in 2001, Congress recognized broad tribal authority over all persons to assure that domestic violence protection orders were enforced. Congress declared that:

> For purposes of this section, a tribal court shall have full civil jurisdiction to enforce protection orders, including authority to enforce any orders through civil contempt proceedings, exclusion of violators from Indian lands, and other appropriate mechanisms, in matters arising within the authority of the tribe.[17]

In part, this section was added to respond to tribal concerns about the 1999 Justice Department report[18] that indicated that 70 percent of the domestic violence perpetrated on Native women was committed by non-Indians, persons over whom the tribe has no criminal jurisdiction. It is also recognition that tribal authority to combat domestic violence is broad even though it may not necessarily include criminal jurisdiction over all offenders. Tribes may use banishment of non-Indians from their communities if these people continually commit domestic violence against tribal members. Tribes may also penalize non-Indians by fines or other monetary penalties that do not involve incarceration. It is important that tribes not accept the commonly espoused view that they have no authority over non-Indians when it comes to domestic violence occurring within Native communities.

The U.S. Supreme Court restricted tribal criminal jurisdiction further in 1990 when it declared that Indian tribes lacked the jurisdiction to prosecute Indians from other tribes who commit crimes within a tribal community.[19] These persons, often referred to as nonmember Indians, were equated with non-Indians for purposes of tribal criminal jurisdiction. Congress reacted quickly to overturn this decision of the U.S. Supreme Court by restoring criminal jurisdiction over nonmember Indians to the tribes.[20] In 2004, the Supreme Court clearly stated that the tribes' inherent jurisdiction over nonmembers had been restored by Congress's action.[21]

When an Indian tribe does have criminal jurisdiction over a particular crime and person, a federal law limits the possible penalties that the tribal court may impose. The Indian Civil Rights Act prevents an Indian tribe from imposing a penalty in excess of one-year incarceration and a $5,000 fine for any crime that it prosecutes. This does not mean that if a person has committed several domestic violence offenses within a tribe's reservation that the tribe could not impose more of a jail sentence than one year for all the offenses combined, but only that the maximum punishment for each violation cannot exceed one year.

Conclusion

Jurisdiction is the combination of the power and obligation to respond to domestic violence in a tribal community. If jurisdiction exists, the appropriate criminal justice system must act to prevent future harm and to provide redress to a victim of domestic violence. Knowing the rules discussed in this chapter will aid in those goals.

Notes

1. 25 U.S.C.§1301.
2. 25 U.S.C.§1153.
3. *Crow Dog, Ex parte*, 109 U.S. 556 (1883).
4. *Crow Dog, Ex parte*, 109 U.S. 556 (1883).
5. 25 U.S.C.§1153.
6. *U.S. v. Rogers*, 45 U.S. 567 (1846). The definition of Indian has evolved through a number of federal cases. Enrollment in an official tribe has not been held to be an absolute requirement, at least where the Indian lived on the reservation and maintained tribal relations with the Indians thereon. *U.S. v. Antelope*, 430 U.S. 641, 647 (1977).
7. 18 U.S.C.§1152.
8. 18 U.S.C.§1152.
9. *U.S. v. Lara*, 541 U.S. 193 (2004).
10. 18 U.S.C.§1152.
11. Lawrence A. Greenfeld and Steven K. Smith, *American Indians and Crime* (Washington, DC: Bureau of Justice Statistics, USDOJ, February 1999, NCJ 173386).
12. *Oliphant v. Suquamish Tribe*, 435 U.S. 191 (1978).
13. 18 U.S.C. § 13.
14. H.R. 3402.
15. 18 U.S.C. §922(g)(8).
16. *Alaska v. Native Village of Venetie*, 522 U.S. 520 (1998).

17. *Violence Against Women Act*, Title IV of the *Violent Crime Control and Law Enforcement Act of 1994* (Pub. L. 103-322) as amended by the *Victims of Trafficking Protection Act of 2000* (Pub. L. 106-386), as amended by the *Violence Against Women and Department of Justice Reauthorization Act of 2005* (Pub. L. 109-162).

18. Greenfeld and Smith, *American Indians and Crime*.19. *Duro v. Reina*, 495 U.S. 676 (1990).

19. Violence Against Women Act, Title IV of the Violent Crime Control and Law Enforcement Act of 1994 (Pub. L. 103-322) as amended by the Victims of Trafficking Protection Act of 2000 (Pub. L. 106-386), as amended by the Violence Against Women and Department of Justice Reauthorization Act of 2005 (Pub. L. 109-162).

20. The *Duro* fix amended the Indian Civil Rights Act to restore the inherent power of Indian tribes to exercise criminal jurisdiction over all Indians. 25 USC 1301(2).

21. *U.S. v. Lara*, 541 U.S. 193 (2004).

Questions

1. How can civil jurisdiction and civil remedies assist Native women to attain justice for the crimes perpetrated against them? How do civil penalties help tribes deal with non-Indian perpetrators?
2. Why is it important for federal prosecutors who work with tribal communities under the Major Crimes Act to be educated about the cycle of domestic violence?
3. Why is it important for tribes to prosecute and follow through with cases against Indian perpetrators without regard for federal prosecutions?
4. Why are the General Crimes Act and the Assimilative Crimes Act so important for domestic violence and sexual assault cases in Indian Country? What jurisdictional gap do they fill? Why was there a need to pass these acts?
5. What laws are in place through the Violence Against Women Act that assist tribal nations and the federal government in prosecuting domestic violence or sexual assault on reservations? What are some of the realities of these laws in tribal communities? Why do tribes need to look to federal law in drafting protection orders?
6. Why is state and tribal cooperation so important for domestic violence and sexual assault victims in PL 280 states? What happens if there is a lack of cooperation?

In Your Community

1. What are creative ways that your tribe works within the legal systems and restrictions placed on tribal jurisdiction to punish non-Native perpetrators? What are some ideas that you have to deal with non-Native people who assault women in your community?

2. Jurisdiction is confusing and difficult to understand in Indian Country; however, it is important for fighting domestic violence and sexual assault in tribal communities. How would you explain jurisdiction to your family, friends, community?
3. What ideas do you have for getting federal prosecutors to understand and better work with your tribal community to prosecute domestic violence and sexual assault? If you are in a PL 280 state, what ideas do you have for state law enforcement to better cooperate with your community?

Terms Used in Chapter 14

Enumerate: To name a number of things on a list.

Inherent rights: Refers here to the rights that a tribe or government has because it is a tribe or government. Rights are not given by another.

Preponderance: The lower burden of proof in a civil case; more probably than not.

Restitution: Restoring a person to their original position prior to the loss or injury.

Trust relationship: A relationship in which the U.S. government has certain duties or obligations to look after and care for tribes. These fiduciary duties are defined by case law, statute, and treaty.

Suggested Further Reading

Fletcher, Matthew L. "Affirmation of Tribal Criminal Jurisdiction Over Nonmember American Indians." *Michigan Bar Journal* (July 2004).

Garrow, Carrie E., and Sarah Deer. *Tribal Criminal Law and Procedure.* Walnut Creek, CA: AltaMira Press, 2004.

Radon, Amy. "Tribal Jurisdiction and Domestic Violence: The Need for Non-Indian Accountability on the Reservation." *University of Michigan Journal of Law Reform* (Summer 2004).

Richland, Justin B., and Sarah Deer. *Introduction to Tribal Legal Studies.* Walnut Creek, CA: AltaMira Press, 2004.

Ritcheske, Kathryn A. "Liability of Non-Indian Batterers in Indian Country: A Jurisdictional Analysis." *Texas Journal of Women and Law* 14 (2005): 201.

Free Man Walking

I ignored the voice
      that told me I was in danger.
And he showed up,
      with a gleam in his eye.
Wrenched me in half,
      and planted his seed.
As I swallowed my tears,
      not wanting to wake his angel.
Have her come down
      and see the monster that her master was.
So I stayed quiet,
      and held his secret.
Afraid.
    Ashamed.
        Alone.
When I finally spoke,
      society blamed me.
His family told me to hush,
      not to repeat those words.
So I was left,
      with his venom,
          and his sentence.
While he walked
      and lived,
          happy
              and free.

              Mary BlackBonnet (Sicangu Lakota)

Representing Native American Victims in Protection Order Hearings

Chapter 15

KELLY GAINES STONER

Domestic violence[1] is a pervasive problem in today's society.[2] Native American women are battered at a higher rate than any other group.[3] Research indicates that Native Americans are less likely to report assaults, leading to the conclusion that they are victimized at an even greater rate than already reported. Domestic violence incidents involving Native Americans involve more severe physical violence and often include deadly weapons.[4] One of the most common methods for obtaining court ordered protection from domestic violence is known as the protection order.[5]

The Violence Against Women Act (VAWA) sets forth that a protection order is any injunction or other order issued for the purpose of preventing violent or threatening acts or harassment against, or contact or communication with or physical proximity to, another person. According to VAWA, the order must be issued in response to a complaint, petition, or motion filed by, or on behalf of, a person seeking protection. Protection orders may also be called "restraining orders" or "injunctions" as well as a variety of other names.[6] Each jurisdiction may have its own definition and/or terminology regarding protection orders and the practitioner should consult jurisdictional statutes for those definitions.

Protection orders provide court ordered protections that are specifically set out in the order language itself. In addition, various jurisdictions make it a crime to violate the terms of a protection order, signaling criminal sanctions such as jail time for violations. Finally, protection orders may create a special relationship with the state or issuing jurisdiction, enhancing the duty to protect. Failing to protect the recipient of a protection order may give rise to a cause of action in federal and/or state law or a tort claims action.[7]

Native American women[8] face unique obstacles as they attempt to obtain a protection order in a state court, tribal court, or a Court of Indian Offenses (hereafter referred to as CFR courts.) These women must cope not only with the ravages of the violence, but may also face a court system that is uneducated regarding the dynamics of domestic violence or is unwilling to hold the batterer accountable. In fact, some of these women will face a court system that is engaged in institutional racism or ignores the culture and traditions that are critical to the victim's healing.

This chapter describes many of the challenges that attorneys and victim advocates face as they represent Native American victims of domestic violence. We address victim characteristics and safety issues, followed by the behaviors and manipulations of the batterer. This section sets forth how to prepare your case and what to expect at the protection order hearing. Since we are a mobile society and victims move readily across jurisdictional lines with their protection orders, this section details how to craft a protection order that is enforceable in other jurisdictions.

Profile of a Native American Victim

I was so ashamed to even speak of what he had done to me. I thought I would embarrass my family and his. These things were sacred and private.

—A NATIVE AMERICAN SURVIVOR OF DOMESTIC VIOLENCE

Representing Native American victims of domestic violence in protection order hearings often presents difficult challenges for the practicing attorney and victim advocate. To adequately represent your client, you need to have a basic understanding of the dynamics of domestic violence, including the types of behaviors that the victims may present. It is also important to understand and respect the intense life struggles the victim may be encountering. Your actions as an attorney or victim advocate[9] will do one of two things for your client—help make her safer or put her in even more danger.[10]

Victims of domestic violence may suffer from a variety of problems that will impede your ability to gather the information and evidence necessary to prepare the case. The victim may present with a variety of symptoms, such as trouble concentrating, night terrors and flashbacks, depression, feeling suicidal, feeling lonely, feeling isolated or confused. Your client is also sixteen times more likely to be using drugs and/or alcohol to deal with her painful situation. You should inquire regularly about any drug or alcohol usage if you suspect that behavior. The best way to address drug and alcohol issues in court is to identify the issue early on and get treatment to demonstrate to the court the client recognizes the problem and is taking positive steps to correct it.

The victim may have a profound and justified fear of losing her children. In many cases, the children are the pawn by which the batterer will try to maintain his control. Unfortunately, research shows that more than half the men who abuse their partners beat their children.[11] In cases where the mother leaves because of homicide dangers, the children often become the direct target of the father's anger.[12] The client may determine that she should stay with her abusive husband to keep her children.

She may return to the batterer despite your best efforts. Despite the difficulty for all involved, you must respect her decisions. Research indicates that a victim on average will attempt to leave the batterer at least seven or eight times before she finally breaks free. She may return to him despite all of the concerted efforts to allow her to remain safe and free from the abuse. Many attempts have been made to explain why the victim stays with or returns to the batterer (see chapters 3 and 12). Research reveals that she blames herself for the violence, she has no money, she fears she will lose her children, she has been isolated and has no one to reach out to that she can trust, and she feels the system will fail her as it has in the past.

A Native American victim may be struggling with additional issues regarding her extended family. She may be fearful of the batterer's family if that family is politically powerful in the tribe or particularly aggressive in their behaviors towards her. She may be mourning the loss of the batterer's extended family as her own. She may be fearful of having to trust nonmembers or non-Indians with her safety and the secrets of her abuse. She may be extremely embarrassed to speak of these things to an outsider. Further, the community attitude regarding domestic violence comes into play when you are representing victims in Indian Country.

A Native American juror once told me that a black eye and broken ribs did not equal domestic violence because many of the Native American women in the community were suffering severe injuries at the hands of their partners and not complaining about it. This internalized oppression is a direct result of the attitudes and beliefs of the community towards domestic violence. I have had many of the women who sought services from our project tell me that they did not know they were being abused. The abuse these victims suffered was entirely acceptable and even expected in the communities in which they resided. Many of these women were brought up to believe that abuse was acceptable. Further, the only apparent punishment was by the community, which sanctioned the victim for bringing family issues before the court and embarrassing the family. You must understand the community's attitude towards domestic violence and plan your case accordingly.

Profile of the Batterer

He was such a smooth talker. He always got what he wanted. He made it seem like it was all my fault. I just froze when the Judge asked me questions and I knew the Judge wouldn't believe me.

—A NATIVE AMERICAN SURVIVOR OF DOMESTIC VIOLENCE

While no one profile fits all batterers,[13] a discussion of typical characteristics or behaviors that the batterer might exhibit may assist you in better representing your client. Batterers use a variety of different methods to control their victims (see chapter 3). You may expect some or all of the following characteristics from the batterer: may be a control freak observing rigid role-play (won't allow the victim to work); may distance himself from the victim and refuse to give her any type of emotional contact (this is extremely damaging to the victim's self-esteem); may have an extensive criminal history; may be extremely jealous; may express remorse after an episode; and the batterer may take offense easily. A look or even the mildest attempt at limit setting can trigger a violent episode.

Batterers may be well-liked by others and respected in the community. The batterer may view himself as the victim. Some of the punishments and tactics used by batterers are similar to those tactics used on prisoners of war. The victim becomes psychologically broken down and becomes emotionally and physically drained. Moreover, the majority of batterers I have encountered in the last eleven years are extremely good talkers and masterful manipulators of the system. In the majority of my cases, the batterer has slowly but steadily isolated the victim financially, physically, and emotionally. Pay close attention to the isolation issues during your domestic violence screening.

The batterer will usually not cooperate with you or anyone connected to the case for any extended period of time. It has been my experience that the batter will usually not even cooperate with his own attorney. He will continue to intimidate the victim through financial means, the children, or any other method he can find that works. He most likely will not pay his child support regularly, especially if the victim is financially dependent on receiving that money. The victim may be facing economic hurdles. Keep this in mind when you are advising her and work with the victim advocate to find other sources of financial support.

Preparing the Case

Interviewing Tips

Because of the trauma they have experienced, many survivors can find the legal process very confusing and frustrating. You can assist and empower your client by paying special attention to your interview techniques. Interview her in a quiet place to avoid any exaggerated responses that she may have developed due to the battering. Interview her in a place where the staff is instructed not to interrupt you. Remember, she may have trouble concentrating and may be experiencing difficulty with her memory so interruptions should be avoided.

Establish a relationship with the client. Focus more on listening during the first interview. I begin by asking general questions to see if the victim is able to speak freely. If not, I focus instead on specific questions such as "Has he hit you with his fist?" or "Has he touched you in a way that hurt you or scared you?"

You should also interview her on several occasions for no longer than an hour at a time. Be extremely cautious about following your interviews with a letter. Batterers often return to the client's home either by invitation or trespass and have on occasion confiscated those letters.

One question that is often asked is whether to allow the victim advocate to sit in on the attorney's interview sessions and whether that waives the attorney-client privilege.

Carefully consider whether to allow third parties (who are not your employees) to sit in on the interview process. Allowing third parties to be present during the interview may waive the attorney-client privilege thereby allowing opposing council to put the third party on the stand during a court hearing to testify as to what the client said during the attorney's interview.

Some jurisdictions provide by statute that the victim advocates' records are privileged and cannot be disclosed unless the client consents. The attorney may also have the victim and victim advocate sign an agreement allowing for the free exchange of information between the victim advocate and the attorney, setting forth that the victim advocate is working with the attorney on case preparation. The agreement presents a strong argument that the victim advocate and attorney are working together on case preparation resulting in a work product that is protected by the attorney-client privilege.

If your jurisdiction makes you a **mandatory reporter** regarding child abuse/neglect, let your client know this up front. In some jurisdictions, statutes require an attorney or victim advocate to report suspected abuse or neglect and state forthright that the statute defeats any privilege. Some states make it a misdemeanor to fail to report.

Ensure that the victim advocate is serving the client's needs. The foremost reason that victims return to their batterers is unmet need. The Apache Tribe of Oklahoma has set up a model where the victim advocate works closely with the civil legal attorney and reports to the attorney on a weekly basis regarding the client's needs and whether those needs have been met. This gives the attorney the opportunity to better guide the client and avoid some legal issues by early intervention. It also provides the attorney with a better understanding of the client's daily life struggles.

Empower the client with information. Do not make decisions for her. Instead, strive to give her all the information necessary for her to make an informed decision.

Counsel her on the pros and cons of her decision, but respect her choice. Continually update your lethality assessment.

Lethality Assessments

> *This case looked a lot like every other domestic violence case coming through our office—but this one ended in our client's murder. He stalked her, he blamed her and he killed her. You should treat every case as if it were the beginning of a homicide.*
>
> —AN ATTORNEY WHO REPRESENTS DOMESTIC VIOLENCE VICTIMS

The lethality assessment attempts to measure the present danger and assists the attorney when advising the client in ways that promote safety. To perform an assessment, the most important aspect of the process is to listen to your client. She knows the batterer far better than you ever will.

The following signs should be red flags that indicate the batterer is or is becoming unstable and plans should be made immediately to address the client's safety:

- The abuse has changed forms (from verbal to physical)
- The batterer has shown signs or made threats of homicide or suicide against himself or family members (the more detailed the plan the greater the danger)
- The batterer idolizes his partner and depends upon her heavily (for instance financially)
- There have been repeated calls to law enforcement for domestic incidents
- The batterer's actions demonstrate he does not fear legal consequences
- The batterer has killed or mutilated a pet, or is a hostage-taker or a stalker

The most dangerous time for a victim is when she is attempting to separate.[14] The lethality assessment must be continually updated as the case progresses. The victim advocate and the client are critical sources of information when conducting the assessment.

If you determine the lethality risks are mounting, there are certain steps you and your client should take. First, have the victim advocate and the client prepare a detailed safety plan. This plan should include the collection and safe storage of important papers (such as birth certificates, tribal enrollment cards, and insurance cards) and an extra stash of money. Further, an extra set of keys and detailed instructions on an escape route and safe place to stay must be addressed. Victim advocates often develop key "code" words that alert the victim advocate of the danger without the client having to specifically state she is in danger. In some cases, it may be necessary to have a relocation plan in place. Finally, letters to local law enforcement agencies indicating the issuance of a protection order and setting forth in detail the fear of danger and need for protection may be in order in those cases where the client is struggling with lackadaisical law enforcement personnel.

I have written detailed letters to chiefs of police in areas where the officers have refused to respond quickly to my client's calls for help or have made comments to my client to the effect that she was a bother to the officers because she had called for help so often. My letters set out in detail the date the protection order was issued, the terms of the order, the dangers facing my client, and details regarding why my client felt law enforcement was not performing sufficiently to her calls for help. In all cases I have handled so far, these letters to the chiefs of police have proven effective in changing response times and outward attitudes towards my client's calls for help.

Finally, you must do a systemic assessment of the community resources and attitudes towards domestic violence. It does you no good to win a victory for your client in court if law enforcement will not respond when the enraged, emotional batterer appears at her door to make her pay for embarrassing him in court. It does no good to win a victory in court if the judge will not hold the batterer accountable for his actions. A sound determination of community support will assist you in the lethality assessment and better enable you to advise the client.

Gathering and Using Evidence

An attorney can use the services of the victim advocate when gathering evidence. Often the victim advocate will have a strong relationship with the victim. Many times the victim advocate has taken pictures of injuries, may have torn or bloody clothing, and may even have pictures of the scene that can be very helpful if the batterer has destroyed the victim's property. However, the attorney and the victim advocate must be aware of the foundational requirement known as the "chain of custody" for tendering items in the victim advocate's possession during a court hearing. In court, the victim advocate must state what the article is, how she came to have possession of it, identify any unique marks on the article, state where the article has been kept, and who, if anyone, has had access to the article. The victim advocate must then indicate that the article is in the same condition as it was when the victim advocate took possession of it.

Some types of evidence that will support allegations of abuse are: your client's testimony, testimony of witnesses, visible injuries, 911 tapes, other protection orders, criminal records showing the abuser's domestic violence offenses, diaries recording incidents of abuse, evidence of past abuse, and expert testimony regarding the dynamics of domestic violence and regarding defensive actions or injuries to the batterer caused in self-defense.

Usually witnesses cannot testify about the words spoken by another person. However, there are exceptions to the **hearsay** rule and those exceptions work well in domestic violence cases. The "then existing mental, emotional or physical condition"[15] rule allows for an array of evidence to be introduced. For instance, the victim may have stated, "my neck hurts and my back is stiff." Those statements will be admissible under this rule. In addition, the victim's fear or her state of mind is admissible pursuant to this rule.

"Present sense impression"[16] is another useful rule of evidence to use in domestic violence cases. This rule allows the witness to state what they heard the **declarant** say while perceiving an event or immediately thereafter. For example, a 911 dispatcher may be able to testify that a victim yelled "He's banging on the front door!" on the telephone.

"Excited utterances"[17] are also very useful. To use this rule, the attorney must show that the statement is relevant and the witness heard the client make the statement while still under the stress or excitement caused by the event or condition. There is a time restraint that varies according to jurisdiction regarding how long the statement may be made after observing or experiencing the event or condition, so the attorney must check the applicable rules of evidence. A police officer may be able to testify that the victim yelled "He's going to kill me!" while visibly shaking.

Finally, "prior bad acts" is a useful tool in domestic violence cases. Since domestic violence is a pattern of behavior, it is relevant to introduce other acts of the batterer to demonstrate the pattern. This rule is a little complicated but basically allows evidence of prior bad acts to come in if used to prove motive, opportunity, intent, preparation, plan, knowledge, identity, or absence of mistake or accident.

Medical records are also useful evidence. The victim advocate may have referred the victim to health care professionals and those medical records, such as emergency room admissions or doctors' notes, may prove very telling in the case.

The attorney should use discovery in domestic violence cases where time permits. In my own practice, protection order hearings rarely allow time for formal discovery. However, you can gather some information such as police reports and interview possible witnesses. If time permits, consider using interrogatories, request for production of documents, and request for admissions. I have found that request for admissions sometimes work extremely well for my clients as the batterers are often hard for opposing council to contact and the admissions have to be answered within a certain time frame or they are deemed admitted. What a wonderful tool! In more than one case, I have had such admissions as "I admit that I have physically and emotionally abused my wife on a regular basis and continue to do so" to be deemed admitted for a failure to timely respond.

Drafting the Pleadings

If the victim has not already completed an affidavit requesting protection from the court, the attorney or victim advocate should assist her in doing so. Keep in mind that the facts that constitute the statutory definition of domestic violence must be set out in the petition or affidavit. The definition and requirements may vary from jurisdiction to jurisdiction.[18] Be specific regarding the remedies your client seeks. Don't hesitate to request a "no direct or indirect contact" order. You may request exclusive use of the home and automobile as well as payment of certain debts and bills. However, a word of caution, batterers historically will not comply with court orders, especially in jurisdictions where the court will not hold the batterer accountable. Make sure your client has alternative financial resources to help her through this critical time.

Consider requesting custody of the children if the jurisdiction where you practice allows you to obtain custody in protection order cases. If not, consider adding the children to the protection order if you have enough evidence to do so.

If children are involved, you should request supervised visitation. Despite the fact that many jurisdictions have statutes that require a batterer must have supervised visitation unless the court makes findings that an alternate type of visitation will provide for the safety of the children, I have found the courts will rarely comply with that particular statutory provision. I tend to locate a supervisor and bring that person to court with me to agree to supervise the visitation. This burden should not fall on my client, but in reality if she wants supervised visitation she has to provide the option and do the groundwork.

Preparing and Interviewing Witnesses

Witnesses have varying storytelling abilities and personalities. You should ask your client and the victim advocate to write down a list of potential witnesses, including a summary of what their testimony will be. Ask the client if she discussed the abuse with anyone. Try to determine whether there were any eyewitnesses. When preparing your case, you should interview each witness and assess whether his or her testimony is helpful or harmful to your case. Prepare your witnesses for testimony, including what to do when objections are made. Only use those witnesses you feel the court will find credible unless unusual circumstances are present in your case.

Some typical witnesses in a protection order hearing might be: family members, neighbors and other bystanders, friends, co-workers, mental health providers, doctors, and law enforcement officers. Expert witnesses may also be needed in the case to educate the court with respect to domestic violence. One key reason I use expert testimony is to explain why the victim keeps going back to the batterer or why she has obtained and dropped numerous protection orders in the case. Expert witnesses can be domestic violence victim advocates that may or may not have worked on the case but who have extensive experience in the field. Be cautious about calling your own victim advocate as an expert witness as you may waive the attorney-client privilege against disclosures of confidential information. I typically use victim advocates from other counties or tribes.

Identifying the Theory and Theme of the Case

While you do not have to be elaborate in developing the theory and theme of your case, it is helpful to go through these steps in order to make your client's story more organized and sequential in its telling. The theory is the "what happened in what order" of the case. It is sometimes useful to make a chronological list of the story. Do not forget to explain why the victim has acted as she has, especially if the batterer is alleging your client is the aggressor or if your client has obtained and dropped protection orders on other occasions. Make a flowchart with each piece of evidence or testimony that supports a fact the statute requires you to prove. Choose the most important facts and be simple and brief.

The theme of the case will most likely be that "the opposing party is an abuser." You can refer to the characteristics of the batterer set forth above to help you develop your theme further. The facts of your case must support the theme. The attorney or victim advocate must tell the client's story through the facts presented, supported by the evidence and testimony. Repeat your theme at least two times during your presentation.

The Protection Order Hearing

Safety

The protection order hearing is often stressful and emotional for your client. Safety to and from the courthouse must be addressed at the outset. The victim advocate typically accompanies the client to and from the courthouse. Safety plans are reviewed prior to the hearing as emotions may run high during and after the hearing. You should strategically place your client away from the batterer and away from the batterer's eye contact if possible. Try to visit the courtroom with your client a day or so prior to the hearing when the room is vacant. Instruct your client where she will sit and prepare her for cross-examination. Preparation in these areas not only assists you in the presentation of the case, but it makes the victim feel empowered because she knows what to expect.

Direct Examination

Direct examination will require you to meet each one of the statutory requirements to establish domestic violence through testimony of your witnesses. Do not neglect to call elders as experts in tribal court when custom and tradition are necessary for the court to have an understanding regarding the theory of the case or any remedies you are requesting. Most tribal codes require the tribal court to give deference to custom and tradition.

Let your client tell her story. Your role is to guide the story to ensure that all of the statutory requirements are met. Listen to your witness. Try to paint a clear picture for the court with respect to what has gone on and what your client needs to be safe.

If there is damaging evidence about your client, get it out when you present your side of the case. It is always less damaging if it comes from your witnesses and you have an opportunity to allow those witnesses to explain in a light more favorable to your client.

Cross-Examination

Cross-examination is perhaps the most difficult aspect of the case. Discuss with your client body language the batterer might exhibit to indicate he is losing control. It is also important to bring up that the batterer may not be represented by counsel and thus may be cross-examining your client himself. Instruct your client whom to look at and what to do when objections are made. Good cross-examination requires endless preparation and protection order hearings do not typically allow that luxury. You should consider three reasons to conduct cross-examination of defense witnesses. First, cross-examine to bring out evidence that is good for your case; second, to impeach the witness due to prior inconsistent statements; and finally, to show that the witness cannot be trusted because of some bias. If none of these reasons are present, be cautious and consider whether to cross-examine at all. Remember, a batterer will almost never admit that he has abused.

Listen for partial admissions from the batterer. Can you place him at the scene at the right time? Ask short questions in logical sequence. Use leading questions that require a yes or no answer. If the batterer is rambling, request that the court issue an instruction to the batterer to answer the question yes or no. Some courts will give the instruction and the batterers do not enjoy losing that control.

Crafting Enforceable Orders

It is not unusual to have a client that lives in one jurisdiction, works in another jurisdiction, and may visit still another from time to time. The attorney should strive to ensure that each protection order contains language that increases the chance of enforcement in other jurisdictions.

Congress enacted the Violence Against Women Act (VAWA), which contains full faith and credit mandates[19] (see chapter 16). In order for a protection order to comply with the VAWA,[20] four components must be present in the language of the protection order. First, the order must indicate that the party who is being awarded the **relief**, or someone on that party's behalf, has filed a request for the relief; second, the order must set forth that the court that issued the order had subject matter jurisdiction and in personam (personal) jurisdiction over the parties.[21] The order language must indicate that due process has been satisfied by setting forth what measures were used to give notice and opportunity to be heard to the respondent.[22] Dual protection orders will not be given full faith and credit unless the language indicates that each party filed a request for such an order and the court made specific findings of fact with respect to the need for the dual protection order.[23]

Ensure that the protection order sets forth specific, detailed findings regarding the danger to the victim and the need for the protection order. The duration of the order should be indicated. The order should give contact information such as the clerk's name and telephone or fax number. The order should state that all parties have been informed of the scope and terms of the order. Some jurisdictions even note what constitutes a violation of the order, such as any contact through a third party. All parties should be provided a copy of the order and that fact should be noted in the order language.

Some jurisdictions provide a cover sheet for protection orders that set out that the provisions of the VAWA have been met requiring full faith and credit be given to the protection order. Tribes can create their own cover sheets. Law enforcement officers tend to enforce orders that look familiar to them

In addition, it is critical to note that the VAWA federal gun laws require the order to set forth a finding that the defendant is a credible threat to the physical safety of the intimate partner or the child or the terms of the order must explicitly prohibit the use, attempted use, or threatened use of physical force against the intimate partner or child that would reasonably be expected to cause bodily injury. Consequently, all protection orders should contain that language.

Violations of Protection Orders

No piece of paper can protect me from him.

—A NATIVE AMERICAN SURVIVOR OF DOMESTIC VIOLENCE

A recent study reports that more than 60 percent of the women who obtained temporary restraining orders reported the order was violated within one year.[24] More than two-thirds of the restraining orders obtained by women against intimate partners who raped or stalked them were violated.[25] Finally, approximately one-half of the orders obtained by women against intimate partners who assaulted them were violated. Equally troubling statistics indicate that those violations were rarely prosecuted.[26]

There are some steps you can take in the event of a violation to enhance the probability that your client's case will be prosecuted. First, advise your client to report all violations to the proper law enforcement agency as well as reporting those violations to your office. The client should document as clearly as possible any violations in great detail, such as the time, what the violator was wearing, what he was driving, and any other details that can be safely obtained. If possible, have your client record the batterer's telephone contacts on a message machine or tape recorder. The client should make note of any witnesses that might have observed the violation and relay that information to the law enforcement agency as well as the victim advocate and the attorney. Next, take appropriate safety planning precautions with your client. Safety should always be your paramount concern.

If the case is prosecuted, the victim advocate or attorney should make sure that a victim witness coordinator is obtained, if such a person is provided by the prosecuting jurisdiction. The victim witness coordinator's role is to prepare the victim for trial and accompany the victim to court appearances in the criminal justice system. However, if no victim witness coordinator is available, the victim advocate may assist the victim throughout the criminal trial.

Conclusion

> *You gave me hope and helped me be strong. You changed my life by helping find the strength to start over. My children and I are free.*
>
> —A NATIVE AMERICAN SURVIVOR OF DOMESTIC VIOLENCE

Representing Native American victims of domestic violence presents unique challenges for the attorney and victim advocate. To properly and safely represent these clients in protection order hearings, the attorneys and victim advocates must have a thorough understanding of the dynamics of domestic violence as well as the cultural needs of the client. Protection order cases must be carefully and strategically prepared and all protection orders must contain specific and detailed language to comply with VAWA's full faith and credit parameters.[27] Representing Native American victims of domestic violence can be so rewarding when your efforts have played a part in enabling your client to break free from the cycle of violence to begin a new life. Even if the victim chooses to return to the batterer, the victim has been empowered through education and the knowledge of domestic violence and how the systems work. Power makes her stronger. Keep in the mind that the next time she chooses to break free just might be the time she stays free. Your work can help her change her life.

Notes

1. Defined in this chapter as a pattern of coercive behavior aimed at controlling the behavior of another in an intimate or familial relationship.

2. Patricia Tjaden and Nancy Thoennes, *Extent, Nature and Consequences of Intimate Partner Violence: Findings from the National Violence Against Women Survey* (National Institute of Justice and Centers for Disease Control and Prevention, NCJ 181867, July 2000), p. 25.

3. Tjaden and Thoennes, *Extent*, p. 26.

4. Tjaden and Thoennes, *Extent*, p. 26.

5. Margaret Martin Barry, "Protective Order Enforcement: Another Pirouette," *Hastings Women's Law Journal* 6 (1995): 348.

6. 18 U.S.C. §2265 (1994) (amended 2000).

7. See *Valistreri v. Pacifica Police Dept.*, 855 F.2d 1421 (9th Cir. 1988) and *Dodish v. City of Allentown*, 665 F. Supp. 381 (E.D. Pa 1987). But see *DeShaney v. Winnebago County Department of Social Services*, 489 U.S. 189 (1999) (setting forth the requirements of what constitutes a special relationship for purposes of 1983 claims). Note also that tort claim actions against state or tribal officials will require the claimant to overcome the issue of sovereign immunity from suit.

8. Research demonstrates that women are victimized at a rate higher than men. Tjaden and Thoennes, *Extent*, p. 17.

9. The term "victim advocate" is used to mean the service provider, safety planner, and lethality assessor that accompanies the victim through the civil and sometimes criminal systems. This term should not be confused with a "lay victim advocate." A lay victim advocate is usually an elder or tribal member that has permission to practice tribal law and represent clients in a particular tribal court.

10. Genevieve James, speaking at the Tribal Trial College, Seattle, Washington, July 9–11, 2003.

11. Lenore E. Walker, *The Battered Woman Syndrome* (New York: Springer, 1984), p. 59. More than 50 percent of the perpetrators who batter spouses will also batter children, and the pattern of spouse abuse usually precedes the abuse of the child.

12. Maria Roy, *Children in the Crossfire* (Deerfield Beach, FL: Health Communications, 1988), pp. 92–93.

13. Donald G. Dutton and Susan K. Golant, *The Batterer: A Psychological Profile* (New York: Basic Books, 1995), pp. 24–35.

14. Tjaden and Thoennes, *Extent*, pp. 37–38.

15. F.R.E. 803(3). The attorney must check the rules of evidence in the appropriate jurisdiction. I cite the Federal Rules of Evidence in this chapter.

16. F.R.E. 803(1).

17. F.R.E. 803(2).

18. For instance, 22 Okla. Stat. Ann. § 60.1 (Westlaw 2002) states that "domestic abuse means any act of physical harm, or the threat of imminent physical harm which is committed by an adult, emancipated minor, or minor child thirteen (13) years of age or older against another adult, eman-

cipated minor, or minor child who are family or household members or who are or were in a dating relationship." In contrast, the Spirit Lake Tribe's Law and Order Code sets forth that "domestic abuse means inflicting or attempting to inflict physical injury on an adult by other than accidental means, physical restraint, emotional abuse or malicious damage to the personal property of the abused party."

19. 18 U.S.C. §2265 (1994) (amended 2000).
20. 18 U.S.C. §2265 (1994) (amended 2000).
21. In personam jurisdiction is jurisdiction over the person. Unlike subject matter jurisdiction, in personam jurisdiction may be consented to and may be waived by the parties. See *Hoffman v. Blaski*, 363 U.S. 335 (1960). Basically, there are three ways to acquire in personam jurisdiction: serving a defendant while he or she is present within the forum; if the defendant has minimum contacts with the forum (see *International Shoe v. Worldwide Volkswagon Corp. v. Woodson*, 100 S. Ct. 559 (1980)); or if the defendant comes into the forum and commits an act while there.
22. Due process protects against fundamental unfairness by requiring that parties receive notice and opportunity to be heard. See *Armstrong v. Manzo*, 380 U.S. 545, 550 (1965).
23. 28 U.S.C. §2265(d)(1994)(amended 2000).
24. Tjaden and Thoennes, *Extent*.
25. Tjaden and Thoennes, *Extent*, p. 53.
26. Tjaden and Thoennes, *Extent*, p. 51.
27. Tjaden and Thoennes, *Extent*, p. 51.

Questions

1. What point of view is this chapter written from? Why is it important for a victim and her lawyer to understand the details of court proceedings in protection order hearings?
2. Why does Stoner point out that the client or victim might be using drugs or alcohol? Why does she suggest drug and alcohol issues should be brought up in court by the victim's side? Why might the victim be abusing drugs or alcohol? How does it relate to her situation?
3. Why is it important for the victim to make the decisions concerning her case and not her lawyer?
4. Why is it essential to define the terms of child visitation in a protection order? What sort of dangers does this situation present for the mother and her children?
5. How can elders be important in tribal court domestic violence cases?
6. At the end of the chapter a victim indicates that protection orders are only pieces of paper and Stoner identifies statistics that indicate they are often violated by the abuser. Why are they still so important to obtain? What should be done in addition to a protection order to assure the victim's and her children's safety?
7. How can law enforcement and the legal authorities work to hold abusers accountable when they violate a protection order?

8. How can tribes craft their protection orders to better serve and protect victims while still retaining the necessary components to make them compliant with VAWA's full faith and credit section?

In Your Community

1. What can your tribal community do to hold batterers accountable when they violate a protection order?
2. What can a victim do if she cannot afford to hire a lawyer to handle her case? Can she represent herself? What resources are available to assist her through this civil proceeding?
3. Why is it important to understand the specific statutory definitions of domestic violence and the requirements that need to be met to obtain a protection order in your jurisdiction or tribal community?
4. What types of challenges does the Anglo-American legal system that requires the lawyer and witnesses to theorize and tell their story in a clear chronology present for tribal members in your community?

Terms Used in Chapter 15

Declarant: The person making a statement.

Hearsay: Second-hand evidence in which the witness is not telling what he or she knows personally, but what others have said to him or her.

Mandatory reporters: People who are required by law to report any suspicion of child abuse or neglect to authorities.

Relief: Deliverance from oppression, wrong, or injustice.

Untitled

PAIN PAIN PAIN
A SHOWER OF BROKEN GLASS
YELLING, SCREAMING, HURTFUL WORDS
FEAR, NOWHERE TO HIDE.
HORROR IN LITTLE CHILDREN'S EYES
NIGHTS THAT LAST FOREVER
good morning dear

        Sharon Lynn Reyna (Stockbridge-Munsee/Mohican)

Using Full Faith and Credit to Protect Native American Survivors of Domestic Violence, Stalking, and Sexual Assault

Chapter 16

DANIELLE G. VAN ESS AND SARAH DEER

> *After being battered by her husband for many years, Frieda decided to try to leave the relationship to find safety. She **petition**ed for and received a protection order from tribal court. While driving to visit her mother off-reservation, Frieda noticed her husband's car following her. She made it to her mother's house, ran inside, and called 911. "I have a protection order against him!" she told dispatch. An officer from the local city police arrived, but when he saw that her order was from the tribal court, he said, "I'm sorry—I don't have authority to enforce a tribal court order."*

The above scenario has been a common occurrence for many women who are victims of domestic violence. In 1994, the U.S. Congress addressed this problem through the Violence Against Women Act (VAWA), which included new federal laws about protection orders and full faith and credit (FFC). This chapter provides an introduction to the federal law, and how it can work to improve the situation for women who are seeking safety.

Introduction: What Is Full Faith and Credit?

The phrase "full faith and credit" can be confusing for nonlawyers. "Full faith and credit" is a legal phrase meaning that a legal document from one jurisdiction will be acknowledged as valid and enforced in another jurisdiction. In the legal phrase, "faith" does not refer to religion and "credit" does not refer to money.

The concept of full faith and credit is not new. Perhaps the most common example of full faith and credit in practice is in your wallet right now. If you drive from California to New Mexico, you do not have to stop in Arizona and then in

New Mexico to get new driver's licenses. Your driver's license is valid and enforceable throughout the country and in many other countries as well. If you get married in California and later move to Washington state, you do not have to get married again in Washington state. If you then get divorced in Washington state and move to North Dakota, you do not have to get divorced again in North Dakota. These are all examples of full faith and credit in action between states.

Traditionally, the concept of full faith and credit has been limited to state governments. The U.S. Constitution specifically addresses the issue in Article IV, Sec. I:

> Full Faith and Credit shall be given in each State to the public Acts, Records, and judicial Proceedings of every other State. And the Congress may by general laws prescribe the Manner in which such Acts, Records and Proceedings shall be proved, and the Effect thereof.

Despite the full faith and credit clause in the U.S. Constitution, many states historically failed to recognize or enforce protection orders from other states or tribes. Although the states were enforcing other types of orders from other states, domestic violence protection orders were a relatively new type of order. European Americans had long considered domestic violence a private matter and were very slow to accept the new trend of state intervention.

Full faith and credit in the context of violence against women and protection orders is far more complex than in the context of driver's licenses, marriage certificates, or divorce decrees. As with most topics in federal Indian law,[1] full faith and credit in the context of violence against Native women is even more complex.

One tool for addressing violence against Native women is to use full faith and credit to help build a flawless safety net that bridges across all jurisdictional boundary lines. In building this net, tribal nations reaffirm their sovereignty, affirmatively acting to protect all women, including Native women. Wherever that net is in place, survivors of domestic violence and stalking can travel, taking their protection orders with them for safety.

Violence Against Women Act and Full Faith and Credit

In 1994, the U.S. Congress enacted the Violence Against Women Act (VAWA). VAWA is a series of federal laws designed to protect all women in the United States from domestic violence, dating violence, stalking, and sexual assault. Although VAWA is a single act, it is actually **codified** in various places throughout the federal code. In 2000, and again in 2005, Congress made significant changes and amendments to VAWA.

Two provisions included in the original VAWA and amended in 2000 and 2005 relate specifically to enforcing protection orders across jurisdictional lines. The first is the federal definition of "protection order" found at 18 U.S.C. § 2266(5). The second is the full faith and credit provision, with several subsections found at 18 U.S.C. § 2265.

VAWA and its full faith and credit provisions are federal laws. In the U.S. Constitution there is a clause that says whenever the states have laws that differ from federal law, the federal law "trumps" or supersedes that inconsistent state law. That clause reads:

> This Constitution, and the Laws of the United States which shall be made in Pursuance thereof; and all Treaties made, or which shall be made, under the Authority of the United States, shall be the supreme Law of the Land; and the Judges in every State shall be bound thereby, any Thing in the Constitution or Laws of any State to the Contrary notwithstanding.[2]

This clause is called the "Supremacy Clause" because it declares the U.S. federal Constitution, and all federal laws and treaties, to be the "supreme law of the land." Lawyers and professors disagree about whether the Supremacy Clause also applies to tribal governments. Since tribal nations are separate sovereigns with their own constitutions, many experts believe that the U.S. Constitution does not apply directly to tribal governments. However, a line of U.S. Supreme Court cases dating back to 1896 have established the idea that Congress has "plenary power" to regulate Indian affairs.[3] According to the Supreme Court, Congress can enact certain kinds of laws to limit tribal nations' sovereign powers of self-governance and has done so several times. Therefore, most scholars of the VAWA view the act as binding law for tribal governments as well as state governments.

Defining "Protection Order"

The definition of a "protection order" under the VAWA is very broad.

> The term "protection order" includes
>
> (A) any injunction, restraining order, or any other order issued by a civil or criminal court for the purpose of preventing violent or threatening acts or harassment against, sexual violence, or contact or communication with or physical proximity to, another person, including any temporary or final order issued by a civil or criminal court whether obtained by filing an independent action or as a pendente lite order in another proceeding so long as any civil or criminal order was issued in response to a complaint, petition, or motion filed by or on behalf of a person seeking protection; and
>
> (B) any support, child custody or visitation provisions, orders, remedies or relief issued as part of a protection order, restraining order, or injunction pursuant to

State, tribal, territorial, or local law authorizing the issuance of protection orders, restraining orders, or injunctions for the protection of victims of domestic violence, sexual assault, dating violence, or stalking.[4]

Notice first that the definition says "any **injunction**, restraining or other order." The order does not have to be called a "protection order" or "restraining order" or "no contact order." The definition is broad enough to include all orders, regardless of what they are called, so long as they were issued to prevent violence, threats, sexual violence, harassment, contact, communication, or physical proximity to any other person. The person the order protects does not have to be married to or dating the person subject to the order. The order may be temporary, as with an **ex parte order** or emergency order. The order also may be of a limited duration, for example, one year, or the order may be permanent or good for the life of the protected party. The protected party could have gone before a court to ask for a protection order, or the judge may have issued the order on his or her own as part of an ongoing criminal case. So, temporary or final, civil or criminal, "a rose by any other name," it is a "protection order" under the VAWA.

The Full Faith and Credit Provision of the VAWA: § 2265(a)

The VAWA full faith and credit provision reads:

> Full Faith and Credit—Any protection order issued that is consistent with subsection (b) of this section by the court of one State, Indian tribe or territory (the issuing State, Indian tribe or territory) shall be accorded full faith and credit by the court of another State, Indian tribe or territory (the enforcing State, Indian tribe or territory) and enforced by the court and law enforcement personnel of the other State, Indian tribal government or Territory as if it were the order of the enforcing State or tribe.[5]

The VAWA defines "State" to include, "a State of the United States, the District of Columbia, and a commonwealth, territory, or possession of the United States" in 18 U.S.C. § 2266(8).

Interestingly, the term "Indian tribe" is not clearly defined in 18 U.S.C. § 2265. Most experts agree that the term refers to federally recognized tribal governments.

As long as a protection order, as defined under 18 U.S.C. § 2266(5), is consistent with the requirements of 18 U.S.C. § 2265(b), federal law requires that it must be given full faith and credit and enforced by the courts and law enforcement officers of another state or tribe. For example, if a Passamoquoddy tribal court enters a lifetime protection order against a non-Native man to protect a Native woman, a Maine state court must enforce that order as long as the order meets the basic requirements for fairness set out in the next subsection of the full faith and credit law.[6]

What Are the Requirements of § 2265(b)?

In order to be entitled to full faith and credit and be enforced in another jurisdiction, a protection order must satisfy some basic requirements. The statute reads:

> Protection Order—A protection order issued by a State or tribal court is consistent with this subsection if—
> (1) such court has jurisdiction over the parties and matter under the law of such State, Indian tribe or territory; and
> (2) reasonable notice and opportunity to be heard is given to the person against whom the order is sought sufficient to protect that person's right to due process. In the case of ex parte orders, notice and opportunity to be heard must be provided within the time required by State, tribal or territorial law, and in any event within a reasonable time after the order is issued, sufficient to protect the respondent's due process rights.[7]

The first part of this subsection means that a state, tribal, or territorial court had to have the power, according to that state, tribe, or territory's laws, to issue a protection order concerning those people named in the order. For example, a bankruptcy court might not have power to issue a domestic violence protection order, but a court of general jurisdiction probably would. Courts generally have jurisdiction over the people (or the "parties") if both have some sort of connection to the state, tribe, or territory. However, there are some challenges regarding tribal jurisdiction over nonmembers and non-Indians (see chapter 14).

The second part of this subsection says that the person subject to the order also had to have had advance notice that the order would be entered and an opportunity to be heard to argue why the court should not issue the order. **Due process** is a legal term that refers to the requirement that courts treat people fairly. This requirement of notice and opportunity to challenge the order serve to protect the due process rights of the person subject to the order. If the order is issued on an emergency basis or ex parte, meaning that only one of the parties is present, then the person subject to the order must have an opportunity to contest the order within a reasonable period of time after the emergency order is issued. Typically the time frame is about ten to twenty days after the order, but this varies widely from one jurisdiction to another. This protects the due process rights of the person subject to the order.

No "Mutual" Protection Orders!

What about the due process, or basic fairness rights, of the person who sought protection from abuse in the first place? A widespread problem nationwide can be illustrated by the following example.

> Penny goes to court and fills out a written petition for a protection order asking the court to help protect her from further threats or acts of violence by her boyfriend, Ron. The court issues a temporary protection order and sets a date for Penny and Ron to come back to court two weeks later so the judge can decide whether to issue another order for a longer amount of time. In the meantime, a law enforcement officer serves Ron with a copy of the temporary protection order and the petition Penny wrote out to the judge. The officer tells Ron that he has to go to court to see the judge in two weeks if he does not want the temporary order extended or a new order issued against him.
>
> Two weeks later Penny and Ron both appear before the judge as scheduled. The judge reads over Penny's written petition again, and then asks Ron a question. Ron tells the judge that Penny is exaggerating and that she is the one who is really violent in their relationship and that she throws things at him and has even slapped him across the face in the past. The judge, frustrated and thinking about the twenty other domestic violence hearings she has that morning, says, "It sounds like you're both acting violently and immaturely in your relationship. I'm issuing an order that neither of you is to communicate with the other in any way. You can pick up a copy of the order with the clerk's office. Next case!" What this judge has just done is issue a "mutual protection order." That is, it is an order that contains cross-relief[8] against both of the parties, the **Petitioner**, Penny, and the **Respondent**, Ron. It would not be a mutual order if Penny obtained one order from one court and Ron obtained another order from another court. In that case Penny and Ron would have two competing orders, rather than one mutual protection order. In one of the competing orders Penny would be the Petitioner and Ron would be the Respondent. In the other, Ron would be the Petitioner and Penny would be the Respondent.

Was it fair of the judge to issue a mutual protection order including relief against Penny? What about her right to due process? Ron did not fill out a written petition for protection. Penny was never served with notice that Ron was going to argue that she was violent toward him. Penny did not have a two-week opportunity to prepare to defend against those accusations or to hire an attorney, if possible, to represent her at the hearing. Often, mutual protection orders will appear as if the judge had an afterthought. They will say, "Respondent shall not contact, abuse, threaten, harass, and so forth, the Petitioner in any way." And, then, at the end, the order will say, "Petitioner shall not contact the Respondent either for the duration of this order." Sometimes a court will order a Petitioner into counseling for alcohol or drugs if the court sees that she may be "self-medicating" to cope with the trauma to which the Respondent has subjected her. This is also a type of mutual protection order because it is making an order against the person who sought help and protection from the court instead of just against the person alleged to have committed acts of violence against her. In such situations, the Petitioner, here Penny, is deprived of her right to due process. Judges are often very concerned with protecting a Respondent's right to due process but they sometimes forget to afford Petitioners the same right.

To address this common problem, Congress responded by amending the full faith and credit provision of the VAWA to include the present subsection (c), which reads:

> **Cross or Counter Petition**—A protection order issued by a State, tribal or territorial court against one who has petitioned, filed a complaint, or otherwise filed a written pleading for protection against abuse by a spouse or intimate partner is not entitled to full faith and credit if—
>
> (1) no cross or counter petition, complaint, or other written pleading was filed seeking such a protection order; or
>
> (2) a cross or counter petition has been filed and the court did not make specific findings that each party was entitled to such an order.[9]

This change means that if Penny travels into another jurisdiction with that mutual protection order and Ron violates that order, law enforcement officers and courts in that new jurisdiction must enforce the order against Ron but not against Penny. That is because she is the one who petitioned for protection against abuse, Ron did not file a written cross-petition, and the judge did not make specific findings that Ron was also entitled to protection under such an order. In that case, the judge was merely frustrated and issued a mutual order without protecting Penny's right to due process by requiring Ron to file a written cross-petition and without making specific findings that perhaps this was one of the very rare instances in which both parties might need protection from abusive acts of the other. In short, under the VAWA, mutual protection orders are usually enforceable only against the Respondent and not against the Petitioner.

Registration, Filing, and Notice

Another change Congress made to the full faith and credit provision of the VAWA in 2000 was to prohibit states, tribes, and territories from requiring women to register or file their protection orders from other jurisdictions before law enforcement officers and courts in the new jurisdiction would enforce them. Although registration[10] may be beneficial to survivors of domestic violence and stalking in some instances, it may also be dangerous in others.

One way in which it might be helpful to a survivor to register her protection order is where the order may not have been entered into the national protection order registry, the National Crime Information Center Protection Order File (NCIC POF) maintained by the Federal Bureau of Investigation (FBI). Currently, almost all of the states are contributing at least some of their protection orders to this national registry. This can be beneficial in several ways. If a survivor does not have a paper copy of her protection order or a critical part of her order is not legible to law enforcement officers responding to the scene of an apparent protection order violation, anywhere in the United States, those law enforcement officers have the ability to check the NCIC POF to verify the existence and key portions of her protection order if it has been entered into that national registry.[11]

Another reason a survivor might wish to register her protection order is that if it is entered into the NCIC POF, it may help stop the person subject to the order from legally purchasing a new firearm. If someone subject to a protection order tries to purchase a firearm lawfully, the FBI may deny the sale under certain conditions. That is because it is illegal under federal law for anyone subject to a current, qualifying protection order to possess firearms or ammunition for the duration of that protection order.[12]

Finally, it might be important for a survivor to register her protection in those tribes or with those state officials who may still require registration as a prerequisite to enforcement. Remember that that practice is contrary to the federal law and ignores the safety concerns that prompted the amendment. Nonetheless, many local officials have not yet been educated about the changes in federal and state law, so they may still advise survivors that they need to register their protection orders. Presently, Alaska is the only state in the United States with a state law that still requires registration of **foreign protection orders** prior to enforcement.[13] All forty-nine other states have amended their laws to reflect the change in the federal law. Many tribes also require "recognition" of foreign protection orders prior to enforcement. This is a requirement that the tribes may wish to reconsider in light of the serious safety concerns that may be involved in that process.

When a woman registers her protection order in a new jurisdiction, she must first find out where she must register. This varies from state to state and tribe to tribe. For example, in some jurisdictions registration is through the courts, while in others it is through the state police. She must also know the hours of operation during which she can bring her order there for registration; for example, the court may only be open for business between 8:30 a.m. and 4:30 p.m. She might also find out once she arrives at the courthouse that she must have a certified copy of her protection order, which she may not have with her, in order to register it. She may also need to make childcare arrangements while she goes to court, and she may have to find a means of transportation or money to travel to the courthouse. In the past, many jurisdictions also required a filing fee for registering a foreign protection order. Although this is now contrary to federal law and most states' laws as well, that has not yet filtered down to a few court clerks and other officials who might mistakenly request payment of fees prior to accepting a protection order for registration.[14] In short, it is often very inconvenient and even impractical for survivors of domestic violence or stalking to register their foreign protection orders in a new jurisdiction.

In addition, registering an order can actually be dangerous for some survivors of abuse. If a woman has just fled an abuser, she may not have had the time to get to court or the law enforcement office in the new jurisdiction before she needs to have the order enforced for her safety. If a woman is worried that her abuser or stalker may try to find her, she may not want to register her order. That is because once a woman registers her foreign protection order it may become a searchable public record. If so, an abuser who may have some idea where she might have fled can try to track her down by the public record paper trail. Moreover, some jurisdictions include protection orders along with other court records on the Internet, although most experts discourage the practice. Here, the concern is that a moderately computer-savvy abuser sitting in North Dakota may be able to locate his ex-girlfriend who fled his abuse and then registered her protection order against him in a particular county in Alabama. He may decide to get in a car or on the next bus, plane, or train to Alabama to find her there. For all of these reasons, Congress changed the federal law to prohibit the requirement of registering one's protection order before it will be enforced in a new jurisdiction. The relevant subsection of the full faith and credit provision of the VAWA reads:

> (2) No Prior Registration Or Filing As Prerequisite For Enforcement.—Any protection order that is otherwise consistent with this section shall be accorded full faith and credit, notwithstanding failure to comply with any requirement that the order be registered or filed in the enforcing State or tribal jurisdiction.[15]

Additionally, Congress recently changed the law to ensure that states and tribal governments were not providing access to information via the Internet that should be protected:

> (3) Limits on Internet publication of registration information.—A State, Indian tribe, or territory shall not make available publicly on the Internet any information regarding the registration, filing of a petition for, or issuance of a protection order, restraining order or injunction, restraining order, or injunction in either the issuing or enforcing State, tribal or territorial jurisdiction, if such publication would be likely to publicly reveal the identity or location of the party protected under such order. A State, Indian tribe, or territory may share court-generated and

law enforcement-generated information contained in secure, governmental registries for protection order enforcement purposes.[16]

Another safety concern Congress recognized and addressed in the 2000 amendments to the VAWA was the practice some jurisdictions had of sending notice to the Respondent when a survivor registered her protection order. The following example illustrates the problem:

> Jenn is married and lived with her new husband in Oklahoma until recently when he became violent and abusive. She then fled to a small town in Texas where a cousin of hers had moved and where she thought her husband would never look for her. Her husband, Jim, was trying to find her and calling all of her friends and relatives for information about where she might have gone. In one of those conversations he learns that she has a cousin who moved to Texas and he finds that cousin's phone number and calls. Jenn goes to the local sheriff's department and asks the officers to keep an eye out for her cousin's home in case Jim happens to arrive there. The sheriff's officer, who has not yet been properly trained on full faith and credit, tells Jenn she must first register her protection order. She does and, without first informing Jenn, the court clerk sends notice to Jim back in Oklahoma informing him that a protection order against him was filed in that county in Texas. When Jim receives that notice he knows exactly where to find Jenn. Without warning to Jenn, Jim arrives at her cousin's home a few days later.

The safety issues raised in this scenario are precisely why Congress changed the federal full faith and credit law to prohibit the practice of sending notice to the Respondent when a survivor does choose to register her protection order in a new jurisdiction. The law now reads:

> (I) Notification.—A State, Indian tribe or territory according full faith and credit to an order by a court of another State, Indian tribe or territory shall not notify or require notification of the party against whom a protection order has been issued that the protection order has been registered or filed in that enforcing State, tribal or territorial jurisdiction unless requested to do so by the party protected under such order.[17]

As the statute indicates, there is an exception to the prohibition against sending notice. That is, when a survivor expressly requests, preferably in writing, that the court or other agency responsible for registering her order send notice to the Respondent informing him that her order will be enforced in that new jurisdiction. This may be helpful in a situation where, for example, the Respondent has insisted that a different jurisdiction has no authority to enforce the protection against him. The following hypothetical helps explain this issue:

Stephanie is a Native woman living and working in Tucson, Arizona. She has been dating Bill, a non-Native man. Stephanie is an enrolled member of the Tohono O'odham Nation, and she regularly visits her family and friends back on the reservation. When Stephanie obtained a protection order against Bill after he assaulted her, he told her, "I'll just wait for you on the reservation to talk some sense into you because that order is no good there. Those tribal cops can't touch me; I'm not an Indian." Stephanie, who has a well-trained advocate in Tucson, knew about full faith and credit, so she decided to register her Arizona order with the tribal court and specifically request that the court send notice to Bill that the order would be enforced against him on the reservation. In that case, Bill already knew the other jurisdiction to which Stephanie was going to travel (she was not fleeing somewhere secret), so it made sense for her to request that he receive notice that she registered her order there.

Tribal Authority over Non-Indians

When Congress amended the VAWA in 2000, it clarified the right of tribal courts to use their full civil powers to enforce protection orders on tribal lands:

> Tribal Court Jurisdiction—For purposes of this section, a tribal court shall have full civil jurisdiction to enforce protection orders, including authority to enforce any orders through civil contempt proceedings, exclusion of violators from Indian lands, and other appropriate mechanisms, in matters arising within the authority of the tribe.[18]

Tribal courts are fully able to civilly enforce protection orders against all people, Native and non-Natives alike. The tribes may choose to impose one or more civil remedies, including, for example, fines and banishment or exclusion from tribal lands.

The question of whether tribal law enforcement authorities may arrest a non-Native offender depends on a variety of factors, including: (1) whether the tribal lands are surrounded by a PL 280 state or a non-PL 280 state; (2) whether there have been any **cross-deputization agreements** between tribal law enforcement authorities and state or federal counterparts; and (3) what the powers of tribal law enforcement officers under tribal code to arrest for particular offenses are (see chapter 14).

Conclusion: Put It In Writing!

The Violence Against Women Act has made it more evident to states and tribes that there is a need for a comprehensive, clearly written code for issuing and enforcing protection orders. Without clear guidance from the codes, victims can easily fall through the gaps of the system. Each tribal government, as a sovereign nation, can write, adopt, and enforce its own protection order system. Without a clear code, women who seek protection orders can be given contradictory information—and this information can be considered a matter of life or death for a victim of domestic violence.

Notes

We use the term "survivor" instead of "victim." A survivor is considered to be more empowered and healthier, as a survivor has strength, experience, and wisdom, all lacking in a victim.

1. William C. Canby Jr., *American Indian Law in a Nutshell,* 3rd ed. (St. Paul, MN: West Group, 1998), p. 1.
2. U.S. Constitution, art. VI, cl. 2.
3. *Talton v. Mayes,* 163 U.S. 376, 384 (1896); *Santa Clara Pueblo v. Martinez,* 436 U.S. 49, 56 (1978).
4. 18 U.S.C. §2266(5).
5. 18 U.S.C. §2265(a).
6. 18 U.S.C. § 2265(b).
7. 18 U.S.C. § 2265(b).
8. "Cross-relief," in legal terms, means a court decision that recognizes the claims of both parties in a dispute.
9. 18 U.S.C. § 2265(c).
10. Registration may also be called "filing," "domestication," "recognizing," or another similar term. These all essentially mean the same thing and are all prohibited as prerequisites for enforcement of foreign protection orders.
11. This system is not foolproof, however, as not all states are contributing, most tribes are not yet contributing, and even those states that are contributing are not contributing all of their protection orders.
12. 18 U.S.C. § 922(g)(8). A "qualifying" protection order is one that a judge issues after a hearing of which the respondent had actual notice and an opportunity to be heard. 18 U.S.C. § 922(g)(8)(A). The order must restrain him from harassing, stalking, or threatening an intimate partner or her child, or engaging in other conduct that would place her in reasonable fear of bodily injury to herself or the child. 18 U.S.C. § 922(g)(8)(B). The order must also contain either a finding that the respondent represents a credible threat to the physical safety of the survivor or the child, or the order must expressly prohibit the use, attempted use, or threatened use of physical force against her or the child that would reasonably be expected to cause bodily injury. 18 U.S.C. § 922(g)(8)(C). There is also a relationship requirement before a qualifying protection order will trigger this federal firearm prohibition. The person protected by the order must be the Respondent's wife, ex-wife, girlfriend, mother of his child, or they must live together or have lived together in the past, or the protected party must be a child of either the Respondent or his intimate partner. 18 U.S.C. § 925(a)(32).
13. §18.66.140(b) (2003).
14. See, e.g., 42 U.S.C. §3796hh, 42 U.S.C. §3796gg-5. Federal law now requires those jurisdictions receiving Grants to Encourage Arrests ("GTEA" or "Arrest" grants), STOP grants, and others to certify that their "their laws, policies, and practices do NOT require, in connection with the prosecution of any misdemeanor or felony domestic violence offense, or in connection with the filing, issuance, registration, or service of a protection order, or a petition for a protection order, to protect a victim of domestic violence, stalking, or sexual assault, that the victim bear the costs associated with the filing of criminal charges against the offender, or the costs associated with the fil-

ing, issuance, registration, or service of a warrant, protection order, petition for a protection order, or witness subpoena, whether issued inside or outside the State, tribal, or local jurisdiction." The reason for this change in the federal law is that Congress recognized the "chilling effect" the practice of charging fees for such services has on survivors of domestic violence, stalking, and sexual assault. Congress does not want survivors to be discouraged, dissuaded, or unable to file such complaints or seek the protection they need from the courts and law enforcement agencies.

15. 18 U.S.C. § 2265(d)(2).
16. 18 U.S.C. § 2265(d)(3).
17. 18 U.S.C. § 2265(d).
18. 18 U.S.C. § 2265(e).

Questions

1. What is full faith and credit? Why is it important to domestic violence survivors?
2. What is the Supremacy Clause of the U.S. Constitution? Why is it necessary to have such a provision in the Constitution? If the Constitution had no Supremacy Clause, what are some potential problems that could develop?
3. What requirements must a protection order satisfy before full faith and credit under VAWA applies?
4. What are the benefits to a survivor who has her order entered into the National Crime Information Center Protection Order File (NCIC POF)?
5. Why was it important to survivors for VAWA to eliminate the requirement of filing a foreign protection order in all jurisdictions?

In Your Community

1. Does your tribal court require the registration of a foreign protection order before enforcement? What is their rationale for noncompliance with VAWA? How does this increase the risk to survivors? If your tribe no longer requires registration, discover the history of change.
2. Does your tribe have laws that authorize protection orders? Are there possible civil penalties in your tribal code, which could be enforced against non-Indian protection order violators?
3. Are there any problems with state enforcement of tribal protection orders in your community? If so, explain the problem and propose a possible solution.

Terms Used in Chapter 16

Codified: Laws that have been collected and arranged systematically, usually by subject matter, have been codified.

Cross- or counter-petition: A formal request to a court or other authority asking for some type of action against one who has filed a petition against you; as in a cross-petition for a protection order.

Cross-deputization agreement: An agreement between governmental units with different jurisdictions (commonly between tribe, state, and/or federal governments) authorizing law enforcement officers from one of the parties to the agreement to have the same power and authority as law enforcement officers from the other party.

Due process: Refers to certain safeguards that assure fundamental fairness.

Ex parte order: Refers to an order where only one side has presented their case. Often used for emergency proceedings.

Foreign protection order: Refers to a protection order from another jurisdiction (not a foreign country).

Injunction: An order prohibiting someone from doing something.

Petition: A formal request to a court or other authority asking for some kind of action; as in a petition for a protection order.

Petitioner: One who presents a petition to a court or other authority.

Respondent: One who responds to a petition.

Suggested Further Reading

Deer, Sarah, and Melissa Tatum. "Tribal Efforts to Comply with VAWA's Full Faith and Credit Requirements: A Response to Sandra Schmieder." *Tulsa Law Review* 39 (2003): 403.

Tatum, Melissa. "A Jurisdictional Quandary: Challenges Facing Tribal Governments in Implementing the Full Faith and Credit Provisions of the Violence Against Women Acts." *Kentucky Law Journal* 90 (2002): 123.

———. "Law Enforcement Authority in Indian Country: Challenges Presented by the Full Faith and Credit Provisions of the Violence Against Women Acts." *Tribal Law Journal* 4 (2004), available at http://tlj.unm.edu/articles/volume_4/tatum/index.php.

Divorce, Child Custody, and Support Issues in Tribal Courts

Chapter 17

HALLIE BONGAR WHITE

Tribal courts can provide an important forum for Native survivors of domestic violence seeking to regain autonomy and safety. Formal legal proceedings for divorce and child custody and/or support can often be heard in tribal courts where Native women may feel more comfortable initiating legal action. Tribal court proceedings take place within a familiar community sharing similar values and worldview. Transportation difficulties may be minimized for survivors, their families, victim advocates, and witnesses when proceedings are held within the community. Proceedings in tribal courts may sometimes be held in a woman's native language.

Tribal courts may also be more user-friendly for victims representing themselves **pro se** (without an attorney). Native women may find that they maintain some advantages in gaining child custody under the laws of many tribes. It may also be easier to secure the testimony of tribal police officers in tribal courts and to bring forth other evidence of the abuse located on the reservation. Filing fees, fees for service of process, and other court costs may also be far lower than those of state courts.

Conversely, some Native women may feel more comfortable initiating divorce, custody, and/or support proceedings off-reservation. There is a shortage of free or low-cost legal services in many reservation communities. Facing an abuser in formal legal proceedings without legal counsel can be daunting. This is especially true when the abuser is represented by an attorney. Access to legal services off-reservation may be a decisive factor influencing a domestic violence survivor's decision to file in state court. Native women in off-reservation shelters may also find it more convenient and may feel safer filing in state courts. Some Native women may feel more comfortable litigating sensitive issues involving physical and sexual violence in communities where they are unknown.

Most tribes have empowered their tribal courts with the authority to issue final divorce orders (sometimes called dissolution of marriage orders) that formally terminate a legal marriage and legal relationship between two parties. Divorce actions in tribal courts can also include formal determinations of child custody, visitation, division of property, assignment of debt, child support, and spousal maintenance (sometimes called "alimony"). Some tribal courts also issue protection orders within divorce proceedings.

When parties are not legally married but have a child or children in common, tribal courts may also have the authority to issue child custody and child support orders. These orders often include determinations of visitation rights and may also include protection orders.

The Importance of Obtaining a Formal Divorce, Custody, and/or Support Order

Survivors of abuse who choose to walk away from a marriage without legal dissolution may face tremendous obstacles in the future for themselves and for their children. Tribal courts with jurisdiction over the cause of action and over the parties can often issue final divorce, custody, and support orders that enable Native victims to break their legal ties with their abusers and regain autonomy over their lives.

In the absence of a formal divorce decree, an abuser-spouse retains tremendous control over the lives of his victim and their children. The abuser can continue to control the financial destiny of his victim and can continue to make important parenting decisions for their children. Without a divorce decree and court-ordered custody plan, the abuser can also continue to make important medical and educational decisions for their children. Under the laws of many jurisdictions, an abuser-spouse retains equal rights to custody and visitation absent a formal divorce and custody order. He may also be able to legally travel with the children anywhere within the country without the victim's permission, switch the children's schools, authorize surgery, and control their participation in religious ceremonies.

Even when the victim does not live with her abuser, she may remain liable for his continuing debts as long as a valid, legal marriage still exists. An abuser can fail to make payments on a new vehicle, furniture, or home. He can open new credit accounts and fail to pay the monthly charges. The abuser can accidentally injure a third party in a car accident or run up large medical or dental bills. In all of these cases, the victim may be held financially responsible for the debts of her abuser even if they have informally separated for many years.

In many jurisdictions, an abuser will inherit all of the victim's property upon her death if she dies intestate (without a will) and there is no legal divorce in place. Without a legal divorce, the abuser may also retain rights to the victim's 401(k), pension, or other retirement plan.

Financial abuse is a common form of control exercised by abusers over their intimate partners. In the absence of a formal divorce decree, an abuser may continue to run up debts that will destroy the victim's credit and make it impossible for her to obtain a home mortgage, credit cards, or a car loan in the future. A victim may have to resort to formal bankruptcy proceedings (after completion of a legal divorce) in order to discharge her legal obligations for the debts of her abusive spouse. A formal divorce order releases the victim from liability for any future debts of her abuser-spouse.

Formal custody, support, and visitation orders are also important in cases where the abuser and intimate partner are not legally married but have one or more children in common. If **paternity** has been established, an abuser retains equal rights to custody and visitation of the children in the absence of a formal court custody and visitation order. An abuser can continue to make the same medical, educational, and religious decisions as a father who is legally married to the children's mother. In the absence of a formal child support order, an abuser may cease to pay for the care of his children and shift the entire financial burden on to the mother.

Tribal Court Jurisdiction in Divorce, Custody, and Support Cases: Where to File

Tribal courts must have both subject matter and personal jurisdiction to grant an order for divorce, custody, and/or support. Subject matter jurisdiction is the power to hear the general topic being brought before the court. Personal jurisdiction is the power to hear a case involving the specific parties involved in the case.

The tribe must authorize its tribal court to hear divorce, custody, and support actions under the laws, custom, or tradition of the tribe. Many tribes authorize their courts to hear divorce, custody, and support actions brought by tribal members, nonmember Indians, and non-Indians married to a tribal member or with a child in common with a tribal member. Some **tribal codes** only allow their courts to hear divorce, custody, and support cases where both parties are tribal members, where both parties are Indians, or where one of the parties is an Indian and both parties reside on the reservation. Other tribes allow their courts to hear divorce and custody cases where both parties are tribal members and reside off-reservation. A few tribes and pueblos do not permit divorce. Their tribal courts are not authorized to issue divorce or dissolution of marriage orders under any circumstances.

On the most basic level, tribal codes authorize tribal courts to issue divorce decrees when there is proof that a valid, legal marriage exists. Similarly, tribal codes provide authorization to issue child custody and support orders when legal parentage has been established (that is, by formal paternity proceedings, adoption, and so forth).

The definition of a legal marriage varies from tribe to tribe. Most tribes recognize marriages performed on their own reservation as well as marriages performed off-reservation under the laws of states or other tribes. Tribal courts often recognize traditional marriages performed according to the custom and tradition of their own tribe. Tribal law may also recognize "common law marriages" where the couple has lived together as "man and wife" for a number of years and the community has acknowledged their relationship as a valid marriage (even in the absence of any formal ceremony or license).

Many tribes recognize legal parentage of children whenever a child is born to two married people. Tribes may also establish legal parentage by formal paternity proceedings, court adoption proceedings, and by traditional tribal adoption.

Within certain limits, tribes, as sovereign nations, have the right to "make their own laws and be ruled by them."[1] Tribal courts have **exclusive** jurisdiction to hear divorce actions between two Indians (member or non-member Indians) residing on a reservation.[2] Exclusive jurisdiction means that the tribal court is the only court that can hear the action. The parties cannot file for divorce in state court because the state court does not have subject matter jurisdiction to hear the matter. This presents a problem for victims of domestic violence living on reservations or pueblos where divorce is not permitted. These women may be foreclosed from obtaining a divorce in any jurisdiction as long as they continue to reside on-reservation.

Tribal courts, if their codes permit, can issue divorce orders in a marriage between an Indian and a non-Indian residing on the reservation when the petitioner (person initiating the case) is a non-Indian.[3] The law is unsettled when the Indian spouse residing on the reservation with their non-Indian spouse initiates the divorce action.[4] Indian spouses initiating divorces against their non-Indian spouses where both parties reside on the reservation may have the option to file in either state or tribal court.

Tribal courts have exclusive jurisdiction to hear divorce and custody cases involving an Indian child where at least one of the parents is Indian and one of the parents resides on the reservation with the Indian child.[5] Tribal courts may also have exclusive jurisdiction to hear divorce and child custody cases where one of the parties and an Indian child reside on the reservation and the other party resides in a state.[6] This applies to marriages where both spouses are Indians as well as to marriages between non-Indians and Indians. Tribal courts cannot hear divorce or custody cases involving two non-Indians residing on the reservation even if they voluntarily submit to the jurisdiction of the tribal court. Non-Indians, even if they are longtime residents of a reservation, must file for divorce, custody, and support in state court.[7]

Victims who leave the reservation and then reside in a state may be able to file for divorce in state court after they have resided in the state for a time period determined under the laws of each state. Every state has a statute outlining the minimum length of time a person must reside in that state before they can file for divorce in state courts. It may be easier for a victim relocating to a state to obtain an order for dissolution of marriage in state court than to obtain child custody, support, and final orders assigning property and debts. State courts may decide to exercise the doctrine of comity (mutual respect for the court of another sovereign or state) and allow tribal courts to make final custody and property determinations, especially when evidence concerning child custody or the actual property to be divided is located on the reservation.

Victims leaving a reservation may have to wait up to six months to establish residency in a state in order to file for child custody in state courts.[8] However, Native victims of domestic violence fleeing their reservation with their children may be able to file for emergency child custody in state courts without fulfilling a lengthy residency requirement under the provisions of the Parental Kidnapping Prevention Act (PKPA).[9] The PKPA is a federal law passed by Congress designed to discourage conflicts in interstate custody cases, deter interstate child abductions by parents involved in custody disputes, and promote cooperation between states about interstate custody matters. While the PKPA does not directly apply to tribes,[10] it can allow Native women fleeing from reservation-based domestic violence to gain some relief in state courts. The PKPA allows states to assume emergency jurisdiction in child custody cases where the child, a sibling, or a parent of the child has been subjected to or threatened with mistreatment or abuse. Native women filing for emergency child custody in state courts under the PKPA should allege in their petitions that they or their children are victims of domestic violence or have been threatened with acts of domestic violence by the other parent.

Initiating Divorce, Child Custody, and Support Actions in Tribal Courts

Divorce, custody, and support proceedings can be an emotionally and financially trying experience for a Native survivor of domestic violence. The period in which proceedings are initiated can also be a dangerous time for the survivor and her children. Statistics show that the risk of death or injury dramatically increases for a victim once she leaves her abuser. The risk may also increase when the abuser is arrested and charged with abuse or when he is served with protection order, divorce, custody, or support documents. Safety planning with an experienced victim advocate is the first important step for any Native survivor contemplating divorce, child custody, protection orders, and/or support proceedings in tribal courts.

Many tribes have adopted formal rules of procedure that must be followed in all divorce, custody, and support actions. Other tribes have retained their more traditional procedures for making divorce, custody, and support determinations. Victims may wish to consult with an attorney or a legal advocate licensed to practice in their tribal court before filing. This is especially important in tribal courts that follow more formal rules of procedure. If an attorney or legal advocate is not available, victims may consider asking the tribal court for a copy of the rules of procedure and copies of any standardized forms the court uses in divorce and custody actions. The rules of procedure contain important deadlines for filing pleadings (also known as petitions) in tribal court. Pleadings or petitions are formal, written requests to the court requesting certain "forms of relief" (specific things the party wants the court to order).

Some tribal courts provide standardized forms for use in divorce, custody, and support actions. These standardized forms can serve as a template or model for victims filing on their own without the help of an attorney or lay legal advocate. They can help to ensure that victims have covered all of the important areas the court needs to consider in divorce, custody, and support cases.

Many tribal courts charge a filing fee for the party initiating a divorce or custody action. The fee is generally paid when the formal petition for divorce, custody, or support is filed with the tribal court. Many courts also charge a fee for filing a response (formal, written answer) to a petition. Sometimes a party can request that the filing fee be waived for economic hardship. A fee waiver can be requested in writing in most courts. Other tribal courts may waive fees if the victim orally requests a waiver.

A petition in tribal courts can usually include a request to dissolve the marriage, divide the property, assign debts, issue support orders (spousal support and/or child support), restore a maiden name, and issue a child custody order. Victims of domestic violence may also wish to ask the court to issue an order of protection if they have not done so already. Some tribal courts will consolidate the protection order with the divorce, custody, and support proceedings. Other tribal courts require a separate action to be filed to obtain a protection order.

It can also be important for victim safety to inform the court if the abuser owns or possesses any firearms and ammunition and to request an order prohibiting his possession of firearms or ammunition as part of the court's initial orders. The tribal court may then consider ordering the abuser to surrender firearms and ammunition to the court or to law enforcement during the course of the proceedings.

The pleading filed in tribal court usually states the names of the parties, dates of birth, tribal affiliation, physical address, and length of time at that address. Some courts require a social security number or tribal enrollment number for the parties. Victims of domestic violence may ask the court to keep their address confidential, especially if they are in shelter or if revealing their physical address would endanger them. They may supply another address where they may safely receive mail instead.

Victims seeking custody of children generally include information about the legal names of their children, their tribal enrollment (or eligibility for enrollment), dates of birth, current address (if revealing the address would not endanger the victim or children), and length of time the children have resided on the reservation. It may also be important to inform the court if the victim is pregnant with her abuser's child.

On the most basic level, the petition tells the court who the parties are, what the victim wants the court to do, and provides reasons for the court to grant the victim what she has requested. Tribal courts vary as to whether a party must allege grounds for divorce such as physical or mental cruelty or adultery. Many courts allow "no fault" divorces where one of the parties must simply state that the marriage is irretrievably broken or that they wish to dissolve the marriage.

Tribal courts are beginning to adopt a formal presumption against giving custody of children to an abuser. These courts recognize that a batterer's violence against the mother is a strong indicator of poor parenting skills and of an increased likelihood of violence against the children. Tribal courts have also ruled that domestic violence against a mother in the presence of her child is the same as abusing the child mentally and emotionally.[11]

Victims may gain significant advantages in tribal court custody cases when they allege domestic violence in their petitions. As a general rule, victims should state in their custody petitions that domestic violence has been perpetrated against the victim by the abuser and should supply specifics of the violence (injuries, arrests, hospitalization, and so forth). Victims should also state in their pleadings whether the violence occurred in the presence of the children, while they were pregnant, or against the children.

In addition to considering whether domestic violence has occurred in the relationship, tribal courts also consider which parent has served as the children's primary caretaker when making custody determinations. A primary caretaker is the person who has physically cared for the children the majority of the time. Primary caretaking duties can include providing childcare, taking children to doctors, taking the children to and from school, bathing, feeding, and dressing the children, and so forth.

Many tribal courts decide custody along matrilineal or patrilineal lines. For example, the matrilineal Hopi Tribe traditionally gives custody of the children to the mother. If she is unfit or unable to care for the children, custody is then given to the father. If he is unfit or unable to care for the children, custody is then given to the mother's female relatives. Similarly, in some patrilineal tribes it may be difficult for the mother, even if she and/or the children are victims of domestic violence, to obtain custody.

Victims should also suggest a reasonable schedule and plan for visitation in their pleadings. Native victims of domestic violence should be aware that they are at an increased risk of injury when custody of the children is exchanged. It may be important for the woman's safety to request custody exchange through a third party such as social services or a mutually trusted friend or relative. Usually third-party custody exchanges are performed in public places with staggered drop-off and pick-up times for the victim and abuser. This may reduce the chances that the victim and abuser will meet face to face and may increase the victim's safety at this dangerous time.

Victims can also request in their petition that the court order the opposing party into drug or alcohol treatment before they are allowed visitation with the children. Tribal courts can order an abuser to successfully complete parenting classes and/or batterer reeducation classes prior to being allowed visitation with the children.

In divorce cases, the petition for divorce should also contain a list of property acquired during the marriage ("marital property"), a list of each party's separate property, and a list of separate and mutual debts. Generally, property or debts that each party possessed before the marriage are considered separate property. Property that is inherited or given by gift to one of the parties may also be considered separate property. All property otherwise acquired during the marriage is usually considered joint or marital property. However, tribal law, custom, and tradition may define "separate" and "marital" property and debts quite differently.

Property can include houses, land, livestock, furniture, money, retirement accounts, vehicles, stocks, jewelry, and other items. The victim should tell the court in her petition how she would like the property to be divided. She may also ask the court to issue a preliminary injunction forbidding both parties from disposing of any joint marital property before the court can formally divide the property. This may help to prevent an abuser from "looting" or disposing of all of the property to punish the victim for leaving.

Victims may petition the court to allow them to retain exclusive use of the family home. However, problems can arise when the victim is non-Indian or a member of a different tribe, the lease to the couple's reservation home is held under the abuser's name, or the family is residing on the abuser's reservation. Some

Tribal Housing Authorities allow a domestic violence victim to remain in a tribal home leased to a tribal member, especially if she has children who are enrolled or eligible for enrollment with the tribe.[12]

Victims seeking child or spousal support from tribal courts should include wage and employment information for themselves and for the abuser in the petition. Victims who do not know the exact wages of their abuser should make a good faith estimate of their abuser's wages and submit that estimate to the court. They should also tell the court that they have submitted an estimate of the wages.

Many tribal courts have adopted formal child support guidelines. On the most basic level, these guidelines help the judge to decide how much money the non-custodial parent must pay to the custodial parent. The primary factors in many of these child support guidelines are the incomes of the parties, the number of children involved in the action, and the amount of physical custody or parenting time each party has with the child.

Courts must carefully weigh the abuser's unemployment or underemployment status. Underemployment means that the person has the ability to work full-time but chooses to work part-time. It can also include circumstances when the person intentionally works in a low-paying position when they have the ability and skills to work at a higher-paying job. Some tribal courts compute child support using minimum wage figures when an able-bodied abuser is unemployed.

Some tribal courts may order the victim to attend mandatory mediation or couples counseling with their abuser during divorce or child custody actions. This practice can endanger victim safety and should not be used. During mandatory mediation or couples counseling the victim is forced to face her abuser. She may be intimidated by the batterer's continuing tactics of abuse into relinquishing demands in her case. He may attempt to follow her after the hearing to locate her current residence or to perpetrate new acts of violence against her. There is often great discrepancy between an abuser's public and private behavior. Many abusers know how to terrorize their victims with subtle words and gestures that may go undetected by others in the room. A victim may appear to be hysterical and irrational to a court-appointed mediator while the abuser may appear calm and rational. Abusers may use court-mandated mediation sessions as opportunities to regain control over the victim or to terrorize her. True mediation requires a level playing field between the parties. Domestic violence is a pattern of power and control. In cases of domestic violence there is always an uneven power differential.

The presence of a victim advocate in the courtroom can help provide important support for the victim throughout the legal proceedings, especially if she is unrepresented. It can be helpful for the victim to "practice" testifying and telling her story prior to the actual court date. Effective testimony by victims of domestic violence includes a clear and concise history of the abuse. Persuasive testimony of the abuse includes information about the type of abuse, the locations where the abuse occurred, a description of any injuries, and a listing of others who witnessed the abuse or injuries. Victims may also be able to introduce evidence of the abuse, such as photographs of their injuries, medical records, school records for the children, and police reports.

Sometimes expert witnesses are used in tribal court to explain the dynamics of domestic violence, lethality risk factors for the victim, self-defense claims of the victim, the effect of domestic violence on children, and other areas. An expert witness is any person who has a greater knowledge of the subject matter than the average layperson. Victim advocates and law enforcement officers with specialized domestic violence training can often qualify as expert witnesses in tribal court. The use of an expert witness in a tribal court custody, support, or divorce action can greatly assist a Native victim in fully presenting her claims to the court.

Enforcement of Tribal Court Custody and Support Orders

Abusers who violate tribal court custody, support, and visitation orders can be held in contempt of court for failure to comply with a valid court order. Some tribal codes include criminal penalties for willfully disobeying a tribal court order. Tribal members and nonmember Indians of federally recognized tribes can be criminally prosecuted in many tribes for failure to comply with a court order. Non-Indians cannot be criminally prosecuted for failure to comply with a tribal court order.[13]

Garnishment proceedings are one means of enforcing a tribal court support order against an abuser who refuses to pay. Garnishment is usually an involuntary procedure whereby the opposing party's employer deducts the amount of support from their wages before the employee receives his paycheck. The money is then remitted to the court.

Cases involving an abuser who works for the tribe or on the reservation are usually fairly simple to resolve. A victim or her attorney can usually provide a copy of the tribal court garnishment order to the employer and begin the garnishment process.

If the abuser works off-reservation, the victim must usually "domesticate" the order in state court by demonstrating to the state court that the garnishment order is a valid tribal court order. The victim must file a formal, written request with the state court and demonstrate that the tribal court had subject matter and personal jurisdiction over the abuser and that a valid support order has been issued. Generally, proof of subject matter and personal jurisdiction and the existence of a valid order are contained in the tribal court's final order granting divorce, custody, and support. Under a federal law, the Full Faith and Credit for Child Support Orders Act, states must fully honor and enforce support orders issued by tribes or by other states.[14]

Notes

1. See *Williams v. Lee*, 358 U.S. 217 (1959) at 220.
2. See *Whyte v. District Court*, 140 Colo. 334, 346 P. 2d 1012 (1959), cert. denied, 363 U.S. 829 (1960).
3. See *Williams v. Lee*.
4. See *Williams v. Lee*.
5. See *In Re Marriage of Shane Colin Skillen*, 287 Mont. 399, 956 P.2d 1 (Mont 1998), *Malaterre v. Malaterre*, 293 N.W. 139, 1980 N.D. 240 (1980), and *Martinez v. County of La Paz*, 152 Ariz. 300, 731 P.2d 1244 (1987 Ariz. App.).
6. See *In Re Marriage of Shane Colin Skillen*, 287 Mont. 399, 956 P.2d 1 (Mont 1998).
7. See *White Mountain Apache Tribe v. Smith Plumbing Co.*, 856 F. 2d 1301 (9th Cir. 1988)
8. See the residency requirements of the Uniform Child Custody Jurisdiction Act or Uniform Child Custody Jurisdiction Enforcement Act adopted by the state in question.
9. 28 U.S.C. §1738A.
10. For a contrary view of the applicability of the PKPA to tribes, see an opinion of the Cheyenne River Sioux Tribal Court at *Eberhard v. Eberhard*, no. 96-005-A (Chy R. Sx. Ct. App. Feb. 18, 1997).
11. *Cherokee Nation Judicial Appeals Tribunal v. Cherokee Nation*, No. JAT-01-13 (Nov. 26, 2002).
12. The Pascua Yaqui Tribe maintains this policy.
13. See *Oliphant v. Suquamish Indian Tribe*, 435 U.S. 191, 98 S. Ct. 1011, 55 L.Ed.2d 209 (1978).
14. 28 U.S.C. §1738B.

Questions

1. What are some of the reasons a Native survivor of domestic violence might prefer a tribal court divorce to a state court one? What are some reasons a state court divorce might be preferred?
2. Describe the situations when a tribal court generally has exclusive jurisdiction to decide a divorce or custody case.
3. Describe when the Parental Kidnapping Prevention Act could be used to assist Native women fleeing domestic violence situations.
4. How could a victim advocate help in a divorce proceeding in tribal court?

In Your Community

1. What type of laws does your tribe have relating to custody of children or divorce? Who can divorce in your tribal court?
2. What services are available to assist domestic violence victims in court proceedings in your community? Are there legal service programs in your

area that do not practice in tribal court? What action could be taken to encourage them to provide services in tribal court?

Terms Used in Chapter 17

Exclusive: Sole; excludes all others.

Garnishment: A legal taking of the property or wages of another.

Paternity: The legal determination of a man's status as a father.

Pro se: When someone represents him- or herself and appears in a legal proceeding without an attorney.

Tribal code: The laws of the tribe.

The Deafness of Domestic Violence

Can you hear my fear when I stand in front of you,
the Judge, and lie?
what about when I say nothing at all?
If I wasn't scared then I would talk
I would tell everything that's true.
A lack of words becomes my downfall
and you take my abuser's side.
Protection order denied!

Listen!

Listen when I say nothing at all
Listen when it sounds like a lie
Listen and understand
Educate yourself
and learn how domestic violence takes its victims by the hand
and makes them feel smaller than a grain of sand.
Listen and learn how victims' fear of greater violence
keeps them silent, causes them to lie about the abuse
Listen before you choose.

Can you hear my abuser laugh when you,
the police, arrest me for fighting back?
and he gets nothing, maybe 24 hours in jail,
this is how the system sets itself up to fail.

Listen!

Listen as my abuser laughs on the inside
Listen and understand
develop a protocol and a guide
strengthen your police force
stand on the victim's side

Take your time,
observe the surroundings
think before you decide
who began the hitting and the pounding.

Can you hear your own selfishness when you,
the tribal government and the state government,
refuse to work hand in hand?
We are talking about my life, and my pain
not your land.
How can we end the violence when what each of you seek
Power
is the very thing that feeds the abuse and makes sure certain people become the weak?

Listen and put your differences aside
call community meetings,
join forces, cross deputize.
Create a jurisdiction that doesn't thrive on boundaries or lines,
One that doesn't ignore the "End Domestic Violence" signs.

States, uphold tribal decisions
make punishing the criminal the ultimate mission.
Tribes, don't get lost in your pride,
when one of your own is an abuser
don't create laws that help them hide.

Tribes and states, sit down together when making your laws
This illuminates unforeseen flaws.

If the state is closer, tribes,
allow them to intervene.
Time wasted could be the difference between
life and death to a victim,
do you hear what I mean?
See that each entity has a voice.
Create a way for victims to have a choice

Can you hear my child's cries
when you, the Children's Services,
judge my parenting skills
by my two black eyes?
Instead of taking my child away
and making me be the one to pay

create an environment where it is safe for my child to play
Stop the abuser from getting his way.

Tribes, here is your chance, step up and be a role model for the state,
teach them good traditional values and how to appreciate women
before it's too late.

Can you, all who are listening, hear my voice
the victim's voice, at all?
The sound of my abuser's voice has silenced me
It has deafened you,
The sound of my abusers voice has hidden, my voice, in stories told of history
in interpretations and practices of religion.
and it has deafened you.

Listen!

Hear me, ask me, include me the victim in all the decisions
of my life, of my abuse.

   Kimberly Mullican Querdibitty

The Indian Child Welfare Act and Violence Against Women

Chapter 18

JAMES G. WHITE AND SARAH MICHÈLE MARTIN

For many victims of domestic violence, fear of losing custody of their children may hinder their efforts to assert their legal rights. In situations where children are in the victim's home, batterers may threaten to report the mother to child protection services for alleged abuse of her children. If the children are members of the abuser's tribe, he may try to use the Indian Child Welfare Act (ICWA) to intimidate and manipulate his partner in circumstances where the law has no applicability. Many times, an abuser will incorrectly threaten that ICWA will give him priority in a custody dispute between the two of them. ICWA never applies in cases of custody disputes between two parents. However, in situations where the act does apply (such as removal of children due to abuse or neglect), it may sometimes work against the victim, particularly if those assisting her do not understand the act. It is therefore important that advocates working with victims of domestic violence gain a working knowledge of the purposes and applicability of the Indian Child Welfare Act.[1] A thorough understanding of the Indian Child Welfare Act must begin with its history.

Historically, American Indians have struggled to maintain their cultural identity and traditional ways. Throughout the United States, American Indian children have been removed from their families by federal, state, and private agencies in numbers that far exceed those of non-Indian children. In the 1950s and 1960s, the Indian Adoption Project placed hundreds of Native American children with white parents, the first national effort to place an entire child population transracially and transculturally.[2]

In Minnesota, for example, an average of one of every four Indian children younger than age one was removed from his or her Indian home and adopted by a non-Indian couple. Many of these children were taken from their homes simply because a paternalistic state system failed to recognize traditional Indian culture and expected Indian families to conform to non-Indian ways.[3]

In California in the 1970s, there were 2.7 times as many Indian children in foster care as non-Indian children. The adoption rate for California's Indian children was 8.4 times greater than that of its non-Indian children and 6.0 times greater than that of any other minority. Of California's adopted American Indian children, 92.5 percent had been placed with non-Indian families.[4]

In Arizona, home to twenty-one federally recognized tribes, there were three times as many Indian children in foster care as non-Indian children. Government statistics for 1973–1976 reveal that one of every ninety-eight Indian children was in foster care in contrast to one of every 264 non-Indian children. Of these foster children, one of every fifty-three Indian children was adopted in contrast to one of every 220 non-Indian children. This represented, by proportion, four times as many Indian children in adoptive homes as non-Indian children.[5]

These statistics reveal that the American Indian family was being separated at a rate greater than any other culture in the United States. Most of these children were not being given the opportunity to grow up with a sense of their heritage. Congress was presented with studies "showing recurring developmental problems encountered during adolescence by Indian children raised in a white environment."[6] These concerns are reflected in the congressional findings set forth in the act:

> [T]here is no resource that is more vital to the continued existence and integrity of Indian tribes than their children and that the United States has a direct interest, as trustee, in protecting Indian children who are members of or eligible for membership in an Indian tribe; (4) that an alarmingly high percentage of Indian families are broken up by the removal, often **unwarranted**, of their children from them by nontribal public and private agencies and that an alarmingly high percentage of such children are placed in non-Indian foster and adoptive homes and institutions; and (5) that the States, exercising their recognized jurisdiction over Indian child custody proceedings through administrative and judicial bodies, have often failed to recognize the essential tribal relations of Indian people and the cultural and social standards prevailing in Indian communities and families.[7]

What Are the Purposes of the Indian Child Welfare Act?

In order to properly address a victim's concerns regarding the act, it is important to always keep in mind the public policies that form the basis of the law. The primary purposes of the Indian Child Welfare Act are set forth in its "congressional declaration of policy," which states:

> The Congress hereby declares that it is the policy of this Nation to protect the best interests of Indian children and to promote the stability and security of In-

dian tribes and families by the establishment of minimum Federal standards for the removal of Indian children from their families and the placement of such children in foster or adoptive homes which will reflect the unique values of Indian culture, and by providing for assistance to Indian tribes in the operation of child and family service programs.[8]

The act is primarily concerned with preserving the continued existence and integrity of Indian tribes by preventing the unwarranted removal of Indian children from their families by nontribal public and private agencies.[9] It is based upon the fundamental assumption that it is in the Indian child's best interest that its relationship to its tribe be protected.[10] As the U.S. Supreme Court noted in the seminal case *Mississippi Band of Choctaw Indians v. Holyfield*, the main effect of the Indian Child Welfare Act is to curtail state authority.[11] ICWA has no applicability to custody proceedings in tribal courts.

Advocates working with victims of domestic violence must be able to distinguish between circumstances in which the act applies and those in which it does not. In state proceedings where the act does apply, the protection of the Indian child's relationship to his or her tribe can have a major impact upon custody determinations. Under such circumstances, the mother's advocate can assist her by working with tribal advocates and social workers to ensure that the abused parent has support and can safely exercise visitation, free from threats and manipulation of the abuser. Moreover, advocates can help an abused mother in providing her children with opportunities to connect with healthy tribal members and develop positive relationships with the tribe.

When Does the Indian Child Welfare Act Apply?

The Indian Child Welfare Act applies to state "child custody proceedings" involving an "Indian child," as those terms are defined in the act. The term "Indian child" is defined by the act as "any unmarried person who is under the age of eighteen and is either (a) a member of an Indian tribe or (b) eligible[12] for membership in an Indian tribe and is the biological child of a member of an Indian tribe." It should be noted that "enrollment" is not necessary to a determination of tribal membership under the act.[13] As the court stated in *In re Jeffrey A.*,

> "Determination of tribal membership or eligibility for membership is made exclusively by the tribe." (Rule 1439(g).) "[O]ne of the primary purposes of giving notice to the tribe is to enable the tribe to determine whether the child involved in the proceedings is an Indian child." (*In re Desiree F.* (2000) 83 Cal.App.4th 460, 470, 99 Cal.Rptr.2d 688.) Enrollment is not determinative of membership in a tribe. (Rule 1439(g)(2); Guidelines at p. 67586.) "The Indian status of the child need not be certain to invoke the notice requirement. Because the question of

membership rests with each Indian tribe, when the juvenile court knows or has reason to believe the child may be an Indian child, notice must be given to the particular tribe in question or the Secretary." (*In re Desiree F.*, supra, 83 Cal.App.4th at p. 471, 99 Cal.Rptr.2d 688.) Furthermore, the ICWA and any federal or state statutes or regulations implementing the ICWA "shall be liberally construed in favor of a result that is consistent with the [ ] preferences" expressed in the ICWA. (Guidelines at p. 67586.)[14]

Most courts have held that a child's actual enrollment in a tribe is controlling regardless of the child's eligibility for enrollment in another tribe.[15] Once a child who is eligible for enrollment in two tribes is enrolled in one of them, a parent from the second tribe cannot change the child's enrollment in order to gain jurisdiction.[16] If a child is enrolled in one tribe, eligibility for enrollment in a second tribe does not give the tribal court of the second tribe jurisdiction under the ICWA.[17] If the child is a member of more than one tribe or is unenrolled but eligible for membership in more than one tribe, the act defines the child's tribe as "the Indian tribe with which the Indian child has the more significant contacts."[18] Jurisdiction is based upon the child's tribal affiliation, not on the parent's tribal membership.[19] The "Indian tribe" must be any Indian tribe, band, nation, or other organized group or community of Indians recognized by the federal government as being eligible for the services provided to Indians by the Secretary of the Interior because of their status as Indians.[20]

The term "child custody proceeding" is defined to include court proceedings for foster care placement, termination of parental rights, and preadoptive and adoptive placement.[21] It does not apply to a custody action solely between the two parents of an Indian child, such as in a divorce action. This is one of the biggest misunderstandings of ICWA and is often the source of batterer's threats and manipulation (he might say "if you leave me, ICWA will give me the children and you'll never see them again"). The term "custody" refers to legal as well as physical custody.[22] The act applies to both voluntary and involuntary proceedings.[23] It does not apply in placements arising out of status[24] offense delinquency actions or in custody disputes arising in divorce actions.[25] It is important to note that if a non-Indian mother were to petition the termination of rights of an Indian father, as might occur in a stepparent adoption, the Indian Child Welfare Act might apply.[26] This can have a major impact upon whether the Indian parent's rights can be terminated, since the act presumes that it is in the child's best interest that his or her relationship to the tribe be protected.

Some state courts have created the "Indian Family Exception," which allows courts to more easily terminate rights to Indian parents. Although the U.S. Supreme Court in *Mississippi Band of Choctaw Indians v. Holyfield*[27] unequivocally stated that Congress intended that the act receive uniform nationwide application, some state jurisdictions have created a judicially created exception, the "Indian Family Exception" first applied by the Kansas Supreme Court in *In re Adoption of Baby Boy L.*[28] The Kansas court declared that "the legislative history behind the Act and the Act itself discloses that the overriding concern of Congress—was not to dictate that an **illegitimate** infant who has never been a member of an Indian home or culture, and probably never would be, should be removed from its primary cultural heritage and placed in an Indian environment over the express objections of its non-Indian mother."[29] This was followed by the Washington Supreme Court in *Matter of Adoption of Crews*,[30] and the Second District Court of Appeals in *In re Bridget R.*, which added a requirement that the proponent of application of the Indian Child Welfare Act demonstrate that either the child or the child's parent "maintains any significant social, cultural or political relationships with Indian life."[31] Although state courts remain significantly split on application of the "Indian Family Exception," many state courts have rejected its application because it ignores the tribe's separate and distinct interest in the child.[32]

Which Courts Have Jurisdiction over Child Custody Actions Involving Indian Children?

The term "jurisdiction" refers to a court's power to decide a case or issue a decree.[33] The Indian Child Welfare Act is a preemptive federal law that governs all state custody proceedings involving Indian children except those incident to divorce, similar actions, or to criminal acts committed by a child.[34] Because federal law is supreme, the jurisdictional provisions contained in the act are controlling where applicable.[35] This is of particular significance where state authorities have removed children because of domestic violence issues in the home.

All too frequently, children are removed by state authorities who accuse the victim of failing to protect her children from witnessing the abuse, or the abuser makes false claims of child abuse as a controlling tactic. The abused parent in cases where ICWA applies may be assisted by the act, as it requires a higher standard or proof of abuse be met before removal of children or allowing the continuation of removal. However, it can also hinder her efforts to regain custody of her children, particularly if she is a non-Indian, by ICWA's preferences that the children be placed with members of the batterer's family or tribe, who may not be supportive of reuniting her with her children.

Exclusive Tribal Court Jurisdiction

The Act provides for exclusive tribal court jurisdiction over any ICWA child custody proceedings involving an Indian child who resides or is **domiciled** within the reservation of such tribe.[36] "Exclusive tribal court jurisdiction" means that only the tribal court has the power to decide a case or issue a decree in an ICWA custody case involving an Indian child who lives or is domiciled on the reservation.[37] The U.S. Supreme Court has held that "domicile" is to be determined by federal law, stating "it is most improbable that Congress would have intended to leave the scope of the statute's key jurisdictional provision subject to definition by state courts as a matter of state law."[38] The parents' domicile is established by physical presence in a place in connection with a certain state of mind concerning one's intent to remain there.[39] A child's domicile is that of its parents. However, if the parents are unmarried, the child's domicile is generally that of his or her mother.[40] Where a child is a ward of a tribal court, the tribal court retains exclusive jurisdiction notwithstanding the residence or domicile of the child.[41]

The act does, however, gives state courts authority to remove an Indian child from his or her parents, who live or are domiciled on a reservation but are temporarily located off the reservation, and place the child in foster care under applicable state law in emergency situations to prevent **imminent** physical harm to the child.[42] The act also imposes a duty upon the state to ensure that the emergency removal terminates immediately when it is no longer necessary to prevent imminent physical harm to the child.[43] Therefore, in removals based upon domestic violence where the mother does not present a risk to the children, having her leave the batterer and obtain a protection order ends the emergency and should require return of the children.

Concurrent Jurisdiction

The act provides for **concurrent** state and tribal court jurisdiction over any child custody proceeding involving an Indian child who does not reside and is not domiciled within the reservation of such tribe.[44] "Concurrent jurisdiction" means that either the state or tribal court has the power to decide the case. However, the U.S. Supreme Court has stated that there is a **presumption** in favor of tribal court jurisdiction.[45] The act also provides that the state court *must* transfer the case to tribal court if either parent, the Indian custodian, or the child's tribe petitions the state court to transfer jurisdiction unless (1) either of the child's parents objects, (2) the tribal court declines jurisdiction, or (3) the state court finds "good cause to the contrary."[46] The party opposing the transfer has the burden of establishing "good cause" to deny transfer of the case to tribal court.[47] It is important for advocates to note that a parent has the absolute right to object to transfer. Therefore the advocate should inform the victim's attorney of any potential problems that could affect the choice of courts. For example, if the tribe's judges are related to the batterer, this could create a conflict of interest. On the other hand, this could militate in either direction depending upon the batterer's family's attitude toward his conduct. The advocate should investigate thoroughly and not assume bias where none may exist.

The Bureau of Indian Affair's Guidelines provide that "good cause" not to transfer the proceedings to tribal court may exist if any of the following circumstances exist: (1) the proceeding was at an advanced stage when the petition to transfer jurisdiction was filed, and the petitioner did not file the petition promptly after receiving notice of the hearing; (2) the Indian child is over twelve years old and objects to the transfer; (3) the evidence necessary to decide the case could not be adequately presented in tribal court without undue hardship to the parties or the witnesses; and (4) the parents of a child over five years old are not available and the child has had little or no contact with the child's tribe or members of the child's tribe.[48] Additionally, the Guidelines specify that socioeconomic conditions and the perceived adequacy of tribal justice systems or social services may not be considered by the state court in making a "good cause to the contrary" determination.[49]

What Evidentiary Standard Must State Courts Use in Indian Child Welfare Act Cases?

In dependency and termination of parental rights proceedings, the act requires state courts to make two findings: (1) that "active efforts" have been made to provide remedial services and rehabilitative programs designed to prevent the breakup of the Indian family and that such services and programs have been unsuccessful[50] and (2) that continued custody of the child by the parent or Indian custodian is likely to result in serious emotional or physical damage to the child.[51]

The primary difference between the evidentiary standards applicable in dependency and severance matters involving Indian children and those involving non-Indian children is the **burden of proof** required. In temporary deprivations of custody of Indian children, such as dependency matters, the findings must be established by **clear and convincing** evidence. This is a higher standard than the **preponderance of the evidence** standard of proof required for non-Indian children. In termination of parental rights proceedings involving Indian children, the findings must be established **beyond a reasonable doubt**. This is a higher standard than the clear and convincing standard of proof required for terminations applicable to non-Indian children. These can be very significant distinctions when attempting to prove domestic violence allegations. Some state courts have required that the "active efforts" finding of 25 U.S.C. § 1912(d) also be proven beyond a reasonable doubt.[52]

Additionally, cases governed by the act require "testimony of expert qualified witnesses."[53] "Qualified expert witness" is meant to apply to expertise beyond the normal social worker qualifications.[54] Such expert testimony based upon familiarity with the tribal cultural standards is needed to provide the state court with knowledge of the social and cultural aspects of Indian life to diminish the risk of any cultural bias.[55] The Bureau of Indian Affairs Guidelines provide that:

> Knowledge of tribal culture and childrearing practices will frequently be very valuable to the court. Determining the likelihood of future harm frequently involves predicting future behavior—which is influenced to a large degree by culture. Specific behavior patterns will often need to be placed in the context of the total culture to determine whether they are likely to cause serous emotional harm.[56]

The act requires that the court make findings that "active efforts" have been made to provide remedial services and rehabilitative programs designed to prevent the breakup of the Indian family. This can provide a substantial protection to the mother in that she can demand that the court provide her with the services she needs to keep her children safe. The advocate should be involved in the child custody case to the extent that the advocate can provide support to the mother and verify that appropriate services are being provided. The advocate should then be able to testify as to the mother's safe behavior and her participation in appropriate services.

What Are the Indian Child Welfare Act's "Placement Preferences"?

An Indian child may not be placed in foster care unless the judge finds by clear and convincing evidence that parental custody is likely to result in serious physical or emotional harm to the child.[57] The act's emphasis on the social and cultural aspects of Indian life is reflected in its mandatory preferences when placing an Indian child in foster, preadoptive, or adoptive homes. The act mandates that the standards to be applied in meeting the preference requirements be those "prevailing social and cultural standards of the Indian community in which the parent or extended family resides or with which the parent or extended family members maintain social and cultural ties."[58]

The act requires that, in the absence of good cause to the contrary, when a state court places an Indian child in foster care or in a preadoptive placement, preference in placement must be given to: (1) a member of the Indian child's extended family; (2) a foster home licensed, approved, or specified by the Indian child's tribe; (3) an Indian foster home licensed or approved by an authorized non-Indian licensing authority; or (4) an institution for children approved by an Indian tribe or operated by an Indian organization that has a program suitable to meet the Indian child's needs.[59] The act also requires that in the absence of good cause to the contrary, when a state court places an Indian child in an adoptive placement, preference in placement must be given to: (1) a member of the Indian child's extended family, (2) other members of the Indian child's tribe, or (3) other Indian families. Given the fact that some courts have stated that "when the act is read as a whole, it is clear that Congress has made a very strong policy choice that Indian children, including those who have a non-Indian parent, belong in an Indian home," such preferences can have a significant impact upon child custody considerations in domestic violence situations.[60]

Conclusion

While the Indian Child Welfare Act has limited application in the context of domestic violence, in those situations in which it does apply it can have a significant impact on the outcome of custody determinations. It is essential that both advocates and attorneys involved in assisting victims of domestic violence in child custody matters be sufficiently informed about the applicability and consequences of the act. This will permit them to make use of the act's helpful provisions and avoid any negative consequences.

Notes

1. *The Indian Child Welfare Act*, 25 U.S.C.§1901 et seq.
2. The "Indian Adoption Project," available at http://darkwing.uoregon.edu/~adoption/topics/ICWA.html.
3. B.J. Jones, "The Indian Child Welfare Act: The Need for a Separate Law," available at http://www.abanet.org/genpractice/magazine/1995/fall/indianchildwelfareact.html.
4. American Indian Child Resource Center, "American Indian Child Welfare Act," available at http://www.aicrc.org/icwa.html.
5. Arizona Department of Economic Security Reports, "Provision of Child Welfare Services to Indian Children and Families," Arizona (1977). Unpublished report.
6. *Mississippi Band of Choctaw Indians v. Holyfield*, 490 U.S. 30, 50 n. 24. (1989).
7. 25 U.S.C. §§1901(3), (4) and (5), Congressional Findings.
8. 25 U.S.C. §1902, Congressional Declaration of Policy.
9. *Matter of Adoption of Child of Indian Heritage*, 111 N.J. 155, 543 A.2d 925, 930 (N.J. 1988).
10. *Matter of Appeal in Pima County Juvenile Action No. S-903*, 130 Ariz. 202, 204, 635 P.2d 187 (Ariz.App. 1981), cert. Denied 455 U.S. 1007 (1982).
11. *Mississippi Band of Choctaw Indians v. Holyfield*, 490 U.S. 30, 45 n. 17 (1989).
12. Eligibility for enrollment is determined by the law of the child's tribe. In *re Adoption of Riffle*, 902 P.2d 542, 545 (Mont. 1995).
13. *People ex rel D.T.*, 667 N.W.2d 694 (S.D.2003).
14. *In re Jeffrey A.*, 103 Cal. App.4th 1103, 1107, 127 Cal. Rptr.2d 314 (Cal.App.2002).
15. *People ex rel T.I.*, 707 N.W.2d 826, 834 (S.D.2005).
16. *In re Welfare of Children of J.B.*, 698 N.W.2d 160, 166 (Minn.App.2005).
17. *People ex rel* T.I., op. cit.
18. 25 U.S.C. §1903(5), Definitions.
19. *John v. Baker*, 982 P.2d 738, 759 (Alaska 1999).

20. 25 U.S.C. §1903(8), Definitions.
21. 25 U.S.C. §1903(1), Definitions.
22. See *J.W. v. R.J.*, 951 P.2d 1206, 1213 (Alaska 1998), and cases cited therein.
23. 25 U.S.C. §1913, Parental rights; voluntary termination, and 24 U.S.C. §1912, Pending court proceedings.
24. A status offense is an offense committed by a juvenile that is only an offense because of the child's status as a juvenile and that would not be an offense if committed by an adult, such as drinking and truancy.
25. 25 U.S.C. §1903(1), Definitions.
26. *In re Crystal K.*, 226 Cal.App.3rd 655, 276 Cal.Rptr.619 (1990).
27. *Mississippi Band of Choctaw Indians v. Holyfield*, 490 U.S. 30 (1989).
28. *In re Adoption of Baby Boy L.*, 231 Kan. 199, 643 P.2d 168 (1982).
29. *In re Adoption of Baby Boy L.*, op. cit.
30. *Matter of Adoption of Crews*, 118 Wash.2d 561, 825 P.2d 305 (1992).
31. *In re Bridget R.*, 49 Cal.Rptr.2d 507, 529-30 (Cal.App.1996).
32. See *Michael J, Jr. v. Michael J., Sr.*, 198 Ariz. 154, 7 P.3d 960 (App.2000); *State, In the Interest of D.A.C.*, 933 P.2d 993 (Utah App.1997); *In re Adoption of Child of Indian Heritage*, 111 N.J. 155, 543 A.2d 925 (1988).
33. *Black's Law Dictionary*, 7th Ed., p. 855 (1999).
34. *Matter of N.S.*, 474 N.W.2d 96, 100 (S.D.1991) (Sabers, J. Concurring).
35. *Matter of Adoption of Halloway*, 732 P.2d 962, 966 (Utah 1986).
36. 25 U.S.C. §1911(a), Indian tribe jurisdiction over Indian child custody proceedings; (a) Exclusive jurisdiction.
37. See, 49 C.J.S., Judgments §§449-451, regarding validity of judgments.
38. *Mississippi Band of Choctaw Indians v. Holyfield*, op. cit. at 45.
39. *Mississippi Band of Choctaw Indians v. Holyfield*, op. cit. at 48.
40. *Matter of Appeal in Pima County Juvenile Action No S-903*, 130 Ariz. 202, 204, 635 P.2d 187 (Ariz.App.1981), cert. Denied 455 U.S. 1007 (1982).
41. 25 U.S.C. §1911(a), Indian tribe jurisdiction over Indian child custody proceedings; (a) Exclusive jurisdiction.
42. 25 U.S.C. §1922. Emergency removal or placement of child; termination; appropriate action.
43. 25 U.S.C. §1922. Emergency removal or placement of child; termination; appropriate action.
44. 25 U.S.C. §1911(b), Indian tribe jurisdiction over Indian child custody proceedings; (b) Transfer of proceedings; declination by tribal court.
45. *Mississippi Band of Choctaw Indians v. Holyfield*, 490 U.S. 30, 36 (1989).
46. 25 U.S.C. §1911(b), Indian tribe jurisdiction over Indian child custody proceedings; (b) Transfer of proceedings; declination by tribal court.
47. *Matter of Appeal in Maricopa County Juvenile Action JS-8287*, 171 Ariz. 104, 108, 828 P2d 1245, 1248 (App.1991).
48. 44 Fed.Reg 67591; see also, House Report No. 95-1386, 1978 U.S.C.C.A.N.
49. 44 Fed.Reg 67591.
50. 25 U.S.C. §1912(d), Pending court proceedings; (d) Remedial services and rehabilitative programs; preventive measures and 25 U.S.C. §1912(f), Pending court proceedings; (f) Parental rights termination orders; evidence; determination of damage to child.
51. 25 U.S.C. §1912(e) and 25 U.S.C. §1912(f).
52. *Matter of Appeal in Maricopa County Juvenile Action JS-8287*, 171 Ariz. 104, 113; 828 P.2d 1245, 1254 (App.1991).

53. 25 U.S.C. §1912(e) and 25 U.S.C. §1912(f).
54. House Report No. 95-1386, 1978 U.S.C.C.A.N. at 7545.
55. *Matter of N.L.*, 754 P.2d 863, 867 (Okla.1988).
56. 44 Fed. Reg. at 67593.
57. 57 25 U.S.C. § 1912(e)
58. 25 U.S.C. §1915(d), Placement of Indian children; social and cultural standards applicable.
59. 25 U.S.C. §1915(b), Placement of Indian children; (b) Foster care or preadoptive placement; criteria; preferences.
60. *Matter of Appeal in Coconino County Juvenile Action J-10175*, 153 Ariz. 346, 349, 736 P.2d 829, 832 (Ariz.App.1987).

Questions

1. A common threat made by a perpetrator of domestic violence to a Native victim is "I am going to report you to social services for child abuse." If you are a Native victim living off the reservation, how might the Indian Child Welfare Act help you, if a report is made?
2. What are "active efforts"? How do you think "active efforts" are different than efforts in a non-ICWA case?
3. What type of cases does ICWA apply to?
4. What were the key purposes for enacting ICWA? Do you believe it has made a difference since its enactment?
5. What are the pros and cons of transferring an ICWA case from state court to a tribal court for a Native woman, if the tribal court is the tribe of the abuser, not her tribe?

In Your Community

1. Does your tribe respond to ICWA cases throughout the United States? What type of structure or infrastructure do they have to ensure that they can assertively respond? Describe a common response?
2. Do social services in the state in which you reside adequately train social workers and judges on the requirements of ICWA? If not, what can be done to adequately provide training?
3. Do the state courts in your area follow ICWA requirements in child protection cases? What could you or your tribe do to improve their response?

Terms Used in Chapter 18

Beyond a reasonable doubt: Proof that results in being fully satisfied and entirely convinced of a fact and circumstance.

Burden of proof: In the law of evidence, the necessity to affirmatively prove a fact, facts, or issue.

Concurrent: Existing at the same time.

Clear and convincing: Proof that results in a reasonable certainty of the truth or fact. Requires more than a preponderance of the evidence and less than proof beyond a reasonable doubt.

Dependency proceeding: A formal court proceeding to determine if a child's welfare requires a state or tribe to intervene. Other names: child protection proceeding or child abuse and neglect proceeding.

Domicile: A person's legal home.

Illegitimate: Born to parents who are not married to each other.

Imminent: About to happen, near at hand.

Preponderance of the evidence: A degree of proof that is more probable than not.

Presumption: An inference (something that is implied) in favor of a particular fact.

Unwarranted: Not justified or deserved.

Suggested Further Reading

Indian Child Welfare Act: California Judges' Benchguide (2000), available at www.calindian.org/icwa.htm.

Larrington, Jane. *Overview for Judges on the Indian Child Welfare Act and Domestic Violence* (12/22/03). Southwest Center for Law and Policy, available at www.swclap.org/article5.pdf.

National Indian Child Welfare Association website, www.nicwa.org.

Spears, Linda. *Building Bridges Between Domestic Violence Organizations and Child Protective Services.* (February 2000), available at www.vawnet.org/NRCDVPublications/BCSDV/Papers/BCS7_cps.php.

Tribal Law and Policy Institute website: http://www.tribal-institute.org/lists/icwa.htm.

NO ESCAPE

Anger erupts from anger delivered,
living day to day, night to long night,
trying to avoid the pain that is always home.
Home is the ache of cruel words, and
the silence that is required to survive.
Like the air we breathe, we cannot avoid it, and we cannot see it; we live with it,
and don't know how to survive without it.
It's a trap we know is set, to step around, and accidentally trip.
Long shadows mean that safety is over, it's time.
Walking into the ambush is the daily routine.

That necessary invisibility that was learned as a child lives on.
It seeps through my skin, controls my words, and makes my choices.
I participate unwillingly, thinking this is love, this is home . . .
Until I realize that it's safer to be alone.

I can't talk, because then I would have to admit what is real and what is not.
I want to go back and be a child.
I want to sing, I want to play, I want to be numb.
Until, one day, the swollen river overflows its banks,
The storm is raging; you can't control nature, or understand its power.
It doesn't matter if I love you, it is power, and it is everywhere.

What about my people,
can this be tradition?
No, we are lost, following a new familiar path:
Wanting to hurt, but not hurt ourselves?
We dance, we sing, we laugh, we have ceremonies,
and we have funerals.
We poison ourselves and each other,
watch one another in slow deliberate suicide,
grasping, clutching, thinking: this is life itself.

     Anonymous

The Role of Probation in Providing Safety for Native Women

Chapter 19

GEORGE TWISS

The role of **probation** in domestic violence cases, a rapidly developing area in the criminal justice field, is fueled by an increased awareness of the dynamics and societal consequences of domestic violence. Criminal justice systems, including probation departments, must adjust to new laws addressing violence against women. Established probation strategies are recognized as woefully inadequate (and often dangerous) to the victims. They tend to be ineffective in dealing with the manipulative domestic violence offender.

Nowhere is this problem more apparent than in Indian Country, where Native women[1] have the horrifying distinction of being three and a half times as likely to be victims of physical and sexual violence as any other ethnic group in the United States.[2] Federal funding provided for the addition of law enforcement officers to tribal departments without a corresponding increase in jail space. New tribal domestic violence codes result in an increased number of identified offenders with no place to incarcerate them for their violence. Yet something must be done to make them accountable for their behavior, while providing rehabilitation and hope for successful reintegration back into our Indian communities.

One answer is to increase the number of Indian Country probation officers with funds from the Violence Against Women Act. Cultural and community resources also must be identified to enhance probation efforts. A customized strategy of intensive supervision appears to be our best hope for enhancing the safety of our women and children. That strategy must incorporate the specific customs and traditions of individual tribal jurisdictions to make it a viable sentencing option for tribal courts.

Probation must be redefined, because it has become a static entity, with procedures and processes becoming the primary force behind supervision and enforcement. The needs and safety of the victim, and even the offender, are routinely secondary to the process itself. The challenge for Indian Country domestic violence probation officers is to develop a new strategy that gives priority to the safety and needs of the victims.

The majority of this chapter focuses on developing or enhancing tribal probation strategies to best provide for the safety of women in Indian Country. However, many Indian nations lack the resources, infrastructure, or personnel to implement a functioning probation department. This chapter concludes with strategies that could provide a tribe with some level of supervision and accountability for domestic violence offenders without having an established probation officer or probation department.

Evolution of Indian Country Probation

In precolonized Native communities of North America, probation as we know it today was an alien concept. Social and community standards were constantly monitored and reinforced by all the members of the community, instead of by a designated individual or group. Teachings of respect and responsibility promoted individual accountability for inappropriate or harmful behavior. Timely intervention and support of family and community members reinforced individual responsibility.

The consequences for noncompliance with the standards of the community were commonly understood to be traditional reparations, such as **mediation** by an elder or medicine person, **shunning**, a request to leave the group, forced **banishment**, or death, depending on the seriousness of the violation. Everyone monitored adherence to the rules of the community, which were passed from generation to generation through oral tradition. It was the responsibility of each individual to find out what reparation was necessary and what changes in behavior were required for inappropriate behavior. The offending individual could accept guidance and was expected to seek it from elders, relatives, and other community members in his or her efforts to change his or her ways. The responsibility for rehabilitation was the individual's and the individual's alone. Consequences were clear, and the offending person knew the community was watching to see if he or she did change.

This traditional form of justice, although seemingly unstructured and simplistic to European outsiders, did have structure, **precedent**, and procedures that were determined by the community. Some Native nations had more formalized processes and some had less-structured ways of addressing bad behavior. But all used a community-based form of offense monitoring and rehabilitation that placed the responsibility for change directly on the individual offender. Help was available, but the offender had to accept responsibility for his or her actions and ask for that help.

With the advent of colonization and military occupation, traditional Native tribal justice practices were discouraged or forbidden. Subsequent Indian Country policies helped shape tribal criminal justice systems that mirror those of the Anglo-American system.[3] Most Native court systems have lacked the resources to implement and maintain a consistent and effective probation effort. Those tribes with functional probation departments implemented probation following Anglo-American processes, procedures, values, and priorities. They were more concerned with **restitution** for property damage than rehabilitation and reintegration of offenders into the community. Probation efforts addressing domestic violence offenders followed the same practices.

For many tribes, this was the case until the Violence Against Women Act of 1994 provided an influx of resources for tribal criminal justice systems, allowing tribes to expand existing probation departments or establish domestic violence probation services within their courts for the first time. Additionally, many tribes now have the resources to develop and implement new probation strategies for domestic violence offenders that are culturally consistent with traditional Native concepts of justice.

Currently Indian Country's westernized criminal justice system depends on the courts, law enforcement, and probation officers to function as the enforcers of community standards. This system replaced the underlying teachings and participation of the family. Unfortunately, this Western response has not stopped violence against women in Indian Country. Indian Country probation practitioners recognize that it is time to implement new strategies that include higher levels of supervision and the assistance and coercive power of the community to shape and change criminal behavior.

Historical Native Justice and the "New" Non-Native Justice Strategies

For those unfamiliar with traditional Native justice practices, one only has to look to several supposedly "new" national criminal justice strategies to understand the traditional Native community-based response to crime.

For millennia, Native warrior or social societies were asked to carry out policing and security duties at events, special occasions, or during times of conflict.[4] These societies enforced strict community guidelines at all events. Their authority derived from the community and from the respect they earned by demonstrated strength of character and integrity. They may have played a traditional role or they may have been appointed on an as-needed basis. They were answerable to the community, responding to the immediate needs and concerns of that community. The warrior and social societies actively solicited the input of the community and requested community assistance in carrying out their responsibilities. This community-oriented policing was practiced by Native law enforcement long before non-Indians set foot in North America or thought to **emulate** this practice.

Every **infraction** of the rules of the community was met with an immediate consequence, no matter how minor the offense. The idea was to prevent major infractions by addressing minor ones before they escalated. These societies were also expected to proactively address issues through education, mentoring, and role-modeling proper behavior to avoid conflict. The community assisted by reporting the actions of individuals causing concern, or situations that might lead to a conflict within the community. The society then addressed the issue before anything further happened. These are the primary goals of the contemporary "Broken Windows"[5] theory of crime intervention: address minor infractions, as reported by the community, before they escalate into major crimes.

The American Probation and **Parole** Association (APPA) has developed a model domestic violence probation policy that promotes appropriate and effective strategies for domestic violence offender probation, including enhanced supervised probation.[6] The idea is to incorporate an interagency and community-based monitoring effort with direct feedback from the woman, her family, the offender's family, and other people in the offender's community. The program is developed on a case-by-case basis, to reflect the specifics of the crime, the needs of the victim, the needs of the community, and the needs of the offender. The offender takes an active part in formulating his program and is aware of the specific consequences of noncompliance at the start of his probation. The goal is to reeducate the domestic violence offender and modify his behavior by making him accountable not only to the probation officer but also to individual members of the community. The approach is victim-based with a focus on strict offender accountability. Historically, Native communities employed this same approach to rehabilitation and accountability, but with each member of the community providing supervision and monitoring on a daily basis.

Although the above-noted strategies may be oversimplified here, the underlying point should give hope to Native communities. Our people had effective ways to deal with inappropriate behavior before the influence of the predominant culture. Combining these strategies into an effective and culturally consistent probation approach with domestic violence offenders in our current system is the challenge.

The "Paper Chase"

Domestic violence offenders are chronic offenders who are extremely manipulative. They do not voluntarily change their behavior.[7] Without effective intervention and programming, they will keep offending, the violence becoming more frequent and more severe. The probation officer must use the coercive power of the law and community pressure to draw attention to any subsequent violent behavior, otherwise the offender escapes responsibility. If the system allows him to continue his violence without holding him accountable, and community members either condone or ignore his behavior, the offender feels he has been given the green light to use violence against his partner whenever he pleases.

Past probation efforts were a "paper chase." The probation officer made reports to the court based on monthly check-ins by the offender, accompanied by a printout of the offender's interim criminal activity, on-time check-ins, and proof of employment. If an offender wanted to successfully complete probation, all he had to do was snow his probation officer during check-ins, keep his job, and avoid being arrested. The message to the offender was to avoid getting caught committing a crime. It did not address whether his partner was still being victimized.

Fortunately, the inadequacies of this approach with domestic violence offenders have become increasingly evident as the dynamics of intimate partner violence are researched and articulated. We now recognize that system manipulation is especially prominent among domestic violence offenders.[8] A batterer likes nothing more than a predictable bureaucratic response to his violence. They are adept at playing mind games with their victims and spreading disinformation among acquaintances, family, friends, and law enforcement personnel. Why should it be a surprise that they also strive to manipulate their probation officers? Their main goal is to convince any probation officer they are not dangerous or violent and that they do not warrant more than a cursory check-in now and then. They might be cooperative, rational, and docile with their probation officers, while still intimidating, harassing, and assaulting their partners. As far as they are concerned, the less attention or monitoring their probation officers gives them, the better.

For those on probation in tribal courts, playing the game was even easier. Tribal courts and state courts do not regularly share information on offenders. An offender was less likely to have anything come to the attention of either a tribal or state probation officer if the activity occurred in the other jurisdiction. Consequently, an offender could have had several arrests in one jurisdiction while being considered fully compliant with probation conditions in the other. In addition, neither system was actively looking for violent behavior, only reported crimes.

Enhanced monitoring was usually the exception rather than the norm, since statistics were not available to make it a viable option. So probation falls back on its established paper chase in addressing all crimes. Closely watching those on probation or parole is not a new idea. The strategy was implemented in the late 1980s and throughout the 1990s to address child sexual abuse, abduction, and exploitation. Parents and other concerned citizens demanded that authorities actively monitor the activities of child sex offenders on probation or parole. Probation strategies have since adapted to include enhanced monitoring for all offenders who may be especially dangerous and highly likely to reoffend, including batterers.

Indian Country domestic violence probation must develop similar strategies. Supervision must focus on whether or not the violence is still occurring, not whether the offender has been arrested for a crime. The result is monitoring the current behavior rather than waiting for the next crime. Domestic violence probation is thus more effective and focused on keeping victims safe, rather than focused on satisfying a specific probation process.

Realigning the Focus

Victim Involvement in Supervision

It is important to answer the following questions when developing a domestic violence probation strategy:

- What was the reason for passing a domestic violence law on our reservation?
- Was it to increase the workload of law enforcement and the court?
- Was it to provide more offenders for probation to supervise?
- Or was it because our women were being battered and abused at an alarming rate?

The social and criminal injustice evidenced by the numbers of Native women suffering at the hands of those who profess to love them was the force behind such laws. The resources available under the Violence Against Women Act made it possible for tribes to finally address this problem. Correcting the injustice requires that the focus of all agencies be on the safety of the women we serve instead of on our individual procedures.

Since law enforcement officers, prosecutors, and judges adjust to new laws, priorities, and procedures, probation departments and probation officers need to make adjustments as well. Probation strategies must adapt to address the specific behavior these new laws are designed to correct. But how do we best monitor and correct that behavior?

Unlawful behavior is easy to spot when it is reported to police and becomes a crime. Domestic violence, however, is characterized by a pattern of conduct by which one individual exercises power and control over another. In that cycle of abuse, most of the violence occurs outside the view or knowledge of the police. So, who in law enforcement can actively monitor that behavior to make sure the violence and abuse are not still occurring? Probation officers develop the type of contacts over time with the offender that can identify and curtail recurring abuse and violence.

To concentrate on the behavior of the offender, probation officers need to make the probation term an ongoing investigation of the offender's behavior. Probation officers have the ability to become more involved with probationers. They also have the administrative authority to make offenders accountable for a wide range of behaviors and activities that do not fall within the jurisdiction of law enforcement.

Probation officers must be quick to address even the smallest infraction with immediate sanctions. Offenders will test whether the probation officer and the tribal court are serious about holding him accountable. The first sanction should be to extend the offender's term of probation to an additional year of supervision, if possible. This reinforces the importance of compliance and demonstrates how serious the court and the tribe view the offender's behavior. This may also temper any rage he may feel later after he finally realizes that his supervision is a reality and not merely an inconvenience.

Probation officers must be prepared to use all of their resources to investigate and monitor offender behavior during the probation term. This includes establishing and maintaining effective lines of communication with those who know the offender best, including his victim. This approach does not only require safety checks with the victim, it also entails promoting a relationship in which she feels comfortable speaking with the probation officer anytime.

Often probation officers get caught up in official function and do not consider the impact of probation activities on the victim and her children. For example, a probation officer may feel an offender needs alcohol treatment as soon as possible, and can then pursue other programming needs. Getting the offender into treatment, in the long run, should be beneficial for him, the victim, and their children. However, does the officer take into consideration the welfare of the victim, presuming to know what is best for her? That is very arrogant and condescending. The officer has taken the place of her batterer in trying to control her life. What if the offender is a seasonal worker and the sole support of his family and the officer plans to send him to treatment during his employment season? Has he stopped to think how this will affect his family? Who will feed them and provide for them while he is, in the words of one victim, "off discovering himself"? A probation officer must take the time to obtain the woman's input.

Often an ill-timed probation requirement or activity can place the victim at greater risk of violence, or sabotage the offender's rehabilitative programming. For example, if the probationer's main excuse for his violence was jealousy, sending him away from his family for thirty to sixty days might not be the best strategy. He has convinced himself that she is just waiting for an opportunity to leave him for someone else, so not knowing what she is doing may trigger violence when he returns or he may become distracted and not benefit from the rehabilitation. Knowing what makes him tick by talking to his partner may minimize those situations. She may help develop more effective programming strategies.

Victim "safety checks" should be in-person. She is a real person and not just part of a procedure. She will be impacted by any supervision decisions the officer makes. In person the probation officer can also pick up on her body language any indication that she may be hiding an incident of the offender's inappropriate behavior or an undisclosed fear:

> Battered women are often very attuned to their partners' moods as a way to assess their level of danger. They focus on their partners' needs and "cover up" for them as part of their survival strategy. Battered women's behaviors are not symptomatic of some underlying "dysfunction," but are the life-saving skills necessary to protect them and their children from further harm.[9]

Even if safety checks are done for their safety, many women will not relish visits from their partners' probation officer. They may not be willing to discuss their fears and concerns.

A safety check should never change into an interrogation of the woman or the allegation that she is "covering" for the offender. The probation officer must realize that any evasion, denial, or half-truth elicited from the victim is part of her survival strategy. Being truthful and informative with her is imperative. She may never feel fully able to trust or confide in her partner's probation officer, but she needs to know, through repeated efforts by that officer, that she can come to him or her if she is in danger or has concerns.

If anything appears amiss during the visit with the woman, it should be part of the ongoing investigative function of the probation officer to find out which of her partner's behaviors has made her afraid or wary. Ask her what is wrong, but do not expect her to answer right away, or at all. No matter how a woman responds to probation safety checks, it still sends a direct message to her batterer that someone is watching and checking on his behavior.

Keeping the safety of the victim as the focus of the supervision has a twofold purpose: observing the offender's behavior and validating the woman in the eyes of the community. Probation officers have noted that the community seems to report subsequent violence or abuse more readily when the woman is recognized as a crime victim. Also, community members will report an activity to a probation officer more readily than they will report to the police.

Establish a system of contacts with those people who are involved regularly with the probationer and his victim. Develop a close working relationship with the victim's advocate. Her advocate will often be the safest conduit for the victim to keep in contact with probation. Others who can serve as contacts to the victim can be family members, friends, counselors, or other service providers.

No matter the source, any report of physical threats, death threats, or suicide threats by the offender should be immediately shared with police. The threat constitutes an immediate danger to the offender's partner and should be followed by immediate efforts to get him into custody.

Lethality Assessments

There are many lethality assessment tools in use and practitioners disagree on which is the most effective. Regardless of which tool is used, some type of assessment must be done to document the potential for further violence by individual offenders. The assessment should also be a key determinant in adopting a specific probation case strategy for each offender. Assessments should be ongoing throughout the probation term:

> Some batterers are life-threatening. While it is true that all batterers are dangerous, some are more likely to kill than others and some are more likely to kill at specific times. Regardless of whether or not there is a protection order in effect, one should constantly evaluate whether an abuser is likely to kill his partner, other family members, and/or police personnel . . . It is important to conduct ongoing assessments, no matter how many times the abuse has occurred or no matter how many times police have been called to the same household.[10]

Use the assessment to determine the likelihood and possible severity of future violence against others by the offender. Any recent escalation in the frequency and severity of violence should automatically indicate a high-risk status, which should trigger the need for increased supervision and other measures to provide for victim safety.

Risk assessments are not an exact science. No measure of lethality has been found that takes into account all the variables of individual personality, individual history, and situation. The best a probation officer can determine is a general likelihood of continued or escalating violence. In order to establish these tendencies, the probation officer must first rely on available information, past history, and his or her own experience working with domestic violence offenders.

Courts and probation departments are constantly trying to establish scientific and measurable criteria in this area. Some jurisdictions require the use of an established assessment tool to give the court a basis for special conditions, high bail amounts, or added victim safety measures. Existing lethality assessment tools range from a subjective checklist[11] to more rating-based tools, such as the Woman Abuse Scale,[12] Conflict Tactics Scale,[13] Field Assessment Danger Risk Factors,[14]

Spousal Assault Risk Appraisal Guide (SARA),[15] and Partner Abuse Prognostic Scale (PAPS).[16] Whether a probation department utilizes one of these tools can depend on policy, or whether the department can afford the cost of the software and/or materials.

Although these more widely used assessment tools differ in format and rating system, each concentrates on the victim's perception of risk and the offender's history of violence as basic determinants of lethality. In the absence of a formal assessment tool, probation officers can still provide an informed perception of lethality and prepare an initial strategy for probation:

> Case Assessment: Assessment activities include both offenders and victims. Offenders are told that victims will be contacted by the probation officer initially and throughout the supervision period. Victims' accounts of the violence are heard as credible and used as a basis for making case decisions. Victims are advised during the assessment process, and subsequently, of their rights and actions they may take to increase their safety. All family violence offenders are initially classified as high-risk and assessed for substance abuse problems.[17]

In the interest of safety, all domestic violence offenders should be initially classified as high-risk for lethality, especially in the absence of established jurisdictional standards or accepted use of any specific assessment tool.

Safety of Sources

Confidentiality is vital to protecting victims against retaliatory violence. Any information gained about the offender's behavior can be used by the offender as an excuse to inflict further injury and abuse on his victim. When held accountable for his behavior, he will usually first assume that the victim has "betrayed" him, giving him what he feels is a reasonable justification for retaliation against her. If the source is not the victim, the offender may still retaliate against whoever gave the probation officer the information. Probation officers should always be aware that confronting the offender with any information, gained from any source, might result in violent retaliation.

Probation officers do not need to disclose the source of their information to the offender. Confronting him with what this person or that agency said about him works in movies and television cop shows for dramatic affect, but it is not good technique for a probation officer. If a probation officer puts one source at risk, all available informational sources may be afraid to volunteer information. Feed the mystique and his uncertainty. Declining to reveal sources of information enforces the idea that everyone is watching him and that the probation officer has access to every aspect of his life.

Keep in mind that no one lives completely outside the observation of others. Just because something happens behind closed doors does not mean that others are not aware that something has happened. Often separate versions of an incident may be provided to the probation officer, whether by family, friends, neighbors, children, neighborhood watch members, law enforcement workers, or the victim herself. Details of each version help to create a picture of what happened, and the overall picture of what happened is what the officer uses in the interview with the probationer to confront him on his behavior.

Before the offender can worry about where the information came from, the probation officer can press for an answer from the offender and lock him into a response. If he denies that anything happened, the officer can ask about specific details of the incident. If certain details, such as a loud argument or breaking glass, could have been heard and reported by almost anyone, it will be very difficult for the offender to deny that something occurred or determine the source of the information.

If the probationer admits that something did occur, he will no longer worry about where the probation officer got the information, only about portraying his actions in the most innocent way. A domestic violence offender usually is so compelled to justify his actions that he will sometimes readily admit the behavior, focusing more on how logical his action was or how the victim caused his actions.

That admission is more than sufficient to justify for the court any corrective action the probation officer needs to pursue. The court will not be interested in how the admission was solicited, as long as the probation officer did not make promises, use force to get the admission, or otherwise coerce the probationer into admitting to a violation. Remember, probation is an administrative function and does not have to adhere to a probable cause standard or beyond a reasonable doubt standard of proof for a finding that a violation has occurred. A lower standard of proof, reasonable belief, applies. When compiling a sworn report for the court or testifying in a revocation hearing, the officer need only state that he or she asked the probationer about numerous indications that a violation had occurred and that the probationer had admitted to certain actions or activities. Miranda warnings also do not apply to this administrative procedure.

This technique allows victims to feel safe in disclosing further violence or abuse, confident that the probation officer can confront the abuser without disclosing the source of any information concerning violations. The same holds true for community, family, or neighbors who might be added sources for information.

The probation officer should also keep his or her sources confidential when dealing with positive reports on the probationer's behavior. Appropriate response to probation conditions may quickly erode or result in retaliation if the probationer can verify that his partner, or any other specific person, has been providing information to his probation officer.

Offender Supervision

Supervision means active supervision, not sitting at a desk waiting for probationers and information to come to you. Actively checking with persons and entities having regular contact and interaction with the probationer can provide a wide-angle deterrent effect to the probationer. It also extends the resources and ability of the probation officer to monitor more of the probationer's behavior by enlisting the eyes and ears of others in the community.

The following is a list of some of the more common investigative sources probation officers might rely on for information on the probationer's behavior:

- The woman herself
- The woman's advocate
- Shelter services
- The probationer
- Scheduled check-ins
- Safety checks on victim
- Home visits with probationer
- Work-site visits, both announced and unannounced
- Probationer's children
- Other household members
- Family (both his and hers)
- Friends (both his and hers)
- Law enforcement
- Neighborhood Watch volunteers
- Service providers (social services, housing, child protection, CASA, and so forth)
- Health care providers (EMS, emergency room, midwives, dental, prenatal, acute care, community health representatives, and so forth)
- Employers (his and hers)
- Babysitters or daycare workers
- Teachers
- Counselors (mental health, medicine persons, elders, occupational, and so forth)
- Criminal court personnel and records
- Civil court personnel and records
- Civic or traditional Native societies, organizations, clubs, and so forth
- Psychological evaluations
- Chemical dependency evaluations
- Random drug testing

- Liaisons or agreements with adjacent or other law enforcement and/or probation agencies
- Administrator of community service time

These types of contacts and information-gathering efforts involve an active probation response rather than a static one. The probation officer does not just sit in the office waiting for information to come to him or her, but actively pursues information through contacts in the community, in person, by phone, by fax, and/or by e-mail.

Utilizing some information sources has the potential to place the victim at increased risk or at least make life with her batterer very uncomfortable for her. The supervision plan should be discussed with her at the initial victim contact to minimize risk and to keep her informed. She should be told that there will be frequent safety checks and why. The probation officer should encourage her to call at any time and allow her to ask any questions she may have. Requesting a release of information to speak with her advocate should also be a priority of this first meeting.

This type of supervised probation strategy appears time-consuming at first. Establishing a contact network for each offender does take time and energy; however, the probation officer working in a Native community will soon recognize that many of the contacts will be the same for most of the probationers.

Exchanging probationer lists with state and/or federal probation agencies and surrounding law enforcement agencies should be done on a regular basis. Routine cross-reporting can be established by a memorandum of understanding or interagency agreement. The probationer should get the feeling that all law enforcement agencies everywhere are watching him and reporting on his behavior.

Scheduled probationer check-ins and periodic evaluation meetings remain an important part of intensive supervision. The stability of regularly scheduled meetings with the probation officer strengthens the probationer's relationship with the probation officer, while regularly affirming the probationer's accountability for a crime of domestic violence. On the other hand, implementing only scheduled weekly, bi-weekly, or monthly check-ins as the primary source of supervision allows too much time between contacts to deter violence. Offenders may end up "scheduling" their abusive behavior to coincide with their probation reporting schedule.

Partners of some probationers have reported renewed abuse, sometimes escalating to violence, immediately after a scheduled check-in. Those same offenders later admitted they wanted to show their partners that, although on probation, they could still have control. Offenders reasoned that they had the interval until their next check-in or announced home visit to intimidate or placate their partners into not reporting the abuse to the probation officer.

Still other probationers said they were abusive to their partners during the several days before a scheduled check-in, hoping to intimidate and threaten their partners into remaining quiet about any abuse or other probation violation that might have occurred.

To intervene, probation officers can use unannounced and random home visits, drug tests, worksite visits, or partner safety checks, along with scheduled reporting conditions. Random telephone contacts can also be used. Periodic unscheduled notices to report, whether by telephone or mail, can also derail any planned abusive behavior on the part of the probationer.

These unannounced visits and supervisory activities might appear unduly harassing or unwarranted infringements on the probationer's time and privacy. They are, however, totally in keeping with established probation practices. Probation is a sentence and unannounced safety checks are a part of that sentence. Detention guards would not announce such checks if the offender was in jail and neither should a probation officer.

The frequency of additional supervisory activities varies by individual offender. Several weeks of monitoring strategies at the beginning of the probation term or following a probation infraction may be needed for some individuals. Others may warrant a longer or shorter period, depending on the level of threat perceived by the victim, the individual's attitude, and the level of past violence. Still other probation officers may choose to inject several days of unannounced checks and visits at random intervals throughout the probation term. Whatever strategy is used, the idea is to keep the probationer aware that there are restrictions on his life and activities during the term of probation that are a direct result of his conviction and his choice to use violence against his partner.

Rehabilitation

The community expects the tribal criminal justice system to provide for the rehabilitation and reintegration of these offenders back into the community. Probation programming is the vehicle for that rehabilitation. Accordingly, specific problems and needs of each probationer must be considered when deciding what programming is appropriate. Rehabilitative programming must also serve to undermine and strip away the probationer's carefully developed excuses and justifications for using violence.

Rehabilitation plans must be developed individually for each probationer. Assembly-line and cookie-cutter approaches to rehabilitation will not work because each probationer has a specific history, needs, degree of dangerousness, life situation, and excuses for the violence.

Alcohol/drug abuse plays a large part in many types of criminal behavior in Indian Country, including domestic violence crimes. In fact, many batterers use alcohol and/or drug dependence as an excuse for their violence. When alcohol and/or drug abuse is a substantial problem in the community, chemical dependency assessments and treatment referrals should be a basic probation condition for all offenders. The community and the court will readily support this strategy, and addressing this issue will strip the offender of one of his excuses. Also, a probationer who is still using alcohol or drugs is not clear-headed enough to fully accept responsibility for his actions or take an active part in any rehabilitation measures.

Many Native people suffer from depression and other stress-related psychological disorders, due in part to conditions of abject poverty, unemployment, and related social factors. This includes many domestic violence offenders. Probation officers should not hesitate to require psychological evaluations for probationers. Mental illness can be a major contributor to violence. Impaired cognitive abilities and delusions will seriously hamper any other rehabilitative efforts and reeducation programming.

Domestic violence offenders also rely on other socioeconomic justifications for using violence against their partner, including unemployment, poor anger management, lack of parenting skills, lack of education, housing issues, and job-related stressors. These issues need to be addressed because any excuse that appears viable by the offender, the community, and his family will prevent acknowledgment of the root cause of his violence, which is predominantly the need to establish and maintain power and control in the relationship. Some solutions are to send the probationer to anger management classes, parenting classes, educational programs, employment training, or any other resource available in the community to address what he feels is the real problem.

Of course such programming must be supplemental to domestic violence awareness and batterer reeducation programming. The probation officer should consult with the reeducation facilitator as to whether the probationer should continue attending reeducation classes while other programming is implemented, or if reeducation classes should be required only after other programming has been completed.

No single strategy has been demonstrated as being effective with all offenders, although one promising strategy uses a combination of culturally appropriate reeducation and programming with supervised probation that is mandated through the coercive power of domestic violence laws.[18] The law requires adherence with specific probation conditions, one of which is attendance at domestic violence reeducation classes, as well as mandated cultural classes and traditional role-model education. Addressing ready-made excuses and soliciting community involvement with batterers is also an essential part of this strategy.

New probation strategies have not been implemented in any jurisdiction long enough to establish a statistical basis that proves one specific strategy will work for all Native offenders. Individual cultural considerations and community expectations make establishing one domestic violence probation strategy for all of Indian Country highly inappropriate.

Pre-Sentence and Pre-Arraignment Investigations

Probation officers are also routinely asked by the court to prepare **pre-sentence** and/or **pre-arraignment reports** on offenders who have pled guilty or who may plead guilty at arraignment. This is an extremely important function of probation because it provides the court with a picture of past criminal behavior and enables the judge to make informed decisions as to bond conditions or sentencing. This function is entirely investigative and requires that the probation officer locate and articulate any facts that may have a bearing on the offender's likelihood of reoffending, the dangerousness of the offender to his victim, and his likelihood of returning to court for trial.

There is an old saying in law enforcement about sex offenders, which also applies to domestic violence offenders: "There are no first time [domestic violence] offenders, only ones who have been caught for the first time." Domestic violence offenders develop a pattern of behavior that has usually manifested itself in prior offenses or in specific incidents in the past, both documented and undocumented. To find and present that information to the court, the probation officer must use all available sources of information, including public records, past probation history, past release history, documented incidents of violence, and prior orders for protection. By interviewing previous partners and/or victims of the offender, the probation officer can uncover information on undocumented behavior. Even rumored incidents should be investigated and documented, if possible.

Those coming from a traditional law enforcement or legal advocate background might question the use of unsubstantiated rumors or undocumented incidents in preparing a pre-sentence or pre-arraignment report for the court. The argument is that the offender should not be held accountable for alleged behavior if it cannot be proven in court. To the contrary, any information uncovered will be presented to the court as the result of an "administrative investigation" and not an adversarial criminal proceeding. He is not being tried for the unsubstantiated rumors or undocumented incidents. They may only be considered in deciding if he will return for court or if he presents a substantial risk to his victim or the community at large.

An offender pleading not guilty has already been advised of and afforded his due process rights in the criminal procedures during arraignment. Although he has a right to reasonable bond, the court can consider any information pertinent to past or likely behavior when deciding what bond to place upon him. The judge has the ability to decide whether that information is relevant and should be considered.

Likewise, an offender who has been afforded his due process rights at trial and has been found guilty, or changes his plea to guilty, has completed the due process phase. His sentencing is only an administrative proceeding under the authority and responsibilities of the court. Information that could have been ruled prejudicial, irrelevant, or hearsay at trial can all be considered for the purpose of determining appropriate sentencing conditions.

A complete pre-sentence or pre-arraignment report should document all information available about the offender, whether favorable or unfavorable. It should detail the family, social, community, and financial status of the offender. The judge needs to know if his bond has been revoked before or he has failed to appear, if he has a position in the community or a job that pays well, if he has a drinking or gambling problem, and if he has a pattern of abusive behavior toward his partner/victim after prior domestic violence arrests. In short, everything should be included in the pre-sentence or pre-arraignment report, whether it reflects badly or favorably on the offender. Such a report is often the only way a judge can be informed about what type of person the offender is.

Case Management and Caseloads

An ongoing debate exists in the general probation and parole community concerning the caseload a probation and/or parole officer should carry. At one time the number fifty was adopted as the "best" caseload size for probation. However, since 1967, the accepted optimum caseload size has stayed at thirty-five cases per probation officer.[19] That is not to say that the caseloads of every probation officer are restricted to thirty-five cases, but that this is a general standard for most non-Indian probation departments.

With severely limited resources, tribal court systems do not have the luxury of restricting caseload size for probation officers. Most are lucky to have received funding to establish any probation effort at all. Many tribal courts are still unable to fund a general probation officer, let alone one to specifically handle domestic violence.

In tribal systems that do have a probation officer or officers, setting caseload size is usually not an option. They are what they are. Caseloads can vary from six to six hundred easily, so the main considerations have to be matching the supervision strategy adopted by the agency to the probation officer's caseload and prioritizing cases to provide the highest levels of supervision to those offenders who need it most. Since the Bureau of Justice Statistics' 1999 report *American Indians and Crime*[20] has documented the peril faced by Native women from intimate partner violence, tribal criminal justice systems can justify increasing their efforts at providing a greater level of safety to women, including specialized probation services for domestic violence offenders. Securing the resources to accomplish this is another matter.

Probation as a Long-Term Strategy

The lack of comprehensive statistics from Indian Country probation efforts is problematic in determining what may or may not be working in Native communities. Yet, Native communities with supervised probation as a sentencing option may be experiencing some success with a probation strategy customized to fit their cultures, communities, and their specific laws.

Establishing a probation strategy that works for a specific community may require reorganizing resources and/or changing strategies several times before the right combination is found. Each tribal community is different and several attempts might be needed before a specific strategy makes an impact. These efforts to make changes will not be accomplished overnight. The problem took centuries to develop in our communities, and it may take years to develop a probation strategy that is effective in our communities.

In their report to the Oglala Sioux Tribe Judiciary Committee in 2002, the Cangleska, Inc., Domestic Violence Probation Department on the Pine Ridge Indian Reservation of South Dakota summed up the effectiveness of their initial strategy:

> In 1998, statistics determined that there was a 44.8% **recidivism** rate among domestic violence offenders on the Pine Ridge Indian Reservation—a rate that had stayed consistent for nine years. By March 2001, we had reduced the re-offense rate to 22.3%, a reduction of over 50%. We were then hit by funding difficulties and had to let go most of the probation staff and offenders' program staff. By August of 2001, recidivism was back up to 46.4%. When we were able to re-staff those departments, the rate reduced to 24.2% within a month. During that entire period, 1998–2001, the number of domestic violence arrests declined by 18% as well. It is clear from these numbers that our dual approach at offender rehabilitation is working, but only when the criminal justice system responds appropriately.[21]

These results came from an underfunded probation department composed of five probation officers monitoring 1,800 offenders. The department was energized by these figures and became determined to increase the department's effectiveness with the resources at hand.

Cangleska, Inc., restructured their probation response and supervision strategies to maximize available resources. Continuing contact with individual victims was made a requirement of probation staff. Enhanced supervision was implemented with repeat offenders where the level of violence was high or had escalated sharply between assaults. Processes for ongoing communication between probation and advocates, men's group facilitators, and other members of the coordinated community response were formalized and utilized to keep probation officers aware of a broader range of offender activities. Culturally relevant education, role-modeling, and character development activities were included in probation and reeducation programming.

The effect in the Oglala Sioux system is flexibility of the probation response, which can be adjusted during the probation term to meet the specifics of the crime, available resources, and the changing needs of the victim, the offender, and the system. This individualization of supervision allows the probation officer to target areas of the offender's behavior that encourage or trigger the use of, or the excuse for, violence. This type of supervision strategy is so time intensive it is impossible to use with all domestic violence offenders. Only the "worst of the worst" offenders can be targeted for this type of monitoring, leaving a majority of first-time or less-violent offenders to be monitored by "paper chase" methods. Although this probation scheme appears to be reducing recidivism, the Oglala Sioux do not have the capacity or the research base at this time to determine the long-term effects of their approach.

Just as it took years to shape a domestic violence offender's feeling of privilege and need for dominance, formulating the appropriate probation strategy for a specific Native community may require years of experimentation, innovation, and fine-tuning. Yet, the future safety of Native women and their children relies on just such a long-term commitment from tribal probation programs.

Tribes without Tribal Probation Resources

Tribes without probation officers or probation departments can still develop strategies for tribal monitoring of domestic violence probationers. The first step is developing policy stating the need for such supervision, then examining what resources the tribe and community have that might be used to monitor offender behavior.

Active Monitoring by Law Enforcement

The tactic of enlisting community and family members to keep an eye on offenders can still be implemented without probation officers. This effort can be combined with other community-based policing techniques. Police officers can work to actively enlist the help of community members, as a function of their jobs. Anyone can report crime and police officers need to promote community responsibility for the mutual safety of its members.

Police officers historically have used informants and public-minded citizens to keep them apprised of potential trouble spots and criminal activities in the community. Including the specific activities of domestic violence probationers in this enforcement strategy can send a strong message to offenders that their activities are actively being monitored by law enforcement. Officers hearing of further violence by a probationer can then conduct safety checks on the probationer's partner. The officer can confront the probationer on the reported behavior, whether or not probable cause exists to take action at that time.

Officers can gather and keep confidential information on the offenders. As discussed previously in this chapter, this type of monitoring has a strong deterrent effect on individual offenders. The fact that the offender does not know how the officer is getting the information can be extremely effective, causing the offender to believe that "everyone" may be watching him and that any acts of violence, no matter how concealed he thinks they are, will result in an immediate response by law enforcement.

System procedures, such as effective information sharing between criminal justice and service providers, no-tolerance policies, and coordination of victim services also further provide a strong signal to offenders that the community will hold them accountable for their violence. Law enforcement can develop strategies to use the coordinated community response system as an active monitor of offender activities and behavior. If the regular duties of law enforcement or other court officers can also be amended to include monitoring activities, probation supervision without probation officers can be implemented by a tribal community.

PL 280 Probation Initiatives and Problem Solving

Monitoring probationer activities and behavior in jurisdictions falling under PL 280 can be especially problematic if tribal/state animosities exist or if the tribe is attempting to reestablish its jurisdictional authority. The difficulties often lie in the miscommunication and the incompatible practices between the tribal community and the state employees. Nonetheless, probation monitoring can be enhanced to provide for greater levels of safety for Native women and their children.

Providing for the safety of individual Native women must be stressed as a priority by the tribal community. In tribal communities falling under nontribal probation programs,[22] the tribe can initiate meetings with probation and law enforcement to formulate innovative processes to meet their specific probation and safety needs. Tribes may need to educate nontribal agencies to their specific needs and concerns. Non-Native probation officers working in Indian Country can take the initiative to seek out the specific concerns and needs of the Native community. Tribes should also look to advocacy programs as good examples of ally building. They may try to target a receptive probation officer for recruitment or reassignment to the tribal community. Establishing cooperative agreements and relationships with state or local county probation programs is essential.

Conflicts might be addressed through collaborative allocation of resources. Specific funding sources that might be available to the tribe, but not to state or county programs, could be sought and obtained by the tribe. Offering these added resources to existing nontribal probation services can serve as an incentive to realigning probation priorities in the tribal community. This could include funding a tribal probation officer who will work directly for the state or county court to only monitor domestic violence probationers within the tribal community.

No matter what form any development efforts take, providing for the public safety in a PL 280 jurisdiction should be a joint effort. Each side needs to make the safety of Native women a priority.

Tribal Development of Probation Services

Some Indian communities may have the ability to establish a probation response, but the tribe does not see probation service as necessary. In those instances, community education and awareness might be the starting point for making domestic violence probation a priority for the tribal criminal justice system. National Indian Country and local statistics can be stressed to clarify the need for an effective probation response. Probation can be brokered as a sentencing option in the face of insufficient jail space. Emphasizing the need to conform the probation response to the tribe's customs, values, and cultural priorities is also an effective selling point.

Maintaining probation programs is usually at the mercy of available federal funding or monies from casino revenues, private grants, or state-based initiatives with Indian set-asides. The other challenge is maintaining the enforcement aspect of the probation program. Someone has to be acting to enforce domestic violence sentencing conditions, or any sentence of probation issued by a tribal court is meaningless. Having no consequences only encourages an offender's use of violence and means increased danger to women in the community. Some type of probation enforcement must be implemented to make a tribal domestic violence code effective.

Conclusion

Underresourced tribal communities must explore alternative ways to hold domestic violence offenders accountable for their violence and provide for greater safety. One alternative, which has similarities to traditional methods, is enhanced supervision probation. Community resources are used to provide supervision and violation reporting. This effort should be established by the community and should take into account tribal custom, culture, and expectations for rehabilitation of offenders. No matter what resources a Native community has or does not have, keeping their women safe should be a priority, and some type of effort should be maintained to monitor the violent and abusive behavior of domestic violence offenders.

Notes

1. Throughout this chapter the term "woman" will be used as often as possible instead of the word "victim," for two reasons. First, statistics show that between 85 and 95 percent of domestic violence victims are women. Second, we need to view these women as individual persons and relatives. The objectification and dehumanizing of women who are battered by criminal justice and health care systems is a form of collusion with the batterer. Our goal should be to always put a face and name to these women when dealing with those who choose to use illegal and culturally abhorrent violence against them.

2. Lawrence A. Greenfeld and Steven K. Smith, *American Indians and Crime* (Washington, DC: Bureau of Justice Statistics, USDOJ, February 1999, NCJ 173386), available at http:www.ojp.usdoj.gov/bjs.

3. Greenfeld and Smith, *American Indians and Crime*.

4. Greenfeld and Smith, *American Indians and Crime*.

5. Fay S. Taxman and James M. Byrne, "The Truth about 'Broken Windows' Probation: Moving towards a Proactive Community Supervision Model," *Perspectives* (Journal of the American Probation and Parole Association, spring 2001).

6. American Probation and Parole Association (APPA) Working Group, "Model Domestic Violence Enhanced Probation Protocols" (Council of State Governments, Lexington, KY 2003), available at www.appa-net.org.

7. Fernando Mederos, Denise Gamache, and Ellen Pence, *Domestic Violence and Probation* (Minneapolis, MN: Battered Women's Justice Project, under a grant from Violence Against Women Office, Office of Justice Programs, USDOJ, 1998).

8. Carl Reddick and Don Chapin, "Domestic Violence: A Probation Officer's View," *Perspectives* (APPA, spring 1999).

9. Barbara Hart, *Assessing Whether Batterers Will Kill* (Battered Women's Justice Project, Pennsylvania Coalition Against Domestic Violence, 1997).

10. Hart, *Assessing Whether Batterers Will Kill*.

11. Women's Justice Center, "Domestic Violence Homicide Risk Assessment Checklist" (2004), available at http://www.justicewomen.com/tips_dv_assessment.html.

12. M. A. Straus and R. J. Gelles, "Physical Violence in American Families: Risk Factors and Adaptations to Violence," *Families* 8 (1990): 145, available at http://wps.ablongman.com/ab_marriage_family/0,6256,473448-,00.html.

13. M. A. Straus, "Modified Version of the Conflict Tactics Scales," from "Measuring Family Conflict and Violence: The Conflict Tactics Scales," *Journal of Marriage and the Family* 41 (1979): 87.

14. C. M. Murphy, T. M. Morrel, J. D. Elliott, and T. M. Neavins, "A Prognostic Indicator Scale for the Treatment of Partner Abuse Perpetrators," *Journal of Interpersonal Violence* 18 (2003): 1087–1105.

15. P. R. Kropp, S. D. Hart, C. D. Webster, and D. Eaves, *Manual of the Spousal Assault Risk Assessment Guide*, 2nd ed. (British Columbia Institute on Family Violence, 1994).

16. S. V. Tyagi, *Risk Assessment Measures in Prediction of Domestic/Interpersonal Violence: Brief Overview of Some Measures and Issues User Report* (Professional Education for Community Practitioners: Technical Paper Series, Counterpoint Counseling and Educational Co-operative, 2003), 1.

17. P. R. Kropp and S. D. Hart, "The Spousal Assault Risk Assessment (SARA) Guide: Reliability and Validity in Adult Male Offenders," *Law and Human Behavior* 24, no. 1 (February 2000): 101–18.

18. Reddick and Chapin, "Domestic Violence."

19. *Caseload Standards: Issue Paper* (American Probation and Parole Association Issues Committee, Council of State Governments, 1990), available at http://www.appa-net.org.

20. Greenfeld and Smith, *American Indians and Crime.*

21. George Twiss, *Status of the Tribal Domestic Violence Response: A Report to the Oglala Sioux Tribe Judiciary Committee* (2002); unpublished (on file with author).

22. Dianna Davis, Blair Rudes, and Laura Williams, *To Protect and Serve: An Overview of Community Policing on Indian Reservations* (Community Policing Consortium Monograph, Development Associates, Inc., 1997).

Questions

1. Why does the author make a distinction between the words "victim" and "woman" in the writing of this chapter?
2. When the author refers to the "paper chase," what does he mean? What information does the probation officer normally require at check-in? Why is this type of check-in ineffective with domestic violence offenders?
3. What are some examples of precolonial forms of tribal probation? Although probation or restitution varied by tribal community, what were some important common aspects?
4. Why is it important for the probation officer to react to even small infractions of the offender?
5. How can tribes work effectively with state and federal courts and law enforcement to monitor offenders to make sure that they do not escape the system and violate probation?
6. Why is victim involvement in probation monitoring so essential? Why is this traditionally left out of the Anglo-American system?
7. Why is it so important to hold offenders accountable in domestic violence probation cases? How does this play into the cycle of domestic violence?
8. Why should tribal community members be involved in the monitoring aspect of probation?
9. How should rehabilitation be addressed and who should decide how to deal with an offender's excuses for his violent behavior, such as alcohol and drug abuse? Who should offer the batterer reeducation programs and how should they be made culturally appropriate?

10. How can tribal laws be strengthened to recognize the importance of probation work in domestic violence and sexual assault cases?

In Your Community

1. Does your community fall under a federal, state, county, or tribal probation program? If it is nontribal, what suggestions do you have for strengthening the relationship with non-Native agencies to educate them so they can better serve victims in your community? If it is a tribal program, what improvements need to be made?
2. What ideas do you have for probation programs to make them more responsive to the particular needs and cultural traditions of your community?
3. What arguments can you conceive of to convince tribal employees and council members or federal, state, or county workers of the importance of a probation program for domestic violence offenders in your community?

Terms Used in Chapter 19

Banishment: The forcible expulsion of somebody from the community.
Emulate: To imitate another.
Infraction: The failure to obey or fulfill a law or agreement.
Mediation: The intervention by a third party between two sides in a dispute in an attempt to help them reach an agreement.
Parole: A period after incarceration during which the offender is required to meet certain conditions, such as good behavior, regular reporting, and so forth.
Pre-arraignment report: A report provided to the court before the accused comes to court to respond to a criminal charge. Report used by the judge to help in setting bail and conditions of release pending trial.
Precedent: An action or decision that can be used as an example for a similar decision or to justify a similar action.
Pre-sentence report: A report provided to the court after a guilty verdict or plea, used by the judge to determine the punishment for the crime.
Probation: The supervision of a criminal offender by a probation officer.
Recidivism: The tendency to relapse into a previous undesirable behavior or crime.
Restitution: Compensation for a loss, damage, or injury.
Shunning: Avoiding somebody or something intentionally.

Testament

What are words
Pictures of my soul in symbols
Letters from a heart that is so sore
It only wants to write beauty.

Past is past
Healing is today
Moving on is tomorrow
Words could never hold all the pain.

Words were most often
SHOUTED
They were never a soft caress
Nor the sound of praise.

Maybe that is why
My words flow best
When they capture the beauty
Of the life I surround myself with.

Words are my escape
My grasp on the future
My joy at having survived
All the ugly words of the past.

Words are my lifeline
My celebration
Ecstasy of recovery and rebirth
In my ancestral homelands.

I can soar with eagles
Dance in the reflections on the river
Drown in the smell of cedar.
Bask in the warm sun.

All because I survived
All because I can touch Life

Touch Nature with my mind
Sing to Her with my words.

The healing is here
In the letting go of old words, old wounds
As I sing the beauty of life
I need no testament to pain.

        Judi Brannan Armbruster (Karuk)

Glossary

Ambiguity: A situation or expression that can be understood in more than one way, and the meaning may be unclear.
Assimilation: Refers to the process of becoming a part of or more like another.
Banishment: The forcible expulsion of somebody from the community.
Beyond a reasonable doubt: Proof that results in being fully satisfied and entirely convinced of a fact and circumstance.
Biased: Unable or unwilling to form an objective opinion about something.
Bisexual: Someone who is physically, sexually, and emotionally attracted to persons of the same and different genders.
Burden of Proof: In the law of evidence, the necessity to affirmatively prove a fact, facts, or issue.
Clear and convincing: Proof that results in a reasonable certainty of the truth or fact. Requires more than a preponderance of the evidence and less than proof beyond a reasonable doubt.
Codified: Laws that have been collected and arranged systematically, usually by subject matter, have been codified.
Colonization: The act of establishing colonies, where one dominant culture settles an area generally inhabited by another culture.
Coming out: Coming out of the "closet," acknowledging who we are as LGBTTQQ individuals. Coming out is a form of being true to ourselves and is often terrifying because of rejection from those biased and phobic against LGBTTQQs. It can also be exhilarating to accept oneself.
Common law: Unwritten law of the tribe, developed through custom and tradition.
Complacency: Self-satisfaction; contentment with the way things are.

Concurrent: Together, having the same authority; at the same time.
Consent: To voluntarily agree to an act.
Continuum: A spectrum; succession.
Covenant: A binding agreement; a promise.
Cross- or counter petition: A formal request to a court or other authority asking for some type of action against one who has filed a petition against you; as in a cross-petition for a protection order.
Cross-deputization agreement: An agreement between governmental units with different jurisdictions (commonly between tribe, state, and/or federal governments) authorizing law enforcement officers from one of the parties to the agreement to have the same power and authority as law enforcement officers from the other party.
Customary law: A law based on custom or tradition.
Declarant: The person making a statement.
Dependency proceeding: A formal court proceeding to determine if a child's welfare requires a state or tribe to intervene. Other names: child protection proceeding or child abuse and neglect proceeding.
Domicile: A person's legal home.
Due process: Refers to certain safeguards that assure fundamental fairness.
Egalitarian: Promoting equal political, economic, social, and civil rights for all people.
Emulate: To imitate another.
Enumerate: To name a number of things on a list.
Eroded: Caused to diminish or deteriorate.
Escalate: To increase in intensity or extent.
Eunuch: A man whose sexual organs have been removed.
Ex parte order: Refers to an order where only one side has presented their case. Often used for emergency proceedings.
Exclusive: Sole; excludes all others.
Fee lands: Land that is owned free and clear without any trusts or restrictions.
Felony: A crime carrying a minimum term of one year or more in state prison.
Flashback: A recurring, intensely vivid mental image of a past traumatic experience.
Foreign protection order: Refers to a protection order from another jurisdiction (not a foreign country).
Futility: Lack of usefulness or effectiveness.
Garnishment: A legal taking of the property or wages of another.
Gay: A term for someone who forms physical and emotional relationships with a person of the same gender. Gay can be used to talk about both men and women, but commonly refers to men.

Genocide: The systematic killing or attempted killing of all people from a national, ethnic, or religious group.
Government-to-government: A relationship between equal or near-equal nations that prevents one having control over the individuals in another.
Hearsay: Second-hand evidence in which the witness is not telling what he or she knows personally, but what others have said to him or her.
Heterosexism: The assumption that everyone is, or should be, heterosexual and that heterosexuality is the only normal, natural expression of sexuality. It implies that heterosexuality is superior and, therefore, preferable.
Holistic: Refers to a method of healing that focuses on the whole person (physical, mental, emotional, and spiritual aspects), not just one aspect.
Homo/Bi/Trans/Queer-phobia: Fear and hatred of gays, lesbians, bisexuals, and the transgender and queer community. The fear and hatred usually comes in forms of prejudice, discrimination, harassment, threats, and acts of violence.
Illegitimate: Born to parents who are not married to each other.
Illicit: Unlawful.
Immemorial: Reaching beyond the limits of memory, tradition, or recorded history.
Imminent: About to happen, near at hand.
Indenturing: Binding one person to work for another.
Infiltrate: To penetrate, especially with hostile intent.
Infraction: The failure to obey or fulfill a law or agreement.
Ingenuity: Inventive skill or imagination; cleverness.
Inherent authority: An authority possessed without its being derived from another.
Inherent rights: Refers here to the rights that a tribe or government has because it is a tribe or government. Rights are not given by another.
Injunction: A court order prohibiting a party from a specific course of action.
IUD: Intrauterine device—a form of birth control.
Jurisdiction: The area in which a government has the right and power to make decisions.
Lesbian: A woman who is gay; loving other women.
Lethality: The quality of being deadly.
LGBTTQQ: Acronym for lesbian, gay, bisexual, transgender, two-spirited, queer, and "questioning" folks.
Mandatory reporters: People who are required by law to report any suspicion of child abuse or neglect to authorities.
Mediation: The intervention by a third party between two sides in a dispute in an attempt to help them reach an agreement.

Misdemeanor: A lesser crime punishable by a fine and/or county jail time for up to one year.

Mother's right: The right of a mother to her children.

Oblivious: Lacking conscious awareness.

Oppression: The act of subjecting a person or a people to a harsh or cruel form of domination.

Out: To "out" someone, to tell others about their sexual minority status—to bring that information out into the world without the individual wanting it known. Although "coming out" usually involves voluntarily doing so, "outing" someone is generally not done in a positive way.

Parole: A period after incarceration during which the offender is required to meet certain conditions, such as good behavior, regular reporting, and so forth.

Paternalistic: Like a father; benevolent but intrusive.

Paternity: The legal determination of a man's status as a father.

Per capita: "By heads"; by the number of individual persons.

Perpetrator: The person responsible for a crime.

Petition: A formal request to a court or other authority asking for some kind of action; as in a petition for a protection order.

Petitioner: One who presents a petition to a court or other authority.

Plea bargain: In criminal procedure, a negotiation between the defendant and his or her attorney on one side and the prosecutor on the other, in which the defendant agrees to plead "guilty" or "no contest" to some crimes in return for reduction of the severity of the charges, dismissal of some of the charges, the prosecutor's willingness to recommend a particular sentence, or some other benefit to the defendant.

Pre-arraignment report: Report provided to the court before the accused comes to court to respond to a criminal charge. Report used by the judge to help in setting bail and conditions of release pending trial.

Precedent: An action or decision that can be used as an example for a similar decision or to justify a similar action.

Preponderance of the evidence: A degree of proof that is more probable than not.

Preponderance: The lower burden of proof in a civil case; more probably than not.

Pre-sentence report: A report provided to the court after a guilty verdict or plea, used by the judge to determine the punishment for the crime.

Presumption: An inference (something that is implied) in favor of a particular fact.

Proactive: Taking the initiative by acting rather than reacting to events.

Probation: The act of suspending the sentence of a person convicted of a criminal offense and granting that person provisional freedom on the promise of good behavior.

Pro se: When someone represents him- or herself and appears in a legal proceeding without an attorney.

Prosecute: In criminal law, to charge a person with a crime and thereafter pursue the case through trial on behalf of the government.

Proselytize: To induce someone to convert to one's own religious faith.

Protocol: An accepted system of behavior or procedure.

Psyche: Spirit or soul.

Punitive: Inflicting or aiming to inflict punishment; punishing.

Queer: "Umbrella term" for the social/political/intellectual movement that seeks to encompass a broad range of sexual identities, behaviors, and expressions.

Questioning: Someone who is questioning his or her sexual orientation. This can often be an exciting and terrifying time because often we thought we were heterosexual and then we notice certain feelings have surfaced for another from the same gender, which sometimes causes confusion.

Recidivism: The tendency to relapse into a previous undesirable behavior or crime.

Rehabilitate: To restore someone to a useful place in society.

Relief: Deliverance from oppression, wrong, or injustice.

Relocation: Refers to the U.S. policy of moving large numbers of Natives from reservations to urban areas.

Respondent: One who responds to a petition.

Restitution: Compensation for a loss, damage, or injury.

Retaliation: To pay back (an injury) in kind.

Rites: A ceremonial act or series of acts.

Sentencing hearing: The period in a criminal case devoted to determining the sanctions to be imposed on the defendant.

Sexual orientation: How a person identifies sexually, physically, and emotionally in the way he or she is attracted to someone of the same gender, another gender, or both genders.

Shunning: Avoiding somebody or something intentionally.

Skiff: A flat-bottom open boat of shallow draft, having a pointed bow and a square stern.

Sojourn: A short stay or visit.

Sovereign: To act independently as a person or nation.

Stalking: Behavior where an individual repeatedly engages in harassing, unwanted conduct directed at another. It could include phoning, following, e-mailing, threatening to harm an individual or his or her family members, or many other types of actions.

Stoic: Seemingly indifferent to or unaffected by joy, grief, pleasure, or pain.

Subjugation: The act of bringing under control; conquering.

Subpoena: A written legal order summoning a witness or requiring evidence to be submitted to a court.

Sustenance: Something, especially food, that sustains life or health.

Taboo: A ban or an inhibition resulting from social custom or emotional aversion.

Transgender: Self-identifying term for someone whose gender identity or expression differs from "traditional roles."

Tribal code: The laws of the tribe.

Trigger: Something (smell, sight, action, noise) that causes a sexual assault victim to remember the experience.

Trust relationship: A relationship in which the U.S. government has certain duties or obligations to look after and care for tribes. These fiduciary duties are defined by case law, statute, and treaty.

Two-spirited: A term used to identify First Nations/Native Americans/Alaska Natives who are lesbian, gay, bisexual, or transgender. Before white European intrusion, many tribes treated two-spirited folks with respect. The term "two-spirit" evolved out of a Native American gay/lesbian international gathering in Minneapolis in 1988. Today, many LGBTTQQ First Nations/Native Americans/Alaska Natives use the term "two-spirited" to identify their sexuality/gender.

Unwarranted: Not justified or deserved.

Validating: Confirming and strengthening.

Writ: A written order issued by a court, commanding the party to whom it is addressed to perform or cease performing a specified act.

Index

adoption, 17, 216, 284, 297–98, 300–301
advocacy: general, 60–61, 181–89, 193–12; personal experiences with, 117–18, 120, 210–11
Alaska Native people, 11–12, 71–82, 115–26, 131–46, 167–72
Alaska Native villages: Allakaket, 19; Hydaburg, 9; Perryville, 77–78; Sitka, 132, 138–39; Venetie, 71
Alaska Native Women's Coalition, 79, 81–82
alcohol/alcoholism. *See* drug/alcohol abuse
Allen, Paula Gunn, 57, 217, 219
allotment. *See* General Allotment Act
American Probation and Parole Association, 314
Anchorage, Alaska, 72
Apache Tribe of Oklahoma, 253
Arizona, 298
Artichoker, Karen, xii, 6, 19
assimilation, 17, 91, 99, 151
Assimilative Crimes Act, 240
Attla, Catherine, 74
Awiakta, Marilou, 194

banishment, 12, 42–43, 75, 77–78, 80, 226, 244, 312
Battered Women's Justice Project, 208

bisexual. *See* two-spirited
Black Bear, Tillie, xi–xiii, 5, 7, 20
Black Elk, 219–20
boarding schools, 17–19, 36–38, 57, 61, 73, 91, 143–44, 149, 151, 218–19, 224
Broken Leg-LaPointe, Adeline Stella, 31
Bureau of Indian Affairs, 17, 144, 151, 217–18, 303–4
Bureau of Justice Statistics, 89, 92, 328

California, 10, 20, 88–89, 126, 149–62, 242, 298
Cangleska, Inc., 328–29
Carlisle Indian Industrial School, 36–37, 218. *See also* boarding schools
ceremonies, 43–44, 53, 73–74, 186–87, 216–17
CFR courts, 249–50
Chickasaw Nation, 14
children, 32, 51, 71, 73, 90, 93–94, 112, 158–59, 205–6
child sexual abuse: general, 71, 185, 222, 315; personal experiences with, 35, 37–38, 133, 154–55
Choctaw Nation, 14
Clairmont, Jim, xviii, 220
Clan Star, Inc., xi

343

colonization, xi, 5–10, 19–20, 50, 57, 60, 63, 75, 90–91, 96, 99, 149–51, 153, 161, 181, 194–96, 219, 222, 313
confidentiality, 61, 186–87, 199–202, 206, 258, 287, 321, 320, 330
coordinated community response (CPR), 211–12
Court of Indian Offenses. *See* CFR courts
Crow Dog, 237
customary law, 6, 8, 10, 73–76, 81, 151, 312

Deer, Sarah, xv, 4
Deloria, Vine, Jr., 7, 195
divorce, 107–11, 132, 281–91, 300–301
domestic violence: general, 49–64, 196; myths about, 53–57; personal experiences with, 105–12, 155, 169–70, 250, 251, 260, 261
double jeopardy, 239
drug/alcohol abuse, 39–40, 43, 55, 75–77, 88–93, 95, 117, 124–26, 132, 135, 143, 156, 182, 196, 238, 250, 273, 325
due process, 80, 260, 271–273, 326–327

elders, 6, 19, 32, 74–75, 81–82, 123–24, 146, 150, 181, 215, 219, 225, 259, 312
emergency contraception, 186

Federal Indian Law: general, 4, 10, 18–20, 151–52. *See also* General Allotment Act, Indian Child Welfare Act, Indian Civil Rights Act, Major Crimes Act, Public Law 83-280, United States Supreme Court decisions

Fienup-Riordan, Ann, 73–74
firearms, 89, 106, 133, 136, 145, 170, 204, 242, 260, 274, 286
full faith and credit, 79, 267–78. *See also* protection orders

gay. *See* two-spirited
General Allotment Act, 16
General Crimes Act, 238–41
Grand Portage Band of Ojibwe, 226
guns. *See* firearms

Hall, Tex, 9–10
Harring, Sidney L., 153–54
healers, traditional, 34, 187, 219–26
Henry, Terri L., 212
Ho-Chunk Nation, 216
Hopi Tribe, 151, 288

incarceration, 111–12, 122, 126, 135–37, 143, 149–62
Indian Child Welfare Act, 94, 159, 297–305
Indian Civil Rights Act, 13, 235, 245
Indian Country, federal definition, 237
Indian Country Crimes Act. *See* General Crimes Act
Indian Health Service, 18, 20
Iroquois Confederacy, 5–6, 11

Jackson, Moana, 5
jail. *See* incarceration
Johnnie, Jessie, 6
Jones, Eliza, 74
jurisdiction: gaps in, 4, 211; general, 233–45

Kansas, 115–26, 301

Ladiga, Sally, 16–17
LaDuke, Winona, 225

law enforcement, 56, 61, 76–80, 95, 108–9, 136–37, 141–43, 187, 255, 329–30
lesbian. *See* two-spirited
lethality, 54, 254–55, 290, 319–20
"The Long Walk," (Navajo), 57

Majel-Dixon, Juana, 7, 20
Major Crimes Act, 13–14, 151, 237–41
Mankiller, Wilma, 63
Mann, Henrietta, 50
medicine man/woman. *See* healers
Mending the Sacred Hoop, xi, 64
Minnesota, 112, 222–23, 226, 242, 297–98
Mousseau, Marlin, 6, 19
Multigenerational Trauma Cycle, 87, 90–93

National Coalition Against Domestic Violence, xii
National Congress of American Indians, 9–10

Office on Violence Against Women, xviii
Oglala Sioux Tribe, 328–29
order of protection. *See* protection orders
Osage Nation, 16

Parental Kidnapping Prevention Act (PKPA), 285
Pratt, Col. Richard, 36, 218
probation, 311–32
protection orders, 77–78, 80, 109, 204–6, 210–11, 236, 243–44, 249–62, 267–78
Public Law 83-280, 14, 71, 77–78, 237, 240, 242–43, 277, 330–31

racism, 5, 49, 57–58, 61, 89, 91, 134, 150, 152, 157, 169, 171, 195, 199, 250

relocation, 91, 99
Ross, Gayle, 60
Ross, Luana, 152, 156, 157, 161

Sacred Circle, xi, 52, 58, 63
sexually transmitted diseases, 41, 160, 186, 188
sexual violence: general, 161, 181–89, 223; myths about, 182–84; personal experiences with, 31–44, 107–9, 115–26, 138–39, 145, 155, 169; in prison, 160–61. *See also* child sexual abuse
shelters, 60–61, 94–95, 111–12, 170, 197, 201–2, 206, 211, 225, 287, 322
slavery, 91, 153
Smith, Andrea, xv, 221
Smith, Tuhiwani, 73
social change, 62, 172, 181, 188–89, 195, 197–99, 202
South Dakota, 20, 36, 149
South Dakota Coalition Against Domestic Violence, xii
stalking, 38, 99, 170
Starr, Arigon, 62
statistics, 3–4, 49, 71–72, 78, 88–90, 116–17, 149, 240, 249, 261, 297–98
sterilization, forced, 17–18, 20, 186
Strong Hearts of the Circle, 223
suicide/suicide attempts, 31, 35, 51, 75–76, 91, 124, 140, 145–46, 155, 254, 319

traditional law. *See* customary law
"The Trail of Tears," 16, 57
treaties, 11–12, 14–16, 91, 152, 269
trust responsibility, 13, 152, 237
two-spirited, xii, 167–72

United States Supreme Court decisions: *Alaska v. Native Village of Venetie*, 71; *Cherokee Nation v. Georgia*, 11; *Johnson v.*

McIntosh, 15; *Mississippi Band v. Holyfield*, 299–301; *Oliphant v. Suquamish*, 13–14, 240, 244; *United States v. Lara*, 239
urban Native women, 87–97

Violence Against Women Act, xii, xv, 3, 20, 193, 206, 240–41, 244, 249, 260–61, 267–78, 311, 313, 316; Safety for Indian Women Title (VAWA III), xii, 3, 19

Ward, Nancy, 9
Washington, 301
White Buffalo Calf Woman, 5, 6, 20, 217
White Buffalo Calf Woman Society, Inc., xii, 5–7
Williams, Effie, 19, 74
Wilson, Shawn, 74
Wounded Knee massacre, 20

Zuni, Christine, 6

About the Advisory Board

Genne James, Navajo, is an enrolled member of the Navajo Nation and has worked in the area of domestic violence for over fifteen years. She is board member of Monero Mustangs, a nonprofit committed to protecting and preserving the wild mustangs of northern New Mexico.

Tina Olson, Yaqui, has worked on issues surrounding domestic violence for over twenty years. As project coordinator for Mending the Sacred Hoop TA Project she has organized such domestic violence trainings as Law Enforcement, Building a Coordinated Response, Creating a Process of Change for Men Who Batter, Regional Trainings, Sexual Assault Response for Advocacy, and In Our Best Interest. She has taken various roles in the work to end violence in the Duluth, Minnesota, community, working as a women's advocate and men's group facilitator, as well as aiding in the development of Mending the Sacred Hoop's coordinated response in Carlton and St. Louis counties in northeastern Minnesota that began in 1990. Tina is currently the board chair for Women in Construction, an Economic Justice Project developed to provide livable wages to women by training low-income women to work in the construction trades. Tina is the proud mother of four daughters who are all working in helping field careers, law, social work, nursing, and law enforcement. She is also grandmother of four grandchildren. Tina lives in Duluth, Minnesota, with her partner of thirty years, Paul Olson.

Mary L. Pearson, Muscogee Creek descendant, has been a tribal judge since 1989 and has been admitted to the Oregon, Idaho, and Washington bars. Mary has served as chief judge for Coeur d'Alene Tribe since February 2004 and court administrator since March 2006. She has assisted in training court personnel in how to hear, try, and advocate and assisted in developing domestic violence materials since 1998. Mary has three grown children, six grandchildren, and two great-grandchildren.

Beryl Rock, Minnesota Chippewa Tribe, enrolled at Leech Lake Indian Reservation, is the mother of three, grandmother of five. She recently graduated with a B.S. in social work from the College of St. Scholastica.

Rose Mary Shaw, Osage Indian from Pawhuska, Oklahoma, currently serves on the Oklahoma Department of Mental Health and Substance Abuse Board. She is the first person of color to be appointed to this state governing board. She has served on numerous national and state advisory boards for victim assistance agencies and co-founded the first Indian tribal domestic violence and sexual assault coalition in Oklahoma. She graduated from Northeastern State University of Oklahoma with her B.S.W. and continued at Washington University at St. Louis for her M.S.W. She currently holds a license for social work with a clinical specialty. She currently is the director of the Osage Nation counseling center, which oversees the chemical dependency, mental health, and domestic violence programs for the Osage Tribe of Indians.

Rebecca St. George, Anishinaabe, is the mother of a young son and a young daughter. She is also an auntie, a niece, a daughter, a sister, a cousin, and a granddaughter. Rebecca has been working to address violence against Native women since 1993. She has volunteered at a battered women's shelter, facilitated batterers' reeducation groups, volunteered with the sexual assault crisis line in Duluth, Minnesota, and works with Mending the Sacred Hoop, both in the area of technical assistance and, currently, as an advocate for Native women in Duluth and the surrounding areas.

Tammy M. Young, Chookaneidi Clan, Tlingit, has been a co-director of the Alaska Native Women's Coalition since it was born in 2001. It is a nonprofit, nongovernmental agency dedicated to working with families affected by violence in rural Alaska. She is a founding mother of a new shelter in interior Alaska called Our Grandmother's House. Tammy also is a faculty member of Clan Star, Inc., providing technical assistance to the Tribal Coalitions across the country as the mentoring director. She lives in her father, John A. Young Jr.'s, home village of Sitka. Her mother, Jessie Johnnie, is from Hoonah, Alaska, but resides now in Sitka. Jessie has been the guiding force in Tammy's life, raising her to follow her maternal traditions. Tammy was born to the Chookaneidi, the Brown Bear clan. Her children James (thirty; recently married to Pamela (Howard), also thirty) and Heather (twenty-six) also reside in Sitka, and Stormy (twenty) resides in Anchorage with her newborn son Tristen. Advocacy for women and children has been a lifelong pursuit, while paying attention to elders and the stories.

About the Contributors

Jacqueline Agtuca is director of Public Policy of Clan Star, Inc, a nonprofit incorporated under the laws of the Eastern Band of Cherokee Indians, dedicated to increasing the safety of Native women; former USDOJ deputy director for the Office of Tribal Justice (1999–2001) and senior policy advisor for the Office on Violence Against Women (1995–1999); Family Violence Prevention Fund Director Criminal Justice (1988–1995); Legal Assistance Foundation of Chicago staff attorney (1986–1988).

Anonymous, Apsáalooke, Crow Tribe.

Judi Brannan Armbruster, Karuk Tribe of California, direct descendant. Judi was raised in a blue-collar suburb of Phoenix, Arizona. Not wanting to get caught up in the cycle of pain, prejudice, anger, and abuse led her on a search for the roots of her Native ancestry. Ten years ago she "came home" to the Karuk ancestral lands (the very top of California), where she was able to reignite her poetic voice and find healing. Her contributions to several anthologies and her strong online presence as a poet are indeed a "testament" to that process. Judi is a fifty-eight-year-old retired registered nurse, married with one daughter.

Diane E. Benson, Lxeis', Tlingit, (enrolled Sitka Tribe of Alaska), owner of Tleix Yeil' Drama & Commentary, provides consultation, historical research, and writing services for film or other performance or educational programs, particularly involving issues of diversity or politics. Diane is a published writer of poetry and nonfiction, and she holds a Master of Fine Arts degree and is completing a Master's in public policy. She often speaks publicly on social and recovery issues and is a facilitator of the "Finding Your Voice" workshop. She lives in Chugiak, Alaska, with her dog-team.

Mary BlackBonnet, Sicangu Lakota, received her B.A. in creative writing from the University of South Dakota. She believes writing is a powerful way to deal with all the challenges life can throw you, stating: "You can either sit down and mope, or you can pick up your pen and take back your power." She hopes to give writing workshops to women and teenagers on the empowerment of writing. Her work has been published in *Nagi Ho Journal, Tribal College Journal, Frontiers: A Journal of Women's Studies, Potomac Review,* and *Genocide of the Mind, Eating Fire, and Tasting Blood.*

Frances M. Blackburn, Northern Arapaho Tribe, is the proud single mother of six beautiful children and resides on her home reservation in Wyoming. She no longer considers herself a victim, but a "work in progress" of becoming a survivor. She now dedicates her life to helping victims of violence among her Native people.

Sally Brunk, Ojibwa/Lac du Flambeau, states, "I was born and raised on the Keweenaw Bay Reservation, but belong to the Lac du Flambeau band. I have been writing for about twenty years and use my family for the basis of my writing. I have written short stories also, but poetry is what drives me."

Lea Krmpotich Carr, White Earth Band of the Minnesota Chippewa Tribe, states, "I am a half-century old woman, working in the American Indian Learning Resource Center, as an advisor/counselor, at the University of Minnesota, Duluth. I am currently tackling my master's of education degree in a Tribal Cohort program. I started to write poetry as a teenager to cope with problems that I couldn't talk about. I am a domestic abuse survivor, and 'Run' is a representation of my leaving my ex-husband."

Rose L. Clark, Navajo, is a member of the Navajo Nation and was born and raised in Albuquerque, New Mexico. She received her B.A. in psychology with a minor in alcohol and drug studies from Loyola Marymount University in Los Angeles, and her Ph.D. in clinical psychology with an emphasis in multicultural community clinical issues from the California School of Professional Psychology in Los Angeles in June 1998. She is a licensed psychologist and the behavioral health consultant for the California Area Indian Health Service. Clark sits on numerous boards advocating on behalf of American Indian issues, including the Indian Health Service National Suicide Prevention Committee, the Indian Health Service Youth Regional Treatment Center Network Task Force (YRTC), the California

Rural Indian Health Board Access to Recovery Steering Committee, and the Steering Committee for the American Indian/Alaska Native National Resource Center for Substance Abuse Services. She was the recipient of the American Psychological Association Early Career Award in the Public Interest in 2006.

Amanda D. Faircloth, Lumbee, is a native of Lumberton, North Carolina, where she resides with her mother and sister. She is a graduate of Dartmouth College with a B.A. in English. She currently works as the Administration and Public Relations manager for Lumbee Regional Development Association, Inc., a nonprofit corporation that provides a variety of community services to the Lumbee tribal members. She was also recently selected to serve on the Lumbee Tribal Youth Council to represent her tribal district.

Lisa Frank, Neets'aii Gwich'in Athabascan, states, "I am the youngest board member for the Alaska Native Women's Coalition. I am interested in helping other Native brothers and sisters to face the violence we all deal with. I hope to continue to help others out there."

Joy Harjo, Mvskoke (Creek), a member of the Mvskoke Nation, is an award-winning poet, musician, and performer. Her most recent works include *How We Became Human, New and Selected Poems* and "Native Joy for Real"—a CD of original music. She also co-wrote the NMAI Signature Film, *A Thousand Roads*. She is an endowed professor of creative writing at the University of New Mexico and lives in Honolulu, Hawaii.

Brenda Hill, Siksika Blackfeet, is education coordinator for Sacred Circle in Rapid City, South Dakota. Brenda assists in the creation of Sacred Circle's annual training schedule, coordinates the Workshop Partnership and On-Site Programs, facilitates workshops, specializes in provision of advocacy and shelter development, and provides technical assistance to tribal groups. She also is responsible for the development of information packets and other Sacred Circle materials. Brenda is the founding mother and former director of the Women's Circle Advocacy Program on the Lake Traverse Reservation. She has been actively involved in the South Dakota Coalition Against Domestic Violence and Sexual Assault since 1990. Though she holds a BA and an MA degree, she attributes her expertise to the grassroots women who have honored her with their stories, her personal experience of being battered, and the South Dakota Coalition Against Domestic Violence and Sexual Assault. Regardless of title, Brenda is an advocate for women who have been battered. She has two children and six beautiful grandchildren.

Eileen Hudon, Anishinabe, White Earth, Crane Clan, has been an advocate to end violence against Native women since 1979. She began writing poetry at age nineteen to transcend violence. "Oppression in its many forms may mold aspects of my experience, however, when the day ends, and more importantly when it begins, I maintain control over my thoughts. May the Creator forever keep me as a *Songidee Biimadazwin*."

Carrie L. Johnson, Dakota Sioux, received her Ph.D. in clinical psychology with an emphasis in multicultural and community psychology from the California School of Professional Psychology, Los Angeles. Johnson is a licensed clinical psychologist and the director of United American Indian Involvement's Seven Generation Child and Family Counseling Services, which provides services to American Indian children and families throughout Los Angeles County. Johnson also provides consultation, training, and workshops to American Indian programs and communities on an American Indian Community and Family Healing Model she has developed. She is involved in administration, program development, research, and direct services for the American Indian community.

B. J. Jones is the chief judge for the Sisseton-Wahpeton Oyate and Prairie Island Indian Community tribal courts, as well as an associate and special judge for several other tribes in the Dakotas and Minnesota. He also serves as the legal consultant for Sacred Circle, the national support center to end domestic violence against Native women and, in that capacity, trains tribal court personnel nationwide on appropriate tribal justice responses to domestic violence. He formerly worked for an Indian legal services program where he represented thousands of victims of domestic violence in various legal matters and still represents victims on a pro bono basis. His recent cases include the South Dakota Supreme Court decision in *Medearis v. Whiting* in 2005 where the court declared it unconstitutional for a court to compel a rape victim to allow visitation with the perpetrator's family against her wishes and, *Matter of Grand Jury Subpoena*, an 8th Circuit federal case regarding the right of the United States to compel the production of confidential records on victims of domestic violence. He is a 1984 graduate of the University of Virginia School of Law.

Karlene, Tlingit Indian from Southeast Alaska, has been involved in the antiviolence movement for twenty-two years, doing trainings on ending violence against women; sexual assault; child abuse/neglect; elder abuse; and on other forms of oppression such as racism, anti-Semitism, ageism, and hate crimes against people of color and GLBTTQQ folks. "My greatest joys are my family, friends, and nieces and nephews, and of course my connection to the Creator."

Margaret "Augie" Kochuten, Quinault and Chinook, states, "Unaware of my First Nation heritage until 1995, when my mother discovered her inherited land on the Quinault Reservation, my uncanny sense of home for fifteen years in the Aleut village of False Pass, first, largest and most beautiful Island of the Aleutian Chain, suddenly became very logical. My three lovely Aleut daughters and I left the little house on the big Island for a smaller Island with a larger community, Unalaska, in 1990. I currently work for the State of Alaska in the Office of Children's Services and am finishing my B.S.W. I have six grandchildren. The womanly art of survival is passed invisibly through this poem, a tribute to all Telzan, Milne, McBride, Serebernikoff, Helmholz, Weber, and Kochuten women who each, in their own way, passed spiritual strength down through the generations in heeding kitchen table wisdom."

Charlene Ann LaPointe, Sicangu Lakota, was born December 13, 1948, on the Rosebud Reservation in South Dakota. Charlene is the eldest daughter of Rev. LaVerne LaPointe and Adeline (Broken Leg) LaPointe. She is the proud mother of one son (Marc) and has five grandchildren, six biological brothers, four adopted brothers, three sisters, numerous nieces, and nephews, and one great-granddaughter. Preservation of extended family history, relationships, and kinship teachings are important aspects of Charlene's upbringing and ongoing work.

Jayci Malone, Stockbridge-Munsee Band of Mohicans, is currently employed part-time and attending school full-time, where she is pursuing a bachelor's degree in nursing. She currently resides on the Stockbridge-Munsee reservation with her son Aweh'lapaew.

Sarah Michèle Martin is the director of the Tohono O'odham Nation's Advocate Program, a tribally funded law office that represents tribal members in family, probate, consumer, and juvenile law matters and criminal defense cases. Prior to joining the Tohono O'odham Advocate Program in 1997, she taught law and criminology at Florida State University's satellite campus in the Republic of Panama. She has also served as an assistant Arizona attorney general in the area of child abuse and neglect. She earned her M.S.W. degree, with an emphasis in family and child welfare, from Arizona State University in 1979, and her J.D. from the University of Arizona in 1983.

MariJo Moore, Cherokee, is a writer/poet/essayist/editor/publisher/artist and the author of *The Diamond Doorknob, Red Woman with Backward Eyes and Other Stories, Spirit Voices of Bones,* and several other books, as well as editor of *Genocide of the Mind:*

New Native Writings. Her website is marijomoore.com. She resides in the mountains of western North Carolina.

Tracie Jones Myrick Meyer, widow of Timothy Meyer, is Kalapuya Indian and enrolled in the Confederated Tribes of Grand Ronde Community of Oregon. Tracie devoted much of her life to social service with Indian People, until retiring due to health reasons. Her greatest joy comes from being mother to her three daughters, Angie, Jessica, and Shayla, and teaching "Things Indian" to her five grandchildren. She continues to write poetry and has started her first novel.

Eleanor Ned-Sunnyboy, Allakaka' Tribe, states, "I am an Athabascan woman from the village of Allakaket. My involvement with the violence against women movement began informally many years ago. Coming from an Alaska Native perspective, I am a very strong believer in the promotion of our inherent sovereign right to govern ourselves as indigenous people of this land and in the restoration of our 'Traditional Law' of respect for all."

Nila NorthSun, Shoshone-Chippewa, has been publishing since 1975. Her fifth and latest book, *love at gunpoint*, is available through West End Press, University of New Mexico distribution. Nila publishes in numerous anthologies and currently is a grant writer for her tribe in Fallon, Nevada, where she now makes her home. Nila was recently awarded the Indigenous Heritage Award for Literature.

Stormy Ogden, Tule River Yokuts and Kashaya Pomo. As a former prisoner, Stormy knows firsthand the violence that follows our Native women into prison. Since her release she has continued to advocate for women. She has written several articles along with presenting on the Prison Industrial Complex and Colonialism. "Growing up Indian made me an Activist and surviving prison has made me an Advocate."

Juanita Pahdopony, Comanche, teaches full-time at Comanche Nation College and is an advocate for Native American Graves Protection and Repatriation and the retention of Native students. She is a published writer, professional artist, and filmmaker.

Kimberly Mullican Querdibitty, Choctaw/Chickasaw descent, has a B.S. degree in psychology, is working on her master's degree, and is currently employed by the domestic violence program at the Apache Tribe. Although she does not claim a certain racial background, her Native roots are a distinct part of who she is. She hopes this poem will inspire all that read it, as it was created from personal experiences.

Sharon Lynn Reyna, Stockbridge-Munsee Mohican Nation, states, "I am from the Stockbridge-Munsee tribe in Wisconsin. I am fifty-four years old and a Mother of three. We need to break the cycle of violence."

Kim Shuck, Tsalagi, Sauk/Fox, and Polish, has an M.F.A. in Textiles from San Francisco State University. She is the mother of three children who range in age from eleven to sixteen. Her first book of poetry, *Smuggling Cherokee*, won the Diane Decorah Award from the Native Writer's Circle of the Americas.

Petra L. Solimon, Laguna/Zuni, is the daughter of Elliot and Lucina Solimon of Laguna Pueblo. She is an enrolled tribal member of Laguna. Her clans are Big Sun and Little Eagle.

Venus St. Martin, Colville/Nez Perce, resident of Lewiston, Idaho, is currently a full-time student at Lewis-Clark State College and a full-time employee for the Nez Perce Tribe Wildlife Management Program. She is married to Haace St. Martin and is a full-time mother, mentor, and confidante to two daughters, Kaniesha and Mariah, two sons, Isha and Sydney, and a stepson, Pesha.

Kelly Gaines Stoner, is the director of the Native American Legal Resource Center and director of Clinical Programs at Oklahoma City University School of Law. Stoner teaches Indian Law-related classes and Domestic Violence Law at Oklahoma City University School of Law. Stoner has worked in the domestic violence field representing Native American victims of domestic violence in state courts, tribal courts, and CFR courts for the past eleven years. She is the supervising attorney for the Apache Tribe of Oklahoma and Oklahoma City University School of Law's Native American Domestic Violence Project.

George Twiss, Oglala Lakota, is a veteran of twenty-three years of Indian Country law enforcement. He has served in many capacities—a tribal and BIA police officer, BIA criminal investigator, and, most recently, as the director of the only private, nonprofit domestic violence probation department in the nation, Cangleska, Inc., on the Pine Ridge Indian Reservation. He is a nationally recognized expert in the issues of child sexual abuse, sexual assault, and domestic violence investigations. His experience in Indian Country law enforcement and law enforcement administration serves him well in his role as head of Law Enforcement Technical Assistance and Training for Sacred Circle, the National Resource Center to End Violence

Against Native Women (a project of Cangleska, Inc.). He believes he has an obligation not only to the women of his nation, but also to other women in Indian Country. Twiss seeks to help other Native men rediscover their sacred trust to provide for the safety of women, including role-modeling and living a sober and nonviolent life as an example for their children and grandchildren. Part of that trust is advocating for and protecting the rights of Native women to be safe from violence and safe in their own bodies, spirits, and thoughts.

Danielle G. Van Ess has been studying, rallying, and working to end men's violence against women for more than fifteen years. Danielle spent three years working as a staff attorney and lead trainer for the National Center on Full Faith and Credit in Washington, D.C., a project that was then part of the Pennsylvania Coalition Against Domestic Violence Legal Department. Danielle provided technical support from her office and traveled extensively, including several visits to Indian Country, to conduct trainings on federal and corresponding state and tribal laws related to domestic violence and firearms. Since 2004, she has moved three times and had two babies, taking a temporary break from full-time work. She is happy to be finally settled down with her husband and their daughters just outside of Boston, Massachusetts. Danielle is now anxious to resume her domestic violence legal work as well.

Hallie Bongar White is the executive director of the Southwest Center for Law and Policy, a tribal Technical Assistance provider for the USDOJ, Office on Violence Against Women. She is an attorney licensed to practice before the courts of several tribes, the state of Arizona, the U.S. Federal District Court for the District of Arizona, the 9th Circuit Court of Appeals, and the U.S. Supreme Court. White trains nationally and regionally on issues related to sexual assault, domestic violence, stalking, abuse of persons with disabilities, firearms violence, and abuse of elders in Indian Country. She is the former director of the Indian Nations Domestic Violence Law Program and is a graduate of the Native American Studies Department of the University of California at Berkeley. White attended the Master's Degree Program in American Indian studies and the College of Law at the University of Arizona. She has served as an assistant attorney general and as a clerk of the Court for the Pascua Yaqui Tribe. White has also assisted numerous tribes in drafting domestic violence and protection order codes. She is the mother of five children and has two grandchildren who are enrolled members of the Citizen Potawatomi Nation. She and her family reside in Tucson, Arizona.

James G. White is an attorney and member of the Citizen Potawatomi Nation. He serves as a justice on the Nation's Supreme Court. He is licensed to practice in Kansas (1984), Arizona (1992), federal district courts, the 9th Circuit Court of Appeals, and the U.S. Supreme Court. He is the legal director of the Southwest Center for Law and Policy, a nonprofit organization, which, in cooperation with the Office on Violence Against Women, provides training and technical assistance to tribal communities and to organizations and agencies serving Native Americans/Alaska Natives on domestic violence, sexual assault, stalking, and other topics.

Coya Hope White Hat-Artichoker, Sicangu Lakota, is Lakota from the Rosebud Reservation in South Dakota. Coya loves poetry and the spoken word. Much of Coya's work deals with the interconnections of her various identities and communities she exists within.

Victoria Ybanez, Navaho, Apache, and Mexican, is currently the Tribal Technical Assistance coordinator for Praxis International, working with Rural Domestic Violence and Child Victimization Tribal Grantees to strengthen their ability to develop tribal domestic violence responses. Victoria has been involved with the battered women's movement for twenty years, bringing a depth of experience with domestic violence, homelessness, poverty, and racism to her work. She holds a bachelor's degree through the University of Minnesota, Duluth, and is a graduate of the Institute for Renewing Community Leadership, University of St. Thomas, Minneapolis, Minnesota.

About the Editors

Bonnie Clairmont, HoChunk, citizen of the HoChunk Nation of Wisconsin and member of the Bear Clan, resides in Saint Paul, Minnesota, where she is employed with the Tribal Law and Policy Institute (TLPI) as the Victim Advocacy Program specialist. Prior to her employment with the TLPI, Bonnie was Outreach/Client Services coordinator for Sexual Offense Services of Ramsey County, a rape crisis center. She's worked for more than twenty years advocating for victims of sexual assault and domestic violence, providing multidisciplinary training/collaboration on the needs of women and children who are raped and battered. She has dedicated much of her work to providing and improving services for victim/survivors of sexual assault, battering, and child sexual abuse, particularly those from American Indian communities. She has been a member of the Ramsey County Sexual Assault Protocol Team (a project for which she co-authored a grant and provided primary leadership). For four years she coordinated the Strengthening the Circle of Trust conference, a conference focusing on sexual assault and exploitation perpetrated by American Indian "spiritual leaders/medicine men." Bonnie, and her partner Jim, have two children, Lakota Hoksila and April Rainbow, and five grandchildren.

Sarah Deer, J.D., Mvskoke, is currently employed as Victim Advocacy Legal Specialist for the Tribal Law & Policy Institute in Saint Paul, Minnesota, and is an on-line instructor of tribal legal studies at UCLA Extension and former lecturer in law at UCLA Law School. Formerly, Sarah worked as a grant program specialist at the USDOJ in the Office on Violence Against Women in Washington, D.C. Sarah received her J.D. with Tribal Lawyer Certificate from the University of Kansas School of Law and her B.A. in women's studies and philosophy from the

University of Kansas. While a law student, Sarah was employed as assistant director of Douglas County Rape-Victim Survivor Service, Inc. Sarah serves on advisory boards for numerous antiviolence organizations and projects, including the ABA Commission on Domestic Violence and the National Alliance to End Sexual Violence. Sarah is a co-author of two textbooks published by AltaMira Press: *Introduction to Tribal Legal Studies* and *Tribal Criminal Law and Procedure*.

Carrie A. Martell is currently attending law school at the University of New Mexico. She plans to focus on Indian law. Carrie wants to work with Native women who are victims of domestic violence and sexual assault, developing laws that protect women's place within their communities, as well as representing women in the courtroom. Carrie was employed by the Tribal Law and Policy Institute prior to law school and was fortunate to work with Sarah Deer and Bonnie Clairmont on the later stages of this book. Carrie thinks it is important to educate people about violence against Native women through Native women's voices. Carrie received her master's degree in American Indian studies from UCLA.

Maureen L. White Eagle, Métis/Turtle Mountain Chippewa, has practiced law as an attorney in North Dakota, Minnesota and in several tribal jurisdictions since 1981. She developed and managed the civil legal services program for Native survivors of sexual assault and domestic violence at the Minnesota Indian Women's Resource Center from 2002 to 2005. She received a Bush Leadership Fellowship for 2005–2006 to study the status of women throughout the world. Upon her return to the United States, she formed Partners for Women's Equality, an international organization that supports human rights for all women, and she currently serves as executive director.